Essentials of Marketing: Text and Cases

Essentials of Marketing: Text and Cases

Geoffrey Lancaster
Reader in Marketing
Huddersfield Polytechnic

Lester Massingham
Principal
MTMS Ltd

McGRAW-HILL BOOK COMPANY

London · New York · St Louis · San Francisco · Auckland
Bogota · Caracas · Hamburg · Lisbon · Madrid · Mexico
Milan · Montreal · New Delhi · Panama · Paris · San Juan
São Paulo · Singapore · Sydney · Tokyo · Toronto

Published by
McGRAW-HILL Book Company Europe
Shoppenhangers Road
Maidenhead · Berkshire · England SL6 2QL
Telephone Maidenhead (0628) 23432
Cables MCGRAWHILL MAIDENHEAD Telex 848484
Fax 0628 770224

British Library Cataloguing in Publication Data

Lancaster, Geoffrey A.
   Essentials of marketing: text and cases.
   1. Marketing
   I. Title   II. Massingham, Lester
   658.8   HF5415
   ISBN 0-07-084181-0

Library of Congress Cataloging-in-Publication Data

Lancaster, Geoffrey.
   Essentials of marketing.
   Bibliography: p.
   Includes index.
   1. Marketing.   2. Marketing—Case studies.
I. Massingham, Lester.   II. Title.
HF5415.L2625   1988   658.8   87-25979
ISBN 0-07-084181-0

678 CL 921

Printed and bound in Great Britain by Clays Ltd, St Ives plc

CONTENTS

PREFACE

The importance of marketing in a dynamic business environment is now more fully appreciated. Those organizations that have not been prepared to look to the needs of their customers first have found it increasingly difficult to survive in today's competitive business climate.

This contemporary marketing text synthesizes marketing knowledge and does not purport to break new ground. It is highly readable and does not assume previous knowledge of marketing. It is unique in that it contains a number of longer marketing cases previously written by one of the authors and used by the Institute of Marketing, and is brave enough to suggest solutions to the questions asked. The text is, therefore, 'different' in that it is not merely a distillation of theoretical knowledge, but it is practical through the medium of 'real life' cases and their solutions. It thus translates theory into practice.

It has been written by two of the Institute of Marketing's senior examiners as the fundamental text that underpins any introductory marketing course. Throughout the text, other specialists' texts in the series are referenced and recommended for more advanced and specialist reading, so the entire series becomes a course in marketing in itself from undergraduate to postgraduate levels. In terms of Institute of Marketing studies it is appropriate to purchase this text at Certificate level, in the knowledge that it will not become redundant as the Diploma stage case study is catered for in terms of advice on how to tackle marketing case studies. Most case study texts tend to concentrate more upon business policy and are thus not generally applicable to the area of marketing. This text is relevant, as the cases are the actual ones used in recent examinations. Indeed, some of these cases are now used on university MBA and postgraduate programmes.

The text is attuned to the needs of both students and tutors and contains supporting references and end of chapter questions. It is appropriate to the needs of all basic marketing courses from higher national to postgraduate levels. It is also appropriate for marketing courses where case study analysis forms a component of that course.

With the increasing application of the marketing concept by marketing-oriented organizations, the text is indeed timely. Business institutions are changing rapidly – evidenced particularly in modern retailing – and this makes the text all the more relevant. It is particularly relevant to modern marketing, and unlike most comprehensive marketing texts it is written by British authors, who being Institute of Marketing senior examiners can concur with the Institute's logo that 'Marketing means business'.

ACKNOWLEDGEMENTS

In producing a text of this length and coverage we have had to seek advice and help from a number of colleagues and experts who have provided us with some of the raw material and given their critical and constructive evaluations.

We, therefore, gratefully acknowledge the contributions of Terence Johnson, Peter Murphy and Paul Reynolds of Huddersfield Polytechnic; Jeryl Whitelock of the University of Salford; David Jobber of the University of Bradford; Richard Pearson, Export Manager of Drake Fibres; Howard Baron, Marketing Consultant, and Norman Waite, Director of Education, of the Institute of Marketing.

PART
ONE

MARKETING PERSPECTIVE

MARKETING—ORIGIN AND DEVELOPMENT

INTRODUCTION

The marketing way of management is not a particularly complex or original notion; indeed the saying 'the customer is always right' is as old as business itself. Marketing is really a business orientation based on this principle which has grown and developed into a management discipline over the years. Marketing is not narrowly confined to a particular office or department; it is an attitude of mind, an approach to business problems that should be adapted by the whole organization, from the chairman and chief executive down to the lowest levels.

Marketing is based on the concept that the customer is the most important person to the company. In order to prosper or even survive, every company must work hard to retain its existing markets and continually strive to secure new and profitable customers. The marketing concept puts the emphasis on *customers* and the identification and satisfaction of customer requirements. Such an orientation to business consequently results in the customer becoming the focus of the company's activities, and most successful companies in the world owe their prosperity to the adoption and application of this marketing concept.

In starting our discussion of marketing it must be stated that although the concept of marketing is relatively straightforward, the term 'marketing' often means different things to different people. This confusion is not restricted to the ordinary person in the street. There are still many business people who have not fully grasped the importance of the marketing concept. The objective of this first chapter is to explain clearly what the marketing concept is all about and to compare and contrast it with less sophisticated approaches to business which, even today, are still practised by many business firms.

A DEFINITION OF MARKETING

It was explained in the introduction that the marketing approach to business is really quite straightforward and the basic principles of marketing have been used to a greater or lesser degree for as long as mankind has engaged in trading activity. In this sense marketing is a rather old subject, although the name marketing is relatively new.

As far back as 1776, Adam Smith,[1] the father of modern economics, wrote the following passage in his famous work *The Wealth of Nations*:

> Consumption is the sole end and purpose of all production and the interests of the product ought to be attended to, only so far as it may be necessary for promoting that of the consumer.

In the above statement Adam Smith has given the essence of what modern marketing is all about. The very word is *consumer* as it is the identification and satisfaction of a *consumer's requirements* which forms the basis of modern marketing.

Although the essence of marketing is as old as trade itself, marketing has only emerged as a serious subject of study and been accepted as a major management discipline since some time after the middle of the present century. In this sense marketing is a very new subject concerned with the analysis of conditions and forces that make for successful commercial exchanges.

In certain commercial subjects, for example accountancy, it is possible to give a reasonably accurate definition of the scope of the subject in a few lines. Such a straightforward, simple, definition is however more difficult to find in the case of such a wide ranging subject as marketing. This is not because a definition of marketing does not exist. On the contrary, the problem is choosing the most appropriate one as there are so many definitions.

Because marketing is such a wide ranging topic, different people often look on the subject from different viewpoints or give the subject a particular emphasis. To some extent such different viewpoints result from the academic background or the area of employment of the person giving the definition. For example, many people often go into marketing after studying economics and tend to give the subject an economic slant. Others have worked for many years in a specialized area of marketing, e.g., market research or advertising, and hence tend to regard their particular area as the most important facet of marketing.

The following list is a sample of the wide range of definitions given for the subject:

Marketing is a social process by which individuals and groups obtain what they need and want through creating and exchanging products and value with others.[2]

The marketing concept is a philosophy, not a system of marketing or an organizational structure. It is founded on the belief that profitable sales and satisfactory returns on investment can only be achieved by identifying, anticipating and satisfying customer needs and desires.[3]

Marketing is the delivery of a standard of living to society.[4]

Marketing is the primary management function which organizes and directs the aggregate of business activities involved in converting consumer purchasing power into effective demand for a specific product or service[5] and in moving the product or service to the final consumer or user so as to achieve company set profit or other objectives.[6]

Marketing is the process whereby society, to supply its consumption needs, evolves distributive systems composed of participants, who, interacting under constraints – technical (economic) and ethical (social) – create the transactions or flows which resolve market separations and result in exchange and consumption.[7]

The generally accepted UK definition is the one given by the *Institute of Marketing*, which reads as follows:

Marketing is the management process which identifies, anticipates, and supplies customer requirements efficiently and profitably.

The reader will appreciate that although there are many generally accepted definitions of marketing, there is no one unified definition. All of the definitions given above are correct while at the same time being slightly different. Because of the difficulty of incorporating all the facets of marketing into a simple definition let us instead look at a number of key points which will help clarify the situation:

1. Marketing focuses the firm's or individual's attention towards the *needs* and *wants* of the marketplace.

2. Marketing is concerned with *satisfying* the genuine needs and wants of specifically defined target markets by creating products or services that satisfy customer requirements.
3. Marketing involves analysis, planning and control.
4. The principle of marketing states that all business decisions should be made with a careful and systematic consideration of the *user*.
5. The distinguishing feature of a marketing-oriented organization is the way in which it strives to provide *customer satisfaction* as a way of achieving its own business objectives.
6. Marketing is *dynamic* and operational, requiring action as well as planning.
7. Marketing requires an improved form of business organization in order for marketing to be able to lead and catalyse the application of the marketing approach.
8. Marketing is both an important functional area of management and an overall *business philosophy* which recognizes that the identification, satisfaction and retention of customers is the key to prosperity.

This last point is particularly important, as much of the problem of definition and misunderstanding over the term 'marketing' stems from the confusion between the *function* of marketing and its *philosophy*. The term 'marketing' is used to describe both the techniques used by the marketing department and the overall marketing orientation of the firm. Marketing is in fact both a functional area of management and a business philosophy. Let us look at these two views of marketing in a little more detail.

MARKETING AS A FUNCTIONAL AREA OF MANAGEMENT

One of the main sources of confusion for someone approaching the subject for the first time is the fact that marketing is a complex phenomenon that combines both the *philosophy* of business and its *practice*. Hence marketing consists of two interrelated phenomena:

1. A basic concept that focuses on customers.
2. A set of management techniques.

Many organizations have a marketing department made up of both marketing generalists, e.g., the marketing manager, and specialists, e.g., sales manager or marketing research manager. Such a marketing department will obviously be based in a physical location within the organization in the same way as say personnel or purchasing. The people involved with the day-to-day running of the marketing department will have at their disposal a range of management techniques often referred to as the marketing spectrum or mix. These techniques cover such areas as sales and sales management, advertising and promotion, pricing, packaging, product development, marketing research, planning, distribution and after sales service. The concept of the marketing mix will be discussed further in Chapters 2 and 4. Many of the functions of marketing offer separate career opportunities and are often undertaken by specialists, with the marketing manager responsible for coordinating all the separate but interrelated activities.

Looked at from this point of view marketing is indeed a functional area of management which is usually within the firm and which uses a number of highly developed techniques in order to achieve specific objectives. As a function, an important part of marketing's role is to identify correctly both the current and future *needs* and *wants* of specifically defined target markets. This information is then acted upon by the *whole organization* in bringing into existence the products and/or services necessary to satisfy customer requirements. It is the marketing function that forms the interface with the firm's existing and potential customers. Marketing provides entrepreneurship by identifying customer requirements and through which the rest of the firm is able to mobilize resources to capitalize on them.

Although it can be seen that marketing has a very important functional role within the organization, the influence of marketing should not be restricted to the marketing department. A marketing-oriented business has implications for the way people *throughout the organization* respond to the initiatives that are forthcoming from marketing.

MARKETING AS AN OVERALL BUSINESS PHILOSOPHY

Many successful companies see marketing as the keystone of their business. Such firms do not see marketing simply as yet another functional area of management but more as an overall business philosophy, a way of thinking about business, and a way of working which runs through *every aspect* of the firm's activities. Hence, marketing is viewed not as a separate function, but rather as a profit-oriented approach to business that permeates not just the marketing department but the *entire business*. Looked at from this point of view marketing is seen as an attitude of mind or an approach to business rather than a specific discipline.

This holistic view of the role of marketing within the firm has been expressed by a leading authority on management thinking, Peter F. Drucker,[8] who stated:

> Marketing is not only much broader than selling, it is not a specialized activity at all. It encompasses the entire business. It is the whole business seen from the point of view of its final result, that is, from the customer's point of view. Concern and responsibility for marketing must therefore permeate all areas of the enterprise.

This marketing-oriented business philosophy is referred to as the *marketing concept*. It is a philosophy that puts the customer at the very centre of the firm's corporate purpose. Marketing cannot exist in a vacuum. To be really effective it must permeate the whole company. What is needed is an integrated approach, not just the creation of a marketing department. It is the company's whole approach to business problems that is the key issue. It is the adoption of a business philosophy that puts *customer* satisfaction at the *centre* of management thinking throughout the organization that distinguishes a marketing-oriented firm from other less enlightened companies. Such an approach to business propels the marketing-oriented company into new activities and new opportunities and away from the narrow preoccupation with selling existing products to existing customers. Marketing cannot begin to be effective within a company unless it has the *firm support* of general management and penetrates every area of an organization.

The question we must ask ourselves is why, if the marketing concept is so simple and straightforward, has it only been relatively recently that firms have adopted it as a serious business philosophy? To answer this question and to see how the marketing concept has evolved over the years into the form accepted today, we need to take a historical perspective and look at the development of trade.

MARKETING IN A HISTORICAL CONTEXT

Marketing is principally concerned with exchange or trade. Trade in its most basic form has existed ever since mankind has been capable of producing a surplus.

In historical terms surplus was usually agricultural produce which would then be traded for other goods such as pots or cloths. This early process of exchange brought about the existence of the local market and later the village fair to facilitate trading. The emergence of trade allowed people to specialize in producing particular goods and services and exchange them in markets for other goods they needed.

THE ECONOMIC ROLE OF EXCHANGE

If individuals and organizations within our society were totally self-sufficient and could survive without the need for exchange, there would be no need for marketing. However, in a modern society, virtually everyone depends upon exchange for economic welfare. An organized system of exchange, based on formalized procedures and an explicit legal framework, is fundamental to the working of any modern industrial economy.

Exchange is the act of obtaining something of value, usually a product or service, from another party, an individual or organization, by offering something of value to the other party. The thing of value offered can be another product or service resulting in a simple barter agreement, although in modern exchange transactions, money is usually used as a medium of exchange. The act of exchange is an important economic process because it actually *creates value*. The act of production creates wealth, but the value of this wealth is greatly enhanced through the exchange process by allowing an individual or organization a greater range of consumption possibilities, resulting in greater satisfaction and utility all round.

Hence, the exchange process is central to the subject of marketing which, broadly speaking, can be said to be concerned with how, why and when consumers choose to satisfy needs and wants through exchange.

THE INDUSTRIAL REVOLUTION

Before the Industrial Revolution the production and distribution of goods tended to be on a small scale. Producers generally sold their products to a very localized market. The period 1760–1830 saw the British economy transformed from its dependence on agriculture with a dramatic increase in industrial production. With industrialization and the development of machines, production became more geographically concentrated, carried out in purpose-built mills or factories. Enterprises were now on a much larger scale and manufacturers produced relatively large volumes of products, not only for a localized market but for a national and even an international market. Although this period brought many social problems, economic activity and production expanded dramatically, particularly from the end of the eighteenth century. The development of the heavy industries such as iron and coal, the availability of steam power to drive machinery, the greater use of machines in all industries particularly textiles, and the equally dramatic developments in communications, transport, agriculture and commerce transformed the economy, resulted in the growth of the factory system and saw the migration of the population from the countryside to the new industrial towns.

During this period trade flourished, but because consumption had now become more dispersed over greater geographical distances, producers no longer had immediate contact with their markets. In order for producers to be able to manufacture goods and services that would sell in such markets it became necessary for them to *analyse* carefully and *interpret* the needs and wants of customers and to manufacture products that would 'fit in' with those needs and wants.

This process of matching the resources of a firm to the needs and wants of customers was termed entrepreneurship. Generally the entrepreneur was the individual who 'carried' the firm, for example Josiah Wedgwood epitomizes the traditional entrepreneur. In a sense, the entrepreneurs were practising an early form of marketing although they did not actually call it such.

This period also saw advancements in production techniques based on job specialization and the division of labour. Prior to industrialization, production was carried out by the craft industries. In the craft industries, work was based on specialization in the production of a particular product, with the producer engaged in all the processes of production. The craftsmen would then trade their specialist product in order to obtain goods and services produced by other craftsmen, who of course also specialized in the production of a particular product. A skilled craftsman, e.g., a blacksmith or a cobbler, develops a high degree of skill in carrying out a particular activity. The craft industries were based on an early form of division and specialization of labour, productivity and output.

Industrialization saw the process of specialization and division of labour taken even further. The process of producing a product was broken down into stages or activities. Individuals then specialized in a particular operation. This resulted in a higher level of skill and speed and a greater amount of output than was possible when individuals had to carry out all the operations in the production of a product. The increase in job specialization increased the need for *exchange*. Specialization resulted in greater productivity which in turn reduced costs and hence the price of products. Larger scale production meant that channels of distribution had to be created to enable the effective demand from a much larger market to be met. The period of the first Industrial Revolution laid the foundations of the modern industrial economy, in which we now have a sophisticated system of institutions and economic organizations carrying out specialized activities in manufacturing, distribution, communication and finance to facilitate modern-day commercial activity, which of course is still based on the fundamental concept of trade or exchange.

THE MID-NINETEENTH CENTURY TO THE PRESENT DAY

From the middle of the nineteenth century to almost the beginning of the twentieth century, Britain was a dominant force in the world's economy. Throughout the nineteenth century both Britain's industrial output and the world's demand for that output had dramatically increased. The main factor underlying this industrial growth was the development of international trade. Britain was still seen as the 'workshop of the world' and held a virtual monopoly in the supply of manufactured goods to the relatively underdeveloped countries of the British Empire.

The latter half of the nineteenth century saw the emergence of other countries as competing industrial powers, most notably the United States of America and Germany. The rapid development of industry in these countries resulted in a significant increase in total output. Although Britain faced fierce competition in the areas of coal, steel and textiles, the period up to the First World War continued to be one of industrial expansion. Although Britain's share of world trade declined the actual value of her trade increased as the incomes generated in other countries resulted in an increase in total demand.

During the First World War Britain's economy was concerned with the war effort. After the war Britain discovered that many of her previous overseas markets were now trading with her new industrial *competitors*. The financing of the Second World War resulted in Britain selling off many of her overseas investments. As a result trade was even more important to the country's future. The period since 1945 has seen a decline in the importance of the traditional Empire and Commonwealth countries as overseas markets. Attention is now focused on the United States, Japan, and particularly countries in the European Community.

Despite an overall growth in world demand, the increase in world productivity has resulted in the excess supply of many products, e.g., steel and textiles. The international situation has changed from a sellers' market, where there was once a virtually insatiable demand for everything produced, to a buyers' market. Today we have a large number of producers competing to supply a finite market. Modern industry, as we have seen, is based on the process of mass production which necessitates *mass consumption*. Today, in order for a product to be commercially successful, it must be produced in sufficient volume. In order for producers to achieve a sufficient level of demand they must produce products that the market *wants to buy*. Simply to produce is no longer enough. To be competitive, firms not only have to take the needs and wants of the market into consideration, they have to *start with them*.

Today's modern organizations have become larger and more complex to manage. Markets too have changed and consumers' tastes have become more sophisticated. In the modern firm the entrepreneurial function is rarely left to one individual, but has developed into a management function and overall business philosophy that we now term marketing.

It can be seen then that marketing has its historical roots in trade and entrepreneurship. Marketing to a greater or lesser degree has always been practised by successful firms, albeit in a rather unsophisticated manner. It is only in modern times that marketing has developed as a formalized business concept with a codified philosophy and set of techniques. The realization by producers that they needed to take the buyers' points of view into account has slowly developed since the onset of industrialization. However, it has only been over the last 30 years that this growing realization matured into the ideological breakthrough we now call marketing. Manufacturers eventually realized that not only must they take the buyers' needs and wants into account, but that they were the starting point in the production of goods and services. This 'marketing maturity' did not happen overnight, but was a gradual process. Even today there are many firms that really only pay 'lip service' to the marketing concept and have still some way to go before they can truly claim to be *marketing oriented*.

THE PRODUCTION-, SALES- AND MARKETING-ORIENTED FIRM

Many organizations pass through programme stages of business orientation before fully adopting the marketing concept. Broadly speaking, even today there are three types of company:

1. Production oriented.
2. Sales oriented.
3. Marketing oriented.

Most marketing-oriented companies have evolved over the years, passing through the first two stages before reaching the third. Let us look at these various stages in a little more detail.

Production orientation

We saw earlier that in the nineteenth century and early part of the twentieth century the fundamental role of business was seen as production. Manufacturers were in a suppliers' market and faced with a virtually insatiable demand for goods and services. Firms concentrated on production and productive efficiency in order to bring down costs. Product decisions were taken first and foremost with production implications in mind. Firms tended to manufacture and offer products that they were *good at producing*, with customers' requirements and satisfactions of *secondary* importance. Firms tended to be 'production oriented' and the production man was the most important person in the organization as it was thought that he held the key to the firm's prosperity. This production mentality was a workable philosophy as long as a sellers' market existed. However, many firms had to change their attitude as the world economy drifted into recession in the 1920s and 1930s and to produce was no longer enough.

Manufacturers who focus their attention on existing products and pay little or no attention to the changing needs and wants of the marketplace are in danger of one day discovering that they have no customers. Such firms suffer from what is often termed 'marketing myopia'. This is a very shortsighted viewpoint where firms are so busy concentrating on their products that they fail to take *customers' requirements* into account.

It is strange that even today firms can be found who pay little regard to the needs and wants of their customers and still have the production concept as the guiding philosophy of their business. Such firms take the attitude that they produce excellent products and common sense dictates that people will want to buy them.

Naturally, consumers have to be informed and convinced of the superiority of the company's products, and this task is entrusted to the salesforce. If consumers are not buying the firm's products then as far as the company is concerned there can only be two possible reasons:

1. The customer is ignorant and does not appreciate a good product.
2. The salesforce is inept.

Many firms have, in their own opinions, produced excellent products but not necessarily of the type customers want to buy. The British motorcycle industry produced fine quality machines, but consumers preferred the styling and range offered by Japanese manufacturers.

In a production-oriented company senior personnel such as the chairman and managing director are likely to have production backgrounds. Such companies are likely to have a small sales department which handles traditional marketing functions such as advertising. The greatest importance is placed on production. Under the production concept the salesperson's task is a relatively minor one; he or she has to sell what the firm has produced. Such a firm is typically organized as shown in Fig. 1.1. The sales area is viewed as a service function, and so the sales manager is not part of top level management.

Sales orientation

The world economic recession of the early twentieth century concentrated the minds of business people. Many firms failed and fortunes were lost. Unemployment was high and effective demand slumped. Production capacity was underutilized and there were many unsold goods. Gradually

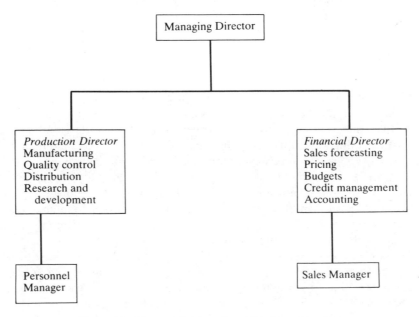

Figure 1.1   The organization of a production-oriented firm

business people began to realize that it was not enough simply to produce goods as efficiently as possible. For profits to materialize such goods had to be sold.

The guiding business philosophy of many firms switched from production to sales orientation. The salespersons and the sales manager now became the most important people in the organization. The firm could manufacture the goods, but these goods still had to be *sold*. The sales concept stated that effective demand could be created by sales techniques and it was thought that the sales department held the key to the firm's future prosperity and survival.

In a sense, sales orientation was a conceptual step forward because although goods and services were still produced with little regard to customer requirements, at least it was realized that products did not sell themselves as a matter of course.

This period saw the development of a number of techniques that are still used today in modern marketing. In order to achieve a competitive advantage greater importance was attached to product differentiation and branding. Advertising, sales promotions and other sales techniques were increasingly used to achieve a 'sales angle'. These techniques were still used to *sell* the product rather than to communicate and inform or to increase customer satisfaction. Although these methods are still used today, it was the ethos with which they were used that distinguishes the sales approach from modern marketing practices, with the emphasis on the *hard sell*.

Even today many people think of marketing as being synonymous with selling and promotion. Although personal selling forms an important part of a firm's marketing programme, especially in industrial markets where personal contact with customers is of particular importance, it is not necessarily the most important element of marketing. In fact, selling is only one of several functions for which the marketing department is responsible. Personal selling is but one of an array of marketing tools, each of which has a particular part to play in the overall scheme of things. Individually, such tools are only part of the firm's overall 'marketing mix' or set of marketing tools which must be finely tuned to achieve maximum impact in the marketplace.

This is not to say that selling is of no importance, rather that if the firm has applied the concept and techniques of marketing, i.e., identified consumer needs, produced appropriate products, priced, packaged, promoted and distributed the product correctly, then consumers should *want to buy* the product rather than the firm having to rely on intense selling. At the extreme Peter Drucker,[9] one of the world's most respected management theorists, has stated:

> There will always, one can assume, be need for some selling. But the aim of marketing is to *make selling superfluous*. The aim of marketing is to know and understand the customer so well that the product or service fits him and sells itself. Ideally, marketing should result in a customer who is ready to buy. All that should be needed then is to make the product or service available ...

In a sales-oriented firm its whole business philosophy is centred around sales. Often these firms believe that with some young, highly motivated salesmen, hungry for success and with a well worked out incentive scheme, they can sell anything. Sales volume is the most important criterion, and planning horizons tend to be relatively short term. The actual customer, and how customers might perceive the value or utility of the goods being 'sold', is of secondary importance. Philip Kotler[10] defines this selling concept as:

> a management orientation that assumes that consumers will either not buy or not buy enough of the organization's products unless the organization makes a substantial effort to stimulate their interest in its products.

From the above definition the implicit premises of the selling concept are:

1. Consumers can always be induced to buy more through various 'sales techniques'.

Figure 1.2   The organization of a sales-oriented firm

2. Consumers tend to resist purchasing and it is the salesperson's job to overcome this.
3. The firm's key task is to organize an effective salesforce.

In a sales-oriented company the sales function is given equal seniority with finance and production. Such a firm is likely to be organized as shown in Fig. 1.2.

The basic assumption of firms practising the selling concept is that their goods and services are 'sold' not *bought*. The aim of these firms is to get the sale and not worry about post-purchase satisfaction; customer satisfaction is considered secondary to getting the sale.

Examples of such selling situations are:

1. Certain double-glazing, burglar alarm, loft conversion, cavity wall insulation and other home 'improvement' companies; once they have a 'lead' from an unsuspecting target they send round a high pressure salesman with a 'foot in the door' approach.
2. Many insurance companies that search out potential customers and 'hard sell' them on the benefits of life insurance.
3. Encyclopedia companies that often disguise their real intention through an 'educational survey' and other devious methods.

A sales approach to business is all very well to those companies that are 'here today and gone tomorrow' but not to firms that want to remain in business and build their business on the basis of trust, respect and genuine *customer satisfaction*. A good high power salesperson can sell virtually anything to anyone – once! For repeat business over the long term the typical selling mentality of many firms is not enough; a more 'customer-' or market-oriented approach is necessary for long-term success.

Marketing orientation

As discussed earlier, the modern marketing concept is a twentieth-century phenomenon. The concept has evolved from the rather myopic production and sales orientation of earlier times as a direct response to the obvious shortcomings of these less sophisticated business philosophies. The concept started to be seriously put into practice in the United States during the 1950s and has, since that time, been adopted as the central business philosophy by many firms throughout the world.

The marketing concept is sometimes referred to as a 'marketing' or 'customer' orientation. Simply stated the marketing concept suggests that in order for a firm to survive in the *long term* and make a profit it must ascertain the genuine needs and wants of specifically defined target markets and then produce goods and services that *satisfy customer requirements*.

Under the marketing concept it is the customer who takes the central place on the business stage. It is the satisfaction of customers that is seen as the key to prosperity, growth and survival. A marketing-oriented firm produces goods and services that customers *want to buy* rather than what the firm wants to make. The emphasis is put on the customer buying rather than the firm selling the goods.

The management of a sales-oriented company tends to be short-run oriented and preoccupied with achieving current sales. In such a company customer considerations are often limited to the sales department alone. To progress from this position to a marketing orientation the firm must be able to cultivate a 'company wide' approach to customer requirements. Marketing cannot begin to be effective within a company unless it has the full support of general management and penetrates every area of an organization, from the lowest to the highest levels.

Levitt[11] has drawn a sharp contrast between the selling and the marketing concept in stating:

> Selling focuses on the needs of the seller; marketing on the needs of the buyer. Selling is preoccupied with the seller's need to convert his product into cash; marketing with the idea of satisfying the needs of the customer by means of the product and the whole cluster of things associated with creating, delivering and finally consuming it.

The contrast is illustrated diagrammatically by Kotler[12] and shown here in Fig. 1.3.

To change from a sales- to a marketing-oriented company, the firm will have to become long-run oriented and preoccupied with planning the right products, the right channels, level of service and marketing strategy to meet the customer's long-run needs. The marketing approach challenges every member of a company, whatever his or her specialist function, to relate his or her work to the needs of the marketplace and to balance it against the firm's own profit needs. Nowhere is this more important than in the area of product design where customers' views, rather than the views of production, should be the starting point.

It was shown in Fig. 1.2 that a sales-oriented company is likely to be organized in the form of specialized departments charged with carrying out different company tasks; each department directly or indirectly will have an impact on customer satisfactions through its own activities and decisions. Under the marketing concept is is desirable to coordinate these activities because the ultimate satisfaction gained by the customer is a function of the *totality* of all company departments acting in *unison*.

Changing from a simple sales to a more sophisticated marketing orientation will mean that marketing will have much more influence and authority over other departments to bring about

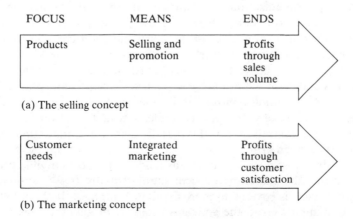

(a) The selling concept

(b) The marketing concept

Figure 1.3   The selling and marketing concepts contrasted

Table 1.1

Department	Emphasis	Marketing's emphasis
Sales	Short-term sales Sales most important One department	Long-term profits Customer satisfaction most important Whole organization
Purchasing	Narrow product line Standard parts	Broad product line Non-standard parts
Finance	Hard and fast budgets Price to cover costs	Flexible budgets Market-oriented pricing
Accounting	Standard transactions	Special terms and discounts
Manufacturing	Long runs Few models Standard orders Long production lead time	Short runs Many models Custom orders Short production lead times

integrated coordinated marketing. The sales department and other functional management departments may resent having to bend their efforts to the will of the marketing department. The major departmental differences or organizational conflicts between marketing and other departments are summarized in Table 1.1.

The main problem facing the sales-oriented firm in progressing to a marketing orientation is the management of organizational change. Marketing will set the strategies and plans in consultation with the departments concerned, but they will retain authority to execute the agreed programme in the way they think best. The human implications of this organizational change should not be underrated, bearing in mind that it will involve a re-allocation of power within the company. Functions previously carried out by other departments will become the responsibility of marketing and every part of the firm will have to conform to a plan drawn up by marketing in consultation with other departments.

In a marketing-oriented firm the Chairman and Managing Director are likely to come from a marketing background. In addition, there is likely to be a Marketing Director with a position of equal status to that of the Production and Financial Directors. Such a firm is likely to be organized as shown in Fig. 1.4.

Although the proper organizational structure is an important element in a firm becoming marketing oriented, such an orientation is not achieved simply by adopting an organizational chart. Management must also adopt and use the marketing concept as a business philosophy. Hence, in a marketing-oriented firm, marketing is not confined to the Marketing Director and the Marketing Department. To be really effective it must permeate the *whole company*. A change of management labels and titles will not achieve the necessary fundamental change in company attitudes. It is the company's *whole approach* to business problems that is the key issue. It is the adoption of a business philosophy that puts customer satisfaction at the *centre* of management thinking throughout the organization. It is this that distinguishes a marketing-oriented firm from a production- or sales-oriented firm.

Although the main thrust of this chapter has tended to reflect tangible products, it should also be remembered that the marketing concept should equally apply to the marketing of services. The theme of services is covered in more detail in Chapter 8. It should also be noted that marketing orientation implies greater consumer awareness through the likes of the 'consumerist movement'. This theme is covered in detail in Chapter 15.

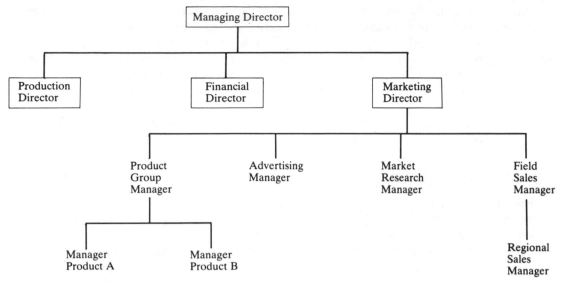

Figure 1.4 The organization of a marketing-oriented firm

CONCLUSIONS

This chapter has traced the development of the modern marketing concept, and compared it with less sophisticated approaches to business. These approaches tended to put the product or product sales, rather than customer requirements, at the centre of business thinking. Even today the marketing concept is still often misunderstood by practising business people and, as a result, is often criticized as a management 'fad' or nothing more than rhetoric. If modern marketing principles are to gain acceptance by the senior managers who must put them into effect, the need is not for more elaborate marketing techniques, but for better communications between the marketing specialist and the general manager.

Unless the marketing way of thinking and caring about the business is practised at a level where effective action can be guaranteed, then the most up-to-date and sophisticated marketing techniques in the world will not succeed. Marketing can provide policies for profitable action, but top management must give the authority to form these policies into action.

Marketing is not narrowly confined to a particular office or department; it is an attitude of mind, an approach to business problems that should be adopted by the *whole organization*, from the chief executive downwards.

Every person working in an organization should realize that without customers there is no business and hence no jobs. If a company cannot attract and retain customers' business it will eventually be forced into liquidation or merger. All departments within the organization should be *working together* as an integrated whole with a common purpose – the satisfaction of customers' needs and wants. They should strive to carry this out more effectively and efficiently than competitors and, in the case of profit-making organizations, make a profit out of the whole operation.

The marketing concept acknowledges that a business geared to serve the needs and requirements of customers will achieve better results over a longer period of time than a company whose orientation is along different lines. When a company is said to be 'marketing oriented' it puts the customer at the very centre of its corporate thinking. It sees its mission in life and its very purpose for existence as being the identification, satisfaction and retention of customers, and this philosophy applies equally to companies providing goods as well as to service organizations.

The firm is attempting to get value from the market in the form of money, through an exchange process, by offering things of value to the market in the form of goods and services. Value is a subjective concept and rests in the minds of individuals. In order to be able to create goods and service that represent 'value' to the market, the firm must understand the value systems of its target market.

This should be contrasted with the selling mentality that puts emphasis on the actual selling of goods rather than on customers and their needs, wants and values.

APPLICATION QUESTIONS

1. How does marketing differ from selling?
2. 'Marketing is often said to be primarily concerned with an exchange of relationships'. Elaborate on this statement illustrating your answer with examples.
3. Define briefly the marketing concept. Explain how a thorough understanding of this concept enables an organization to ensure that it is responsive to changes in consumers' needs and wants.
4. Give examples of three firms which you feel are very marketing oriented. State clearly, using examples, on which basis you made your selection.
5. 'Consumption is the sole end and purpose of all production' (Adam Smith – *The Wealth of Nations*, 1775). What do you think this statement means?

REFERENCES

1. Smith, A., *Wealth of Nations*, Rawdon House, New York, 1937.
2. Kotler, P., *Marketing Management: Analysis, Planning and Control*, 5th edn, Prentice-Hall, London, 1984, p. 4.
3. Barwell, C., 'The marketing concept', in: *The Marketing of Industrial Products*, A, Wilson (ed.), Hutchinson, London, 1965, p. 3.
4. Mazur, P., 'Does distribution cost enough?', *Fortune*, November 1947, p. 138.
5. Christopher, M., M. McDonald and G. Wills, *Introducing Marketing*, Pan, London 1980, p. 9.
6. Rodger, L., *Marketing in a Competitive Economy*, 4th edn, Associated Business Programmes, London, 1974, p. 47.
7. Bartles, R., 'The general theory of marketing', *Journal of Marketing*, XXXII, January 1968, pp. 29–33.
8. Drucker, P. F., *The Practice of Management*, Harper and Row, New York, 1954, p. 56.
9. Drucker, P. F., *Management: Tasks, Responsibilities, Practices*, Harper and Row, New York, 1973, pp. 64–5.
10. Kotler, P., *Principles of Marketing*, Prentice-Hall, Englewood Cliffs, NJ, 1980, p. 21.
11. Levitt, T., 'Marketing myopia', *Harvard Business Review*, July–August 1960, pp. 45–6.
12. Kotler, P., *Marketing Management: Analysis, Planning and Control*, 5th edn, Prentice-Hall, London, 1984, p. 23.

THE MARKETING ENVIRONMENT

INTRODUCTION

We saw in Chapter 1 that the marketing-oriented firm places the customer, and the satisfaction of customers' needs and wants, at the very centre of all corporate thinking. Rather than establishing what the organization can produce and then going out and 'selling' it, the marketing-oriented firm first finds out the genuine need and wants of consumers and then attempts to produce products and services that satisfy these requirements. It was also shown that, in a wider sense, the marketing concept is more an attitude of mind or a customer-oriented business philosophy, rather than merely a functional area of management.

Although a clear understanding of consumers' requirements is of paramount importance in putting such a business philosophy into practice, there are also other factors to consider. The marketing firm operates within a complex, dynamic, external macro-environment. It is the task of the marketing-oriented firm to link the resources of the organization to the requirements of consumers within the framework of opportunities and threats presented by this macro-environment. Hence, the marketing firm not only has to put consumers' requirements at the top of its list of priorities, but it also needs continually to adjust to environmental factors.

The objective of the first part of this chapter is to develop an understanding of the factors making up the marketing macro-environment. Firms cannot usually control their environment, but they can understand, and to a certain extent anticipate and react to environmental forces.

In order to place the macro-environment in its proper context one should be aware that the general term 'marketing environment' is often used to denote both *internal* organizational forces and forces *outside* the control of the firm. For example, Kotler[1] defines the general marketing environment as follows:

> A company's marketing environment consists of the actors and forces external to the marketing management function of the firm that impinge on the marketing management's ability to develop and maintain successful transactions with its target customers.

Such a definition includes *all* environmental forces outside of the firm's marketing management function. This would also include inter-departmental influences. Although the marketing concept is a customer-oriented philosophy that should permeate the whole organization, marketing as a *function* invariably has both to compete and cooperate with other functional areas of management.

Firms are blessed with finite resources. The marketing function often has to compete with

17

other management functions in order to obtain the resources it requires to carry out its job. For example, it needs money to spend on employing sales personnel, advertising and marketing research. Other management departments such as production or purchasing may feel they are equally deserving. The marketing function also *cooperates* with other departments within the firm. For example, the marketing research department may establish a 'gap' in an existing product market. Marketing would then work in conjunction with research and development, production, finance and the legal department in developing a possible new product.

Russ and Kirkpatrick[2] call the interaction between the marketing department and other functional areas of management *intra-firm environment*. It is important, in order to understand the influences of external environmental forces, to appreciate that although the marketing function is the channel through which the firm adapts to changes in external conditions, marketing's ability to carry out this role is also influenced by internal factors. Marketing managers make decisions that have a bearing on other functional areas of the firm. Likewise, the decisions made by other departments have a direct effect on the marketing department's ability to carry out its job. The role of marketing in the company setting and the interaction between marketing and other functional areas is discussed later in this chapter.

The *general* marketing environment, therefore, consists of *all* the factors and forces influencing the marketing function. This includes both internal and external forces. Internal forces, i.e., the intra-firm environment, are largely within the *control* of the firm. It is the generally uncontrollable forces outside the firm in the macro-environment that pose the most important sources of opportunities and threats to the company.

As mentioned earlier, Kotler divides the general marketing environment into two distinct categories which he terms the *micro-* and *macro-* environments. Using this classification, the micro-environment consists of people and organizations in the company's *immediate environment* that affect its ability to serve its markets. As we have seen, this includes inter-departmental influences within the company itself, but it also includes suppliers, market intermediaries, competitors and other 'publics'. Kotler reserves the term 'macro-environment' to denote other external forces such as demographic, economic, political, technological, and socio-cultural forces.

The term 'micro-environment' would seem a somewhat inappropriate term when used in this context. The *Collins English Dictionary*,[3] for example, defines the term 'micro' as 'small or minute: indicating abnormal smallness or underdevelopment'.

While intra-firm relationships and forces could rightly be called micro-environmental influences, it would not seem appropriate to use this term to denote environmental forces outside of the firm. While it is true that certain markets are relatively small and hence involve a limited number of suppliers, distributors and competing firms, it is by no means always the case. Many markets are extremely large and often operate on an international scale. In such markets, the number of suppliers, distributors and competitors may be legion.

In the context of this chapter, the term 'macro-environment' denotes all those forces and agencies *external* to the marketing firm. Some of these outside factors and forces will be somewhat 'closer' to the firm than others, for example, immediate suppliers and competitors. We will term this the *proximate macro-environment* (proximate meaning 'close' as in the word 'proximity'). This will serve to distinguish between the environmental influences close to the firm, and the wider external forces such as economic or political forces, which of course also affect the people and organizations in the firm's proximate macro-environment as well as the firm itself.

PART I   THE MACRO-ENVIRONMENT

The only really certain thing in this world is change. Sometimes change occurs so slowly that it is virtually imperceptible. We are often unaware that change is happening until it is too late to do anything about it. At other times, change is so rapid that even though it is obvious, we find it difficult to react quickly enough. Although none of us possesses the power to foresee the future, we can be sure that it will be *different* from today, and change is a fact of life. We have little power to stop it and the sensible course of action is to welcome change and attempt to adapt to it. However, one can attempt to predict such changes through forecasting, a subject dealt with in more detail later.

Charles Darwin,[4] author of *On the Origin of the Species*, put forward the theory that many living organisms have been able to survive in a constantly changing and hostile world because they were able to adapt successfully to changing conditions. Fossil records indicate that long ago there existed many forms of life that for some reason no longer exist today. Although many theories have been put forward for the demise of prehistoric animals, the main factor seems to have been their inability to adapt.

Firms also operate in a changing, and at times hostile, business environment. They too, in order to survive and prosper, need to take account of, and adapt to, changing environmental conditions. Firms that fail to do so are likely to end up as extinct as the prehistoric mammals.

In order for a firm to be able to adapt successfully to changing circumstances management needs to have an understanding and appreciation of the factors and forces influencing such changes. Ideally a firm should be in a position to adapt to changes as they are occurring or even in advance. Firms should attempt to capitalize upon change rather than merely reacting to it. By identifying environmental trends soon enough, management should be able, at least in part, to anticipate where such trends are leading and what future conditions are likely to result from such changes.

Unless firms are able to identify and react to changes quickly enough, they are likely to be dictated to by circumstances beyond their control. Instead of being part of the changes occurring and *leading* the market, they will, out of necessity, be forced into being market followers. Instead of adapting to change and even going some way in *influencing* events, events will instead influence them, perhaps in an unfavourable way. The 'Mars' company not only makes Mars bars; it makes pet foods, convenience foods, computer software, etc. It makes no secret of the fact that its intention is to be market leader in all its operations.

In terms of their speed of response, and their ability to react to changing conditions, we can generally classify three types of firm:

1. Firms that identify and understand the forces and conditions bringing about change. Such firms adapt and move in line with such changes. To a certain extent, such a firm may itself play a part in influencing events.
2. Firms that fail to adapt to changes early enough to become part of that change. Such firms have little opportunity to influence events, but are usually forced to react to changes eventually, out of the necessity to survive.
3. Firms that fail to realize change has occurred, or refuse to adapt to changing circumstances. Such firms are unlikely to survive in the long term or, even if they do, they are unlikely to prosper.

Controllable marketing variables and the macro-environment

In a mixed economy, such as that to be found in the United Kingdom, firms enjoy a considerable amount of autonomy. Not only does the management of a firm have control over how it organizes and integrates its management functions, but generally it is free to decide what and how to

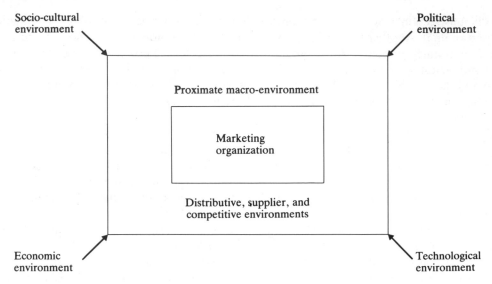

Figure 2.1   Macro-environmental forces influencing the marketing organization

manufacture as well as having freedom in pricing, packaging, advertising and distribution. Generally speaking, the management of a firm is free to carry out its business affairs in any way it pleases and as such a number of marketing variables like price are directly under the control of the firm. Collectively, we call these controllable marketing variables the 'marketing mix' and this concept is discussed in detail in Chapter 4.

While marketing firms control much of their operations, they do not plan strategies in a vacuum. As we have seen, all organizations are influenced by a number of macro-environmental factors which are broadly outside their control. These environmental forces and, in particular, changes in these forces give rise to marketing opportunities and threats. Stanton *et al.*[5] suggest that the ability of a marketing decision-making executive may be measured by the skill with which he can carry out the following tasks:

1. Adjust to the external elements in the changing environment.
2. Forecast the direction and intensity of these changes.
3. Use the controllable variables at his command (the marketing mix) in adapting to this external environment.

The most important factors making up the firm's marketing macro-environment are shown in Fig. 2.1.

We shall look at each of these sub-environments in more detail, starting by looking at those macro-environmental forces closest to the marketing firm.

The proximate macro-environment

The proximate macro-environment consists of people, organizations and forces within the firm's immediate *external* environment. Of particular interest to marketing firms are the sub-environments in which we find:

1. competitors;
2. suppliers; and
3. intermediaries (e.g., distributors).

The people and organizations making up the above sub-environments all have a *direct*, and at times *immediate*, effect on the commercial well-being of the marketing firm.

The competitive environment

There are very few firms that are fortunate enough to have no competitors. While it is true that certain industries such as gas or electricity are near-monopolies, even these industries face competition, if only from each other. For example, gas is a substitute for electricity in many areas of energy use. In fact nearly all firms face competition from other firms within the same industry or from firms in other industries which offer *substitute* products or services.

The competitive environment can often determine the success or failure of a product. Boone and Kurtz[6] discuss the case of 'Corfam', a leather substitute introduced in the United States during the 1960s by Du Pont. The cost of leather in the United States at this time was very high and Du Pont was convinced it had produced a 'winning' product. Years of research had managed to produce a synthetic leather nearer to the real thing than anything else on the market. The new product had many of the attributes of real leather including 'breathability' and the ability to absorb foot moisture. Du Pont was so convinced that Corfam would succeed that it even confidently cut back on advertising the product because it was thought unnecessary. Corfam had to be withdrawn from the market eventually because foreign competition flooded the United States footwear market with real leather shoes which could be sold at a lower price than shoes made from Corfam. Du Pont's Corfam was an excellent product, but the firm failed to judge correctly the reaction of foreign competitors to its introduction. As a result, Du Pont spent millions of pounds on research and development only to end up with a commercial failure on its hands.

The Corfam story illustrates how factors in the competitive environment can affect the commercial prosperity of any firm. It also shows how marketing management must be *alert* to the potential threat of firms marketing product substitutes of both domestic and foreign origin. Many British manufacturing industries such as steel and textiles have been experiencing heavy competition from substitute products, often produced overseas. For example, the UK carpet industry has traditionally had a reputation for producing high quality Axminster and Wilton carpets. Today foreign imported carpets have captured a large share of the market. Many of these carpets are made from synthetic materials instead of the traditional wool pile with jute backing. They are also produced using the cheaper 'tufting' process instead of the traditional 'weaving' process. Many carpet manufacturers have been forced into liquidation over the past 10 to 15 years as a result of these heavy competitive pressures.

In some industries, such as textiles, there may be hundreds or even thousands of manufacturers worldwide to pose a potential competitive threat. In other industries, such as car production, there may be only a few dozen, although the level of competition is likely to be just as fierce. Whatever industry the marketing firm forms part of, it will be necessary for management to identify its competitors. Management will also need to establish exactly what benefits competitors are offering consumers if its firm intends to compete effectively. Having done this, management should then establish how its own firm compares in relation to competition. Only when management has a clear understanding of the factors and forces making up the competitive environment can it hope to compete.

Supplier environment

Suppliers are other business firms and individuals who provide the resources needed by the marketing firm to produce goods and/or services. Nearly every firm, whether engaged in manufacturing, wholesaling or retailing, is likely to have suppliers. Large firms such as Marks and Spencer or the Ford Motor Company are likely to have numerous suppliers. For example, Ford must obtain glass windscreens, headlamp units, brakepads, tyres, steel sheet, fabric for interior upholstery and a number of other materials in order to produce cars. While some of these product constituents will come from major manufacturers such as British Steel, Pilkington's Glass, Lucas and Dunlop, other components, ranging from industrial fasteners to engine gaskets, will often be supplied by a large number of smaller, less well known companies.

As you will appreciate, Ford depends on possibly hundreds of suppliers for its manufacturing capability and commercial prosperity. Likewise, hundreds of firms also depend on Ford for orders. The firms that supply Ford with finished components are also likely to be supplied with raw materials or semi-processed goods by a host of other suppliers.

Purchasing is regarded as a very important management function in many organizations. The reason for this importance is the fact that firms must be able to purchase products and services at an acceptable price and quality. The firm must also ensure that its suppliers are capable of offering an acceptable level of service on such matters as delivery, reliability, stock availability, servicing arrangements and credit facilities.

Manufacturing firms have to decide what preparation of their products actually to make themselves and what parts and components should be sub-contracted out to other manufacturers who are often specialists in their field. For those materials that have to be bought in, purchasing personnel will have to obtain detailed product specifications from engineers and designers, search for suppliers that are capable of producing or supplying materials to specification, rate them on potential suitability, obtain tenders and arrange contracts.

The buyer/supplier relationship is one of economic interdependence. Both parties rely on each other for their commercial well-being. Changes in the terms of the relationship are usually based on negotiation rather than on *ad hoc* unilateral decisions. Such relationships are usually long term with each party realizing its dependence on the other. Both parties are seeking security and long-term stability from their commercial relationship. This is not to say that factors in the supplier environment do not change. Suppliers may be forced to raise their prices and may also be affected by industrial disputes which, in turn, will affect delivery of materials to the buying firm. Some suppliers may find themselves in financial difficulty and be forced into liquidation. In an attempt to limit the effect of such factors many buying firms use a 'multiple sourcing' purchasing policy. This avoids over-dependency on any one supplier and reduces the vulnerability of the buying firm.

Since the illustration has been taken from the motor industry, it is appropriate to discuss the fact that the trend is now for car companies to hold as little stock of components as possible. This trend has been established by the Japanese, and it is not unusual to hold only four hours' stock of certain components. The aim is for 'zero defects' and is an extension of a school of thought called 'just-in-time management'.

The advantages to the car company are that it saves on working capital in that stockholding is minimal. However, the implication is that there must be absolute reliability placed upon suppliers in terms of quality and delivery. The implication to companies marketing to large car firms are that quality and reliable delivery are as important (if not more important) than price.

Marketing firms are also buyers of specialist marketing services. For example, although the larger firms are likely to have their own 'in-house' marketing research department, they will often commission surveys, test marketing programmes and product test facilities from outside specialist agencies.

Whatever the product or service being purchased by the marketing firm, developments in the supplier environment can have an immediate and possibly serious effect on the firm's commercial operations. Marketing management should be continually monitoring changes and trends in order to plan ahead.

The distributive environment

Many firms, particularly in industrial markets where products are often buyer specified, market and deliver their products direct to the final customer. Other firms use some form of intermediate distribution system. The distribution system is then made up of one or more 'middlemen' who can be individuals or other organizations. They range from agents, distributors, factors and wholesalers to retailers.

Because of the seeming permanence of the distributive environment at any point in time, many firms make the mistake of thinking it is static. In fact distribution channels change and evolve just like any other facet of business life. As Davidson[7] explains:

> Distribution channels resemble the hour hand of a watch. They are always moving, but each individual movement is so small as to be invisible in isolation. The cumulative movement over a number of years can, however, be massive.

Because distribution channels change relatively slowly, it is easy for manufacturers to respond too slowly to their evolution. Existing channels may be declining in their popularity or efficiency, while new potential channels of distribution may be developing, unnoticed by the marketing firm. Nowhere is this more evident than in food retailing, a point that is taken up in Chapter 10.

At this stage it is sufficient for you to appreciate that factors in the distributive environment are also likely to be subject to change, especially in the legislative field – a subject taken up later in Chapter 15. As with all the other elements of the macro-environment, the distributive environment is also a source of potential threats and opportunities to the marketing firm. The marketing firm needs to monitor events closely and take appropriate action in order to adapt to changing conditions.

Wider macro-environmental forces

Up to now we have been looking at those macro-environmental factors and forces that are closest to the marketing firm. We termed this the 'proximate macro-environment'. Other macro-environmental forces have a wider influence and affect not only the marketing firm, but also those organizations and individuals (e.g., suppliers) that make up the proximate macro-environment.

Socio-cultural environment

Of all the elements in the marketing macro-environment, the socio-cultural environment probably presents the greatest challenge. People's basic beliefs, attitudes and values are shaped by the society in which they grow up. Their general behaviour, including their purchasing behaviour, is influenced by social conditioning. A more detailed and academic discussion of consumer behaviour is given in Chapter 3.

The main factor influencing a society's attitudes and behaviour is its culture. Core cultural values are firmly established within a society and are generally difficult to change. Such beliefs and values are passed on from generation to generation through the family and other social institutions such as the church, schools and government. Because core cultural values are difficult to change, they act as relatively fixed parameters within which marketing firms have to operate. Kotler[8] states that society also has a set of secondary cultural values. These secondary values are less persistent than society's core values and tend to undergo changes over time. Social and cultural influences are so interrelated that it is extremely difficult to evaluate the effects of one factor without the other. Before we look at the role of culture in more detail, let us first summarize some of the major changes that have occurred in the socio-cultural environment that can have affected marketing.

Changes in social values The 1960s saw the birth of the so-called 'permissive society'. Over a period of about 10 years, society's values went through a period of dramatic change. Society's attitude towards marriage, divorce, sex, religion, drugs, economic and social institutions and authority changed and the values of the previous generation were radically altered. People in general became more responsive to change; in fact they welcomed change. This was the period of 'individualism', 'do your own thing', and 'anything goes'. Today we have seen a reversal of many of the attitudes and beliefs of the permissive society. Today, people value health, economic security and stable relationships and in many ways a lot have returned to the social values and norms of the pre-1960s.

Changes in attitudes towards credit Over the past 20 years society's general attitude towards credit has dramatically altered. As recently as the 1960s, borrowing was generally frowned upon, except for major purchases such as cars and houses. Hire-purchase agreements were usually signed in the store manager's private office and there was something of a social stigma attached to buying something on the 'never never'. Today, credit availability has become an intrinsic part in the marketing of many products. Credit has lost its social stigma and many people own Access, Visa, American Express or individual store credit cards. Credit transactions are now conducted openly, and it is the person who never buys using credit who is considered to be unusual.

Attitudes towards health Twenty years ago people who went jogging or ate specific 'health' foods were regarded as being a little eccentric. Today, people are more aware of the health implications of what they eat and drink, and regular exercise is an important part of many people's lives. The habit of smoking, which was once considered the height of social sophistication, is now thought of as an anti-social habit. Changes in society's attitude to health have resulted in a multi-million pound industry developing and supplying health foods, clothing, books and exercise equipment.

Change in attitudes towards working women Not so very long ago, society's attitude towards working women tended to be chauvinistic. A woman's place was thought to be 'in the home' and the 'career woman' was viewed with a certain amount of suspicion. Today, such attitudes have changed and a high proportion of workers are women. This fact has doubtless contributed to the acceptance of convenience foods as a normal part of everyday life as well as to the widespread adoption of such products as home freezers and microwave ovens. The high proportion of working women has also contributed to the development of 'one stop shopping'. With both spouses working, leisure time is at a premium. Many couples now do a major 'shop' once a month, buy in bulk, store in the freezer, and cook mainly in a microwave oven.

The changes in society mentioned here do not form an exhaustive list, but are illustrative of the sort of changes that have influenced, and will continue to influence, marketing firms. Although social change is not occurring at the speed that it was in the 1960s, it is nevertheless in evidence. Marketing firms need to monitor social trends and be prepared to adapt to social changes if they intend to serve their customers effectively and remain competitive. As mentioned earlier, one of the major factors influencing changes within our society is changes in cultural beliefs and norms. It is to the subject of cultural influence, and in particular cultural change, to which the discussion now turns.

The role of culture

A society's culture is a completely learned way of life which is handed down from generation to generation. Cultural influences give each society its own peculiar attributes. Although the norms and values within a society are the result of many years of cultural conditioning, they are not static. It is cultural change, and the resulting revised norms and values within a society, that is of particular interest to the marketing firm. Nowhere is the aspect more poignant than when the company is marketing internationally, a point discussed in detail in Chapter 14.

The English anthropologist, E. B. Taylor,[9] defined culture as:

> that complex whole which includes knowledge, belief, art, morals, law, custom, and any other capabilities and habits acquired by man as a member of society.

Taylor's definition is an accepted classic in defining some of the major facets of culture, and in emphasizing that culture is very much a learned phenomenon. British culture has historically been largely materialistic, derived as it is from the protestant work ethic of self-help, hard work, thrift and the accumulation of wealth. Arguably, other Western cultures such as the United States, West Germany and Japan are even more materialistically oriented. This factor is often thought to be one of the reasons for these countries' superior economic performance. Cultural values do, however, change over time, and a number of Western core values are currently undergoing major changes. Adler[10] describes some of the changing cultural values which are particularly prevalent among the young:

- A questioning of materialistic pursuits at the peak of our affluence.
- Increasing pressure for social justice.
- A decline in respect for authority and the law.
- A belief in the rightness of militancy and confrontation.
- A love of novelty.
- A passion for style and format – paralleled by a loss of interest in content.

Sub-cultural influences

Within each culture are numerous sub-groups with their own distinguishing modes of behaviour. In the United States black Americans represent the largest racial/ethnic sub-culture. They account for 11 per cent of the total population.[11] While American marketing firms realize that it is impossible to treat such a large group of consumers as a homogeneous mass, a number of studies indicate that their consumption habits are significantly different from those of the remainder of Americans. As a result, American firms are now designing products and advertising campaigns aimed specifically at this large minority market.

Although the UK is more culturally homogeneous than the United States, firms can no longer ignore the cultural differences of the ethnic populations. Ethnic heterogeneity is slowly being recognized by more enlightened firms as a potential source of marketing opportunities. Cannon[12] highlights a number of interesting examples of marketing opportunities and problems:

- Products may need to meet special religious needs (e.g., Kosher foods).
- Marketing intermediaries may be different (e.g., the importance of small, Asian-run, shops).

- Consumer tastes may differ (e.g., Cadbury Typhoo's Poundo Yam aimed mainly at consumers of Caribbean origin).
- Language as a problem in marketing communications (e.g., in the UK, 77 per cent of Pakistani origin women and 43 per cent of Pakistani origin men cannot speak working English).

The culturally aware marketing firm will recognize that sub-cultures represent distinct market segments and will seek to increase their awareness of the needs, attitudes and motivations of sub-groups.

Culture and marketing awareness

An understanding of cultural values is of particular importance to a marketing firm involved with overseas markets. Many countries are geographically distant, but culturally close, while others that are geographically close are culturally distant. For example, France is geographically closer to the UK than say the United States or Australia, although both of these latter countries are 'closer' to the UK from a cultural point of view.

A marketing programme that has been successful in the UK often, because of cultural differences, cannot be applied directly in international markets. Cultural differences exist between different countries, and the differences must be known and evaluated by the marketing firm. A number of factors contribute to a country's overall culture including religion, education and aesthetic appreciation. For a full understanding of a country's culture, management will have to have an appreciation of the factors influencing that culture, a point that it taken up later in Chapter 14.

Political environment

To an increasing extent, the operation of business firms is being influenced by the political framework and processes in our society. Marketing management must be alert to changes in the political attitudes or 'climate' which depend on the policies of the government of the day. The political environment cannot be examined in a vacuum. Political philosophies on their own are nothing without action. The outcome of political decisions can be seen in the legislation and economic policies of government. In this sense, you will appreciate that although for clarity of exposition we are examining the various macro-environmental forces in isolation, in reality they are very much interrelated. Many of the legal, economic and social developments in our society and other countries are nothing more than the result of political decisions put into action. For example, the Conservative Party favours a monetarist approach to the management of the UK economy. It attaches great importance to the control of money supply and hence government public expenditure. The general philosophy is one of 'self-help' and free enterprise, preferring to see business in the hands of private shareholders rather than being owned by the state. Its main concern is with the reduction of the level of inflation which is seen as being vital to long-term economic growth and stability. Expenditure on services such as education and social services has generally been reduced as a percentage of total expenditure since 1979. Business, entrepreneurship, private ownership and profit are seen as being a good thing, vital to the country's future prosperity.

This discussion does not purport to make any normative statements about the running of the country or proffer political ideologies. The important thing to realize is that the political climate is of great significance to the marketing firm and is likely to have a direct bearing on many aspects of the economy and society in general.

To put the opposite political view, it is a fact that the Labour Party is based on a radically different political ideology. Moderates within the party favour Keynesian economic policies which involve larger expenditure on public works programmes. They see social programmes and a reduction in the level of unemployment as their prime objective. While they appreciate that profit is a necessary economic propellant, they look unfavourably upon what they would consider to be 'excess' profits. The Labour Party would prefer to see large sections of the economy under state control, rather than in the hands of private ownership. Under Labour, the country is likely to see an increase in public expenditure, a reduction in unemployment and a rise in the level of inflation as a result of such policies. Wages and prices may be controlled by use of a prices and incomes policy.

Although developments in the domestic political scene are likely to be of prime concern to the majority of companies, many will also be affected by international political developments. Many British firms import from, or export to, foreign countries and may even have subsidiary companies or divisions overseas. In the UK, political change is brought about through the democratic process. The UK enjoys a high degree of political stability which instils confidence in overseas buyers and suppliers and this is good for business. In some overseas countries the political situation is less stable and more volatile. Change and political power are often obtained through force rather than the democratic process. Companies operating in such a climate have to monitor the local political situation very carefully.

The political environment is the starting point from which many other macro-environmental forces originate. Firms themselves can go some way in influencing the political climate through their trade associations or organizations like the Confederation of British Industry (CBI). Organizations such as these are often looked to by the government for advice, or may themselves act as 'pressure groups' in lobbying the government over political or economic issues. Whatever industry the marketing firm is involved in, factors in the political environment at both national and international levels should be carefully monitored and understood.

Economic environment

Marketing management must understand the effects of the many economic variables that are likely to affect their business operations. We see in the mass media that inflation is rising or falling, that exchange rates are affecting the value of the pound or influencing the level of interest rates. We hear discussions on the level of unemployment, industrial output, or the current state of the balance of payments. Such economic factors are of concern to marketing firms because they influence costs, prices and demand.

Marketing firms have had to adapt to significant economic changes over the past 10 to 15 years. The most dramatic of these changes has been the lengthy economic recession originally brought on by the oil crisis sparked off by the Middle East war of autumn 1973. The dramatic increase in oil prices affected the cost of energy (e.g., transportation, power and heating) as well as the cost of many oil-based products like synthetic fibres and plastics.

The oil crisis was not only an economic factor, but also a political one. In fact developments in the economic and political environments are often closely interrelated. As Wilson[13] explains:

> What the oil crisis really signified was the end of the age of certainty, the upsetting of traditional structures and balances in the world and especially in the business environment. For the oil crisis demonstrated that any group possessing resources that were needed by others had much more power than traditionally had been recognised or wielded.

The overall economic picture is perhaps not quite as black as it has been painted. Although many British firms have lost their battle against recession and have been forced into liquidation, much

of British industry remains highly competitive, particularly in the more sophisticated and technologically advanced markets.

A further important economic development for the UK has been her joining the European
Community on 1 January 1973. The 'Common Market', as it is often called, is essentially a customs union. A customs union implies two things: first, that all tariffs between members on industrial products be abolished; and, second, that a uniform tariff be adopted for other nations'
products imported into the customs union area. Membership of the European Community has
subjected British firms to new economic pressures to which many companies are still adjusting.
Changes in economic policy and legislation are continuing developments and it is essential for
marketing firms to monitor continually all business facets affected by the Community's actual or
proposed economic policies.

Although world economic forces are of paramount importance to marketing firms, particularly those involved with either importing or exporting, domestic economic forces usually have
the most immediate impact. The level of domestic unemployment affects the demand for many
consumer products, especially those classed as 'luxury goods'. This in turn affects the demand for
many industrial products, particularly manufacturing plant such as machine tools. The rate of inflation and the cost of borrowing capital affect the potential returns from new investment and in-
hibit the adoption of new technologies. Governments of every persuasion attempt to encourage
economic growth through various policy measures. Tax concessions, government grants, employment subsidies and capital depreciation allowances are some of the measures that have been
used.

The marketing firm needs to monitor continually the economic environment at both the domestic and international level. The 'ebb and flow' of economic forces and the policies which
governments use to attempt to manage their economies could have a significant impact on a
firm's business operations. As with all other environmental factors, economic factors can be
viewed as a source of both opportunities and threats to the marketing firm. By carefully monitoring and understanding the economic environment, a firm's management should be in a better
position to capitalize upon the opportunities and do something about reducing the threats.

Technological environment

Technology is a major environmental influence upon the marketing firm. Not only does it affect
the firm's operations and products, but also consumers' life styles and consumption patterns.
Management must be aware of the impact of technological changes. As Wilson[14] explains in relation to electronics:

> The development of the microprocessor and its large scale production has revolutionised information
> collection, processing and dissemination which in turn is affecting the whole spectrum of marketing
> activity.

The impact of new information technology has been particularly marked in the marketing research area. For example, it is now possible to design and administer questionnaires via computer terminals. At present this method is used on a limited basis, but it is likely to become more
frequently used in the future. Computer assisted telephone interviewing (CATI) has revolution-
ized the speed with which surveys can be completed. Responses are fed immediately into a computer and a report 'hard copy' can be available immediately after the final interview is completed.
As Thomas[15] explains:

> On-line interviewing is now in widespread use in the larger data gathering market research firms. Inter-

views, using telephones, work from a questionnaire which is displayed on a VDU and responses are keyed straight into the computer.

Sales forecasting has always been, and always will be, an important marketing activity. Until recently, the majority of firms tended to use subjective or judgemental sales forecasting methods. The development of computers and available software programs has brought the use of sophisticated forecasting techniques within the reach of all companies. The role of sales forecasting is discussed in greater detail in Chapter 6.

Technology also affects the way that goods are distributed and promoted. Containerized freight and automated warehousing have increased the efficiency with which products can be distributed. Sales representatives can now use audio-visual equipment for presentations and demonstrations. Technology is also affecting marketing at the retail level. Electronic point of sale (EPOS) data capture is now used by the major retailers. The 'laser checkout' automatically records consumer purchases and is used to analyse sales and to control and re-order stock. Operation of the laser checkout system depends on the electronic reading of codes. Many fast moving consumer goods (FMCG) manufacturers have responded to these developments by incorporating 'bar codes' on their product labels.

Technology has influenced the development of products themselves. Calculators, aerosol cans, televisions, compact disc players, video-recorders, word processors and instant cameras have all come into widespread use over the past few decades. While older industries are in decline, whole new industries, sometimes referred to as the 'sunrise industries', have developed and grown to take their place. These new industries have capitalized on developments in the technological environment (e.g., information technology, biotechnology and aersopace).

The rate of technological change would appear to be accelerating. Marketing firms themselves play a part in technological advancement and must make use of current technology. They must ask themselves what products or processes are likely to be demanded and technologically feasible to produce in, say, the next 10 or 20 years that are not available now. Management must not only anticipate the impact of technological change on the firm, but also on all other elements in the macro-environment.

PART II THE COMPANY SETTING

Implementing the marketing concept

An essential element of implementing the marketing concept is the need for the marketing function, or rather the managers in it, to develop effective working relationships and systems for ensuring coordination and cooperation between marketing and the different functional areas. In practice, implementing the marketing concept often gives rise to conflict between marketing and other functions. A company needs to understand the sources and issues of such conflict, and also needs to look for ways to convert potentially damaging dysfunctional conflict into more functional forms of management behaviour.

Perhaps one of the best ways to appreciate the range and nature of the types of problems encountered when translating the marketing concept into practice is to reflect for a moment on the following two problems:

1. Suppose for a moment that you wanted to gauge the extent to which a company had implemented the marketing concept; how would you assess this; what would you look for in the company; what would be the signs?
2. Alternatively, and now that you know what the marketing concept is, if you were made re-

sponsible for turning the production- or sales-oriented company into one which is marketing oriented, what steps would you take?

How problems are approached, and indeed the identification of the problems themselves, is not just one more academic exercise. These questions go right to the heart of the very practical issue of moving from what seems to be a statement of fundamental common sense – the marketing concept – to a position where a company can rightly be judged to be 'good' at marketing. After all, for many years now, politicians, academics, industry pundits, and so on, have extolled the virtues, indeed the necessity, for British companies to improve in this respect. Further, and interestingly, not many practising managers, from whatever function, would deny the central importance of the customer and his or her needs. Fewer, but perhaps still not an insignificant number, of these same managers, including those directly involved in marketing management, would be willing to admit that there is still plenty of room for improvement.

It appears, therefore, that for some reason, translating a concept into practice poses problems which some companies find insurmountable. To explore this further, let us return to the first of our hypothetical problems – that of gauging the extent of implementation.

A doctoral thesis completed at the University of Bradford as long ago as 1969 still remains what is perhaps one of the most thought-provoking and, therefore, useful frameworks for judging the extent to which a company has moved from marketing concept to marketing practice. In his thesis Saddik[16] suggested that in order to make this judgement we should look to seven key areas or aspects of a company's operations, namely:

– Company philosophy/managerial attitudes
– Organizational structure
– Planning procedures – particularly as they relate to marketing planning
– New product development activities and decisions
– Intelligence and information fostering activities and decisions
– Promotional activities and decisions
– Distribution activities and decisions.

Using these seven areas of measurement Saddik's study investigated the extent to which companies in some of the important local industries in the area, engineering and textiles, had implemented the marketing concept. With so much time now having passed since Saddik completed his findings there would be little point in detailing them other than to note that at the time he concluded that the marketing concept was far from being fully accepted and implemented in the industries studied.

Nevertheless, his framework for measurements is still relevant, particularly if we reclassify some of his seven criteria. This reclassification is shown below:

– Company philosophy/business definition
– Managerial/workforce attitudes
– Organizational structure
– Planning and information gathering
– Processes and procedures for decision making.

We shall examine each of these in turn in order to clarify their significance to the implementation issue.

Company philosophy/business definition

We have already seen that the marketing concept is an idea or rather a philosophy of the essential purpose and conduct of a business. This philosophy is based on the notion of *consumer sovereignty*: that the purpose of a business is to create customers, and unless a business satisfies the needs of its customers it will not, in the long run, and under normal competitive conditions, survive and prosper. In order to begin the process of implementation it could be argued that the first step is the acceptance of this philosophy. In the context of the measurement problem, which was posed earlier, we could perhaps gauge the extent to which a company had implemented the marketing concept by examining its philosophy. But where in a company would we look to for evidence of having accepted this philosophy? How could we measure it? Although there is no doubt some difficulty in such measurement – after all companies as such do not have philosophies, rather it is the people in them who have – there are a variety of signs which would indicate the extent to which a company had passed this important first test. For example, an indication of company philosophy can often be gleaned from a company's annual reports or, alternatively, one might look to a company's Articles and Memorandum of Association. Perhaps the clearest, and certainly the most important indication (and therefore the best measure), would be found in how the organization defined its business.

The importance of business definition in the context of implementing the marketing concept was perhaps most clearly highlighted by Levitt.[17] In his 'Marketing myopia' article Levitt illustrates that failure to define what business a company is currently in as a clear indication of a failure, or an unwillingness to implement the marketing concept. An incorrect business definition, in Levitt's terms, is one which is too narrow and/or based on a false premise. For example, how would you define the business of the following companies?

– General Motors
– Max Factor
– IBM

Even with no particular or detailed knowledge of any of these companies, no doubt you could at least guess what business they are in. Certainly you would think that the companies themselves would have little difficulty answering his question. But would you, or they, be correct? More specifically, would your or the companies' answers indicate that progress had been made towards implementing the marketing concept? Let us take one of the companies mentioned above to explore this further: IBM.

IBM represents the initial letters of a company called International Business Machines. Founded in America in the early 1920s, this now large and very successful multinational company currently produces a range of products primarily for use in the business office. IBM is probably best known for its computer products, both hardware and software. In fact this is a market in which it has come to dominate. The answer to the question 'what business is it in?', therefore, would appear to be straightforward. After all the company name itself gives us the answer. Surely this is a company which is in the business of making machines for business, or, alternatively, given the prime focus on computing, this company is in the business computing market.

Perhaps your thoughts were moving along the same lines in terms of defining IBM's business? If so, they may be accused of suffering from Levittt's marketing myopia. If IBM were to define its business in this way it would be a strong indication that the company had not begun to implement the marketing concept.

The reason for this can be found in Levitt's original article. Here Levitt proposed that a company which defined its business in terms of the products it produces is invariably suffering from what was termed in Chapter 1 as production or product orientation. In our terms, its company philosophy – as represented by business definition – would imply that it has not begun to implement the marketing concept. Such a company, Levitt argued, would have a shortsighted and blinkered view of its markets and customers and would, therefore, tend to miss both marketing opportunities and marketing threats. Because of this, eventually a business definition based on products or production would in most cases lead to the long-run decline of a business.

In contrast Levitt suggested that market-/customer-based business definitions should be used to condition company philsophy. Using our earlier example a customer-/market-based business definition for IBM might be represented by the following:

> IBM is in the business of meeting the needs of businessmen for speedy and economical systems for data production, handling and interpretation.

Remember of course that this definition is only hypothetical; business definition is not easy. Some companies have spent considerable time and effort arriving at a meaningful definition. The purpose of this hypothetical definition for IBM is to demonstrate the difference between a marketing philosophy and a product or production philosophy. Our second IBM business definition is based on customer/market needs rather than being couched in terms of what IBM predominantly produces, i.e., computers. There are many advantages to be gained from such a market-/need-based definition, for example:

- It helps to identify competitors, present and potential.
- It acts as a guide for strategic decision making.
- It forces the company to consider what the customer is actually purchasing and why. Customers buy benefits not products.

Because of these and other advantages of properly defining the business we shall return to this aspect again in Chapter 4 when we consider marketing decisions. At this point it should be noted that the redefinition of a business from a product- to a customer-based one represents a fundamental shift in company philosophy and would represent a key signal to the effect that a company had begun to implement the marketing concept. An indication of the significance of such a shift is illustrated in the following extracts from a leading UK management publication.[18]

> ... British Airways of late has made the astonishing discovery that an airline's success, in this age of overcapacity, might actually depend on pleasing its customers ... [now] the focus has shifted squarely to the market and how to please it – a 'quantum leap', according to [BA's] head of marketing ...

Managerial/workforce attitudes

It has been suggested that one of the difficulties of assessing company philosophy stems from the fact that companies do not have philosophies, rather it is the people in them, and in particular their senior management, who do. A customer-/market-based business definition is thus in itself a reflection of a certain attitude on the part of management. Perhaps then, in gauging the extent to which a company has begun to implement the marketing concept, we should focus on the predisposition of the managers in a company particularly as they relate to marketing in general and customer needs in particular. In fact, an essential second step in implementing the marketing concept is the recognition and acceptance throughout a company, in every function, and at every level from shopfloor to chairman, of the importance of satisfying customer needs. The point is that redefining the business alone is not sufficient to ensure that a company has become marketing oriented. After all such a redefinition may reflect an acceptance of the marketing concept by only the senior management of a company or even by only the marketing team itself. Neither of these is sufficient. Implementing the marketing concept requires that the whole of a company and the people in it be oriented towards the needs of the customer. But what are the practical issues and problems to which this assertion gives rise, and in particular what steps can a company take to instil this attitude?

One of the critical issues which this need to change attitudes gives rise to is the possibility of conflict between marketing and other functional areas. For example, the production or accountancy functions have their own jobs to do, their own set of specific problems to solve and activities to perform. Their task is not to take account of customer needs – this is the responsibility of the marketing function. Again, few of these other functional managers would deny the importance of customer needs, but they often find it difficult to relate this to their own activities. If not carefully managed, attempting to instil a consumer-oriented attitude throughout a company can result in antagonism, and often open hostility to the ideas of marketing, in general, and towards the marketing function in particular. A carefully planned, and above all diplomatic, programme of activities is essential in achieving this second step in implementing – instilling the right attitude.

To achieve this some companies have taken the step of organizing seminars, teach-ins, familiarization programmes, etc., for company personnel designed to acquaint them with customer needs and their own role in meeting these. The limited evidence available on the success of such schemes would appear to suggest that they can contribute significantly in turning a concept into a practice. After all, most of us respond well to being kept informed and to being able to see how we can contribute to the achievement of objectives. Some of the best examples of this sort of practice leading to positive attitudes and improved company performance have come from the Japanese companies, many of which hold regular meetings with representatives of the workforce to discuss consumer-related problems. We shall return to some of these ideas later in this chapter when we consider the issue of conflict. You should realize by now, however, that in redefining the business – the first step in implementation – we should not expect, as if by some process of osmosis, for this to filter automatically through the different layers of the company. We need to take steps to ensure that it does.

Organizational structure

As we saw in Chapter 1, the development of the marketing concept can be viewed as a series of evolutionary changes from production, through sales orientation and so on. We saw also that accompanying these different steps of evolution may be changes in the organizational structure of a company. Again, redefining the structure of a company is often seen as being essential to the implementation of the concept. Stanton[19] encapsulates this notion in his two suggestions for translating the philosophy of marketing into action, namely that:

... the marketing activities in a firm must be better co-ordinated and managed ...
[and]
the chief marketing executive must be accorded a more important role in company planning ...

In implementing the marketing concept various activities which traditionally may have been the province of other management functions, for example sales, product planning, and inventory control, should come within the remit and control of the marketing function.

Stanton's ideas about the organizational requirements for implementing marketing are not unique, indeed they are broadly representative of most marketing authors on this topic. Not surprisingly, then, a frequently used indicator of the extent of marketing commitment in companies has been the organizational chart. After all, can a company be said to have implemented the marketing concept if the marketing function and the managers in it occupy a very lowly position in the company hierarchy? More extreme still, can the company which does not have a marketing department at all be said to have implemented the concept? It may surprise you to learn that the answer to both these questions can be yes! In other words, it is possible for a company to have implemented the concept fully without this being accompanied by changes in its organization chart. More importantly, and again reinforcing what was said earlier, you should understand that it matters little what we call it, or where it appears in the organization chart – if at all, so long as someone is responsible for representing the customer and his needs to the rest of the company, and for coordinating those activities necessary to meet those needs.

This should not be interpreted as meaning that organizing for marketing and assessing its overall role or position in company structure is unimportant. Equally, it is the case that often implementing the concept will necessitate changes in company structure. All that is being said is that the organizational chart alone is not sufficient to judge the extent to which a company has implemented the concept. Nor, therefore, are exercises in chartsmanship, changing job titles, elevating the status of marketing in the hierarchy, etc., of themselves, sufficient to bring about marketing orientation.

If anything, if we want to look to organizational factors in assessing the extent of implementation (and if we want to ensure that our company is taking the right steps in its programme of implementing) we would be better advised to look at *what activities are performed*: by whom; involving what relationships and authority; and to what purpose, than simply looking at the job titles in a box on the organization chart. It is to some of these 'activities' parts of marketing that we now turn our attention.

Planning and information gathering

There is no doubt that implementing the marketing concept requires that planning, and the gathering of information on which such plans are based, assumes a greater importance in overall company activities. In addition, in the marketing-oriented company the focus for planning and information-gathering activities centres around the hub of company decision making – customer needs and satisfaction.

These implications of implementing the marketing concept provide yet another basis for gauging the extent to which a company has in fact become marketing oriented. To return to our earlier measurement problem again, if we look at the extent to which a company plans for its future, and in particular the procedures and information on which such plans are based, this will enable us to assess the extent to which the marketing concept has been implemented. In order to appreciate this consider the following example:

> ... your company has just completed its annual marketing plan for the forthcoming year. The planning process commenced with the preparation of a sales forecast based on the pattern and trends of the previous five years' sales. On the basis of this forecast a sales budget has been prepared and translated into production and operating budgets for the company as a whole. The plan includes a detailed schedule of activities and decision making required to implement the plan including product, pricing, distribution and promotion decisions ...

The question is to what extent is your company marketing oriented?

The answer is that we cannot tell without knowing on what basis the plan was prepared, and in particular with what knowledge of the facts about the market and the customers. To continue our example:

> ... your company has recently acquired a new managing director who was previously employed in the capacity of marketing director by a fast-moving consumer goods company. Her experience in marketing is substantial. After considering your company's proposed

marketing plan she calls in the marketing manager responsbile for preparing it. Specifically she is worried that the plan contains no details of the information and market facts on which the plan is based . . .

The marketing manager explains again that the plan is based on his sales forecast. When asked what market research has been carried out in recent years, the marketing manager replies that this expensive luxury has never been considered necessary. After all, both he and most of his staff have worked in the industry for some twenty years.

The newly appointed managing director then proceeds to ask the marketing manager the following questions:

- Who are our customers?
- What do they buy?
- How do they consider value?
- How do they buy?
- When do they buy?

To the marketing manager's consternation he finds these questions difficult to answer. The simple fact is that he has never before considered them.

The evidence suggests that planning is not customer based. No attempt has been made to gather the necessary information and facts on which to base effective marketing decisions. In short, the company has a long way to go in implementing the marketing concept.

The example illustrates that an essential step in implementing the marketing concept is the establishment of planning based on an accurate, factual understanding of customer needs. This, in turn, requires that a company have adequate sensing mechanisms for analysing and interpreting these needs. In most companies this sensing mechanism is provided by the marketing research function. However, you should be careful not to interpret this as meaning that implementing the marketing concept will always require the establishment of a marketing research function. The smaller company may not be in a position to afford this. What matters is not how much a company spends on it, nor who does it, and certainly not what we call it, as long as a company is basing its decision making on an adequate and accurate mechanism for sensing market and customer needs. It is to these decision-making aspects of implementation that we now turn our attention.

Processes and procedures for decision making

Perhaps the clearest indication of the extent to which a company has implemented the marketing concept is contained in its processes and procedures for decision making, and in particular how decisions are made with regard to products, prices, distribution and promotion. Again an example will serve to illustrate this:

. . . your company spends some 2 per cent of its annual turnover on developing new products in its research laboratories. On average, over the past ten years, the company has launched four new products every year. Only three of the last 25 products launched have been successful, but these have earned good profits. The research and development team is given a free hand to develop any products which the company is technically and commercially able to produce and market. Once the technical and production problems have been overcome for a new product, it is passed over to marketing for commercial evaluation and possible launch. This year the company has only two products which it feels are worth launching; these products have reached the stage where a decision has to be made with respect to their market price. In fact the pricing of the company's new products presents few problems. All products, including new ones, are priced on a cost-plus basis. The procedure is that the accountancy department calculates the variable costs of producing the product (raw materials and labour costs) and adds to this a proportion of the fixed costs of factory overheads (rent, rates, etc.). To this 'total cost' is added a percentage profit margin according to the estimated life of the product and the investment required to develop and launch the product. The result is the final price of the product . . .

At first glance the company does not appear to be doing too much wrong – certainly its success rate for new products is low, but this is not unusual as new product development is risky. But to what extent is the company a marketing-oriented company, and what clues are there in the example which would enable us to assess this?

In fact, on the basis of the relatively small amount of information given in the example, it is almost certain that the company has not implemented the marketing concept to any great extent. The evidence for this conclusion lies in the processes and procedures for decision making. There appears to be little communication between research and development and marketing at least in the early, and most crucial, stages of new product development. Similarly, the procedure for pricing of products is distinctly non-marketing oriented. Demand considerations appear to play little part in this decision-making process.

What the example illustrates is the fact that perhaps the most fundamental change which is required to implement marketing in a company is an often subtle, but nevertheless vital, change in how decisions are taken. There are two related aspects to this.

The first change in decision making required to implement the marketing concept is for every department or function, and not just marketing, in the company to place the customer and his needs at the very centre of its decision making. Not only is this a question of what was referred to earlier as education, but also the establishment of a system of processes and procedures for functional decision making which is customer oriented in every department of the company and one which is based on adequate and accurate market facts.

The second aspect of changed decision making in the company which implements the marketing concept is that the different areas of functional decision making, however customer oriented they may be individually, must be effectively *coordinated* to achieve a concerted and consistent, company-wide marketing effort. This is a key function of marketing management, but again if misunderstood (by other functions) and/or badly managed (by marketing or senior management) can give rise to problems and further hostility.

In effect it is in its decision making that a company evidences the extent to which it has been successful in all of the previously discussed facets of the implementation issue. But what of marketing's role in this process, and more specifically what are the functional responsibilities of the marketing department in a company?

The function of marketing and its responsibilities

Our discussion of the requirements of implementing the marketing concept point to a number of key roles for the marketing function in a company. First, the marketing function must act as an intermediary between the company and its customers' needs. In fulfilling this boundary-spanning role, marketing acts as a sort of representative for the customer, interpreting his motives for purchase and ensuring that the company comes closest to satisfying the customer's requirements. This notion is shown in Fig. 2.2.

In addition to this boundary-spanning role for the marketing function, and because of the

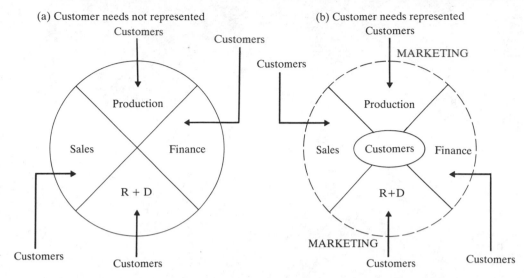

Figure 2.2 The boundary-spanning role of marketing
(*Source*: Adapted from P. Kotler, *Marketing Management: Analysis, Planning and Control*, 5th edn.[1])

importance of planning referred to earlier, a further key role for marketing in a company is the formulation of company and marketing plans based on market facts and information. This notion is shown in Fig. 2.3. The planning role of marketing management is discussed later in the text in Chapters 4 and 13.

Finally, the marketing function must attempt to ensure that decision making throughout the company adequately reflects both company and marketing plans, and the assessment of market and customer needs on which these are based. This is shown in Fig. 2.4.

These three broad areas of responsibility for the marketing function must be translated into a specific set of responsibilities and activities for marketing personnel – a job description in other words. Some marketing textbooks go further than this and list what these are likely to be in the typical company. An example of this approach is that given by Buell.[20] Unfortunately such 'lists' often do not take account of the fact that there is no such thing as the typical company. All companies are different and we should expect to find that within the three broad areas of responsibilities for marketing, described above, specific responsibilities and activities for marketing will differ between companies. We should also remember that as in other functional areas of business, marketing too may comprise of a hierarchy of management levels, each of which will have its own set of responsibilities and activities. The product or brand manager level of the marketing hierarchy, for example, faces a very different (if interrelated) set of issues from those facing the senior marketing manager in a company.

Achieving marketing orientation

We have seen that becoming more marketing oriented may entail an enlarged role for marketing in overall company decision making. Functions and responsibilities which had previously been the province of other functional areas in a company may, under the marketing concept, come within the remit of the marketing department. Although it is not inevitably the case, both enlarged responsibility and increased status are often the outcome of this process. This can give rise to conflict between marketing and other departments. Some of the possible issues of such conflict were discussed earlier and you will recall, for example, that marketing and production

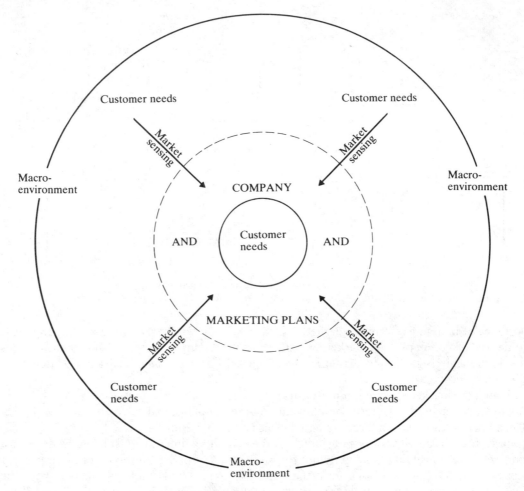

Figure 2.3   Planning and information gathering

may have very different notions as to what constitutes effective management and decision making within each of their respective functions. So too may marketing and research and development, and marketing and sales, and marketing and finance. In fact it would not be an exaggeration to suggest that the potential for inter-functional conflict is at its greatest when we consider the relationship between marketing and virtually every other functional area of a business. Of course, conflict in itself is not always undesirable as Shapiro points out,[21] not unlike market competition, conflict can ensure effectiveness and efficiency. However, conflict can reach such levels as to be dysfunctional; it can effectively disable the participants and reduce efficiency. Unfortunately, some companies have attempted to minimize the potential for conflict between marketing and others (or rather provided a mechanism for reducing the outcome of such conflict situations) by increasing the power and authority of one of the protagonists – marketing. The usual result of enforcing 'agreement' in this way is more, not less, conflict. The reason for this is that simply increasing the authority of marketing over other functional areas does not remove the basic issues which probably gave rise to the conflict in the first place. On the contrary, the nature of marketing's authority and power relationships will often be at the heart of it.

What is required is a mechanism whereby there are no 'losers'. Handy[22] suggests a number

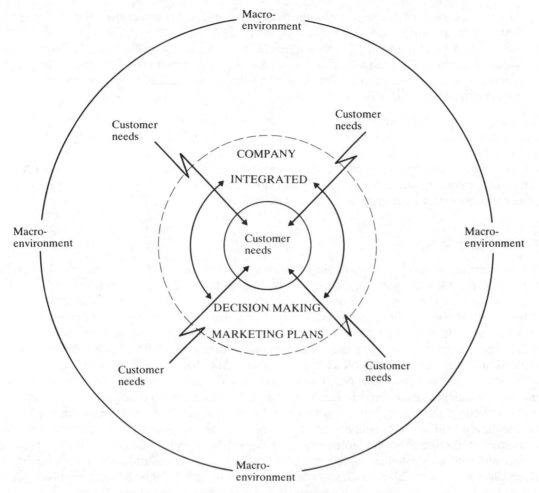

Figure 2.4   Marketing's coordinating role

of procedures which a company might use to achieve this, and which may bring about more effective coordination between the various functional groups. Some of these and their relevance to marketing's relationships in a company are shown below:

1. The agreement of common, overriding and realistic goals or objectives. 'Customer satisfaction' is not a meaningful goal if a department is not judged upon it. Nor is it likely to become an accepted goal if one or more of the parties does not contribute to it or is unsure of how precisely they might contribute.
2. The establishment of information and control systems such that the different departments or parties can appreciate and evaluate their contribution to the goal of customer satisfaction. For example, quality control and inspection might be kept informed of the role of their efforts in increasing sales and reducing customer complaints.
3. The stimulation of high interaction and frequent communication between functional groups. Trust, or lack of it, often lies at the heart of conflict between departments. Regular contact and communication between marketing and other managers can help considerably in building a climate of trust.

4. The establishment of clear *and agreed* terms of reference for marketing and other departments with respect to duties, authority, etc.
5. The establishment of clear and explicit overall company policies within which each functional area will operate. For example, if it is company policy to produce a full-product line, both marketing and production know precisely where they each stand and the potential for conflict between these departments is much reduced.

Even with these mechanisms, conflict can arise between marketing and other departments. Where the parties themselves cannot settle such conflict in a manner which is conducive to effective company management, procedures for arbitration and conciliation will be required. Above all, both effective implementation of the marketing concept and the establishment of effective working relationships between marketing and other functions require positive commitment and support from the most senior management in a company.

CONCLUSIONS

We have examined the role of marketing in various settings. In particular we have looked at the problems and issues surrounding the implementation of the marketing concept.

We have seen that implementing the marketing concept will require that a company pay attention to business definition, managerial and employee attitudes, and the systems and procedures for planning and information gathering. Sometimes, but not always, adopting the marketing concept may also give rise to changes in organizational structure. Perhaps the clearest indication of the extent to which attention to these factors has resulted in increased marketing orientation is in a company's processes and procedures for decision making. To have fully implemented the marketing concept requires that all business decisions, and not just those concerned with marketing, adequately reflect customer and market needs. Furthermore, a company must ensure that individual/functional decision making is coordinated so as to achieve a concerted and consistent marketing effort. In implementing the marketing concept a company must be prepared to face and deal with potential conflict and hostility towards the ideas and activities of marketing. Regardless of the specific mechanisms for improving the relationship between marketing and other departments an essential requirement is the commitment and support of senior management to improving marketing practice.

APPLICATION QUESTIONS

1. To what extent do you consider that factors in the economic environment are the result of decisions taken within the political environment?
2. For a company of your choice suggest:
   (a) a product-oriented business definition;
   (b) a market-oriented business definition.
3. What types of individuals or organizations make up the proximate macro-environment? To what extent are these individuals or organizations affected themselves by wider macro-environmental factors?
4. What do you understand by the term 'boundary spanning' in the context of marketing's role in a company?
5. In implementing the marketing concept careful attention must be given to the relationships between marketing and other functions. Outline the nature of these relationships and discuss what can be done to minimize any conflict.

REFERENCES

1. Kotler, P., *Marketing Management: Analysis, Planning and Control*, 5th edn, Prentice-Hall, London, 1984, p. 77.
2. Russ, F. A. and C. A. Kirkpatrick, *Marketing*. Little, Brown & Co., Boston, MA, 1982, p. 24.
3. *Collins English Dictionary*, William Collins, London, 1983, p. 931.
4. Darwin, C. R., *On the Origin of Species*, 1859.
5. Stanton, W. J., M. S. Sommers and J. G. Barnes, *Fundamentals of Marketing*, McGraw-Hill, New York, 1977, p. 27.
6. Boone, L. E. and D. L. Kurtz, *Contemporary Marketing*, 2nd edn, Dryden Press, Hinsdale, IL, 1977, p. 30.
7. Davidson, J. H., *Offensive Marketing*, Pelican Books, 1979, p. 232.
8. Kotler, P., op. cit., p. 107.
9. Taylor, E. B., *Primitive Culture*, Murray, London, 1971, p. 1.
10. Adler, M., 'Cashing-in on the cop-out: cultural change and marketing potential', *Business Horizons*, February 1970, p. 21.
11. Boone, L. E. and D. L. Kurtz, op. cit., p. 163.
12. Cannon, T., *Basic Marketing, Principles and Practice*, Holt, Rinehart and Winston, New York, 1985, pp. 38–39.
13. Wilson, M., *The Management of Marketing*, Gower Press, New York, 1980, p. 5.
14. Wilson, M., op. cit., p. 7.
15. Thomas, M., 'World of research', *MRS Newsletter*, no. 174, September 1980.
16. Saddik, S. M. A., Marketing in the Wool Textile, Textile Machinery and Clothing Industries (PhD Thesis, University of Bradford Management Centre, April 1969).
17. Levitt, T. 'Marketing myopia', *Harvard Business Review*, July–August 1960, pp. 45–46.
18. 'BA's new flight path', *Management Today*, July 1984, p. 44.
19. Stanton, W. J., *Fundamentals of Marketing*, 5th edn, McGraw-Hill, Tokyo, 1978, pp. 11–15.
20. Buell, V. P., *Marketing Management in Action*, McGraw-Hill, New York, 1966, pp. 23–27.
21. Shapiro, B. P., 'Can marketing and manufacturing coexist?', *Harvard Business Review*, September–October 1977, pp. 104–14.
22. Handy, C. B., *Understanding Organisations*, 1st edn, Penguin, Harmondsworth, 1976, p. 236.

THREE

MARKETING AND CUSTOMERS

INTRODUCTION

This chapter covers the behavioural aspects of the relationship between buyers and sellers – or, more precisely, the relationship between marketer and customer. The distinction here is important because there is a significant conceptual difference between 'marketing' and 'selling', as has already been pointed out in Chapter 1.

Figure 3.1 depicts a model which graphically illustrates this conceptual disparity. Thus selling may be described as an activity which is manufactured and production oriented whereas marketing, conversely, is supply or service oriented.

The key concept is consumer choice. Moreover, it is choice of what can be made available rather than a choice between existing alternatives. Marketing implies a wide choice of products and services; selling implies a finite range of goods and one suspects that the latter has more to do with efficiencies in the production process rather than effectiveness in the marketplace. Indeed, many of the problems presently facing the UK have been ascribed to the difficulty we have in adjusting to a market-based economy as distinct from a manufacturing-based economy. The difference is clearly shown in the comparative performances of such trading nations as Japan, whose employment of the marketing concept has resulted in the dominance of other nations' previously production-oriented attitudes.

The implications of confusing or misapplying these concepts are truly significant. As governments of predominantly manufacturing nations are well aware, the macro-economic effects of competitive market-oriented trading ultimately have to be recognized if such nations are to survive and prosper.

For our purposes, an appreciation of buyer behaviour will look specifically at the way in which such processes of choice occur, the criteria by which products and services are chosen and the implications for marketers of the processes involved.

It is felt that since there is a fundamental difference between the way in which individuals buy privately and individuals (or groups of individuals) buy professionally (that is, on behalf of their organization(s)) two different approaches should be taken. The next section is concerned with organizational buying and a later section with individual consumer buyer behaviour. In order to clarify the processes involved, each section uses models to illustrate graphically the concepts and stages involved in purchase behaviour. Clearly this text is not able to discuss fully such behavioural implications and for a more detailed treatment the reader is directed to Chisnall's pioneering behavioural text.[1]

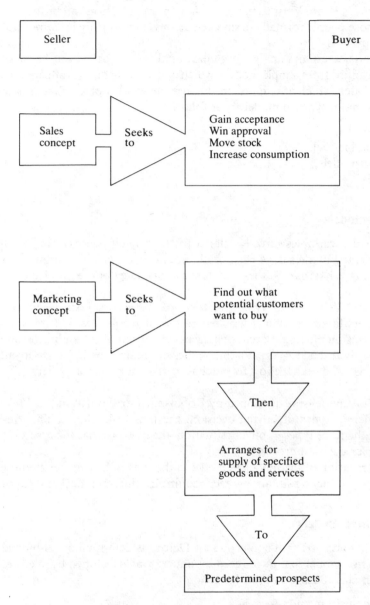

Figure 3.1   Sales versus marketing concept

ORGANIZATIONAL BUYING

Organizational buying can be viewed as a transaction between a number of individuals, rather than an action by one person. Various people within an organization will be involved in the buying process, and those people formally designated as buyers may only be responsible for a small part of the overall process.

Attempts to understand and analyse organizational buying behaviour have been many and varied. They have ranged from simple models, which concentrate on the influence of a single variable, to complex models which attempt to encompass the whole operation and nature of buying decisions. The four major types of model are as follows:

1. Task-oriented models.
2. Non-task-oriented models.
3. Decision process models.
4. Complex models.

1. Task-oriented models

These models consider variables directly related to the buying process, for example, price. A number of task-oriented models have been produced, none of which attempts a comprehensive explanation of buying behaviour. Rather each looks at one facet of the problem.

Source-loyalty model   Webster and Wind put forward the source-loyalty model.[2] This model maintains that buyers favour previous suppliers in that it recognizes that much organizational buying is routine decision making. Purchasing agents will attempt to establish relationships with vendors that are likely to be self-perpetuating and easily maintained. Source-loyalty allows the buyer to minimize risk and search effort by purchasing from a known supplier.

Buy-class model   This model was developed by Robinson, Faris and Wind in 1967.[3] The model identifies three different types of buying decision: the new task, the modified re-buy and the straight re-buy. Of the three types of buying situation, the new task has the greatest degree of risk and the most complex decision process.

The main contribution of the buy-class model to theories of buying behaviour is its recognition of different types of buying situations, each requiring a different marketing approach.

2. Non-task-oriented models

These are primarily concerned with non-economic factors as determinants of buying behaviour.

The perceived risk model first introduced by Bauer[4] was developed by Webster and Wind.[5] They identified four classifications of risk reduction:

(a) Information acquisition and processing.
(b) Goal reduction.
(c) Loyalty.
(d) Investment reduction.

Source loyalty is seen as one of the most effective methods of risk reduction. Research has shown that buyers favour familiar suppliers. In introducing a new product, source credibility gives a well-known supplier an advantage because the buyer perceives lower risk in a decision to buy from that company.

3. Decision process models

Research has been carried out to study the buying process empirically. Cyert *et al.*[6] followed the decision-making process of a company buying data processing equipment. Three aspects of the decision process were observed:

(a) Routine processes that recur within the organization at various stages in the decision.
(b) Communication processes which represent the information flow within the organization.
(c) Problem-solving processes, which attempt to locate solutions to the buying problem.

Other studies have also been carried out. Raymond E. Corey[7] identified four elements of a procurement strategy:

– Procurement scope.
– Supplier selection.
– Price/quantity determination.
– Negotiating strategy.

Decision process models are useful in providing an overall understanding of how an organization buys. This helps the supplier to formulate a marketing strategy. These models may tend to oversimplify the process, but they often form the basic concepts on which more complex models are based.

4. Complex models

Complex models have been developed from earlier models by researchers attempting to explain the multifaceted nature of organizational buying behaviour. Each model incorporates a number of variables and processes. The lack of empirical support means that the usefulness of these models depends upon how well each variable is defined.

Webster and Wind model (Fig. 3.2) This model is concerned with environmental, organizational, interpersonal and individual buying determinants. The model implies that these determinants affect individual and group decision-making processes and final buying decisions. The environmental influences in this model are seen to act as constraints on the buying goals of the organization. Although the marketer cannot control any of these factors, an understanding of the parts they play may be critical to success.

An explanation of the organizational influence relies upon Harold Leavitt's four elements of the buying organization: people, technology, structure and task.[8] The concept of the buying centre is one example of how the model uses these elements. The buying concept recognizes that a number of people participate in the buying decision including individuals and groups from various functions in the organization.

The model also suggests that within the decision-making unit there are a number of roles that people play.

(a) *Users* – they often initiate the buying process and help define specifications.
(b) *Influencers* – these people may have no direct connection with the decision. However, their judgements and perceptions of a product or supplier may affect the final decision.
(c) *Buyers* – the individuals who negotiate the purchase.

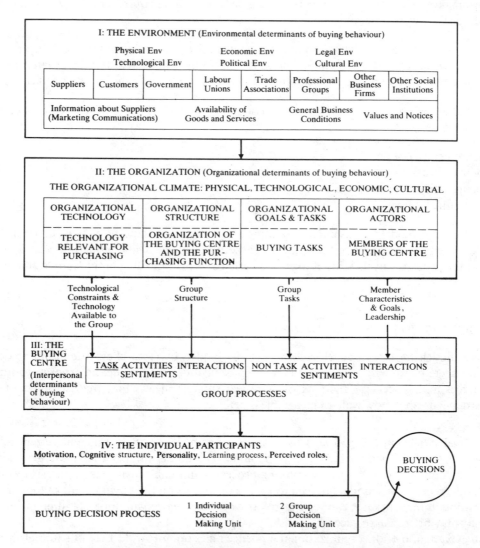

Figure 3.2   Webster and Wind model of organizational buying behaviour
(*Source*: W. Webster and Y. Wind, *Organizational Buying Behavior*, Prentice-Hall, 1972.)

(d) *Deciders* – these people make the actual decision, they are often difficult to identify and they may be formal or informal decision makers.

(e) *Gatekeeper* – this person regulates the flow of information.

An individual may play more than one of these roles.

Although this model is a valuable contribution to the theory of organizational buying behaviour in that it indicates a whole range of factors which can directly or indirectly influence the outcome of a buying decision, it still provides only a static representation of a dynamic situation.

Sheth model (Fig. 3.3) This model was proposed by Sheth in 1973[9] and was developed from the Howard–Sheth[10] model of consumer behaviour. The model concentrates on information sources and portrays a more dynamic situation. The buying centre consists of purchasing agents, engineers, users and others. The actions and expectations of the individuals are influenced by previous experience and the information received by the individuals is subject to their own perceptual distortion.

The model is dynamic in that it considers time and acknowledges that any future decisions which are made will use continually updated information. The Sheth model is successful in four ways:

(a) It demonstrates the complexity of industrial buying behaviour.
(b) It depicts the most important variables in a systematic way.
(c) It is a generalized stimulus–response model of the behaviour of industrial buyers.
(d) A number of theories and concepts are brought together and are supported by empirical research.

The two major weaknesses of the model are that it does not elaborate much on the process of industrial buying and how the relationships of the variables might change during that process. In addition, the model does not look closely at the various methods of conflict resolution that may be involved in decision making.

The models outlined are only a *sample* of the theories that have contributed towards the study of organizational buying behaviour. For a fuller discussion, one is directed towards Chisnall's more specialist text.[11]

Over the past 20 years, attempts have been made to advance knowledge on this subject. Although there has been a considerable output of literature in this area, it has still received little attention in comparison with consumer buying. The majority of research, particularly in the United States, has centred on the industrial buying approach and has concentrated on two main areas. First, there have been studies of the process of industrial buying behaviour and the factors which affect the choice of supplier. Second, there have been studies of the effect of individual elements of the marketing mix on industrial markets.

THEORY VERSUS PRACTICE IN ORGANIZATIONAL BUYING BEHAVIOUR

Industrial marketing practice has not kept pace with the conceptual development of organizational buying behaviour. Initially, models were developed from research carried out in the 1960s which focused on identifying variables that influence behaviour. The framework provided by the models supported the variables and this represented the most advanced thinking in this area. However, the evidence presented by these theoretical models was not backed up by research to show that this was how organizations bought. In addition, the industrial marketer was not

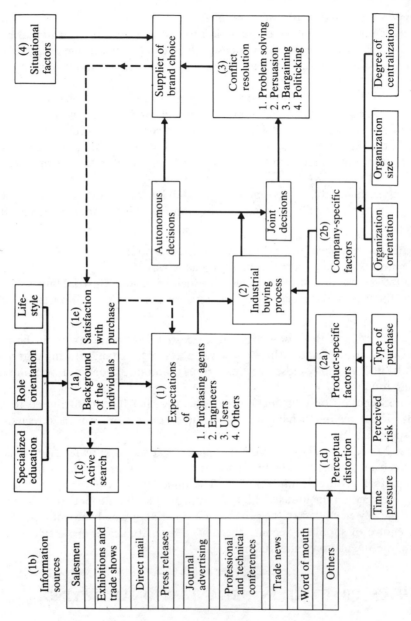

Figure 3.3   The Sheth model of industrial buying behaviour

(*Source*; J. N. Sheth, 'A model of industrial buyer behavior', *Journal of Marketing*, **37**(4), October 1973.[9])

encouraged to implement these concepts. Sheth comments that the work carried out within the area of industrial buying seems to have had little impact on marketing thought and practice. He also considers that marketers may have been led to believe that little is known about industrial buying behaviour. Hence, there has been reluctance among practitioners to move in the direction suggested by conceptual developments in organizational buying.

Another reason for the gap between theory and practice is that data on organizational buying are not available to industrial marketers and, as a result, the usefulness of such data in formulating marketing strategies has not been demonstrated. The difficulty of obtaining reliable data has caused a number of problems. Consumer behaviour has been researched in greater depth than industrial buying behaviour, because consumers are more accessible, more numerous, more identifiable and generally more cooperative than participants in industrial buying decisions. In addition, organizational buying decisions tend to be more complex as do the products purchased.

The industrial researcher is faced with a dichotomy. He can use low cost methods to collect detailed data from a large sample. In this case the researcher is likely to use a questionnaire. However, these focus on a single respondent and tend to ignore the group dynamics of the decision-making unit (DMU). Conversely, the researcher can gather data from the multiple decision participants within a DMU. In this case he is likely to rely on personal interview or group discussion techniques resulting in high research costs, smaller samples and the risk of bias.

The lack of effective methodology for gathering data from decision-making groups is the largest constraint to real progress in this area of research. If industrial marketers could be convinced of the relevance of organizational buying data to them, this would be another step in reconciling theory and practice.

It might then be possible to use buying behaviour to identify segments in the market, but as yet the feasibility of using industrial buyer behaviour for market segmentation has not been demonstrated.

Management needs to see the importance of organizational buying behaviour and segmentation to industrial markets. Industrial marketers need a clearer understanding of how data on buying behaviour can benefit them for segmentation and market strategy and also for maximizing the effectiveness of elements of the marketing mix. Future research in organizational buying should provide some insights into how markets and market segments react to decisions on specific elements of the marketing mix.

CONSUMER BEHAVIOUR

In addition to the development of organizational buying behaviour, there has been much growth in the study of consumer behaviour as a separate discipline.

After the Second World War, when consumer production had been resumed for a number of years, consumers had sufficient choice to exercise discrimination in the goods that could be purchased. In order for firms to survive, consumer needs became their primary focus. The adoption of this marketing concept, especially by American firms, proved the initial impetus for the study of consumer behaviour.

The objective was to identify unsatisfied consumer needs. Research highlighted the complexity of individuals and how their needs and priorities differed dramatically, hence the need to study consumers and their consumption behaviour in depth.

The term 'consumer behaviour' can be defined as the behaviour that consumers exhibit in searching for, purchasing, using, evaluating and disposing of products, services and ideas which they expect will satisfy their needs. The study of consumer behaviour is the study of how individuals make decisions as to how they expend their personal resources, i.e., their money. Another important area is the uses a consumer makes of goods and the evaluation of such goods after use.

Using models of consumer behaviour

The use of models has been a fairly recent development in the study of consumer behaviour. They reflect an effort to order and integrate the various components of information that are known about consumer behaviour. Models are useful in aiding research design to give a deeper understanding of consumer behaviour. Chisnall was the first UK author to document and discuss such work in the mid-1970s and his text provides a detailed discussion of such models.[12]

Howard and Sheth model (Fig. 3.4) Howard and Sheth have provided one of the most comprehensive models of consumer behaviour. The model uses the concept of stimulus–response to explain brand choice behaviour over time, using four major components:

1. Input variables.
2. Output variables.
3. Hypothetical constructs.
4. Exogenous variables.

1. Input variables Input variables are those stimuli which come from the environment. There are three types:

(a) Significative stimuli – these are actual elements of a brand which the buyer confronts, for example, price.
(b) Symbolic stimuli – these are generated by manufacturers representing their products in symbolic form, for example, in advertisements.
(c) Social stimuli – these are generated by the social environment, for example, in reference groups.

2. Output variables The five positions shown in the right-hand portion of the model are the buyer's observable stimulus–response inputs. They consist of the following:

– Attention
– Comprehension
– Attitude
– Intention
– Purchase behaviour.

3. Hypothetical constructs These are intervening variables which can be categorized into two major groups: perceptual constructs and learning constructs.

(a) There are three perceptual constructs – these deal with information processing:

   (i) sensitivity to information – the degree to which the buyer regulates the stimulus information flow;
   (ii) perceptual bias – distorting or altering information;
   (iii) search for information – active seeking of information about brands or their characteristics.

(b) There are six learning constructs – these deal with the buyer's formation of concepts:

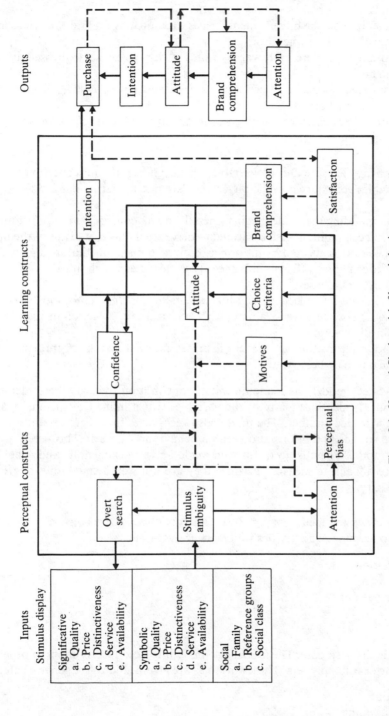

Figure 3.4 Howard–Sheth model of buyer behaviour.

(*Source*: J. N. Sheth and J. A. Howard, *The Theory of Buyer Behavior*, Wiley, 1969.)

(i) motive – general or specific goals impelling action;
(ii) brand potential of the evoked set – the buyer's perception of the ability of brands to satisfy goals;
(iii) decision mediators – the buyer's mental rules for matching and ranking purchase alternatives according to his or her motives;
(iv) predisposition – a preference towards brands in the evoked set expressed as an attitude towards them;
(v) inhibitors – environmental forces such as price and time pressure which restrain purchase of a preferred brand;
(vi) satisfaction – the degree to which the consequences of a purchase measure up to the buyer's expectations.

4. Exogenous variables These external variables can significantly influence buyer decisions. Because these variables are external to the buyer, they are not as sharply defined as other aspects of the model.

The process of operating the model begins when the buyer confronts an input stimulus and it achieves attention. The stimulus is then subjected to perceptual bias as a result of the influence of the buyer's predisposition as affected by his or her motives, decision mediators and evoked set.

The modified information will also influence these variables which in turn will influence his or her predisposition to purchase.

The purchase will be influenced by the buyer's intentions and inhibitions which are confronted. After the purchase the buyer evaluates satisfaction, and satisfaction increases the buyer's predisposition towards the brand.

More information means the buyer engages in less external search for information and exhibits more routine purchase behaviour.

The Howard–Sheth model has made an initial contribution towards the understanding of consumer behaviour. It identifies many of the variables which influence consumers and details how they interact with one another. The model also recognizes that there are different types of consumer problem solving and information search behaviour. There are, however, a number of limitations to the model. There is no distinction made between exogenous and other variables. Some variables are difficult to measure because they are not well defined and its greatest limitation is its complexity.

The Engel–Kollat–Blackwell model[13] (Fig. 3.5) This model considers consumer behaviour as a decision process concerning five activities which occur over time:

1. Problem recognition.
2. Information search.
3. Alternative evaluation.
4. Choice.
5. Outcomes.

These steps provide the basic core. The model also takes into account a number of other variables which influence the decision process. These variables are grouped into five general categories:

– Information input.
– Information processing.
– Product–brand evaluation.

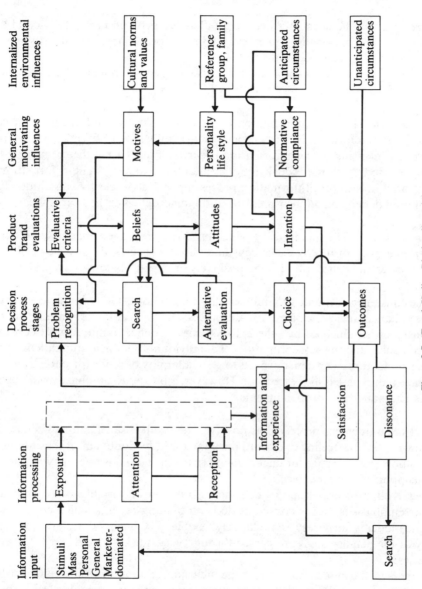

Figure 3.5 Engel–Kollat–Blackwell model

(*Source*: J. Engel, D. Kollat and R. Blackwell, *Consumer Behavior*, Dryden Press, New York, 1978.)

– General motivating influences.
– Internalized environmental influences.

The arrow in the model shows in which direction the influence is exerted.

1. Problem recognition The consumer detects a difference between his or her actual and ideal state of affairs. This may occur through external stimuli, for example, an advertisement, or the activation of a motive, for example, hunger.

In order for action to occur the consumer must perceive a sufficiently large discrepancy between actual and ideal states.

2. Information search The initial information may consist of beliefs and attitudes the consumer already holds. If more information is needed a consumer may look to friends, salespeople or the mass media. The processing of this information is carried out in a number of stages. The individual is first exposed to stimuli which may be attention catching. The information is then received and stored in memory. Information processing is highly selective and individuals may distort information depending on their predisposition to accept what they perceive.

3. Alternative evaluation The standards by which products are judged are derived from the consumer's underlying goals or motives. The consumer also has beliefs about which brands possess which characteristics and hence will respond positively or negatively towards a particular brand.

4. Choice The consumer's attitude will influence his or her choice. Other influences will comprise normative compliance and anticipated circumstances. Normative compliance is the extent to which the consumer is influenced by others, for example, friends, family, etc. It considers their attempts to influence, and the susceptibility of the individual to influence unanticipated circumstances – these are factors a consumer expects (e.g., availability of funds for purchase).

At this stage a purchase is likely to occur. However, a barrier to purchase would be unanticipated circumstances such as a drop in income.

5. Outcome If the outcome is perceived as positive, the result is satisfaction. The alternative to this is dissonance – this is a feeling of discord brought about by doubt about the chosen alternative relative to another, or a range, of unchosen alternatives. The consumer may require more information to support his or her choice.

The Engel–Kollat–Blackwell model considers a number of variables which influence consumers and its emphasis is on the conscious decision-making process which consumers adopt. The flow of the model is fairly easy and relatively flexible, recognizing that in some purchase decisions, many of the detailed steps are passed through very quickly or bypassed, for example in repeat purchases.

One weakness in the model, however, is the inclusion of a number of variables, where their effect on behaviour is not well specified, for example, environmental variables and motives.

The Sheth model of family decision making[14] (Fig. 3.6) This model depicts separate psychological systems, which represent the distinct predispositions of father, mother and other family members. These lead into 'family buying decisions', which may be either individually or jointly determined.

The right-hand side of the model lists seven family and product factors that influence whether a specific purchase will be autonomous or joint. These are:

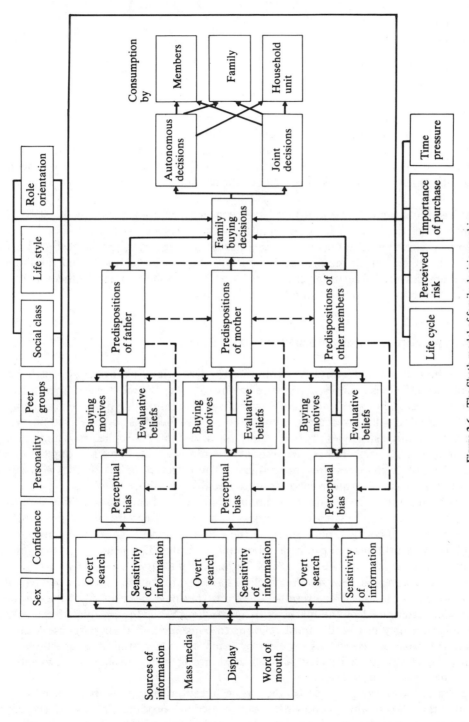

Figure 3.6   The Sheth model of family decision making

(*Source:* 'A theory of family buying decisions', in: *Models of Buyer Behavior*, J. N. Sheth, Harper and Row, 1974, pp. 22–23.[14])

1. Social class.
2. Life style.
3. Role orientation.
4. Family life cycle stage.
5. Perceived risk.
6. Product importance.
7. Time pressure.

The model suggests that joint decision making tends to prevail in families that are middle class, closely knit, with few prescribed family roles, and newly married.

In more specific terms of product purchasing, it suggests that joint decision making is more prevalent when there is a great deal of perceived risk, when the purchase decision is considered to be important and when there is ample time to make the decision.

The models of consumer behaviour that have been outlined are three of the most comprehensive models which describe the decision making or choice processes of consumers.

The Howard–Sheth model is the only one that has been subjected to specific testing. Further studies in consumer behaviour require these models to be developed and tested for them to become useful devices for synthesizing behaviour. As yet, such models tend to be theoretical, and are not of direct practical use to the marketing practitioners.

Theory versus practice in consumer behaviour

Research into the behaviour of consumers continues to evolve, and as it does so it is likely to become more relevant. Consumer researchers are having to justify the relevance of their research, not only in terms of cost, but also in terms of how useful it is to marketing practice and theory.

Researchers are less willing to accept the conclusions of an investigation merely at face value. More frequently, research strategies are being questioned, resulting in replications and critiques of prior research studies. Furthermore, research investigations tend to have a strong theoretical basis and are part of ongoing research programmes. These factors point towards a discipline which is becoming mature, with more valid results and realistic findings.

There has been an increase in awareness about what can and cannot be achieved through consumer research. Part of this increased awareness is the result of better training and tuition in the subject. A number of colleges, particularly in the US, offer specific courses in consumer behaviour, and many institutions run professional seminars. In the US, in the 1970s, the Association for Consumer Research was founded as was the *Journal of Consumer Research*.

With increased awareness, consumer researchers have had to consider the way in which they should approach investigations. For example, questions that have been asked of the consumer have mostly been determined by the marketer or researcher. Yet many product characteristics determined this way may not be the most relevant to consumers in their purchase decisions. Many researchers have overcome this problem by using consumer-originated questions when investigating product attributes. This has been achieved through using group interviews and such techniques as the repertory grid test.[15]

Researchers are also recognizing that the wrong questions may have been asked of consumers, because they did not always know what they wanted in a product. Because consumers are generally not creative enough to be of direct assistance in designing new products, it is often more productive to find out what they do not want.

Future trends in consumer research

There is likely to be a continuous re-evaluation of the concepts, data and techniques being employed in consumer research investigations. Standard approaches to the study of consumer behaviour will continue to be evaluated and if necessary refined or eliminated. Consumer research is likely to come under more interactive examination concerning its managerial implications. Hence studies should become more relevant for decision-making purposes.

As consumer research expands, it is likely that expenditure on this subject will increase. While increased expenditure may be the rule, more attention also needs to be given to the cost/benefit of such projects. This will increase attempts to use the most cost efficient research tools and techniques.

Finally, it is hoped that more integrated research programmes will take place, tracking consumer behaviour over time and monitoring trends in behaviour and attitudes. Despite the fact that integrated research programmes require a high level of commitment in terms of effort, time and resources, the need for them seems to be critical for yielding more valid and reliable data than has previously been available.

CONCLUSIONS

This chapter has covered the processes by which marketers and customers interact. The concepts of marketing and selling were covered in the buyer behaviour context before the two strands of industrial buyer behaviour and consumer behaviour were considered.

For clarity, behavioural models were employed which detailed the decision-making processes involved in the act of purchasing. For organizational buying, these models comprised task-oriented and non-task-oriented models, decision process and complex models. Consumer behaviour models comprised the Howard–Sheth model, the Engel–Kollat–Blackwell model and the Sheth model of family decision making.

APPLICATION QUESTIONS

1. What are the major differences between organizational and consumer buying decisions and why should they be treated as separate and distinct?
2. Do you believe that organizational purchase decisions are made on a more rational basis than that for consumer purchase decisions? Why?
3. How do you think that sellers can be assisted as a result of a knowledge of buyer behaviour?
4. What factors need to be considered when undertaking research into industrial markets as opposed to consumer markets? How would you structure such a task?
5. Do you believe that consumers or industrial buyers behave in a sufficiently consistent manner so as to enable marketers to study them? Give reasons and elaborate on your opinion.

References

1. Chisnall, P. M., '*Marketing: A Behavioural Analysis*', 2nd edn, McGraw-Hill, London, 1985.
2. Webster, F. E. and Y. Wind, *Organizational Buying Behaviour*, Prentice-Hall, Englewood Cliffs, NJ, 1972, p. 12.
3. Robinson, P. T., C. W. Faris and Y. Wind, *Industrial Buying and Creative Marketing*, Allyn & Bacon, Boston, 1967.
4. Bauer, R. A., 'Consumer behaviour as risk taking' in: *Dynamic Marketing for a Changing World*, R. S. Hancock (ed.), American Marketing Association, Chicago, 1966, pp. 389–398.
5. Webster, F. E. and Y. A. Wind, 'A general model for understanding organisational buying behaviour', *Journal of Marketing*, **36**, April 1972, pp. 12–19.

6. Cyert, R. M., J. G. March, H. A. Simon and D. B. Trow, 'Observation of a business decision', *Journal of Business*, **29**, 1956, pp. 237–248.
7. Corey, R. E., 'Key options in market selection and product planning', *Harvard Business Review*, September/October 1975, pp. 119–128.
8. Leavitt, H. J., W. R. Dill and H. Eyring, *The Organizational World*, New York, Harcourt Brace Jovanovich, 1973.
9. Sheth, J. N., 'A model of industrial buyer behaviour', *Journal of Marketing*, **37**, October 1973, pp. 50–56.
10. Howard, J. A. and J. N. Sheth, *The Theory of Buyer Behaviour*, Wiley, New York, 1969.
11. Chisnall, P. M., op. cit., pp. 177–204.
12. Chisnall, P. M., op. cit., pp. 159–176.
13. Engel, J. F., D. T. Kollat and R. D. Blackwell, *Consumer Behavior*, 3rd edn, Dryden Press, Hinsdale, IL, 1978, pp. 21–33.
14. Sheth, J. N., 'A theory of family buying decisions' in *Models of Buyer Behaviour*, Harper and Row, 1974, pp. 22–23.
15. Churchill, G. A., *Marketing Research – Methodological Foundations*, Dryden Press, Hinsdale, IL, 1976, pp. 17–21.

FOUR

MARKETING DECISIONS

INTRODUCTION

We have seen that being marketing oriented requires that all activities of a business, and not just those related to the marketing department, must be focused on the customer and his needs. This, in turn is a reflection of the importance of satisfying customer needs if a company is to enjoy long-term success.

Becoming more attuned to the needs of the market almost inevitably means that the marketing function is required to play a more central role in overall company decisions and plans. Specifically, what this means in organizational terms, and the problems and issues it can give rise to, are those that have been discussed in Part II of Chapter 2. In stressing this role for marketing, we must be careful not to forget the distinction between marketing as a concept – as an overall philosophy for the conduct of a business – and marketing as a function.

In its functional role marketing stands between the company and its customers. It must anticipate, analyse and interpret customer needs into specific action programmes designed to achieve company objectives. The objectives themselves, and therefore marketing activities, are derived from a broader context of overall company planning. Put simply, marketing decisions should be placed into a framework of corporate planning within a company.

This chapter examines the nature of corporate strategic planning from the identification of environmental opportunities and threats to the determining of specific overall company objectives and plans. We shall look carefully at the important, indeed essential, role which the marketing function plays in this process and what this role means for marketing management. In the final part of the chapter we will focus on the framework of marketing decision making with an emphasis on those controllable decisions referred to collectively as the 'marketing mix' – product, price, promotion and place.

CORPORATE STRATEGIC PLANNING

It has been suggested by Henry[1] that corporate planning is essentially an *ad hoc* process. What, essentially, he means by this is that the steps in corporate planning, and the procedure through these steps, are not fixed. Every company is unique and must decide for itself what is the appropriate approach to, and sequence for, corporate planning. Having said this, if we are to make sense of the notion of strategic planning, and if we intend to use it to improve organizational

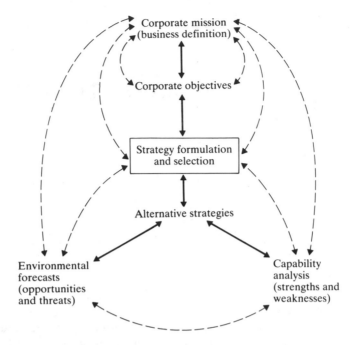

Figure 4.1 The elements of corporate planning

effectiveness, we need some formalized framework of the essential steps. This framework is shown in Fig. 4.1.

The outcome of corporate strategic planning, and therefore the centrepiece of Fig. 4.1, is the formulation and selection of company strategies. In arriving at these strategies, we need to consider the following aspects:

- What is our corporate mission? (What business are we in?)
- What are our relevant strengths and weaknesses?
- What are the relevant opportunities and threats?
- What are our corporate objectives?

The dotted lines in Fig. 4.1 indicate that although we shall deal with these factors sequentially, in practice to arrive at strategic plans we need to consider all these factors in combination. Rather than being a step-by-step process, corporate planning is iterative in nature. Determining what business we are in requires us to look at both our environment and our capabilities as a company. In turn, our assessments of what contributes 'relevant' opportunities and threats, and 'relevant' strengths and weaknesses is determined by our business definition.

With these considerations in mind we will now examine each of the constituent elements of Fig. 4.1 in turn.

Corporate mission

One of the most pervasive distinguishing characteristics of the formal organization is that it exists to serve a purpose. This purpose may take a variety of forms and may be classified in a number of ways according both to our viewpoint and the particular organization. For example, in the context of the overall economy of a country the purpose of the business organization could be said to be the 'creation of wealth'. The purpose of a trade union might be said to be 'the furtherance of the interests of its members'.

In the context of corporate planning, however, generalized statements of purpose such as these have little value. We need something which will provide a clear focus for direction and decision making.

In fact most companies do have a statement of purpose or mission. Normally this purpose is enshrined in a company's Memorandum and Articles of Association which specify at the inception of the business what its broad programme of activities shall be. In most instances, however, this broad statement of purpose is again too general to be of use in corporate planning. What is required as a basis for corporate planning is an up-to-date and relevant statement of corporate mission or purpose. This statement should reflect the essential characteristics of the company, its current environment, its resources and the preferences of the owners and managers of the business.

Determining a corporate mission which fulfils the requirements outlined above is by no means easy. Some companies have spent two or three years redefining their corporate mission and still managed to produce a corporate mission statement which is not particularly useful or relevant. But what precisely is the nature of such a statement?

The corporate mission statement is perhaps best thought of as a *definition of the business*, of the order of 'Our business is . . .'. To be useful and relevant, a business definition should ideally fulfil a number of criteria. The following represents the more important of these criteria when thinking about how to define a business:

1. The definition should be neither too broad nor too narrow . . . Definitions such as 'we are in the business of making profits' or 'we produce pens' are not really useful.
2. Ideally, the definition should encompass the three dimensions of what Abell[2] refers to as the 'business domain'. These three dimensions are respectively:

   (a) customer groups to be served;
   (b) customer needs to be served; and
   (c) technologies to be utilized.

An illustration of how these dimensions might be incorporated into a corporate mission statement is shown below.

> . . . The business of Acme Trading plc is in the provision of *beauty aids* (customer need) to *female students* (customer group) based on *non-allergic, animal-free products* (technology) with the aim of . . ., etc.

This notion of a business domain is a useful extension of the much wanted need to avoid 'marketing myopia' advanced by Levitt[3] in the early 1960s. To avoid a narrow, shortsighted view of one's business, Levitt argues, it is necessary to define the business in terms of what customer needs a company fulfils rather than in terms of what it provides. For example, Austin Rover Group would in Levitt's terms, be said to be in the business of fulfilling the need for transport rather than being in the business of producing vehicles. There is little doubt that this apparently simple piece of 'common-sense' advice from Levitt was instrumental in bringing about an increased marketing awareness in countless boardrooms throughout the United States and later in Europe.

The additional dimensions added by Abell may perhaps have a similar long-term effect on corporate planning in that they add substantially to the relevance and, therefore, usefulness of the corporate mission statement.

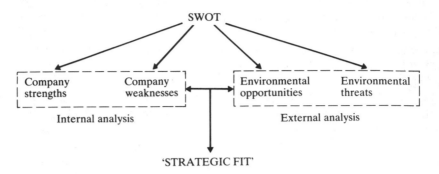

Figure 4.2 Achieving a strategic fit: SWOT analysis

Analysing strengths and weaknesses, and opportunities and threats (SWOT analysis)

It might seem logical to conclude that we can move direct from the corporate mission statement to the determination of corporate objectives. However, in setting objectives we need to appraise both external (environmental) factors, and internal (company) resources. This is essential if a company is to ensure a marketing fit or, as it is sometimes referred to, a 'strategic fit', between itself and the environment. This matching process is essentially one of relating external opportunities and threats to internal strengths and weaknesses and is often referred to by the mnemonic SWOT as shown in Fig. 4.2.

It is important to remember that the external appraisal of opportunities and threats and the internal appraisal of strengths and weaknesses should be considered together. For the time being, however, we shall consider first external (environmental) analysis.

External analysis In Chapter 2 we considered the macro-environment which surrounds and affects each and every company. This macro-environment consists of those factors which are broadly outside the control of the individual company and includes social, political, economic and technological forces. In the context of corporate planning the macro-environment has a number of significant features, in particular:

1. The macro-environment is changing constantly. Some of these changes are long term and relatively predictable, others occur rapidly and often without warning.
2. It is primarily these changes in the macro-environment which cause the most significant opportunities and threats to a company.

One or two examples will serve to illustrate these points.

- Long-term forecasts of world oil reserves suggest major profit opportunities for the developer of alternative energy sources and major threats to those oil exploration companies that do not diversify.
- Sudden revaluations of a nation's currency can represent a significant threat to would-be exporters from that country.
- An unexpected technological breakthrough by a company can represent a significant opportunity for the developer of the technology and a significant threat to his or her competitors.

One significant point you should note from these examples is that any given environmental change can represent a threat to one company and an opportunity for another. A particularly important aspect affecting this is the particular strengths and weaknesses of each company.

For example, a period of particularly rapid technological change and development can pro-

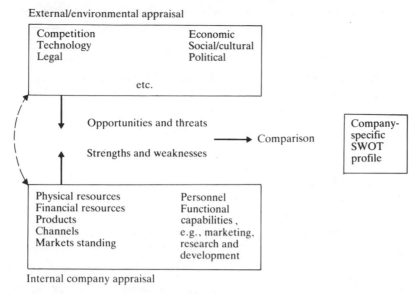

External/environmental appraisal

Competition	Economic
Technology	Social/cultural
Legal	Political

etc.

Opportunities and threats

Strengths and weaknesses

Comparison

Company-
specific
SWOT
profile

Physical resources
Financial resources
Products
Channels
Markets standing

Personnel
Functional
capabilities,
e.g., marketing,
research and
development

Internal company appraisal

Figure 4.3   SWOT analysis

vide a substantial opportunity to a company with the technological and market skills to exploit it and a significant threat to the company lacking these necessary resources.

Similarly a company may pride itself on a 'strength' of being able to produce top quality 'premium' products and yet find itself threatened if economic trends depress levels of disposable income and, therefore, market prices.

The conclusion we may draw from this is that the appraisal of company strengths and weaknesses and an assessment of possible opportunities and threats only make sense if we consider both internal and external factors together. Furthermore, every company will have its own particular and different SWOT profile. As with the overall corporate planning process itself, SWOT analysis requires an iterative approach. This is illustrated in Fig. 4.3 together with some of the more important elements to be appraised.

Clearly, SWOT analysis involves a company in the process of what Argenti[4] has termed 'environmental scanning'. This involves not only keeping abreast of changes in the environments but also, more specifically, attempting to forecast or predict them. This in turn raises a number of questions for the managers of a business. For example: On what external factors should information be obtained? By whom, and at what cost? To what use will this information be put? What forecasting techniques can be used?

These are not easy questions to answer and once again the answers are company specific. In addition, forecasting is made difficult by the possibility of unanticipated events and the fact that the various environmental factors interact one with another. Recent years, however, have witnessed the growth and development of much more sophisticated forecasting techniques to aid management, and some of these are elaborated in Chapter 10.

Objective setting

Both overall company mission statements and SWOT analysis input to this stage of the corporate planning process. The importance of objectives to the planning process cannot be overstated; indeed many texts on planning cite objective setting as being the start point in the process.

Broadly, setting objectives involves a company in considering the following two questions:

– Where do we wish to go?
– When do we intend to arrive?

Without the answer to these questions a company can be likened to a ship without a compass; it can move but it lacks a clear sense of direction. More specifically, among the more important functions which objectives serve in a company are the following:

1. Objectives provide for a *sense of purpose* in a company. Without objectives companies lack the means to focus and organize their efforts.
2. Objectives help a company to *achieve consistency* between the various levels of decision making, and between the different functions.
3. Objectives help to *stimulate effort*; they provide a basis for motivating individuals to achieve them.
4. Finally, objectives provide the *basis for control* in a company. Unless we know precisely what is required it is difficult, if not impossible, to know the extent to which we have achieved it.

In order to fulfil these important functions, it is necessary that objectives have a number of characteristics. Again, among the most important of these characteristics are the following:

– Preferably objectives should be *quantified*. Quantitative objectives with respect to both levels of performance and time reduce the risk of their being vague or ambiguous.
– Ideally, objectives should be *acceptable* and *agreeable* to those charged with the responsibility of attaining them. It is pointless setting objectives if they are not acted upon – or if the effort to achieve them is given grudgingly.
– A frequent reason for objectives being unacceptable is where they are felt to be too difficult or impossible to achieve. Objectives should be *realistic*, pitched neither too high nor too low.
– Finally, objectives should be *consistent*. As we shall see shortly, often companies have a variety of objectives as opposed to one single one. It is important that these multiple objectives do not conflict one with another in such a way that the achievement of an objective in one area is inconsistent with the achievement of objectives in others. For example, an objective of improved profitability may be inconsistent with an objective of maximum sales.

Having discussed the functions of objectives and the characteristics which ideally objectives should possess, if they are to serve these functions, we can now turn our attention to the variety of corporate objectives which a company might set.

In economic analysis it is often asserted that a firm has one, and only one, objective, namely 'to maximize its total profits'. We shall examine this notion of profit maximization in more detail in Chapter 13, which is concerned with pricing. At this stage it is sufficient to note that profit maximizing does not in fact reflect the reality or richness of objective setting in most companies. Clearly, for many companies, profits are enacted for long-run survival and because of this they will normally formulate objectives in this area. Usually, however, these profit objectives are set in terms of some satisfactory level of profits often couched in terms of a specified rate of return on the assets employed.

In addition to profit objectives it is now recognized that companies may have a variety of objectives encompassing a spread of activities. Among some of the most frequently encountered objectives in companies are the following:

– Profit objectives.
– Sales objectives.

– Market share objectives.
– Growth objectives.
– Technical and market standing objectives.
– Survival objectives.
– Social responsibility objectives.

Whatever the mix of objectives, it must be remembered that the objectives themselves relate to some point in the future, hence the importance of specifying a time scale for their achievement. For an existing business there will also be a past. It is possible, therefore, to measure the past and current performance of the company with respect to those areas in which it has objectives for the future. Management can then compare where it wishes to be (objectives) with where it is likely to be on the basis of a projection from past performance. Any difference constitutes what Ackoff has referred to as a 'planning gap'.[5] This notion of a planning gap is illustrated in Fig. 4.4. The planning gap illustrated in Fig. 4.4 stems from the difference between future desired profit object-ives and a forecast of projected profit based on past performance.

   In the face of such a planning gap a number of options are available; the intention, however, is to close the gap which exists. For example, the gap can be closed by revising objectives in a downward direction. Such a step might be taken where the initial objectives are unrealistic. Alternatively, or in addition, the gap can be closed by actions designed to move the company off the projection curve and towards the desired curve. In fact any movement towards a point at some time in the future requires action decisions – even if the action decision is of the order of 'do nothing', i.e., continue much as we have done in the past. More frequently these action decisions require the exploration and evaluation of a variety of options, the selection of courses of action from these options, and the commitment of resources. This next step in the process of corporate planning is the formulation of strategies.

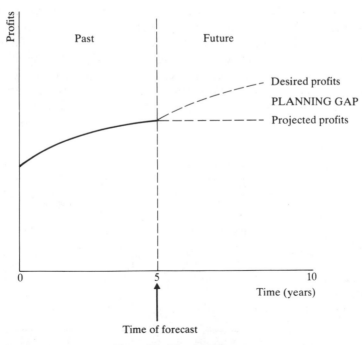

Figure 4.4   The planning gap

Strategy formulation and selection

If objectives relate to the 'where' and 'when' of planning, strategy formulation and selection are concerned with the 'how'.

This idea of strategy is essentially a military one, but it has increasingly been applied in a business context. One of the major difficulties with its application in this context is that the full range of strategic alternatives in business is virtually unlimited and is certainly extremely complex.

In an effort to reduce this variety and complexity to manageable proportions, a number of conceptual frameworks have been developed to aid the company in the delineation and choice between strategic options. Two of the more important of these are outlined below.

Ansoff[6] has proposed the idea of 'product/market scope' to aid in the formulation and selection of strategies, particularly for those companies with growth objectives. The basic framework of this approach is shown in Fig. 4.5. The matrix comprises of 'markets' on the vertical axis, and on the horizontal axis 'products'. In turn, each axis is subdivided into 'existing' and 'new'. Each cell of the matrix so formed represents a different strategic alternative for achieving growth.

Strategic alternative (1), *market penetration*, is a strategy of expanding sales based on existing products in existing markets. Where the total market is still growing the strategy may be achieved, for example, through 'natural' market growth. In markets which are static or declining a market penetration strategy can be achieved only by increasing market share at the expense of competitors.

Strategic alternative (2), *market development*, is a strategy of expansion based on entering new markets, i.e., markets not previously served by the company, with existing products. A good example of this would be a company entering an export market for the first time.

Strategic alternative (3), *product development*, entails developing and launching new products for sale in existing markets.

Strategic alternative (4), *diversification*, involves a company expanding on the basis of new products and new markets. This diversification can take a number of forms. For example, a company might choose to diversify into new product markets by moving through the channel of production and distribution. A car manufacturer taking over a component supplier and both using and marketing the components to other companies would be a good example of this. Alternatively, the diversification may be into an entirely unrelated form of business activity: for example, a tobacco company moving into the production and marketing of children's toys.

Ansoff's product/market matrix is probably one of the best known frameworks for delineating overall corporate strategies.

Product / Market	Present	New
Present	1. Market penetration	3. Product development
New	2. Market development	4. Diversification

Figure 4.5   Ansoff's product/market scope

A second and increasingly popular group of techniques aimed at the identification and selection of corporate strategies is also based on analysing appropriate marketing strategies.

A full discussion of all these techniques is beyond the scope of the text and the interested reader is advised to consult more specialized texts in this area. Excellent reference sources to both texts and techniques are those by Greenley[7] and Chisnall[8]. Together these texts provide an indication of the range of strategy selection techniques available to the decision maker. Some of the more influential of these are outlined below.

Boston Consulting Group's (BCG) growth/share matrix   This technique is based upon an analysis of market growth rate and market share. Strategic business units (SBUs) are positioned in one of four quadrants in a matrix according to whether they are high growth/low share, low growth/ high share, and so on. On the basis of this positioning the approach delineates appropriate strategies for each SBU such as to obtain a balanced portfolio.

McKinsey/General Electric's multifactor portfolio matrix   In this approach 'industry attractiveness' and 'business strengths' form the two principal vectors of the matrix. Industries in which a company competes are assessed as to their relative degree of attractiveness: high, medium or low. The second stage requires an objective assessment of the relative strengths of the company in terms of competing in the markets. Clearly, different strategies are indicated where, for example, a company competes from a position of high strength in a highly attractive market compared to areas where the company is competing on the basis of low strength in an unattractive market.

A. D. Little's business profile matrix   The principal discussions of the matrix are 'competitive position' and 'stage of industry maturity'. So, for example, the analysis may demonstrate that too many of a company's products are in mature or ageing industries and/or have only a tentative or weak competitive position.

Shell's international directional policy matrix   This matrix is composed of the two dimensions; 'profitability prospects' and 'competitive capabilities'. The key to the three classifications of the profitability axis, unattractive, average and attractive, is the rate of market growth. Together with an assessment of a company's competitive capabilities as being either weak, average or strong an assessment can be made as to what might be appropriate strategies to secure the long-term future of the company.

Barksdale and Harris's portfolio analysis/product life cycle matrix[9]   This matrix takes the axis of market growth and relative market share developed for the BCG matrix but adds the further consideration of the stage of product life cycle. The result is an eight-cell matrix (as opposed to only four in the BCG matrix). For example, 'Dodos' are product/market characterized by low share, negative market growth, and the decline stage of the product life cycle.

Using strategic planning selection techniques: problems and limitations   Even this comparatively short list of the range of strategic planning selection techniques is indicative of the growth in interest in this area. Decision makers have increasingly turned to such frameworks as a guide for their strategic decision making in this, one of the most complex areas of marketing. Useful though they may be, however, the techniques are not without their problems and limitations in use. We can perhaps explore this contention further by considering just one of the techniques in more detail, namely that developed by the Boston Consulting Group and frequently called the BCG growth/share matrix.

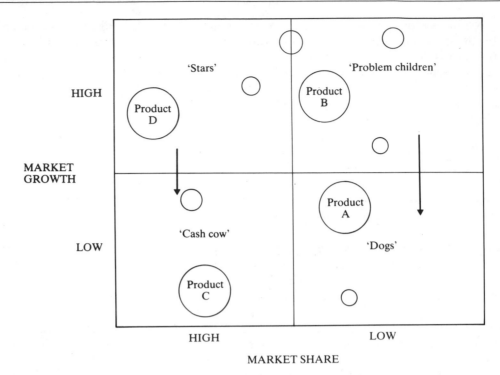

Figure 4.6   BCG's product portfolio matrix

The Boston Consulting Group's product portfolio matrix   This large American consultancy group
has developed an approach to strategic planning based on an analysis of a company's product
portfolio. The essentials of the product portfolio matrix are shown in Fig. 4.6. As we noted
earlier, the matrix is constructed on the basis of two principal factors: *relative market share* and
market growth. Using these factors a company's 'products' are positioned in the appropriate cell
of the matrix, often using a circle with a diameter proportioned to the sales revenue for that
product. According to where they lie in the matrix products are classified as being either 'dogs',
'cash cows', 'problem children' or 'stars'.

The somewhat picturesque technology used for products in the matrix is in fact useful in
understanding what each cell means. A brief description is given below.

'Dogs'   These are products with low market share and slow market growth. These products are
sometimes referred to as 'cash traps' in that they do not generate a significant cash flow to a
company and what little is generated is normally required to be reinvested simply to maintain
sales of the product.

'Cash cows'   These, on the other hand, are products with high market share and slow market
growth. This combination typically means that products in this category generate large amounts
of cash over and above that required to keep the product in this sector.

'Problem children'   These are products with low market share but in high growth markets. These
products can consume cash resources at alarming rates. The overall net drain on cash with these
products is greatest when a company attempts to increase market share.

'*Stars*' These are products in high growth markets with a relatively high share of the market. Stars can generate relatively large cash inflow, but this is more often than not matched or exceeded by the outflow of cash necessary to maintain market share. In net terms, therefore, such products provide, at best, modest net cash flows and are often net cash users.

In using and interpreting the product portfolio a number of factors are important.

1. The portfolio is *dynamic*, i.e., in the absence of any action on the part of a company, products will move their position in the portfolio. Principally because of the product life-cycle effect, products have a tendency to move downwards in the portfolio, i.e., problem children become dogs, and stars become cash cows. This tendency is indicated by the arrows in Fig. 4.6.
2. The notion is to achieve a certain balance in the portfolio. A balanced portfolio would ideally contain few or no dogs, some problem children, some stars and some cash cows. The balance between problem children, stars, and cash cows should be such as to ensure that the company has sufficient net positive cash flow from its cash cows to fund its stars and turn them eventually into cash cows. Funds from cash cows are also used to turn products which are currently problem children, because of relatively low market share, into stars. Not all problem children can be moved in this way and eventually some of them will fall to become dogs. In the long run all dogs are potential candidates for elimination from the product range.

As a consequence of these two factors, a company must take steps to ensure that the future portfolio mix is as the company wishes it to be. In other words it must select appropriate strategies in order to achieve a future, balanced product portfolio. As with most of these techniques, the basic idea of the BCG's product portfolio analysis is in delineating the range of strategies required. The technique, however, is not without its problems and limitations. These are outlined below.

The BCG matrix: problems and limitations The following represent some of the more frequent criticisms of the problems and limitations of the BCG matrix:

- Over-simplification.
- Problems of classification.
- Assumptions.
- Application.

Each of these is considered further below:

1. *Over-simplification* Many critics have argued that the BCG matrix is an over-simplification of product markets and can lead to insufficient management attention to the range of factors which are important in marketing strategy. For example, the matrix is based on only two key factors: market growth and relative market share.
2. *Problems of classification* There are severe conceptual and practical problems associated with defining what comprises a strategic business unit, a concept essential to the analysis. Similarly, there is some doubt as to precisely where the line should be drawn between what contributes a high/low relative market share, and what constitutes high/low market growth.
3. *Assumptions* In common with all the strategic portfolio approaches the BCG model is derived from a number of key underpinning assumptions. If these assumptions are misplaced or wrong then the subsequent value of the technique is reduced or removed completely. For example, a central assumption of the BCG matrix is that higher rates of market share are associated with higher profit rates. While there is some considerable evidence to support this assumption, it is by no means invariably the case that higher share = higher profits.

4. *Application* The BCG approach implies that different SBUs will cooperate by, for example, not objecting to saving up cash or withdrawing certain products. This is essential in order to achieve the objective of obtaining a balanced portfolio. While it is true that the technique itself makes no claims to address such problems there is a danger that management may overlook these problems of application.

In summarizing strategy selection techniques we can state that they are becoming increasingly popular and widespread in use. There is little doubt that they do represent a substantial step forward in management aids to strategic decision making. Having said this great care must be exercised in the selection and use of the techniques with particular attention being paid to assumptions, evidence and so on. Above all, the techniques represent a supplement to managerial judgement not a replacement for it.

Overall it must be recognized that corporate planning is as much judgemental as scientific in nature. Further, it should be noted that the *outcome* of corporate planning – corporate objectives and strategies – provides the framework for functional objectives and strategies, including marketing. We shall examine the nature of marketing planning itself in some detail in Chapter 13. In the remainder of this chapter we shall consider the relationship between marketing and corporate planning and, in particular, the important *input* which marketing is required to make to this process. The chapter concludes with a look at the range of marketing tools available for the achievement of corporate objectives.

MARKETING AND CORPORATE STRATEGIC PLANNING

A considerable degree of confusion and controversy surrounds the precise nature of the relationship between marketing and corporate strategic planning. At one extreme there is a view that marketing and corporate planning are synonymous. If, as has been suggested in this text, a company stands or falls on its ability to satisfy customer needs, then planning on the basis of these needs becomes the focus of all company planning: marketing and corporate planning are one.

On the other hand there is a view that marketing's role in corporate planning is no different from that of other functional areas in a business. Viewed in this way marketing becomes more of a passive recipient of plans and strategies determined at a higher level in the company. These, in turn, become the framework within which marketing activity takes place.

The view taken here is somewhere between these two extremes. There is no doubt that functional plans – including those for marketing – are part of a hierarchy of plans; a hierarchy which is led by corporate strategic planning. This is illustrated in Fig. 4.7.

Nevertheless, markets, customers and competitors are so important to the development of overall corporate plans that marketing must play a key role in their development. Because of this, marketing should contribute to the process of corporate planning and in particular to the SWOT analysis stage, and the selection of appropriate corporate strategies. Among the most important of these contributions by the marketing function would be, for example:

– Information on *past performance*: sales and market share analysis; product life cycle analysis; profit analysis . . .
– Information on *current* market position: competition analysis; major market segments; product portfolio analysis; customer satisfaction . . .
– Information on likely *future trends/changes*: sales and market forecasts, new competition, factors affecting likely future patterns of demand . . .

In this way, marketing and corporate strategic planning interact to produce a clear set of guide-

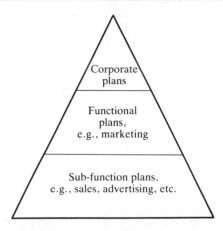

Figure 4.7 The planning hierarchy

lines for both overall company and marketing activities. The tools available to a company in order to achieve company objectives, however, are very much marketing based. Collectively, these tools are normally referred to as *the marketing mix*.

THE MARKETING MIX

We have seen, both earlier in this chapter and in Chapter 2, that a company is affected by, and therefore must take account of, factors which are environmental and hence outside its control. In order to accommodate these factors the company must use those elements over which it has control. The most important of these elements are those which comprise a company's *marketing mix*.

The term marketing mix is attributed to Neil H. Borden[10] and refers to the set of marketing ingredients which a company can use to achieve its objectives. In the same way as a cook can select from a wide range of ingredients and combine them in different amounts to bake a successful cake, so too the marketer is at liberty to pick and choose from an extensive set of marketing components in order to find the right recipe. Because of this it has become conventional to refer to the main elements of the marketing mix as the 'four Ps'. These are, respectively:

- *Product*
- *Price*
- *Promotion*, and
- *Place*

Within each of those four broad categories of marketing decision variables are innumerable subdivisions, examples of which are shown below:

Product, e.g.:
- product range: breadth, depth, and mix;
- product features;
- product quality;
- packaging.
Price, e.g.:
- price levels;

– price discounts;
– credit policy;
– price strategies.
Promotion, e.g.:
– advertising: spend, copy content, media selection and scheduling;
– sales promotion;
– publicity;
– personal selling.
Place, e.g.:
– channels of distribution;
– stock levels;
– delivery.

The marketing manager must combine these various elements of the marketing mix in order to achieve both a competitive advantage in the marketplace and company objectives. Decisions in these elements, over which the company has control, must also accommodate those factors in the company's environment over which it has little or no control. This is illustrated in Fig. 4.8. The importance of marketing mix decisions is such that the whole of Part Three of this text is devoted to examining each element in turn.

As a final corollary to this chapter the importance of coordination between the various elements in marketing mix cannot be emphasized enough. The breakfast cereal manufacturer must ensure that point-of-sale promotional material is available to support a television advertising campaign and that the goods are not only there for customers to purchase, but they should be *seen* to be there. An example of when this clearly did not happen was on the occasion in April 1986 when the *Amateur Photographer* magazine had linked up with a famous high street retailer to undertake a promotion of 50 pence off the retailer's own brand film. This involved a reference to the promotion on the front cover of the magazine and then a one page advertisement inside containing a '50 pence off' cut-out voucher to be exchanged for film. Upon presenting the voucher to the retailer's photographic staff towards the beginning of the redemption period, not only were they totally unaware of the promotion, but they had no 'own brand' film in stock!

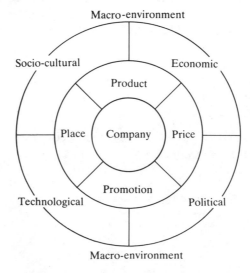

Figure 4.8   The marketing mix and the environment

CONCLUSIONS

This chapter has considered the process of corporate strategic planning from setting objectives through to the identification and selection of overall company strategies. Understanding the steps in corporate planning is important for this sets the framework for functional marketing decision making.

We have seen too, that the marketing function has a key role to play in corporate planning and that the use of techniques such as product portfolio analysis requires a substantial marketing input.

Finally, we have introduced the range of marketing variables through which a company hopes to achieve its objectives – the marketing mix. In the next chapter we shall examine how a company can provide a clearer focus for its marketing mix decision making through effective segmentation and targeting.

APPLICATION QUESTIONS

1. What factors should a company consider in strategy formulation and selection?
2. Outline the role of objectives in company planning. What characteristics should such objectives possess if they are to fulfil those roles?
3. Why is it important to consider strengths and weaknesses, and opportunities and threats together?
4. What do you understand by the product/market matrix and the product portfolio?
5. What is the relationship between corporate planning and marketing?

REFERENCES

1. Henry, H., 'Corporate strategy, marketing and diversification', in: *Perspectives on Management Marketing and Research*, Crosby Lockwood, London, 1971.
2. Abell, D., *Defining the Business: The Starting Point of Strategic Planning*, Prentice-Hall, Englewood Cliffs, NJ, 1980.
3. Levitt, T., 'Marketing myopia', *Harvard Business Review*, July–August, 1960.
4. Argenti, J., *Systematic Corporate Planning*, Wiley, London, 1974.
5. Ackoff, R. L., *A Concept of Corporate Planning*, Wiley-Interscience, New York, 1970.
6. Ansoff, I. H., 'Strategies for diversification', *Harvard Business Review*, September–October 1957.
7. Greenley, G. E., *The Strategic and Operational Planning of Marketing*, McGraw-Hill, Maidenhead, 1986.
8. Chisnall, P. M., *Strategic Industrial Marketing*, Prentice-Hall, Englewood Cliffs, NJ, 1985.
9. Barksdale, H. C. and C. E. Harris, Jnr, 'Portfolio analysis and the product life cycle', *Long Range Planning*, **15**(6), 1982.
10. Borden, N. H., 'The concept of the marketing mix', in: *Science in Marketing*, G. Schwartz (ed.), John Wiley, New York, 1965.

TWO

INFORMATION FOR MARKETING DECISIONS

FIVE

MARKETING RESEARCH

INTRODUCTION

We have examined the place of marketing in business and society, its relationship with customers and how the company can better serve the marketplace through strategic planning. Such planning involves examining this marketplace through techniques of marketing research and sales forecasting which is the focus of this part of the text. This chapter specifically gives an overview of marketing research – its nature, its role and its limitations, followed by some practical discussion of specific techniques. For a more comprehensive and professional treatment of marketing research, the reader is directed to the work of Chisnall.[1]

Information is required to identify marketing problems and opportunities; it is also required to assist with the formulation of an organization's response to problems and opportunities that have been identified. The function of marketing research, therefore, is to generate information that will assist marketers in making decisions. There are two sources of marketing research data: primary (collection of new data) and secondary (data previously collected or data which are already there) which is the focus of a later part of this chapter.

TYPES OF MARKETING RESEARCH

Marketing research can contribute to the decision-making process in all aspects of marketing activity. The major types of marketing research that are conducted can be described as follows:

1. Market research and sales research cover:
   (a) estimates of market size of both developed and new markets;
   (b) identification of market characteristics and segments;
   (c) identification of market trends;
   (d) sales forecasting (although this is sometimes considered to be a separate activity);
   (e) obtaining information on customers and potential customers;
   (f) obtaining information on competitors.
2. Product research covers:
   (a) the generation of new product ideas;
   (b) product concept testing;
   (c) product testing;
   (d) test marketing of products;

(e) investigations into different types of packaging (sometimes called packaging research or package testing).
3. Pricing research is concerned with:
   the identification of the relationship between a product or service's price and demand.
4. Marketing communications research covers:
   (a) research into the effectiveness of marketing communications (this is sometimes called advertising research, but it is felt that the term 'advertising research' is a rather restrictive definition);
   (b) media selection research;
   (c) copy testing;
   (d) sales territory planning.
5. Distribution research covers:
   (a) warehouse location research;
   (b) retail outlet location research.

This listing demonstrates that the term 'marketing research' implies a broader sphere of activity than 'market research'. The term 'market research' could be interpreted not to include key marketing research activities like the generation of new product ideas and pricing investigations and it is restricted to research which merely looks into the marketplace itself.

THE MARKET RESEARCH SOCIETY (MRS)

The Market Research Society is the major professional body for marketing researchers in the United Kingdom. It was founded in 1947 and by 1985 had over 4500 members. Its name is perhaps peculiar in view of the fact that it has already been established that market research is part of marketing research. This is probably because in 1947 it was set up simply as a body of market researchers and it is since then that its remit has widened to embrace the broader aspects of marketing research. Among its many activities, the society publishes, in association with the Industrial Marketing Research Association (IMRA) a code of conduct to which its members undertake to adhere.

The following extract from Part 5.2 of the code is particularly relevant to modern marketing:

No activity should be deliberately, or inadvertently, misrepresented as being market research.
   Specifically, the following activities shall in no way be associated, directly or by implication, with market or social research interviewing:
(a) Sales approaches for profit.
(b) The compilation of lists for canvassing.
(c) Attempts to influence opinions *per se*.
(d) Industrial espionage.
(e) Enquiries about private individuals *per se*.

It has already been explained in Part One that the marketing concept uses the customer as the starting point for planning activities and this essentially means asking customers questions through the medium of marketing research. Thus, as companies adopt the marketing concept, so more marketing research will be undertaken. At the same time, companies will explore other means of obtaining business in an increasingly competitive environment. Many less scrupulous companies have taken to conducting selling activities under the guise of marketing research with a questionnaire aimed at obtaining the respondent's name and address for future selling approaches. Examples of such companies are double glazing/patio door manufacturers and insurance companies (not, we would hasten to add, from the well-known national names, but from lesser known smaller companies whose salespeople are often working only for commission, whose products and services usually cost more than better known companies and who often cease to trade after a short period of time). Such activity gives marketing research a bad name (not to mention reputable double glazing and insurance companies) and serves to make respondents wary when they are approached to take part in a consumer survey.

Perhaps with the above mentioned fears in mind, the Market Research Society has recently introduced a scheme whereby marketing researchers have an identification issued with the authority of the MRS. The problem is that members of the public do not generally know what the MRS is, and unscrupulous companies can still issue a letter of introduction or other form of identification pertaining to claim that the 'researcher' is conducting a bona fide survey (and then use the addresses obtained for subsequent sales canvassing).

IN-HOUSE RESEARCH VERSUS OUTSIDE AGENCY RESEARCH

Sometimes a company may choose to conduct a research study by using internal company personnel. On other occasions it may employ an outside marketing research agency. In this 'make' or 'buy' decision, the following criteria should be considered:

1. *Cost*: many companies believe that it is cheaper to use internal personnel. It is, however, important to consider that while these personnel are conducting research, other aspects of their company employment may be neglected. This is particularly true in the case of salespeople being used for interviewing purposes.
2. *Research expertise*: here one must consider whether or not there is the necessary expertise available internally, particularly when sophisticated research techniques are to be employed in the research project. Similarly, the analysis may call for complicated statistical analysis which might well be outside the scope of internal company personnel. The problem here is that internal personnel, who are not specialist marketing researchers, may not be aware of the existence of such sophisticated techniques in the first place.
3. *Product or service knowledge*: research requiring an in-depth technical knowledge might be more suited to an 'in-house' team, because it would be time consuming (and expensive) to impart such information to a team of outside researchers.
4. *Objectivity*: here, outside agencies are more likely to be objective because an 'in-house' team will perhaps be too familiar with the subject under discussion, and may come to conclusions largely based upon their own prejudices and preconceptions.
5. *Special equipment*: depending upon the nature of the enquiry, it may be that the research calls for specialist computer programs or specialist test equipment, which may not warrant the expenditure by an 'in-house' team for, say, an *ad hoc* (one off) study.
6. *Confidentiality*: although it has already been mentioned that the code of the MRS places importance upon the confidentiality of completed results, it is, nevertheless, a risk to impart confidential information upon, say, new products and processes to individuals from outside the company unless it can be ensured that security can be assured. For this reason some large retailers (e.g., Marks & Spencer, Boots and Sainsbury's) tend not to use outside marketing research agencies.

In order that a company can obtain the benefits of the optimum use of resources, it is often the case that some parts of a marketing research project are handled internally and other parts are contracted out to external agencies.

THE RESEARCH PROCESS

Research should be conducted only when it is expected that the value of information to be obtained will be greater than the cost of obtaining it. Calculating the cost of a research project is a relatively simple matter and merely involves a calculation of interviewer time, equipment used, data processing, etc. The difficulty arises in determining the value of information that will be obtained as a result of the research, and this involves the following considerations:

– The relative profitability of the alternative decisions.
– The likely contribution the information will make to effective decision making.

When it is decided that research value will be likely to exceed the cost of research, the research process can begin. This process usually consists of a series of nine steps, the first five of which are research design phases:

1. Definition of the marketing problem to be solved, together with a specification of the research objectives.
2. Selection of data collection method(s) to be used. In marketing research there are two basic data collection methods: secondary research and primary research. Secondary data are collected mainly for background purposes and not necessarily to solve the specific problem under consideration. Primary data are collected to solve the specific problem at hand. Primary data collection techniques cover: survey research, depth interviews, observational research and experimentation.
3. Selection of sampling method to be used. In some circumstances this may not be appropriate, for instance when the universe is small, it may be decided to conduct a census.
4. Development of an analysis plan. This step specifically involves specifying the data that will be reported together with the selection of the statistical procedures that will be employed in analysing the results.
5. An estimation of the time and resources required to complete the research.
6. Obtaining approval of the research design outlined in steps 1 to 5 from the individual(s) requesting the research.
7. Data collection.
8. Data analysis.
9. Research reporting.

LIMITATIONS OF MARKETING RESEARCH

While it is virtually impossible to remove all sources of error in such a behaviourally based field as marketing research, it is the aim of research design to minimize the probable occurrence of the following types of error:

1. *Sampling errors*: these are errors in the specification of the target population and errors caused by the selection of a non-representative sample.
2. *Non-response errors*: these include a failure to contact all members of a sample and failure by such members to respond to the survey.
3. *Data collection errors*: these include occasions where respondents provide answers to please, impress or irritate the interviewer. For instance, in responding to a question (especially open ended questions where the respondent is encouraged to give a response that is not a predetermined one from a list of alternatives) a respondent may be unable to articulate a response accurately. Data collection errors may also be caused by leading questions and here it is the fault of the questionnaire designer in that the way the question is worded may lead the respondent to give a certain answer (e.g., the question 'Do you believe that children should have a good breakfast?' is almost bound to produce a positive response). Similarly, interviewers

may also produce such biases by the way they read out such questions to respondents with, say, a positive or negative bias in the tone of the voice. Simple clerical errors can also be included under this category where interviewers may record incorrect response information due to misinterpretation or carelessness in recording answers. There will, of course, be a minority of anarchical individuals among respondents who will deliberately set out to give incorrect responses. Such problems, together with the possible problem of interviewer dishonesty, can sometimes be detected statistically wherein such answers will deviate from the 'norm' of answers, or through the use of 'check' questions wherein a question is asked to check upon the validity of a question asked earlier, and where there is a disparity then the questionnaire may be regarded as being 'suspect'.

4. *Analytical and reporting errors*
5. *Experimental errors*: experiments are designed to measure the impact of one variable (e.g., advertising) on another (e.g., sales). Experimental error may arise if uncontrollable events occur during the experiment (e.g., if a competitor launches a new product during a test period – which is quite often done deliberately to confuse the results!).

Before a company embarks upon an expensive primary data collection exercise, it makes sense to use information already in existence. Such data are termed secondary data and are the subject of the next section.

SECONDARY RESEARCH

The major sources of secondary data are as follows:

1. *Internal sources*: these data are generated by the organization itself and include: accounting records, salesforce reports, reports from previous marketing research studies and customer complaints records.
2. *External sources*: these data are generated by sources outside the organization including data produced by the government and publishers of directories, newspapers, periodicals and research reports.

Published data of particular interest to marketers may be grouped into social and industrial statistics, company information, media information (including miscellaneous information from newspapers and periodicals) and market reports. The following listing is a sample selection of major publications relating to the United Kingdom market, and they cover what are commonly termed 'social and industrial statistics'. A fuller listing is given in Chisnall's text.[2]

– *Business Monitors* These provide sales figures, usually by volume and value, on over 4000 individual products and services. Publication frequency may be monthly, quarterly, annually or occasionally, depending upon the product or service.
– *Census of Population* (published every ten years) This is an analysis of the United Kingdom population and it includes statistics for topics such as country of birth, sex, age and socioeconomic groups.
– *Family Expenditure Survey* This annual publication provides an analysis of total household income and expenditure. The analysis is based upon a postal survey of 10 500 households.
– *Overseas Trade Statistics of the UK* This provides monthly and annual import and export statistics by commodity and by country, by both volume and value.
– *Regional Trends* This is an annual publication which gives details of regional trends in the United Kingdom. Subjects covered in the statistics include current and projected population,

housing, health, law enforcement, education, employment, personal income and expenditure, production and investment.

- *Household Food Consumption and Expenditure* This is also known as the *National Food Survey* and it is published annually giving a detailed breakdown of consumption in volume and expenditure in money terms per person per week on all food types. The analysis is also broken down into types of household and by region.
- *Monthly Digest of Statistics* and *Annual Abstract of Statistics* These publications are very popular and are quite often a good starting point for a marketing researcher, before going on to the more specialist statistical publications. Statistics are provided on such matters as population trends, employment statistics, manufactured goods, external trade and shipping. As the titles suggest, these are general publications, and as such they are more useful for background information.
- *General Household Survey* This is an annual publication based upon a continuous sample survey of approximately 15 000 private households on a personal interview basis. It includes data on housing, employment, education and health.

In addition to government statistics, statitistics are also produced by trade associations which reflect their members' interests. It is not the purpose of this text to produce a list of such publications, because the best course of action for any researcher here is to contact the individual trade association and enquire whether or not the information that is required is available. There may, however, be difficulty in obtaining such information if the sponsoring company is not a member of that trade association. There are also a number of independent research report publishers (for example *MINTEL* published by Market Intelligence). The publication *British Statistics Index* provides a useful guide to such publications.

There are a number of statistical publications that provide information relating to individual companies and groups of companies, the principal ones of which are as follows:

- *Guide to Key British Enterprises* This is produced by Dun and Bradstreet on an annual basis. It is arranged alphabetically by company name and has a product index. The addresses, telephone numbers and names of directors are given, together with brief details of company activities, ownership of the company and its approximate turnover and its number of employees. Approximately 20 000 companies are included in this publication.
- *Kompass (UK)* is published annually by Kompass Directories. It is arranged in two volumes, the first of which is arranged geographically, alphabetically and by county, town and name of company. An alphabetical index by company name is also provided. The second volume is arranged by Standard Industrial Classification coding and by company and this volume is probably of more use to purchasers wishing to obtain details of companies manufacturing certain types of products. The guide also gives brief details of company turnover, number of employees and names of directors.

There are also a large number of trade directories for specific industries, e.g., *The Food Trades Directory* (published by Newman Publications) which lists producers, retailers and all other potential outlets for food products. A full list of specialist trade directories is provided in *Current British Directories*. There are a number of other general directories, which although not as ambitious as those mentioned, are useful and easy to use, e.g. Kelly's, Sell's, Stubbs and Ryland's.

- *The Times 1000* is published annually by Times Books Ltd and it contains listings of the top 1000 UK companies by turnover plus 500 European top companies, 100 top American companies and 50 top Japanese companies.
- *Who Owns Whom (UK)* is published annually by Dun and Bradstreet and gives details of parent companies, associate companies and subsidiary companies.

- *Extel cards* provide details of company financial results and chairmen's statements.
- *Datastream*, produced by Datastream International, is a computerized database of company financial results available 'on line'.
- *Prestel* This information can be seen on a domestic television set fitted with a Prestel adaptor. Information is available 24 hours a day and it is continually updated. It works like teletext and gives such information as: stock exchange prices, commodity prices from the international commodity exchanges, advice to importers and exporters, etc.

   Information can also be obtained directly from companies themselves. Such information can include the annual report and product literature. Information of interest to marketers is not limited to information on industrial and social statistics and company performance. Newspapers and periodicals contain a vast amount of potentially useful marketing information. For example, stories about mergers, announcements of new products, new personnel appointments and the opening of new premises can be useful for general background market intelligence.

   To assist in the location of relevant news items there are several indexes of newspaper and periodical articles:

- *Research Index* This is a fortnightly publication and indexes are available for the *Financial Times*, *The Economist*, the *Investor's Chronicle*, *Marketing Week* and *Marketing* among 120 or so other important publications. Each issue of *Research Index* is divided into two sections: the pink pages contain the industry index and the blue pages the company index. The industry section cumulates on a six-monthly basis.
- *McCarthy Information Services* This publication is useful, for example, when the researcher has identified something of interest from the *Research Index*. This information service will then provide fuller details which the client requires. Such data are reprinted on cards and indexed by company and market.
- *Worldcasts* is published by Predicasts eight times a year and it summarizes over 75 000 published projections for products and markets in over 50 countries.
- *Chambers of Commerce* Although this is not a publication, these establishments can sometimes be fruitful sources of information. Many large towns and conurbations have their own Chambers of Commerce. Some have useful libraries which contain reports upon countries and areas of the world, to which export missions may have been sponsored by that particular Chamber of Commerce. They mainly contain useful local commercial information relating to the area which they serve.
- *Market reports* From the number of secondary sources already mentioned (and this is by no means the full listing) the reader will begin to appreciate the volume of work that secondary research can cover. Various research agencies have recognized that companies often require similar collections of published data. Such agencies undertake to collect, analyse and then sell published reports to interested companies. What they are doing is to perform desk research and distil whatever information is available into a concise report. Such published reports are indexed in a publication called *Marketing Surveys Index* which is a monthly publication published in association with the Institute of Marketing.

Most of the publications mentioned are available at major commercial reference libraries; it should be emphasized that there are often surprisingly good commercial sections in modestly sized town libraries. It is always better to investigate these local sources first before visiting one of the major commercial libraries. The reason why this is said is because the larger libraries tend to be more for the professional user, whereas local libraries will contain staff who are more 'in tune' with the needs of 'learners', and will personally show them how to use certain facilities and how to reference the information they require.

PRIMARY RESEARCH

If secondary data do not provide sufficient information to satisfy research objections, primary data must then be collected. In this section primary data collection methods are considered under the following headings:

1. Survey research.
2. Depth interviews.
3. Observation.
4. Experimentation.

Survey research

This is concerned with the administration of questionnaires, and is the most common method of collecting primary data for marketing decisions. When planning a survey there are four major issues to be considered:

(a) Selection of communication method (i.e., mail, telephone or personal survey).
(b) Maximizing response to a survey.
(c) Questionnaire design.
(d) Phrasing of questions.

Mail, telephone or personal survey The general strengths and weaknesses of these three methods are summarized in Table 5.1. An important criterion not featured in this table is 'probable response rate' which is discussed later.

Maximizing response Error caused by a difference between those who respond to a survey and those who do not is termed non-response error. Non-response can involve the refusal to answer an entire questionnaire or just a particular question. It is one of the most significant problems faced by a survey researcher. In general, the lower the response rate to a survey, the higher is the probability of non-response error. However, a low response rate does not automatically mean that there have been non-response errors. Non-response error occurs only when a difference between the respondents and the non-respondents leads the researcher to an incorrect conclusion or decision.

In telephone and personal surveys, reply refusal and respondent non-availability are the major factors that reduce response rates. The number of 'not-availables' may usually be reduced by a series of callbacks at varying times. Refusal rates (the percentage of contacted respondents

Table 5.1

Criterion	Mail	Telephone	Personal
1. Ability to handle complex questionnaires	Poor	Fair	Excellent
2. Ability to collect large amounts of data	Fair	Fair	Excellent
3. Accuracy on 'sensitive' questions	Good	Good	Fair
4. Control of interviewer effects (e.g., respondent–interviewer interaction; unintentional cues from interviewer)	Excellent	Fair	Poor
5. Speech	Poor	Excellent	Fair
6. Cost	Good (but low response rate is a problem)	Good	Poor

who refuse to participate) for telephone surveys have been found to range from 0 to 50 per cent.[3] Interest in the survey topic is a primary factor in the cooperate–refuse decision. Prior communication with the interviewee by letter also helps to reduce the refusal rate. Attempts to increase the response rate to mail surveys focus on increasing the potential respondents' motivation to reply. As with telephone and personal surveys, the respondent's interest in the subject matter is a key factor. Response rates may usually be increased by offering token incentives to reply and sending reminder letters, which include another copy of the original questionnaire.

Questionnaire design A questionnaire can be used to collect data on the respondent's behaviour (past, present or intended), demographic characteristics (age, sex, income, occupation), level of knowledge and attitudes and opinions. Before a questionnaire can be designed and used, answers are required to the following questions:

– What information is required?
– From whom is it required?
– Which method of communication will be used, i.e., mail, telephone or personal interview?
– Are all the questions really needed?
– Is each question sufficient to generate the required information? (Does the respondent have the information? Can the respondent find or remember the information? Is the respondent able to express his or her answer?)
– Will the respondent answer the question correctly? (Is the answer confidential or potentially embarrassing? Do the words used have the same meaning for all respondents? Are any of the words or phrases put in a leading way?)
– Are the questions in a logical sequence?

When designing a questionnaire the following guidelines should be applied:

– The overall questionnaire should move from topic to topic in a logical manner, with all questions on one topic completed before moving to the next.
– Sensitive questions, such as the respondent's income, should be at the end.
– The first few questions should be simple, objective and interesting.
– Is the questionnaire design likely to minimize recording errors and assist analysis?
– Has the questionnaire been pre-tested with respondents similar to those who will be included in the final survey?

Question phrasing There are three types of question format: direct questions, attitude questions and indirect questions.

Direct questions The direct question format may be subdivided into open and closed questions. Open questions allow the respondent to answer in his or her own words. Closed questions include all possible answers, and the respondent makes a choice from among them. Closed questions may be dichotomous or multiple choice. Dichotomous questions allow only two responses; such as 'yes–no', 'agree–disagree' and 'male–female'. The two responses of dichotomous questions are often supplemented by a third neutral category such as 'don't know'. Multiple choice questions allow three or more responses. To clarify the various types of direct questions here are some examples:

Open   'Why did you stop travelling by train?'
Closed–Dichotomous   'Do you like travelling by train?'
                                        Yes ☐
                                        No ☐

Closed–Multiple Choice   'What is your favourite method of travelling to work?'

Car   ☐
Bus   ☐
Train   ☐
Walking   ☐
Bicycle   ☐
Other   ☐

Open questions have the advantage that the respondent is not influenced by stated response categories. The major disadvantages of open questions are respondents' difficulties in articulating answers; interviewer difficulties are in recording answers, introduction of bias through probing and the complexity of categorizing answers.

Closed questions have two main advantages: they are easier for the respondent and interviewer and they aid questionnaire analysis. Closed questions have two disadvantages: first, research is required to ensure that a comprehensive range of alternative responses is presented and, second, considerable skill is required to ensure that the presentation of alternative responses does not sometimes stimulate response bias.

To benefit from the advantages of both open and closed questions, researchers will often use questions in preliminary research situations. Feedback from this preliminary research is then used to formulate closed questions for a final and more extensive survey.

Attitude questions Consumer attitudes and opinions help to predict their future behaviour, and for this reason collection of this type of data is of vital importance to marketers. Attitude data may be collected using direct or indirect questions. We shall discuss some of direct questioning scales used, of which there are four types, for the direct questioning of attitudes. These scales are the non-comparative rating scale, the comparative rating scale, the semantic differential scale and the Likert scale, which can be most easily explained using examples.

Non-comparative rating scale How would you rate the taste of Furgekin Lager?

5	4	3	2	1
Probably the best	Very good, I like it	All right, neither good nor bad	Not at all good, I do not like it	Probably the worst

This scale is non-comparative as the respondent has not been asked to compare one product with another.

Comparative rating scale How do you like the taste of Furgekin compared to Gazekeg?

5	4	3	2	1
Vastly superior	Superior	Neither superior nor inferior	Inferior	Vastly inferior

Semantic differential scale What are your opinions of the Vega Estate car? Please tick the box that best describes your opinions.

	Extremely	Very	Some-what	Neither nor	Some-what	Very	Extremely	
Fast	☐	☐	☐	☐	☐	☐	☐	Slow
Good	☐	☐	☐	☐	☐	☐	☐	Bad
Large	☐	☐	☐	☐	☐	☐	☐	Small
Inexpensive	☐	☐	☐	☐	☐	☐	☐	Expensive

Likert scale The Vega Anglian is the best small car on the market. Do you . . .

Strongly agree	Agree	Neither agree nor disagree	Disagree	Strongly disagree
☐	☐	☐	☐	☐

Research has shown that when the various scaling techniques have been compared the results have been similar across all techniques.[4] Therefore, the selection of a scaling technique will depend largely upon the information that is to be collected.

Indirect questions It is not always possible to use direct questioning to obtain information. People may be either unwilling or unable to give answers to questions they consider to be an invasion of their privacy or that are embarrassing. Projective methods are a group of techniques used to obtain information that cannot be obtained through direct questioning. Projective techniques are based on the theory that the description of vague subjects requires interpretation, and this interpretation can only be based on the individual's own background, attitudes and values. The major projective techniques employed are word association, sentence completion, story completion and cartoon techniques.

Word association requires the respondent to give the first word or thought that comes to mind after the researcher presents a word or phrase. Responses are then grouped into categories of interest to the researcher. The most common use of the word association technique is for the testing of potential brand names.

Sentence completion, as the name implies, requires the respondent to complete a sentence. For example, 'people who smoke are . . .'. In this example the respondent is not required to associate with the answer, and more revealing answers can be obtained than with a direct question such as: 'What kind of people smoke?'

Story completion is an extension of the sentence completion technique. In story completion part of a story is told and the respondent is asked to complete it.

Cartoon techniques present cartoon-type drawings of people in a particular situation. One of the individuals is shown with a sentence in a 'bubble' and one of the others is shown with a blank 'bubble' that the respondent is asked to complete. This technique can show attitudes towards products, purchasing situations, etc., as depicted in the cartoon.

While projective techniques can uncover information not available from direct questioning, their results are difficult to analyse so their use is normally limited to preliminary research.

Panel research A panel refers to a group of respondents who have agreed to provide information over a period of time. In effect, panel research is continuous survey research. Panels are normally operated by research agencies rather than by individual organizations. Two of the most common types of panels operated are retail audits and consumer panels.

A retail audit (such as that produced by A. C. Nielsen Company) records sales to consumers through a panel of retail outlets. The estimate of consumer sales is based on observations. It is arrived at as follows:

Opening stock for + Net deliveries since − Stock held at present = Sales to consumers
period (checked at   last audit   audit   during period
last audit)

The information obtained from such an audit is sold to manufacturers who can see how their brands are performing alongside others. The main problem is in 'representativeness' as certain retail outlets will not allow retail auditors into their premises. Such retailers usually sell a high proportion of 'own label' merchandise, and do not want their success (or otherwise) to become public knowledge.

Consumer panels are typically used to study media exposure and purchasing behaviour. Data are gathered using diaries (data entered by respondents), regular telephone surveys, or instruments (e.g., use of audiometers for monitoring television viewing habits).

Omnibus surveys Omnibus surveys are organized by a research agency on behalf of several clients rather than a single client. As clients participate in a single survey, interviewers ask different questions, but to the same sample of people. The costs of the survey are divided between them. Each client receives only the answers and analysis relating to his or her own questions and there is exactly the same degree of confidentiality as with an *ad hoc* study.

This type of survey is particularly suitable where a client needs original research, but only needs to ask a limited number of questions, as costs are usually based on the number of questions asked. Other factors which usually govern the cost per client are the proportion of the total sample available which the client wants to access. If the whole sample is not required, and the types of questions required are open ended then questions are likely to be more expressive.

There are several large, general omnibus surveys available, plus quite a wide variety of specialized ones. Specialist ones concentrate on particular types of product or customer. Anyone considering using an omnibus survey is advised to look at recent issues of the Market Research Society's newsletter, as this carries advertisements to recruit clients for omnibus surveys.

Depth interviews

Depth interviews normally involve either one face-to-face respondent (individual depth interview) or a group of 5–25 respondents (group discussions).

In the individual depth interview, the interviewer has a list of subjects of interest as opposed to a structural questionnaire. He or she is free to create questions and probe responses in greater depth.

Individual depth interviews are particularly useful in the following situations:

− where the subject matter is of a confidential or potentially embarrassing nature;
− where a highly detailed understanding of complicated behaviour on decision-making patterns (e.g., planning the family holiday) is required. This is usually the case in industrial/organizational research problems where executives are interviewed on a one-to-one basis.

Group discussions are often used for

− generating ideas for new product concepts and new products;
− exploring consumer response to promotional and packaging ideas;

– preliminary research prior to a more structured survey, e.g., to establish consumer knowledge and vocabulary.

Group discussions are normally recorded (on audio or video tape) or viewed 'live' by the client (possibly behind a one-way mirror). The researcher is responsible for leading the discussion, probing interesting comments and preparing a summary of the group's major comments. The major advantage of group discussions over individual interviews is that the interaction process tends to generate more information than could be derived from individuals separately.

There are, however, two problems with both types of technique. First, they can be biased as respondents are normally given an incentive to participate. Second, sample sizes are small and often non-representative. As with projective techniques and open questions, depth interviews are an excellent tool for preliminary research, but results from them normally require validation by more extensive and structured research.

Observational research

An ice-cream manufacturer was concerned that sales of some of its products were not achieving the levels that had been expected (based on survey research). A direct observation study in a sample of shops revealed why. The ice-cream was kept in top-loading refrigerators with sides that were so high that many of the children could not see in to pick out the products they wanted. A picture display was devised for the side of the cabinet to enable the children to recognize each product and to indicate their choice by pointing to it. Sales increased. [5]

Observational research includes viewing and listening to situations. It also emcompasses recording human behaviour with monitoring instruments.

Personal observation is used when it would be impossible or expensive to obtain data through a survey. Examples of its use are:

– monitoring traffic flow both inside and outside a shop;
– studying a retail outlet (e.g., display methods, prices and customer flows;
– viewing competitors' products at an exhibition;
– viewing product usage by, say, children.

Monitoring instruments are sometimes preferable to personal observations for reasons of accuracy, cost or for functional reasons.

Examples of uses of monitoring instruments include:
– monitoring traffic flow through a district;
– monitoring television viewing habits;
– monitoring physiological reactions to promotional and packaging ideas. Physiological measures are measurements of physical responses (including eye movement, brain-wave analysis, perspiration rate, eye pupil size) to a stimulus such as an advertisement.

Computer assisted interviewing This modern technique at present is regarded as a gimmick with which to impress clients. The advantage is that results can be fed in from a remote terminal (where the fieldwork is being conducted) and an instant readout can be obtained at the control headquarters. There must be some advantage in providing the client with 'instantaneous' results, but this might be at the expense of sacrificing accuracy, in that there is little opportunity for verification in the field. In marketing terms, there is little advantage in having instantaneous results rather than having a considered report in a matter of a few days.

A modern variation of the above that has recently been developed is 'computer clipboards' wherein simple questions (with closed responses) can be asked, and actually 'punched' into the computer clipboard. An instant readout can again be achieved. The problem with this device is that it cannot cope with complicated (open ended) questions.

Experimentation

Experimentation involves the manipulation of one or more variables by the experimenter in such a way that its effect on another variable can be determined, e.g., manipulating price in order that its effect on sales can be determined.

Marketing experiments may be conducted in the field or in a 'laboratory' situation.

Field experimentation is also known as test marketing. This involves the duplication of the planned national marketing programme for a product in one or more limited market sectors. Marketing mix variables are manipulated in an attempt to identify the optimum marketing mix for the national launch. Test marketing is not limited to new products. It can be used to evaluate price changes, new packages, variations in distribution strategy or alternative advertising strategies.

In laboratory experimentation, an environment is simulated (e.g., home or shopping environment) and the environment used to test consumer reactions to new products, packaging, displays or advertising themes.

Types of errors affecting experimental results In order that an experiment is useful, care must be taken to ensure that all sources of error are minimized. Such possible sources of error include:

– *Motivation* Respondents may alter their responses to a specific stimulant over a period of time, irrespective of external events. For example, in a prolonged 'taste testing' experiment, respondents may develop more sophisticated palates as the experiment progresses and this may affect their response to a particular flavour.
– *Exogenous occurrences* These are events not controlled by the experimenter, e.g., competitive actions and macro-environmental changes.
– *Selection* Selection error occurs when the groups formed for the purposes of the experiment are unequal.
– *Instrument variability* This refers to changes in the measuring instrument over time. These changes are most likely to occur when the measurement process involves people, either as observers or interviewers; their interest and professionalism may cease or become better as time passes.
– *Lost respondents* After a period of time, respondents in an experiment may refuse to continue their participation. The experimental results at a later stage in the experiment may not be representative of what might have emerged had all the original respondents been present.
– *Experiment effect* The fact that an experiment is being conducted often has an important effect on the respondents. Even pre-measurement can, by alerting the subjects to the topic of study, cause them to change behaviour.

Rodger[6] provides a more detailed discussion on experimental design and shows how this can measure the impact of a single variable or several variables.

Once the optimum research method has been selected, the researcher must decide who and where to study. This decision process normally involves a sampling procedure. After data have been collected, the researcher must then analyse and report research findings. Sampling, data analysis and research reporting are discussed in the next section.

SAMPLING, DATA ANALYSIS AND RESEARCH APPLICATIONS

Sampling

Sampling is a necessary and inescapable part of human affairs. Each of us samples and is regularly sampled. We sample performance of a new car by a test drive, a wine by a few sips and a new acquaintance by an initial meeting.

It is sometimes possible and practical to take a census; that is, to study each member of the population of interest. This is sometimes the situation in industrial market research situations where the numbers of companies to be investigated are small. More often than not, however, a sample is taken due to cost, time, accuracy and research effect. Cost and time benefits are obvious, but the last two reasons require explanation:

– *Research effect* The purpose of marketing research is to collect data about markets: not to influence markets. Yet responding to survey questions forces the respondent to examine attitudes towards the survey topic. This examination may lead to a change in behaviour. To minimize the occurrence of behavioural changes a sample is sometimes preferable to a census.
– *Accuracy* As sample size increases, the occurrence of non-sampling errors may also increase. Non-sampling errors include errors in data collection and analysis.

The sampling process consists of three steps:

– Specify the target population.
– Select the sampling method.
– Determine the sample size.

Specify the target population The target population, or frame, is that part of the total population (universe) to which the study is directed. For example, for a company selling cars in the UK, the universe could be the entire UK population plus foreign visitors, and the frame might be people aged 18 or over. Elements (e.g., prospective respondents) from the target population are selected using reference material (including directories and maps) or selected after preliminary questioning or observation.

Select the sampling method Five basic choices must be made when deciding on a sampling method:

1. *Random v. non-random sampling* In random samples, each member of the target population has a fixed (often equal) probability of being a member of the target sample. Random samples have to be sufficiently large to ensure that all sections of the population are surveyed. In non-random (also known as purposive or quota) samples, on the other hand, respondents are selected to fit a quota designed to mirror relevant characteristics of the population and in this way fewer respondents are required.

A random sample design has two advantages. First, a statistical relationship exists between the sample estimates and population. Second, the composition of the sample is not affected by interviewer likes and dislikes. These two benefits have made random sample designs particularly useful for surveys that are politically sensitive.

A non-random sample may be as reliable as a random sample if the following requirements are met:

– Up-to-date statistics relating to the structure of the population are available.

– Classification questions are carefully designed.
– The interviewer's selection of respondents is carefully controlled.

In a *simple random sample* every individual in the target population has an equal chance of being drawn. Each individual is allocated a number and the sample can be drawn using random number tables. This method is equivalent to the classic lottery where names are placed in a hat and drawn out randomly.

In a *systematic random sample* a random starting point is selected and every Nth unit in the frame is drawn where:

$$N = \frac{\text{Population size}}{\text{Sample size}}$$

This method is quicker and cheaper than simple random sampling as the procedure involving random number tables is avoided.

2. *Single stage v. multistage sampling* If a survey population is large and widely dispersed, a probability sample will often be drawn in more than one stage. For example, a survey of voters could first be sampled by constituencies, then polling districts, then the register of electors. Multistage sampling ensures that interview calls are not too widely dispersed.

3. *Single unit v. cluster sampling* In single unit sampling, each sampling unit is selected separately; in cluster sampling the units are selected in groups, e.g., a household might be a single unit but a street would be a cluster. Cluster sampling has the advantage of reducing interviewing costs, but within-cluster variability may be low.

4. *Unstratified v. stratified sampling* A stratum in a population is a segment of that population having one or more common characteristics, e.g., companies with a turnover of five to ten million pounds annually. Stratified random sampling involves treating each stratum as a separate sub-population for sampling purposes. The reasons for stratifying a population for sampling purposes are:

(a) it may help to ensure representativeness (and thus reduce sampling error);
(b) the required sample size for the same level of sampling error will usually be smaller than for a non-stratified sample.

Stratification is commonly used in industrial marketing research. In consumer research, details of strata are not normally readily available, e.g., individuals' incomes. The ACORN[7] (a classification of residential neighbourhoods) method does enable some stratified random sampling in consumer research. The ACORN method provides 11 classifications of residential neighbourhoods according to type of housing.

5. *Proportionate v. disproportionate sampling* In proportionate sampling an equal percentage of respondents is sampled for each stratum. In disproportionate sampling a small (but important) stratum is over-sampled but restored to its due weight when considering total results. Disproportionate samples are, therefore, most cost effective.

Determine sample size In determining sample size, there are two major considerations:

– Research budget available.
– Degree of precision required.

Research budget Based purely on resources available, sample size may be calculated using the following formula:

$$\text{Sample size} = \frac{\text{Total budget} - \text{Research planning, analysis and reporting costs}}{\text{Variable cost per interview (or observation)}}$$

Precision required For random samples there is a statistical relationship between sample estimates and population values. Using probability theory we are able to relate precision required to sample size. The larger the sample size, the more confident the researcher can be that the results are representative of the population. If the level of precision required can be specified in advance, it is possible to determine the minimum required sample size. This sample size refers to the number of usable responses and allowance should be made for the likely non-response level. A more detailed discussion of sampling accuracy is given by Rodger[8] who explains the statistical methodology behind sample size determination.

Editing and coding responses After data collection the next step is to edit illegible, incomplete and inconsistent responses. There are three ways to deal with imperfect responses:

1. *Ask the respondent to clarify response*: this is usually avoided except in the case of surveys with a small sample size and a high level of imperfect responses.
2. *Use responses*: this approach is often used by research agencies as they are often committed to obtaining a certain number of responses. Tabulation can keep track of non-responses as a separate category. Inconsistent responses might be assumed to average out over the sample.
3. *Discard responses*: the researcher may judge that the end results will be more useful if incomplete responses are discarded.

For small studies (less than 25 respondents) it is possible to conduct analyses manually, provided only basic analysis is required. Data from large studies are coded prior to computer input.

The process of coding involves converting responses to code values on coding sheets. Coding sheets are normally 80 columns wide and one or more column is allocated to each survey question. Each line (horizontal) of the sheet is devoted to one respondent. Closed questions may be pre-coded, that is, a code is allocated to each possible response before the survey. Responses to open questions are normally grouped into convenient categories and a code allocated to each category after the survey.

Figure 5.1 illustrates a typical coding procedure. Two commonly used conversions are used in this example.

– Possible responses are coded from left to right beginning with '1'.
– Non-responses are normally coded 9.

It can thus be seen how the system works from the questionnaire to the coding sheet, and thereafter for computer punching. In this particular example, the partial toothpaste questionnaire has been hypothetically filled in, and the partial coding sheet has been filled in from the response on this questionnaire.

Data analysis

After input to the computer, it is often desirable to create new variables. Two types of new variable may be created.

QUESTIONNAIRE

Respondent No: 890

1–3

Q1   Do you use toothpaste?   ☑ ☐

Yes   No

4

Q2   Please indicate your degree of agreement with the following statements by circling a 6 if you strongly agree, a 1 if you strongly disagree, or somewhere in between depending on your degree of agreement with the statement

Strongly   Strongly
Disagree   Agree
— — — — — — — — —

I am very health conscious   1 ② 3 4 5 6   5

My appearance is very important to me   1 2 ③ 4 5 6   6

I use mouthwash often   1 ② 3 4 5 6   7

Q3   How old are you?   <u>26</u>   8–9

Q4   What is your marital status?

☐ ✓   ☐   ☐   ☐   10

Single   Married   Divorced,   Other
Widowed, or
separated

Q5   . . . etc   **CODING SHEET**   11

Columns

1	2	3	4	5	6	7	8	9	10	11	12	13	14	80
8	9	0	1	2	3	2	2	6	1	⋯⋯⋯etc				

Figure 5.1   Coding procedure

Table 5.2   Simple tabulation

Age of respondent	Absolute frequency	Relative frequency (%)	Adjusted frequency (%)	Cumulative frequency (%)
0–17	1	1.9	1.9	1.9
18–40	20	37.7	38.5	40.4
41–64	21	39.6	40.4	80.8
65+	10	18.9	19.2	100.0
Not ascertained	1	1.9	Missing	100.0
	53	100.0	100.0	100.0

– *Combination of variables* For example, data on a respondent's age, marital status and children may be combined to generate a new variable called 'stage in the family life cycle'.
– *Introduction of secondary data.*

Basic analysis Marketing research analysis usually involves simple tabulation, calculation of summarizing statistics and cross-tabulation.

Simple tabulation involves calculating the number and percentage of respondents who choose each of the available answers. Table 5.2 provides an example of simple tabulation. In this example an adjusted frequency discards data that are missing due to non-responsive or incorrect coding.

There are two kinds of *summarizing statistics*. The first provides measures of the mid-point of the distribution and is known as *measures of central tendency*. The second gives an indication of the amount of variation in the data comprising the distribution and is known as *measures of dispersion*.

Mean, mode and median are the major measures of central tendency, and the reader is again directed to Rodger[9] for a detailed discussion of their computation.

Cross-tabulation involves constructing a table so that responses to two or more questions may be compared. Table 5.3 provides a cross-tabulation example produced using the SPSS(X)[10] software package. Here the response to a question on income groups is compared to the response to a question on weekly food expenditure.

Measurement scales The various ways of phrasing questions have been outlined earlier. From an analysis viewpoint it is useful to categorize questioning/measurement scales into four groups.

Nominal scales Nominal scales are used to categorize responses. For example, the number 1 is assigned to female respondents and number 0 is assigned to male respondents. Nominal scales may be used to calculate the number (or percentage or frequency) of items falling within each category. The calculation of median for nominal data is meaningless, but the mode may be calculated.

Ordinal scales Ordinal scales are used to rank items. For example, a consumer is asked to rank his or her preference for brands A, B and C. In this example, if the consumer ranks B as his or her preferred brand, an ordinal scale will not reveal how much more the consumer prefers brand B to brands A and C. An ordinal scale may be used to calculate frequency, mode and median, but not mean.

Table 5.3   Cross-tabulation of income versus food expenditure

COUNT Row % Col. % Tot. %	Food expenditure (£) Less than £15	15–29	30–44	45–59	60+	ROW
Less than £10 000	33 7.1 84.6 3.5	226 48.7 70.2 24.2	149 32.1 47.8 16.0	45 9.7 23.1 4.8	11 2.4 16.5 1.2	464 49.7
£10 000 – £20 000	5 1.5 12.8 0.5	73 22.0 22.7 7.8	121 36.4 38.8 13.0	102 30.7 52.3 10.8	31 5.3 47.7 3.3	332 35.6
£20 000 +	1 0.7 2.6 6.1	23 16.8 7.1 2.5	42 30.7 13.5 4.5	48 35.0 24.6 5.1	23 16.8 35.4 2.5	137 14.7
Column Total	39 4.2	322 34.5	312 33.4	195 20.9	65 7.0	933 100.0

Each cell contains four numbers:

Count   The number of people in the cell (i.e., 33 respondents had incomes under £10 000 and spent less than £15 per week on food).

Row %   The percentage of people in the row who are in the column (i.e., 33/464 = 7.1 per cent of the people with incomes under £10 000 spent less than £15 per week on food).

Col %   The percentage of people in the column who were in the row (i.e., 33/39 = 84.6 per cent of people who spent less than £15 per week on food had incomes under £10 000).

Total %   The percentage of the total sample in the particular cell (i.e., 33/933 = 3.5 per cent).

Interval scales   An interval scale is a scale where intervals on the scale are equal distances. For example, respondents are asked to state their degree of agreement or disagreement with a statement by selecting a response from a list such as the following one:

1. Agree very strongly.
2. Agree fairly strongly.
3. Agree.
4. Undecided.
5. Disagree.
6. Disagree fairly strongly.
7. Disagree very strongly.

Virtually the entire range of statistical analysis can be applied to interval scales, including frequency, mean, median, mode, range and standard deviation.

Ratio scales   A ratio scale is an interval scale with a zero point. Simple counting of any set of objects produces a ratio scale. Thus sales, costs and number of purchasers are all ratio scales. Ratio scales allow, in addition to the analysis permitted by interval scales, some specialized calculations.

Interval and ratio scales can thus be subjected to more analytical procedures and hence they are easier to analyse.

More complete analyses Most marketing research analysis is limited to the basic analytical procedures described. However, computers now enable more complex analytical procedures to be used by marketers. Many of these procedures are concerned with analysing the degree of association (or relationship) between two or more variables. For measuring the degree of association between two variables Pearson's correlation coefficient is the most common formula employed.[11]

Research reporting The results of a research project may be reported in written or oral format, or both. The importance of effective reporting cannot be overemphasized. Regardless of the quality of the research process and the accuracy and usefulness of the resulting data, the data will not be used if they are not effectively communicated to the appropriate decision makers.

For written reports the following guidelines normally apply:

1. The report sequence is usually title page, table of contents, summary, introduction/research objectives, research methodology, findings, conclusions, recommendations (if appropriate), appendices.
2. Most report readers will not be particularly concerned with the technical aspects of the report, such as sampling procedure and questionnaire design. For this reason, technical details should be placed in the appendix section rather than in the methodology section.
3. Use terminology that matches the vocabulary of the reader.
4. Use diagrams (such as graphs, bar charts and pie charts) whenever possible.

For oral presentations, the report sequence is normally research objectives, research methodology, major findings, conclusions and recommendations and, to maintain audience attention, full use should be made of visual aids.

Application of research techniques

Marketing research techniques may be applied to assist decision making in all the functions of the marketing mix. It should also be borne in mind that 'mixed' research tactics can be used (e.g., personal interviews combined with group discussions). The application of research techniques in product, pricing, marketing communications and distribution research is now briefly outlined; sales forecasting research is discussed in detail in Chapter 6. For a fuller and more professional discussion of the techniques the reader is again directed to the work of Chisnall.[12]

Product research This encompasses the following aspects:

- *Generating new product ideas* Sources of new product ideas include monitoring secondary sources (particularly trade journals, competition's literature), group discussions with consumers and/or industry 'experts', studies of product use and surveys of consumer requirements.
- *Product concept testing* A product concept is a product idea that has been defined in terms of its applications and benefits. Before embarking on the costly process of developing a prototype, it is usually advisable to research demand for the product concept. Product concept testing often involves describing the concept to consumers and asking the following question:

'If this product were available, would you be likely to buy it? Would you say that you:

☐ would definitely buy it
☐ would probably buy it
☐ might or might not buy it
☐ would probably not buy it
☐ would definitely not buy it?'

- *Product testing* In product testing, consumers are asked to use or examine product prototypes. The consumers are then asked if they would buy such a product and to state their opinions of the test product.
- *Test marketing* of products in a limited geographical area.
- *Packaging research* – including laboratory and field experimentation.

A fuller discussion of product research, especially in relation to fast moving consumer goods is given in a text by Watkins.[13]

Pricing research This includes the setting of prices for both new and current products and involves forecasting sales and estimating costs. Methods for forecasting sales are described in Chapter 6, but the estimation of costs is more the subject of accountancy. Pricing also forms part of marketing tactics, whereby prices can be manipulated in the short term to fight a tactical battle (e.g., short-term petrol price reductions) or in the longer term for product positional tactics. A fuller discussion is provided by Greenley within the context of marketing plans.[14]

Marketing communications research This includes the following:

Marketing communications effectiveness research Measuring the effectiveness of advertising, personal selling, sales promotion and public relations activity. This involves measuring its communication effect and/or sales effect. Measuring communications effectiveness is concerned with measuring awareness, attitudes or 'intention to buy' before and after a campaign. Sales effectiveness measurement may be conducted by statistical analysis of past sales versus promotion expenditure. For new products, field experiments with 'control' markets are used.

Media selection research In order to select a suitable publication or medium, a marketer should aim to collect the following data:

- Media distribution (the number of copies or sets carrying the advertisement).
- Audience size (the number of people actually exposed to an advertisement, also known as 'reach').
- Audience exposure (the number of people exposed times the number of times they are exposed, i.e., reach × frequency, also known as 'gross rating points').
- Cost per exposure.

Media distribution details are normally available from the media and these statistics are normally audited by an independent organization, e.g., Audit Bureau of Circulation for the UK. Audience 'reach' and 'exposure' data are collected and published by research organizations such as Research Services Ltd. Media effectiveness can vary greatly for different products and may be measured using the techniques mentioned under 'Marketing communications effectiveness research'.

Copy testing This is concerned with determining the effectiveness of the creative aspects (headline, pictures, etc.) of advertising or promotional material. Creative ideas may be tested using physiological measures, surveys of advertising recall, field and 'laboratory' experiments.

Researching the number and location of sales representations required Two main types of research are used for sales territory planning:

1. *Statistical analysis of sales data*: for current products, an analysis of actual sales versus market potential for each territory will indicate if the optimum number of representatives is being employed.
2. *Sales effort approach*: this approach is particularly appropriate for new products; it involves four stages:
   (a) Compiling lists of prospective customers from secondary sources.
   (b) Estimating the number of sales calls per year required to sell to selected prospective customers.
   (c) Estimating the average number of sales calls per representative that can be made in that territory in a year.
   (d) Dividing (b) by (c) to obtain the number of representatives required.

Distribution research This includes the following:

– *Warehouse location research* In this type of research, the marketing research function is normally required to provide data on customer location (from secondary sources).
– *Retail outlet location research* To assist with the process of planning the location of retail outlets, marketing research can provide a great deal of useful data. Useful data on a prospective site would include volume of pedestrians, number of nearby competitors, and the socio-economic profile of the neighbourhood.

MARKETING INFORMATION SYSTEMS

A marketing information system can be defined as a system designed to generate and disseminate an orderly flow of pertinent information to marketing managers. Thus, marketing research is concerned with the task of generating information, whereas the marketing information system is focused on managing the flow of information to marketing decision makers. This distinction is important because information is worthless unless it is relevant and effectively communicated. This section comes at the end of this chapter because you will appreciate that it is possible to have marketing research without a marketing information system but not vice versa.

The marketing information system of a company is a sub-system of its management information system. A marketing information system, in turn, consists of four sub-systems:

1. The internal accounting system – a system that reports orders, sales, inventory levels, receivables and payables.
2. The marketing intelligence system – the set of procedures and sources used by executives to obtain their everyday information about pertinent developments in the marketing environment.
3. The marketing research system – the systematic design, collection, analysis and reporting of data and findings relevant to a specific marketing situation facing the company.
4. The analytical marketing system – a system for analysing marketing data using statistical procedures and mathematical models.

Systems 1, 2 and 3 are all data collection methods, whereas 4 is an analytical method. The point is that it does work and many marketing-oriented companies are already applying the technique.

CONCLUSIONS

This chapter has covered the subject of marketing research and it has been acknowledged that this subject is an involved and detailed study in its own right. The areas covered have included an introductory description of the development of marketing research followed by secondary research methods. Primary research was then examined under the headings of: survey research, depth research, observation and experimentation. Sampling was discussed followed by data analysis. The chapter concluded with an indication of how marketing research techniques could be applied to the marketing function including the adoption of a marketing information system.

Although it is viewed separately from marketing research, sales forecasting is concerned with 'information for marketing decisions' which is the thrust of this second part of the text. This subject is now dealt with in the next chapter.

APPLICATION QUESTIONS

1. What problems are to be encountered in assessing the cost effectiveness of marketing research?
2. In which research circumstances are observation techniques more suitable than other fieldwork techniques?
3. Distinguish between the universe and the sample frame.
4. What are the essential elements of a marketing information system?
5. Explain what is meant by the following in the context of questionnaire design?
   (a) Open ended questions.
   (b) Closed dichotomous questions.
   (c) Closed multiple choice questions.
   (d) Semantic differential scales.

References

1. Chisnall, P. M., *Marketing Research*, 3rd edn, McGraw-Hill, London, 1986.
2. Chisnall, P. M., op. cit., p. 38.
3. Dillman, D. A., J. G. Gallegos and J. H. Fray, 'Reducing refusal rates for telephone interviews', *Public Opinion Quarterly*, Spring 1976.
4. Kassarjion, H. H. and M. Nakanishi, 'A study of selected opinion measurement techniques', *Journal of Marketing Research*, May 1969.
5. Kitchen, J., 'Observation, ethology and marketing research', *European Research*, January 1981, p. 22.
6. Rodger, L. W., *Statistics for Marketing*, McGraw-Hill, London, 1984, pp. 179–186.
7. ACORN is supplied by CACI London. It is discussed in detail in Chapter 7 'Selection of Markets'.
8. Rodger, L. W., op. cit., pp. 103–22.
9. Rodger, L. W., op. cit., Chapter 2, pp. 22–39.
10. Nie, N. H. *et al.*, *SPSS-X*, SPSS-X, Chicago, IL, 1985.
11. Rodger, L. W., op. cit., for a fuller discussion, pp. 122–32.
12. Chisnall, P. M., op. cit.
13. Watkins, T., *The Economics of the Brand*, McGraw-Hill, London, 1986.
14. Greenley, G. E., *The Strategic and Operational Planning of Marketing*, McGraw-Hill, London, 1986, pp. 124–139.

SIX

SALES FORECASTING

INTRODUCTION

It has now been established that a company's customers are the starting point for business planning activities and this notion lies at the very heart of marketing. In times when demand exceeds
supply it is perhaps less important that individual consumer needs are attended to: indeed, in
such circumstances it is not possible to fulfil all needs and some form of rationing has to be
imposed. This, however, is a rather abnormal occurrence in modern industrialized societies and
generally occurs after a war or an 'act of God'. Such conditions are then only temporary until
manufacturing capacity expands sufficiently to meet the extra demand.

The point that was being made is that the 'norm' is that supply exceeds demand and this is
increasingly the case in the modern world where more efficient forms of manufacturing mean that
the fulfilment of consumer needs becomes easier over time. The problem is thus a matter of
matching supply to demand at a price acceptable to the marketplace. Such a problem demands
that companies engage in pre-planning to ascertain what share of the market they might obtain,
and then plan to achieve it.

FORECASTING AS THE START OF THE PLANNING PROCESS

Individual businesses are becoming more competitive in an increasingly complex and 'inter-
nationalized' environment. Competitive circumstances tend to change more quickly nowadays
and strategic decisions become increasingly critical and binding.

Companies must be able to predict not only their sales, but also plan for profits, cash flows,
etc. The days are gone when companies could afford to have 'slack' in terms of working capital,
labour force, raw materials and finished stocks. Such 'slack' is costly (with high labour and interest rates) and plant and manpower must nowadays be utilized to its optimum capacity. Inefficient
use of such resources is costly and profit margins are such that a company that does not manage
such resources in an efficient manner will be prey to its more efficient competitors.

Forecasting sales must thus be the starting point of the planning process as this is the 'act of
giving advance warning for beneficial action to be taken'.[1]

The main problem that exists within many organizations is that forecasting has traditionally
been seen as a function of the accountant for purposes of budget preparation for the budget
period ahead (normally one year) and this is termed the medium-term forecast. Accountants,

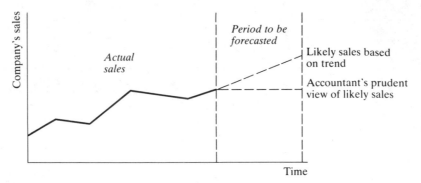

Figure 6.1   Theoretical view of a forecasting scenario

naturally, will not tend to over-estimate and they will tend to forecast on the prudent side. Figure 6.1 illustrates a hypothetical situation. In this situation one might be inclined to level the accusation of excessive conservatism against the accountant. However, at the end of the day the cost/ management accountant is the one who must attempt to ensure that the organization does not over-spend in reaching its anticipated sales, and in the absence of an intimate knowledge of what is happening in the marketplace, one can hardly blame the professional from adopting such a prudent approach.

The reality of this situation is that the market will probably grow as anticipated on the extrapolation, but the company cannot totally meet this growth because it is not prepared for it in terms of budget (e.g., not enough production facilities available to meet increased sales). The company will thus lose sales because it is not in a position to exploit the market. The irony of this situation is that inevitably production can most probably produce more than was budgeted and sales can sell more than was budgeted, so over-achieving on sales in this situation means that the exercise is often viewed as being successful on the basis that 'sales and production have done better than expected'! The fact that sales have in truth been lost is not considered.

One can postulate further and state that if sales proceed better than 'likely sales based on trend' as shown in Fig. 6.1, then the capacity to lose sales will be increased even further. This leads to what McDonald calls a planning gap[2] where action must be brought about to ensure that sales are not lost because production facilities and marketing resources are not available to meet potential demand.

We have thus established that the sales forecast is the start of the planning process and for reasons just outlined, if the company is to achieve its maximum or optimum share of the market, then the marketing department must be the department that is responsible for the sales forecast. This fact is often not appreciated by many non-numerate marketing managers and they are prepared to abrogate what is their direct responsibility to their more numerate colleagues in the finance department.

Once the situation relates to new markets or new products then it is inevitable that marketing must be involved. However, there can be a problem of what Clifton *et al.* refer to as self-protection and inertia.[3] This is where existing suppliers in a market will want to protect their own position and they will tend to overstate the degree of competition and understate the market potential, when approached for information, in order to put off potential new entrants. Equally, inertia might also rule inside the company in that individuals inside the company might not want to extend themselves to addressing the problems of exploiting a new product or market. Needless to say, the problems to be overcome in this forecasting scenario rest with marketing analysts and not with cost accountants.

SENSITIVITY ANALYSIS

This is the technique of attempting to evaluate how changing various marketing inputs will affect sales. Forecasting sales for the market and the company can be done by a variety of techniques explained later in this chapter, but clearly if, say, advertising or personal selling effort is reduced or increased during the period that has been forecasted, then sales will be affected. A forecaster, forecasting company sales, does so with the advance knowledge that certain marketing mix inputs will take place. Manipulation of these inputs and then assessing the likely effect upon sales is known as 'sensitivity analysis'.

SHORT-, MEDIUM- AND LONG-TERM FORECASTS

Before we explain each of the above it is perhaps appropriate to state that there are two methods by which forecasting data may be collected:

1. By making a forecast for the industry or total market and then determining what share of this will fall to the company (sometimes called a market forecast).
2. By forecasting sales direct using previous sales data or anticipating sales directly in some other way.

Usually the method used for market and then sales forecasts is termed a 'top down' approach in that the ultimate forecast is not obtained from an operational level in the organization. The opposite to this is termed 'bottom up' forecasting whereby the data are collected from the marketplace, usually by sales personnel who operate there. This is, however, expanded more in the next chapter.

Battersby produced the first UK written text on forecasting[4] and he differentiated between short-term and long-term forecasts. He introduced medium-term forecasts as being akin to long-term forecasts, but being concerned with minor strategic decisions. Since then, the purpose of medium-term forecasting has become far more important largely because, as has already been elucidated, it is the start of the planning process.

Briefly, each type of forecast may be said to be for the following purposes:

Short term (for up to approximately three months ahead)

Made largely for tactical reasons, e.g., to fulfil seasonal sales demands, for production planning purposes and cash flow requirements.

Medium term (normally for one year ahead)

Made principally for business budgeting. This forecast is the starting point of the company's planning process. The forecast is also used for predicting manning levels required to achieve these anticipated sales and for plant and machinery requirements.

Long term (5 years, 10 years or 20 years ahead)

These forecasts are for major strategic decisions to be taken by the company. What is 'long term' is largely determined by the type of market in which the company operates. A self-evident example would be computers where 'long term' is, say, less than five years and steel production where 'long term' may be 20 years.

Long-term forecasts are used in areas such as management succession, company expansion and long-term financial planning requirements.

Before a company can plan it must first forecast, as this reduces uncertainty. Such plans are thus based upon more scientific criteria. The problem is that if the forecast is incorrect, or is based upon spurious premises, then the whole planning exercise will have been fruitless. The importance of accurate forecasts cannot, therefore, be emphasized enough. Companies can thus prepare for change by planning, in that the forecaster can predict what will happen for a set of decisions in a given set of circumstances. By taking certain actions, the planner can alter the subsequent events relating to a particular situation. A forecast may predict a fall in demand, and in this case management can then make plans to counteract this fall in demand, or at least plan to ensure that it suffers less from the fall in demand than do its competitors.

RELATIONSHIP BETWEEN FORECASTS AND BUDGETS

The forecast determines the budget, and through the sales budget, sales are generated. The company sales budget is an amalgam of each individual salesperson's anticipated sales (their individual sales budgets) broken down in detail by product type, territory by territory and selling area by selling area. Each individual salesperson then receives his or her share of the total sales budget which has to be sold in the period ahead, and this is then termed his or her individual sales quota or sales target.

A budget thus differs from a forecast in that the budget is what is planned to happen, unlike the forecast which is a prediction of what is expected to happen. The forecast is, therefore, more uncertain as it is affected by external factors, whereas the budget is affected by more controllable internal factors.

One rather obvious, but sometimes ignored, fact is that the sales budget must be coordinated with other budgets within the organization. The sales budget for instance should not plan to achieve more sales than production has been budgeted to manufacture.

It must also be borne in mind that budgets should be flexible to allow for changing conditions or unforeseen circumstances. The budget can then be quickly changed to cover such contingencies.

TECHNIQUES OF FORECASTING

This section covers the specific techniques of sales forecasting, although not in sufficient detail to enable the reader to become a *forecasting expert or specialist*. For a more specialist text that starts from first principles the reader is directed to *Forecasting for Sales and Materials Management*, by Lancaster and Lomas.[5]

Basically, sales forecasting techniques are divided into qualitative and quantitative techniques. The first set are often called subjective or judgemental methods as they rely heavily upon opinion in their computation. Quantitative techniques, as the term implies, rely upon mathematics, and such techniques are becoming very popular with the development of computer packages to assist in their application. Quantitative techniques can be split into time series analysis and causal techniques. In time series analysis, the variable that the forecaster considers is time and past events are used to predict the future. However, in applying such techniques, it is difficult to predict downturns or upturns, unless the forecaster deliberately manipulates the data. Such techniques are of little use in markets that are unstable or susceptible to sudden irrational changes. Causal techniques assume that there is a relationship between what is to be forecasted and some other measurable independent variable. The value of this independent variable is put into the equation and the forecast is produced from this. Importance must, therefore, be placed upon the choice of a suitable independent variable, and such variables should ideally precede what is to be forecast by a period sufficient to be able to implement production and marketing plans in good time. One should not attempt to establish the reasons behind such relationships and there is often nothing to suppose that such relationships will hold good in the future. The fact is that a relationship has been established in the past and part of the prediction is that it should probably hold good in the future.

It is logical to look at qualitative techniques first, because these are less scientific in their formulation; in fact they are sometimes referred to as naive methods. They often precede quantitative methods, and it is these latter methods that are now being taken increasingly seriously by progressive management, particularly as more sophisticated computational packages become available.

Qualitative techniques

Consumer/user survey method (market research method) This technique basically consists of asking one's customers about their likely purchases for the period it is desired to forecast and then attempting to ascertain what proportion of these anticipated purchases are likely to fall to one's company. It is quite often undertaken by the salesforce in the case of industrial products. Two problems thus arise: the apportionment of likely sales out of anticipated purchases; and the subjective opinion of buyers when giving their estimates to salespeople.

Sometimes it is not possible to ask customers through the salesforce as is the case for consumer products because they are not usually sold direct to the general public. Here it makes sense to survey a sample of potential consumers through a market research survey (probably as part of an omnibus survey).[6] It is better to assess likely purchasing intentions on a graded answer basis, rather than on a straightforward dichotomous basis, particularly when the product is not a straightforward purchase. For instance, the decision to purchase a carpet is a complicated matter and the purchaser goes through a number of different stages of purchasing intention before making the purchase, unlike, say, a can of baked beans where the decision is far simpler, based upon more immediate needs.

The method is, therefore, quite straightforward, but it is really of most value when there are a small number of purchasers who are likely to signal their intentions to purchase with a reasonable degree of accuracy. The forecaster should also be familiar with competition in the marketplace in order that he or she can assess more accurately what proportion of likely sales will accrue to his or her company out of the assessment for the total market. Consequently, its true value tends to be limited to organizational buying situations where purchasers and competitors are few – a rarity for most buying/selling situations!

Panels of executive opinion (jury method) This method is sometimes known as 'panels of expert opinion' because such 'experts' are counselled about the industry with which they are familiar with the object of producing a forecast. Such experts come from inside the company and from outside the company including management consultants, professional forecasters and investment analysts. Sometimes the panel or jury can include people from client companies who will be in a position to provide advice from a purchasing standpoint.

The group meets in committee and the committee produces a composite forecast which might mean having to average the results in the case of disagreement. The basic precept is that each member of the group should have prepared a forecast beforehand and must be able to support this forecast with hard evidence. Such evidence should be presented to the group and discussed with any inconsistencies being overcome as they arise. As long as agreement is reached after each discussion, a similar set of forecasts should result, because each will represent the majority view, but as was stated earlier, aggregation may be necessary.

'Prudent manager forecasting' is a variation of this approach when company personnel are asked to assume the position of prospective purchasers and evaluate company sales from a customer's point of view and 'prudently' estimate sales, taking into consideration matters like competitors' products in terms of their design, quality, price, service, etc., together with any other external factors that are considered to be of relevance to evaluating the company's sales.

Much of this type of forecasting is based upon opinion and can be expensive in terms of manpower involved in its preparation and discussion. It is a 'top down' method in that a forecast is produced for the industry and it must then be decided what share of this forecast will accrue to the company. Statistics are not collected from market data (from the 'bottom up') and there is a problem in deciding what sales will be in terms of individual products and sales territories. Such information is needed for the budgeting procedure, as was explained in the previous chapter. Thus, it has been demonstrated that there are a number of in-built problems associated with this type of forecasting, particularly the fact that it is a 'top down' method, unlike mathematical forecasting which uses market data.

Salesforce composite   This 'bottom up' method is sometimes referred to as the 'grass roots' approach because it entails each salesperson in the company making an individual forecast for his or her particular sales territory. These individual forecasts are agreed with the area manager who then takes them to the sales manager (or the divisional manager if this stage exists in the sales hierarchy). A similar exercise is then performed between the area/divisional manager and the sales manager until the figures are agreed.

This method is quite popular, particularly in the area of setting sales quotas or targets. There can be less cause for subsequent complaint, because such figures are based on information stemming initially from the salesforce. A slight variation of this method is called 'detecting differences in figures'. Here, the salesperson prepares the figures suitably broken down by individual customers and by individual products. The area manager then produces a similar set of figures independently and they then meet and resolve any differences as they arise. The process continues in similar vein until it reaches the sales manager, when the final sales forecast is agreed.

This appears to be a good method, and in so far as non-mathematical methods are concerned, it probably is. It does, however, fall down when the forecast is to be used for future remuneration (as it invariably is through quotas and targets). There will thus be an inclination on the part of salespeople to produce a pessimistic forecast. This can be overcome in part by linking sales expenses to the forecast. When remuneration is not linked to the sales forecast there might then be a tendency for the salesforce to produce an optimistic forecast. It is well known that salespeople tend to be optimists, perhaps as a result of optimistic noises made by buyers, all being part of good buyer/seller relationships. The salesforce might not, therefore, be an objective enough starting point for sales forecasting and will produce an optimistically or pessimistically biased forecast for the reasons stated. In addition, the salesforce is not necessarily aware of the more global economic factors that might affect future sales, and does not take these into consideration when preparing forecasts.

Delphi method   In this method the project leader selects the team and communicates through the post or telephone, but not in committee. He or she sends a questionnaire to members of the team (who may number 20 upwards) and they are asked to respond to questions of a behavioural nature to begin with. Such questions usually concern matters of a technological breakthrough nature such as new processes for oil refining, new uses for glass products, etc., that have some bearing on the products that the company makes. The answers are then collected and refined and a summary of the answers is sent out with the next round of questionnaires. This time the questioning can be more pointed focusing on such matters as: 'If the new processes for oil refining, as predicted from the results of the first round of questionnaires, can be in production by 1990, how can this company benefit?' The rounds of questioning continue, becoming more specific each time until sufficient useful information is to hand to make marketing and production decisions.

Because the information is not generated in committee the danger of bandwaggon effect of majority opinion is eliminated. However, this method cannot be recommended for the production of a product-by-product and customer-by-customer forecast because it is more concerned with 'futures', and is really only of value for long-term matters like the viability of the company entering a market or developing some new form of product or process for the future.

Bayesian decision theory This method owes its origin to an English cleric of the eighteenth century, but its workings have been refined by statisticians since that date. It is a mixture of subjective and objective material. Its detailed operation cannot be described here, and the reader is directed to more specific texts, like those described at the beginning of this chapter, for a fuller insight into its workings.

A network diagram is used, similar to critical path analysis. Probabilities are estimated by the forecaster for each event in the network. The probabilities thus represent the strength of the decision maker's feeling regarding the likelihood of the occurrence of the various elements in the network. When making business decisions one has to decide among alternatives by taking into account the monetary repercussions of actions taken. When one has to select among alternative investments, consideration must be given to the profit and loss situation that might result from each alternative. When applying Bayesian decision theory this involves selecting an alternative and having a reasonable idea of the economic consequences of choosing that action.

Once the appropriate future events have been identified, and the respective subjective prior probabilities have been assigned, the decision maker works out the expected payoff for each act and chooses the act with the most attractive payoff.

Generating the probabilities described above is a subjective business and for this reason many forecasters reject the Bayesian approach. However, it can be useful in solving business problems for which probabilities are often unknown.

Product testing and test marketing These methods are of most use when little or no previous sales data exist. In such instances it makes sense to anticipate likely demand for the product by testing it on a sample of the potential market beforehand.

The techniques of product testing and test marketing have already been described in Chapter 5. Since product testing only involves a small number of respondents and a summation of their opinions and attitudes towards a new or modified product, test marketing would appear to be the most appropriate medium for producing a sales forecast. Here the product is launched in a limited geographical area and one is thus able to simulate a national launch without committing too many resources in case the product is unsuccessful. Sales are measured during the test and simply grossed up afterwards to provide a forecast.

The main drawback is that this technique is only suitable for new or substantially modified products of a consumer goods nature. There is also the problem of 'novelty', in that if the unit value is relatively small many people will purchase just to 'try it out' and may never purchase again, which might lead one to produce an optimistic forecast for the national launch. It must also be remembered that it has been known for competitors to attempt deliberately to spoil a test marketing campaign by increasing their promotional activity in the test area over the period of the test market.

Quantitative techniques (time series)

Moving averages This is a very simple technique that smoothes the data in a time series. The longer the moving average, the greater will be the smoothing and the principle is that one subtracts the earliest sales figure and then adds the latest sales figure. This figure is then divided by the appropriate number of data periods that have been added together to bring it back to an average. The example that follows provides the best explanation where it can be seen that the longer moving average produces a smoother trend than when using a shorter moving average. The first moving average is for a three-year period whereas the second moving average is over a six-year period and it is this latter one that provides the smoothest pattern of data.

The forecast is produced by extending the trend line and it is up to the forecaster to decide whether three-year or six-year averaging is better. In the case of a steady trend it may not be necessary to smooth the data, and in such cases the process is simply called 'trend projection'. As a rule, the more the data fluctuate, the greater will have to be the averaging period. It is, of course, up to the forecaster to decide what averaging period to use: three years and six years have been used in the example in Table 6.1 for reasons of illustration.

In this particular example it can be seen that the three-year moving average would have been enough to provide a trend for purposes of forecasting and even a two-year moving average would

Table 6.1 Practical example of moving averages technique. Werman Duvet Company Ltd: annual unit sales of double-sized duvets

Year	Number	Three years Total	Three years Average	Six years Total	Six years Average
1971	925				
1972	1023	3111	1037		
1973	1163	3886	1295		
1974	1700	4508	1503	8030	1338
1975	1645	4919	1640	9101	1517
1976	1574	5215	1738	10510	1752
1977	1996	6002	2001	11446	1908
1978	2432	6527	2176	11924	1987
1979	2099	6709	2236	12549	2092
1980	2178	6547	2182	13356	2226
1981	2270	6829	2276	13605	2268
1982	2381	6896	2299	13604	2267
1983	2245	7057	2352	14007	2334
1984	2431	7178	2393	14156	2359
1985	2502	7260	2420		
1986	2327				

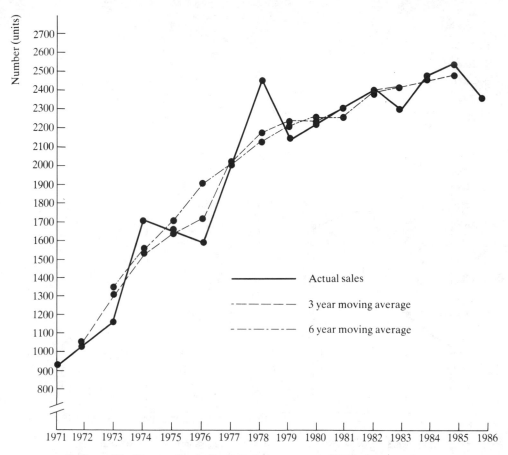

Figure 6.2   Werman Duvet Company Ltd: annual sales of double-sized duvets

have sufficed. Longer moving average periods are of more value to the forecaster when the data fluctuate a great deal. The graph in Fig. 6.2 illustrates this point.

Exponential smoothing   A major drawback with the moving averages technique is that it does not respond immediately to a sudden change in sales and if the sales trend changes it will take one or more periods before the trend is apparent in the forecast (the longer the moving average, the longer it will take to reflect the change). Exponential smoothing helps to overcome this by the apportionment of different weightings to earlier or later parts of the data. The skill lies in how the forecaster judges earlier or later parts of the time series to be more or less typical of the future.

The technique is relatively simple to operate, but it is essentially a technique that needs computer application, particularly if the forecaster is going to 'manipulate' the data to produce a number of different forecasts. The more precise mathematics of the technique cannot be entered into here, and the reader is again pointed to one of the more specialist forecasting or statistical texts mentioned earlier for a more detailed insight.

The technique is best illustrated by reference to the example in Fig. 6.2, annual sales of double-sized duvets for Werman Duvet Company Ltd. The sales are reproduced in Fig. 6.3, and from this it can be seen that weightings have been applied to earlier and later parts of the time series, according to how the forecaster viewed their typicality of how they would reflect the

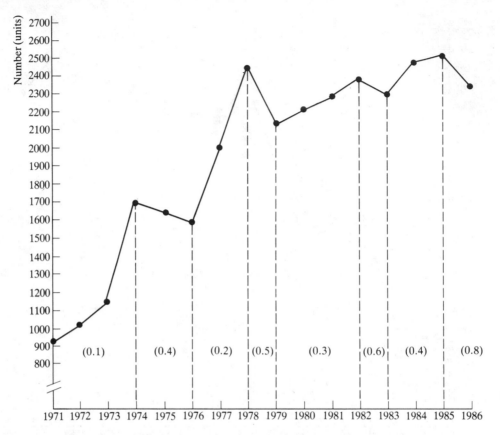

Figure 6.3   Werman Duvet Company Ltd: annual sales of double-sized duvets
(*Note* Figures in brackets represent weightings)

pattern for the future. In this particular example the forecaster has a pessimistic view of the future and has apportioned a greater weighting to the downwards parts of the series and less to the upwards parts. Such weightings will produce a downward trend as the forecast, unlike the moving averages example which produced a flattening yet still increasing trend (see Fig. 6.2).

Time series analysis The sales figures over a time period will fluctuate, but beneath this is a trend which the forecaster wishes to know in order to apply his forecast. This fluctuation is particularly prevalent when the data contain seasonal figures or cyclical material. Bringing these seasonal or cyclical data down to a trend is called the purgative process. This technique, therefore, is of most use when there is a seasonal pattern that is repeated on a regular basis. The time series analysis technique analyses these seasonal movements in terms of their deviations from the average trend and then adds them back into the forecast once the trend line has been extrapolated.

Using the Werman Duvet Company's quarterly sales figures over the past five years best describes how the technique works in practice.

Sales are given quarterly and it can be seen that for a product like duvets the sales fluctuate on a seasonal basis throughout the year as one would expect. Unit sales are added for the four quarters to produce one year's data. The oldest quarterly period is then subtracted and the newest quarterly period added until the latest quarter is reached. The next column adds two years' data, subtracting the oldest and adding the newest. The figure is then divided by 8 to discover the trend (because this contains four quarters over each of two years). Finally, deviations from the trend are calculated by subtracting the trend from the actual sales, or the actual sales from the trend, to produce a positive or negative figure in the form of deviations from the trend.

Table 6.2 gives the quarterly figures for sales of duvets for Werman Duvet Company Ltd and the appropriate calculations to provide the deviations from trend.

It can be seen that when the quarterly deviations are totalled there is a positive sum of 21 remaining. The sum should equal zero, otherwise there will be a positive bias in the forecast. The sum comes equally off each quarter's figures (i.e., in this case five from three of the quarters and six from the other quarter because to fractionalize the amounts exactly would give the forecast a spurious accuracy). In this example we have added four years' data, so the corrected deviations

Table 6.2   Werman Duvet Company Ltd: quarterly sales of double-sized duvets

Year	Quarter	Unit sales	Quarterly moving total	Sum of pairs	÷8 to find trend	Deviations from trend
1982	1	542				
	2	368				
	3	334	2381	4789	599	−265
	4	1137	2408	4825	603	+534
1983	1	569	2417	4848	606	−37
	2	377	2431	4676	585	−208
	3	348	2245	4441	555	−207
	4	951	2196	4417	552	+399
1984	1	520	2221	4482	560	−40
	2	402	2261	4692	586	−184
	3	388	2431	4857	607	−219
	4	1121	2426	4818	602	+519
1985	1	515	2392	4874	609	−94
	2	368	2482	4984	623	−255
	3	478	2502	5028	629	−151
	4	1141	2526	5108	638	+503
1986	1	539	2582	5075	634	−95
	2	424	2493	4820	603	−179
	3	389	2327			
	4	975				

Sum of quarterly deviations from trend

Quarter	1	2	3	4		
Year						
1982			−265	+534		
1983	−37	−208	−207	+399		
1984	−40	−184	−219	+519		
1985	−94	−255	−151	+503		
1986	−95	−179				
Totals	−266	−826	−842	+1955	=	+21
Corrected deviations	−271	−831	−847	+1949	=	0

totals will have to be divided by 4 to bring them back to the correct average deviations. The result is as follows:

Quarter	1	2	3	4	
Deviations	−68	−207	−212	+487	=0

Again, for reasons stated earlier, the sum of the deviations should equal zero.

The graph can now be drawn which will include the actual sales and the trend line. From this, the trend line can be extrapolated. Following this, the deviations from trend should be added in as appropriate to produce the seasonal forecast which is then entered into the sales forecast. Figure 6.4 shows this information graphically.

In this particular case the forecaster has predicted that the downward trend shall continue for a short period and then turn upwards. This is where the skill of the forecaster comes in, and information for such a prediction can come from a variety of sources internal and external to the

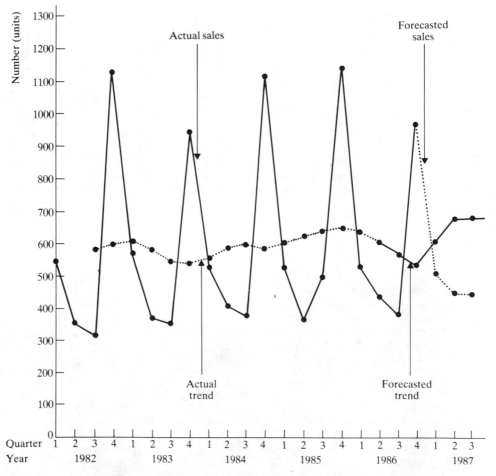

Figure 6.4   Werman Duvet Company Ltd: quarterly sales of double-sized duvets

Table 6.3

Year	Period	Trend	Deviation	Forecast
1986	3	565	−212	353
	4	540	+487	1027
1987	1	600	−68	532
	2	680	−207	473
	3	685	−212	473
	4	690	+487	1177

company. In fact, it is possible to apply some of the qualitative techniques described earlier, which are of more value in attempting to ascertain general trend patterns, particularly 'panels of executive opinion' and the 'Delphi' method.

Figure 6.4 shows quarterly sales and the trend line. The trend line has been extended to produce a forecast trend and the deviations from trend have been entered on to this trend to produce an actual forecast as shown in Table 6.3.

The first two figures for 1986, periods 3 and 4, have been given as a forecast, but these periods have passed, so they cannot be entered into the graph. Figure 6.4 actually produces a forecast for the four quarters of 1987, and it could, of course, have been extended further by extending the trend line and then applying the deviations from the trend.

The technique has much to commend it where there is a seasonality element in previous data. However, there must be an element of subjectivity in the extension of the trend line and it is here that the forecaster must take most care, and apply a soundly thought-out forecast rather than its being merely an extrapolation of the general trend.

'Z' charts 'Z' or Zee charts only provide one year's data. For forecasting purposes, the forecaster must prepare a number of these for previous years and then compare them (usually merely by sight) to see whether there are any general patterns of trend that are repeated, so that a prediction can be made for the future. The technique is thus rather subjective, and its true value probably lies in the presentation of sales data, rather than as a serious medium for forecasting.

Data for two years are needed in order to produce a 'Z' chart and each line of the 'Z' represents previous sales in a different format. The bottom line is the monthly sales, the diagonal line is the cumulative sales and the top line is the moving annual total (calculated by taking off the figure 12 months ago and adding on the new month's figure). The technique is best explained by practical example from the monthly sales of Werman Duvet Company for 1985 and 1986 and this is illustrated in Table 6.4 and Fig. 6.5.

Quantitative techniques (causal)

Leading indicator This method uses the technique of linear regression to establish a relationship between an established measurable observation and what has to be forecasted. Linear regression and its antecedent correlation are described more fully in Rodger's text.[7] Basically, Rodger states that it is possible to infer the existence of correlation (or interrelationship) between two sets of data from the visual inspection of these data on a diagram. One axis measures one set of criteria and the other axis measures another set of criteria. If the measurements come close together in a more or less straight line, the correlation is said to be linear, and there is then a close relationship between the two sets of data. Naturally, for forecasting purposes, if one knows in advance what

Table 6.4   Werman Duvet Company Ltd: monthly sales of double-sized duvets

Month	Unit sales 1985	Unit sales 1986	Cumulative sales 1986	Moving annual total
Jan.	216	240	240	2526
Feb.	136	122	362	2512
Mar.	163	177	539	2526
Apr.	149	179	718	2556
May	121	135	853	2570
Jun.	98	110	963	2582
Jul.	161	103	1066	2524
Aug.	141	111	1177	2494
Sep.	176	175	1352	2493
Oct.	328	294	1646	2459
Nov.	404	412	2058	2467
Dec.	409	269	2327	2327

the data are on one axis, then it is a simple matter to predict what the data will be on the other axis.

However, in real-life forecasting situations matters are not as easy as those just described and in all probability the relationship between the two sets of data will be only approximately linear. We must, therefore, calculate the 'line of best fit' that runs through the data. This line is called the line of regression and it describes in quantitative terms the underlying relationship or correlation between the two sets of data.

The technique needs a computer in its application, and there are a number of statistical packages available through which the technique can be used. The following simple illustration describes how the method can be applied:

The sale of children's clothes will depend upon the size of the child population. Therefore, a clothes manufacturer would use birth statistics as a leading indicator. The number of years that the indicator can precede the forecast, and for which sex of child, depends on the age range and the sex of clothing that the manufacturer caters for.

This is called leading indicator forecasting because the indicator precedes the forecast, but it is of course an over-simplification of how the method operates. Forecasting packages are available that combine a number of leading indicators and then provide a permutation of indicators that best fit known previous sales. It may well be that there is no logical reason why the permutation of a number of indicators relates to previous sales statistics. Such a permutation should be constantly under review as time passes and forecasted sales turn into actual sales. The permutation is then modified to take account of the most recent sales.

Simulation This is a technique that relies heavily upon the computer. It has already been explained that leading indicator forecasting seeks to establish a relationship between something that is measurable and the subject that is to be forecasted. Simulation uses trial and error (or iteration) in arriving at the forecasting relationship.

In a complicated forecasting situation the number of possible outcomes of possibilities is very large. The probabilities of various outcomes can, however, be estimated. This is known as

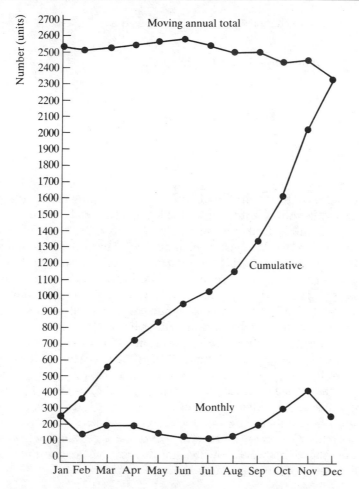

Figure 6.5   Werman Duvet Company Ltd: monthly sales of double-sized duvets

Monte Carlo simulation (the obvious link being gambling on estimated probabilities). It depends upon a pre-determined chance of a particular event occurring.

The technique is difficult to explain any further without going into complicated discussion and explanations. The reader is again pointed to Rodger's text for more of a 'depth' explanation than the one provided in this more basic marketing text.[8]

Diffusion models The first named author has already provided a forecast of the video market using this technique.[9] In keeping with other causal techniques the mathematics are complicated and the reader should seek more specialist help before attempting to apply such methodology. The following explanation attempts to describe the thinking behind the technique.

The techniques that have been explained so far have depended upon a series of past sales from the company or the industry to produce the forecast. When totally new products come on to the market there are no past sales to draw upon, and we must then rely on the application of theory called 'the diffusion of innovations'. This theory is discussed more fully in the next chapter that deals with the product (or service), but it is appropriate to introduce it briefly here in order to describe this technique.

Diffusion theory assumes that new products have four basic elements:

1. The innovation.
2. The communication of this innovation among individuals.
3. The social system.
4. Time.

Innovations can be categorized into the following groupings:

– Continuous.
– Dynamically continuous.
– Discontinuous.

These groupings are a hierarchical listing, with the innovations being more widely removed from previous technology as one moves further down the listing. This leads to a lower degree of likely acceptance of the innovation the further down the list the innovation is placed. In the early stages of a product innovation, knowledge must be communicated to as many potential customers as possible, particularly those who are likely to be influential in gaining wider appeal for the innovation. This process of communication is broken down into formal and informal communication. These two elements are fed into the forecasting model. As such, the model can be applied without large amounts of past sales data. The formal communication is controlled by the company and includes such data as advertising expenditure and sales support for the launch. The informal element relates to such matters as family and reference group influences.

After the innovation has been launched on to the market, a measure of the rate of adoption is needed in order to produce a useful forecast. Products are born, they mature and they die. It is important to the forecaster using this technique that the first few points of the launch sales are known in order to be able to determine the rate of adoption. The forecast can then be made using only a small amount of data points covering the early launch period. The assumption is made that the product has a life-cycle curve and that new product acceptance is through a process of imitation in that later purchasers will follow the innovators. The technique also provides a forecast of first-time users and not for repeat purchasers.

MISCELLANEOUS

There are a number of further forecasting techniques such as Box-Jenkins and X-11 that are very specialized and sophisticated in their application. They are used only in rarefied circumstances and to attempt an explanation here would perhaps imply that their importance is more than they really merit. It is sufficient to say that they have been mentioned and the reader should consider these only if a depth study of sales forecasting is to be undertaken.

CONCLUSIONS

The sales forecast precedes planning and such plans are then needed so that management can organize its activities in an ordered manner. Increasing competition means that businesses have to be more competitive and this means making a more scientific approach to planning. Such an approach is through better sales forecasting.

Forecasting techniques have been split into qualitative techniques and quantitative techniques with the latter being divided into time series analysis and causal techniques.

Qualitative techniques have included: consumer–user survey methods, panels of executive opinion, salesforce composite, Delphi method, Bayesian decision theory and product testing and test marketing. Quantitative techniques (time series) have covered: moving averages, exponential smoothing, time series analysis and 'Z' charts. Quantitative techniques (causal) have included: leading indicator, simulation and diffusion models.

Now that the market has been researched and forecasted, it is possible to select markets on which marketing efforts can be targeted: this is the subject of the next chapter.

APPLICATION QUESTIONS

1. As an information flow from the market to the firm, how important is sales forecasting for marketing? Why should such forecasting be the responsibility of marketing as opposed to finance?
2. Distinguish between qualitative and quantitative forecasting methods. State the advantages and drawbacks associated with each.
3. What is the relationship between the sales forecast and the sales budget?
4. How does a market forecast differ from a company forecast? How does a 'top down' method differ from a 'bottom up' method?
5. For a company of your choice in an industry of your choice (preferably ones with which you are in some way familiar), justify the forecasting methodology you would undertake in providing:
   (a) medium-term forecasts;
   (b) long-term forecasts.

REFERENCES

1. Lancaster, G. A. and R. A. Lomas, *Forecasting for Sales and Materials Management*, Macmillan, London, 1985, p. 1.
2. McDonald, M., *Marketing Plans – How to Prepare Them*, Heinemann, London, 1984.
3. Clifton, P., H. Nguyer and S. Nutt, *Marketing Analysis and Forecasting*, Heinemann, London, 1985, p. 33.
4. Battersby, A., *Sales Forecasting*, Cassell, London, 1968, p. 7.
5. Lancaster, G. A. and R. A. Lomas, op. cit.
6. This has been covered in Chapter 5 and it is where a company can purchase market research questions on a questionnaire shared with questions purchased by other companies. Costs are thus reduced, because it is unlikely that such questioning will take up more than one or two questions, for which it would not be worth mounting an individual survey.
7. Rodger, L. W., *Statistics for Marketing*, McGraw-Hill, London, 1984, pp. 122–132.
8. Rodger, L. W., op. cit., pp. 228–236.
9. Lancaster, G. A. and G. Wright, 'Forecasting the future of video using a diffusion model', *European Journal of Marketing*, **17**(2), 1983, pp. 70–79.

SEVEN

SELECTION OF MARKETS

INTRODUCTION

The central message of the marketing concept is the need for firms to identify and attempt to satisfy the genuine needs and wants of specifically defined target markets, more effectively and efficiently than competitors. As a result of attempting to put this philosophy into practice many firms have realized that in order to relate their product and service offerings to the needs of the marketplace, it is not always possible, except in a few special circumstances, to treat the entire market as a homogeneous mass of potential purchasers. Doing this would be 'product oriented' rather than 'market oriented'. Market orientation means looking at the marketplace through the medium of marketing research and sales forecasting which have been considered in the previous two chapters.

One of the most important developments in the history of marketing has been the realization that many overall markets are made up of significantly different groups or sub-markets. The people or organizations comprising each of these groups are often sufficiently similar as to be treated as a separate 'market' in terms of product offering, communication strategy, pricing policy, distribution and other marketing mix elements.

Hence, in the selection of 'markets', many firms are not so much concerned with the entire population of potential purchasers for a given product category (e.g., a motor car). They are more concerned with the most commercially attractive sectors in segments of the market for a given product form (e.g., the family saloon market or the sports car market).

This process of 'homing in' to particular segments of a given overall market is known as *target marketing*. Before one can do this, an investigation has to be made of the marketplace through various techniques already identified in Part Two. This is the logical culmination of this information-gathering process. This chapter discusses how much target markets can be identified, evaluated and selected.

THE CONCEPT OF A MARKET

The term 'market' often means different things to different people. There are many usages of the term in economics and in business in general. A market may be defined as *a place* where buyers and sellers meet, where goods are offered for sale and where transfer of ownership takes place. A market may also be defined as the total *demand* for a given product or service, for example, the television market or the market for contract cleaning. Markets are also defined in *money* terms, for example, we may say the UK market for Axminster carpets is currently at around £45 million per year. Economists talk of a market as a set of conditions and forces which determine price levels.

We can see from the above examples that modern usage has given several meanings to the word 'market'. Whatever the context in which the term 'market' is used, it generally implies a demand for a product or service. Stanton *et al.*[1] state that in the market demand for any given product or service, there are three factors to consider:

– people with needs;
– their purchasing power; and
– their buying behaviour.

A market, therefore, can be defined as people with needs to satisfy, the money to spend and the willingness to spend it. From a marketing point of view a market consists not only of existing customers but also potential customers. As Foster[2] explains,

> for marketing executives the market is not only present customers but all those persons and organisations who may be persuaded to buy the products or services they offer.

THE DEVELOPMENT OF TARGET MARKETING

The development of mass production and the mass markets of today has been discussed in Chapter 1. We saw that as both domestic and international competition increased from the latter part of the nineteenth century, companies found themselves in a 'buyers' market' rather than a 'sellers' market'. This change required greater sophistication on the part of firms in the marketing of their products and services. This eventually led to the wide-scale adoption of the marketing concept as a central business philosophy from around the middle of the present century.

The concept of target marketing is a refinement of the basic philosophy of marketing. It is an attempt by companies to relate the characteristics or attributes of the goods and services they provide more closely to customer requirements. When mass production techniques were first introduced, out of necessity, they imposed a large degree of uniformity upon consumers. However, such techniques also brought an improvement in most people's standards of living. Mass production reduced unit costs and resulted in cheaper goods. Many products which were once considered luxuries of the rich became available to the ordinary people at affordable prices, and they did not really mind that their cars or sewing machines were of the same design or colour. To be even able to purchase such goods was a new experience for most people. Hence, in the early stages of mass production consumers did not really mind being treated as an homogeneous mass.

As consumers became more affluent, their aspirations also increased. They were no longer satisfied with 'a car' or 'a sewing machine', but wanted a particular type of product with *specific characteristics* that suited their requirements more accurately. Advances in production technology made a degree of product differentiation possible with little reduction in the economies of scale of the former mass production techniques. It was now possible to mass produce a basic product such as a car, which in the later stages of production would take different routes in the assembly process. The result was different variants of the same basic model. The process was applied to many products other than motor cars.

Advancements in production techniques allowed firms to cater for disparities in consumer demand. Today, products are no longer regarded as commodities – like 'coffee' or generic products such as 'cars', but are differentiated to suit the requirements of specific groups of consumers. For example, we now have a plethora of brands of coffee catering to different tastes, e.g., strong coffee, weak coffee, decaffeinated coffee, etc. Likewise, with cars, we no longer have a generic Ford Escort as we did, say, with the Model 'T' Ford. Today, there is such a wide choice of Ford Escorts that it virtually amounts to buying a custom-built vehicle.

The situation today is that while certain firms attempt to service an entire market for a particular product or service, this tends to be the exception rather than the rule. In such cases, the market in question is usually either very specialized and relatively small, or the firm enjoys some form of monopoly power. Many organizations operate in very large markets. Such firms recognize that the overall market is so large that it may not be possible to serve the entire population of that market effectively.

It may be the case that the total market is first too large, and consists of too many potential customers for the firm to be able to deal with. The overall market may be geographically dispersed and the firm may lack the resources to service it properly. For example, the computer 'market' is international. Very often the overall market for a particular product or service is too *heterogeneous*, in terms of the purchasing requirements of individuals or organizations making up the market, for any one firm to service adequately.

By targeting on to specific groups of consumers or 'market segments', instead of attempting to service the demand requirements of an entire population for a particular product category, the firm is able to develop more effective marketing programmes. To speak of the market for shampoo, audio equipment or even industrial valves, is to ignore the fact that within the total market for each of these products there exist sub-markets which differ from one another in some commercially significant manner. This lack of homogeneity may be due to differences in the amount of money consumers are willing to pay, the way in which the product is used, motives for buying or other factors.

STAGES IN TARGET MARKETING

The process of target marketing needs to be carried out systematically and scientifically to be effective. Kotler,[3] states that the process of target marketing has three distinct stages, which are as follows:

Stage One: *Market segmentation* The overall market is divided into distinct groups of buyers who are likely to respond favourably to different product/service offerings and marketing mixes. The firm determines the most appropriate basis for segmentation, identifies the important characteristics of each market segment and develops criteria for evaluating their commercial attractiveness and viability.

Stage Two: *Market targeting* This is not to be confused with the overall process of target marketing. Market targeting is the process whereby one or more of the market segments previously identified are evaluated and selected.

Stage Three: *Product positioning* Even within a given market segment, competitors' products are likely to be positioned in a particular 'niche' or position. Product positioning is the process whereby the product or service and all the other marketing mix elements are designed to fit a given place within a particular segment. Such a position may be more implied than real. It is how the consumer perceives the product's position relative to competitors' products that is important.

We shall now look at each of the three stages shown in Fig. 7.1 in more detail.

Market segmentation

The growth of specialized market segments has resulted in firms producing goods and services which are more *closely related* to the requirements of particular kinds of customers. Instead of treating all customers as a homogeneous mass, firms have identified sub-groups of customers whose precise needs can be more effectively met.

As Levitt[4] explains, the marketer should:

> stop thinking of his customers as part of some massively homogeneous market. He must start thinking of them as numerous small islands of distinctiveness, each of which requires its own unique strategies in product policy, in promotional strategy, in pricing, in distribution methods, and in direct selling techniques.

The whole process of *target marketing* can be illustrated schematically as shown in Fig. 7.1.

Manufacturers have always been aware that certain products were purchased by certain types of people. Rich people tended to buy fine wines and fashionable clothes whereas poorer people tended to buy ale and more basic items of clothing. Much of this early 'segmentation' was accidental. It just so happened that products were purchased by certain types of people. Producers rarely had any particular target groups in mind, or if they did it was largely based on common sense rather than a conscious segmentation policy.

As business people began to pay greater attention to the needs and wants of the marketplace they began to realize that, since the people or organizations that make up a particular market are likely to be heterogeneous, they are unlikely to have identical preferences. Consequently, it was highly unlikely that one product would satisfy everyone. The outcome of this realization can be

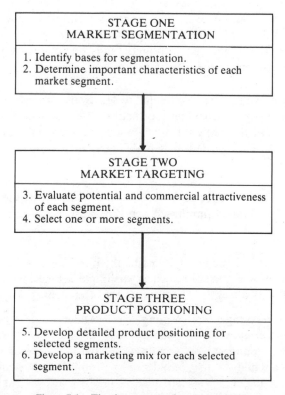

Figure 7.1   The three stages of target marketing

seen today in the many everyday products we see on our supermarket shelves. For example, certain brands of toothpaste, such as Crest, were originally marketed with a simple flavour. However, the fact that people do not have identical preferences suggested the possibility of a number of market segments. In order to serve their customers more effectively Procter and Gamble now market Crest in different flavours, different formulations, e.g., paste and gel, and with different ingredients, e.g., regular or 'tartar control' formula. Hence the total Crest market is broken down into smaller groups or segments made up of people who may be prepared to pay a little more to obtain a toothpaste that suits their personal taste or preference more closely than the 'standard' flavour or formulation.

Bases for segmenting consumer markets There is no 'golden rule' when it comes to segmenting consumer markets. The marketing firm may have to investigate using many different segmentation variables in order to gain an insight into the structure of the overall market. Very often it may be necessary to use a combination of variables in order to define a precise market segment. The sections which follow describe the main discriminating variables used to segment consumer markets.

Demographic variables Demographic factors are perhaps one of the more straightforward bases for segmenting consumer markets, they are also one of the most meaningful. The main demographic variables are given below.

Age For many products purchase behaviour is strongly related to age. For example, the 18–24 year age group tends to buy the latest style of clothing, a large proportion of 'pop' records, eat a lot of 'take-away' food and read certain magazines and newspapers aimed mainly at the 'youth market', e.g., *New Musical Express*. The 'youth market' is a specific market segment as is the 25–35 year and 60+ year segments. Although age is one of the more straightforward segmentation variables it is also one of the most important.

Sex Many product purchases are also related to sex. Some of these products will be obvious to the reader, e.g., dresses, nylon stockings, cosmetics (also purchased by men nowadays) and 'women's' magazines such as *Woman's Weekly*. Some products are not so obvious, for example, certain motor cars tend to be regarded as 'female' cars; this is also true of certain brands of cigarettes.

Family size This is usually categorized as 1–2, 3–4, 5+. Obviously the size of family will have some effect on the types of product purchased and this is especially so of pack size, e.g., family size pack.

Family life cycle In the UK the family remains the basic social unit. The demand for many products, for example, consumer durables such as washing machines, refrigerators, etc., is related to stage reached in the family life cycle. These stages are often defined as:

Young	Young single no children	Young couple youngest child under six	Young couple youngest child six or +	Older couple with children 18+ at home	Older couple no children at home	Older single

Social class income The current convention in the UK is to use a mixture of social class and income. Classifications are based on the occupation of the head of the household.

The socio-economic groupings used in the UK are those established by the National Readership Survey, and fall into the following categories:

A Higher managerial, administrative or professional.
B Intermediate managerial, administrative or professional.
C1 Supervisory, clerical, junior administrative or professional.
C2 Skilled manual workers.
D Semi-skilled and unskilled manual workers.
E State pensioners, widows, casual and lowest grade earners.

In more recent years the use of socio-economic groups as a segmentation variable has been criticized. However, in 1981 the Market Research Society published the findings of a Joint Industry Working Party, entitled *An Evaluation of Social Grade Validity*.[5] The following points were reported:

– Social grade provides satisfactory discriminating power.
– No other classification variable could provide consistently better discriminatory power.
– No evidence was found to show a decline in the discriminatory power of social grade over recent years.

The use of socio-economic grade in market segmentation is discussed in more technical detail by Crimp.[6]

Residential neighbourhoods A relatively recent development in segmentation studies, related to geographic, cultural, socio-economic and other factors is 'A Classification of Residential Neighbourhoods' (ACORN). The ACORN system is a method of 'mapping' geographically the concentrations of particular types of people. The assumption is that the demographic/socio-economic characteristics of people can be correlated to the housing characteristics of a particular area. The ACORN classifications are derived using a multi-variable statistical treatment of Census of Population data and are divided into ACORN groups and ACORN types. The ACORN groups are shown in Table 7.1.

Each ACORN group is subdivided further into ACORN types. By way of illustration Table 7.2 shows the ACORN types given for ACORN Group B (Modern family housing, higher incomes).

Table 7.1 ACORN groups based on the 1981 Census of Population

A	Agricultural areas
B	Modern family housing, higher incomes
C	Older housing of intermediate status
D	Poor quality older terraced housing
E	Better-off council estates
F	Less well-off council estates
G	Poorest council estates
H	Multi-racial areas
I	High status non-family areas
J	Affluent suburban housing
K	Better-off retirement areas

Table 7.2   ACORN types for Group B (modern family housing, higher incomes)

B3	Cheap modern private housing
B4	Recent private housing, young families
B5	Modern private housing, older children
B6	New detached houses, young families
B7	Military bases

The ACORN system has proved useful in many areas of marketing, such as retail store location and poster site location. It is of particular importance when a firm is considering using direct mail. Instead of wasting a lot of mail shots on people who are likely to be interested in the product, ACORN allows the firm to 'target in' accurately to the market segment of interest.

Education Many products are related, in a general way, to the purchaser's level of formal education. Classical music recordings, certain types of books, items of clothing and the purchase of more exotic kinds of food and wine are examples of this. This is very much a generalization as there are many people with little formal education who appreciate such products.

Perhaps of greater importance is the fact that consumers' media habits are related to education. Taken as an aggregate, it would be true to say that the better educated tend to read the better quality broadsheet newspapers such as *The Times* or the *Guardian*. Such people are also more likely to watch the more 'highbrow' commercial television programmes such as 'World in Action' or the 'South Bank Show'.

Education is also related to social class group because, as a rule, the better educated tend to obtain better jobs. Clearly, a firm wishing to advertise a product aimed at the higher socio-economic/better educated segments of the market would be wise to use the appropriate types of media.

As a segmentation variable, education is usually expressed as terminal education age (TEA). A person's TEA is based on age on finishing full-time education. This particular classification is open to criticism, especially today, where cut-backs in full-time education provision have increased the emphasis on part-time studies. Many people today go back to education in later life to study for degrees and professional qualifications. Therefore, the standard question 'How old were you when you finished your *full-time* education' may not really give an indication of a person's true level of educational attainment.[7]

Benefit segmentation Benefit segmentation uses *causal* rather than *descriptive* variables to group consumers. Different people buy the same or similar products for different reasons. For example, some people buy a car purely as a means of transport, others because the shape and design of the car give them pleasure, others as a status symbol or as an extension of their personality, and others for patriotic reasons, e.g., they might always buy British.

Haley[8] first introduced this approach based on the idea that consumers could be grouped according to the *principal benefit* sought. The new classic example given by Haley concerned the benefit segmentation of the United States toothpaste market. Although this is now somewhat 'historical', the example showed that the use of a combination of different types of segmentation variables could lead to the conclusion that the main criterion for segmentation is the 'principal benefit sought'. Hence, although this approach acknowledges the fact that no single variable is likely to be of sufficient discriminatory power adequately to segment a market on its own, it regards the benefit sought as the *main variable*. As Haley himself states:

the benefits which people are seeking in consuming a given product are the basic reasons for the existence of true market segments.

A further illustration of the principle of benefit segmentation is given by Bass *et al.*[9] An investigation into the principal benefits sought by consumers from a milk substitute allowed Cadbury Schweppes to develop the brand 'Marvel' to offer the following benefits:

1. As an emergency standby in case a household ran out of milk.
2. As a fat-free healthy substitute for conventional milk.
3. As an aid to slimming.
4. As a convenient way of using 'milk' for people who only use very little, i.e., less than a whole pint.

In using benefit segmentation the marketing firm needs to determine the major benefits people are seeking from a particular product class, to identify the profiles of the people seeking each benefit and to recognize the existing competitors' products that are close to delivering each of the benefits. Some of the benefits sought may not be serviced by existing products. This will give the firm the opportunity of capitalizing on an unsatisfied market segment.

Segmentation by usage Consumption rates for many consumer products are not evenly distributed across all households. Hence, meaningful segments could be defined in terms of usage of the product itself. As Frain[10] explains:

> Research does indeed indicate that a 'skewed' purchasing pattern often does apply – even to products intended for a mass market: 50 percent to 80 percent of the purchases of some commonly-bought products are made by 20 percent to 30 percent of all UK housewives.

If the firm can identify such heavy users it may be able to develop a special marketing strategy aimed at winning more of them to the brand. For example Bass *et al.* showed that heavy users of beer in the United States tended to be working class, aged between 25 and 50 years of age, watched television more than $3\frac{1}{2}$ hours per day and preferred to watch sports programmes. Consumer profiles such as this are obviously helpful to the marketing firm in developing pricing and communication strategies.

Loyalty status A market can also be segmented according to the degree of consumers' brand loyalty. Kotler[11] divided consumers in four groups according to their loyalty status. To illustrate the principle let us assume we are analysing purchasing behaviour relating to five brands of toilet soap which we will call simply A, B, C, D and E.

- *Hard-core loyals* These are consumers with undivided loyalty to one brand. Their purchasing pattern over six periods would be say, A,A,A,A,A,A.
- *Soft-core loyals* These consumers have divided loyalty between two or more brands. The purchasing pattern of such people may look something like A,B,B,A,A,B.
- *Shifting loyals* These consumers 'brand switch' their loyalty between two or more brands. Their purchasing pattern may look something like B,B,B,A,A,A.
- *Switchers* This class of consumer shows no brand loyalty at all, but instead 'switches' from one brand to another. Their purchasing pattern may look something like B,E,C,A,D.

A company can usually attract switchers, at least in the short term, by price reductions or other forms of sales promotions. A careful analysis of brand loyalty categories can tell the firm a lot about its present marketing strategy and point the way to improvements. For example, from an analysis of 'shifting loyals' the firm may learn about possible inadequacies in its marketing programme that are causing people to switch brands.

Geographical and cultural segmentation In Great Britain the indigenous population tends to be very culturally similar, although some people would argue that there are distinct regional differences (e.g., North and South of England, for beer and certain types of food). There are certainly areas of the country that are suffering more than others from declining industries and unemployment. These factors clearly act as a constraint on purchasing behaviour.

In certain parts of the UK, most notably Northern Ireland, the cultural differences are more marked. This is also true of areas of high immigrant concentration which are often culturally distinct, and hence may be treated as a separate market segment for certain products and services.

Geographic and cultural differences are even more pronounced within certain overseas countries. This would be so of Belgium and to a lesser extent Canada and the United States.

This section has covered the main variables used to segment consumer markets. The list is not exhaustive; there are other variables which can be used depending on the situation. Many of the variables discussed here, and other less frequently used methods of segmentation, are discussed further by Frank *et al.*[12]

Industrial market segmentation

The concept of segmentation can also be applied to industrial markets, although the bases used are likely to be different. A more detailed discussion is given by Brown in an industrial marketing text edited by Hart.[13] The following is an example of the most frequently used industrial segmentation variables:

1. *Size of firm*: the criteria used could be turnover, capital employed or number of employees. Large firms tend to have different criteria for evaluating a supplier and its products than smaller firms. This is partly due to the fact that larger firms are able to employ professional buyers.
2. *Type of industry*: the criteria used may be manufacturing or service industry, nationalized/ private industry, or actual type of activity, e.g., electronics or glass industry. Different industries may have different requirements in terms of product specifications, price, or after-sales service. A firm selling, say, industrial valves may need a different marketing strategy and marketing mix for each industrial segment it deals with.
3. *Geographical region*: some areas of the UK are designated 'Enterprise Zones' or 'Assisted Areas'. The firms operating in such areas often qualify for government grants or other financial assistance. Again, a firm marketing to organizations in such areas is likely to have a different marketing strategy, especially in relation to pricing and communication policy, to that used in other parts of the country. Other geographical criteria may be urban, rural, European Community, Eastern Bloc, developing country, etc.
4. *Type of buying organization*: this segmentation variable is also related to size of firm. How an organization purchases its products affects the way a marketing firm negotiates and communicates to it. Larger firms tend to have a very formal purchasing procedure (e.g., British Gas). Smaller firms tend to be more informal.

Many organizations have factories or divisions located in different parts of the country or in different countries. Some of these firms will have a centralized purchasing system, where the whole company's requirements are purchased from Head Office. Other firms may have a decentralized purchasing system which allows each factory or division a certain amount of purchasing autonomy. How an organization's purchasing system is organized will have an effect on the policies of marketing to that firm.

Industrial buying situations In organizational purchasing, the following situations can be observed:

1. *New buy*: as far as the buying firm is concerned a 'new buy' situation would be:
   (a) the marketing firm was offering a totally new product;
   (b) it had never purchased from this supplier before so it was a 'new' situation;
   (c) the product had been around for some time, but this was the first time the firm had actually bought it.
2. *Modified re-buy*: the buying organization had purchased a similar product before, but this one is slightly different, e.g., a new, more advanced machine tool.
3. *Routine re-buy*: the buying organization had been purchasing the same product from the same firm for a number of years.

In a 'new buy' situation, the buying firm experiences a high degree of perceived risk. Marketing strategies should be aimed at reducing this risk, e.g., through a free trial, after sales service or a guarantee. A modified re-buy is perceived as being less risky although not risk free, and a straight re-buy is perceived as a minimal risk situation.

Service elasticity Very often a firm will be attempting to market the same product to different industries. Service requirements, and the perceived importance of the level of service offered by the marketing firm, is likely to differ between industries. For example, a firm may be marketing industrial valves to both the oil and sugar processing industries. In the oil industry, price is of relatively little importance; delivery, reliability, stock availability and maintenance are very important. In the sugar industry price is likely to be one of the major purchasing criteria. The marketing firm will have to take a completely different approach in marketing these products to each industrial segment.

Price elasticity Some firms or industries are more concerned about price than others. For large successful firms, price differentials between suppliers would have to be relatively large before they would consider switching from an established supplier. Smaller firms are often looking for the cheapest source of supply they can get, although extended credit is often of more importance. A computer firm marketing hardware to public authorities would have to use a different pricing strategy than if it was dealing with, say, ICI or Ford (UK). It can be said that some firms or industries are more price elastic or 'price sensitive' than others.

Market structure When a firm is dealing with a number of different industries it may be possible to segment by market structure. Some industries may be dominated by a few large, powerful firms (e.g., the motor car industry or the defence industry). Other industries may be made up of hundreds of smaller firms. The marketing firms' approach is likely to be different between industries, i.e., they would treat large firms that virtually dominate the market differently to smaller less powerful firms.

Decision-making unit In industrial firms, purchasing decisions are rarely taken by one individual, except perhaps in routine re-buy situations. Very often a number of individuals are involved in the overall purchasing process. The group of people involved are known as the decision-making unit (DMU).

Again, the composition of a firm's DMU is likely to differ by type of industry, size of firm, whether the firm is a nationalized or private sector firm, whether the purchasing function is organized on an informal/formal basis or on a centralized/decentralized basis. The composition of the DMU is, therefore, related to some of the other factors mentioned earlier. However, when used as a basis for segmentation it is the actual structure of the DMU that is used as the *main* discriminatory segmentation variable.

Criteria for effective segmentation The marketing firm not only has to identify potential market segments, but also has to establish whether segments are commercially viable and cost effective. The test is whether the individuals in firms making up the segment can be serviced with a marketing mix probably specific to them. As a rule of thumb, to be commercially meaningful, the individuals or firms making up a segment must be more homogeneous in relation to some exploitable characteristic than the overall market from which they have been chosen. For this to be so, the variation or difference within each segment must be less than the variation between each of the segments. The following factors are useful in evaluating the suitability of a potential market segment:

1. *Measurability*: the marketing firm should be able to identify and quantify the potential of each segment.
2. *Accessibility*: to have any commercial meaning the marketing firm must be able to reach each segment with a specific marketing programme. It must, therefore, be possible to communicate with individuals or firms making up the segment in a cost effective way.
3. *Viability*: to be viable each segment must be large enough or commercially lucrative enough to warrant treating as a separate sub-market.

Benefits of market segmentation Market segmentation should result in benefits for both the marketing firm and its customers. If no such benefits accrue to either party then the segmentation exercise is a meaningless waste of time. The following is an example of possible benefits:

1. Effective segmentation should result in greater sales and profitability.
2. Segmentation should allow the producer to design products and market appeals which are more 'finely tuned' to the needs of the market.
3. Segmentation should result in greater consumer satisfaction.
4. Segmentation allows the marketing firm to focus on those sub-markets with the greatest potential.
5. It allows for greater product differentiation and variety as firms seek further market opportunities by developing new segments.
6. It may result in a better competitive position for existing brands.

Market targeting

Market segmentation is only the first, albeit essential, step in the overall process of target marketing. The firm also has to evaluate each segment and decide how many of the segments to serve. It was discussed earlier that the criteria of measurability, accessibility and viability form the basis of segmentation evaluation. To establish viability we not only need an indication of the size of the segment, but also estimates of likely turnover, profit and an indication of where the segment is going, i.e., forecasts of future trends in demand are also necessary, which was the subject of Chapter 6.

Very often the trend in the overall market is different to that in the individual sub-markets. For example, the overall demand for cigarettes in the UK is declining, whereas the demand for 'low tar' cigarettes is on the increase as consumers switch to less harmful forms of smoking. Many tobacco companies are now exploiting the low tar segment of the market in reaction to consumers' changes in tastes and in order to retain their share of the cigarette market.

For a proper evaluation, each market segment must be expressed in terms of its cost and revenue implications. Buzby and Heitger[14] recommend the use of individual segmentation budgets. These individual segment budgets can then be aggregated to form the firm's overall marketing budget.

Market coverage strategies Once market segments have been identified and evaluated, the marketing firm has to decide on its level of market involvement. It may determine that no meaningful segments exist and decide to cover the whole market with one basic product or service offering. It may establish a number of meaningful segments and decide to service all or a number of them with a differential product and/or marketing mix. It may identify a number of segments, but only decide to service one or very few of them. Hence the firm can adopt one of three market coverage strategies; these are:

1. *Undifferentiated marketing*: with this strategy, the firm focuses on what is common to all potential consumers rather than attempting to exploit differences. One product and one marketing mix are offered to all consumers without any form of differentiation. Its product features and marketing programmes are designed to appeal to as many potential buyers as possible within the overall market. The overall market is treated as a homogeneous mass, and the firm uses mass production, mass communication and mass distribution.
2. *Differentiated marketing*: with this strategy the firm decides to operate in a number of market segments. The firm offers a slightly 'different' product and related marketing mix to each segment. Washing powder, toothpaste and motor car markets are good examples of this approach being used by marketing firms.
3. *Concentrated marketing*: here the firm decides to attempt to cater for one, or possibly a few, market segments. It *concentrates* on a limited group of customers and aims to service them more effectively and efficiently than competitors. This strategy is used by the Savoy Hotel, Rolls Royce cars, and Rolex watches which tend to cater solely for high income groups.

Product positioning

After segments have been identified and a segmentation strategy developed, a firm needs to develop and communicate a product positioning strategy. Product positioning is the act of designing the company's product and marketing mix to fit a given place in the consumer's mind. Using marketing research the firm should establish the position of competitors' products in any given market segment and then decide whether to compete on a 'me-too' basis (to offer a product very close to a competitor's offering) or to attempt to fill a gap in the market.

A technique that has gained popularity, especially in the 'positioning' of products is multidimensional scaling (MDS). MDS is a term that is applied to a variety of techniques for representing brands, stores or products as points in multidimensional space. The dimensions used in the analysis are the attributes which research indicates consumers use to differentiate products.

Tull and Hawkins[15] show how a two-dimensional scale can be used to plot the market posi-

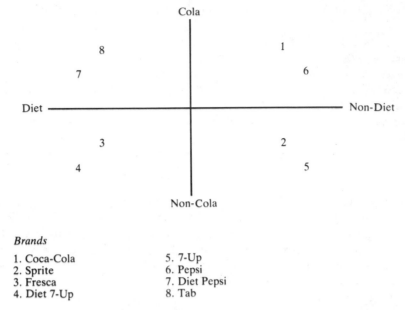

Brands

1. Coca-Cola
2. Sprite
3. Fresca
4. Diet 7-Up

5. 7-Up
6. Pepsi
7. Diet Pepsi
8. Tab

Figure 7.2   Multidimensional space for soft drinks

tion of soft drinks. The two primary dimensions used in the evaluation are 'colaness' and 'diet-ness'. This example is shown in Fig. 7.2.

Tull and Hawkins show that with the aid of a computer an 'ideal' brand position can be developed. Existing brands are ranked in terms of preference by each respondent in the test. This provides the coordinates or scores of the individual's 'ideal' brand on each dimension. The example shows a relatively simple two-dimensional map. The use of computers allows similar analysis on more than two dimensions, thus increasing the usefulness of the technique.

Product positioning is the final stage in the overall process of target marketing. Once the firm has established its product positioning strategy it is then in a position to go on to plan the details of its marketing mix.

CONCLUSIONS

Today, companies are finding it increasingly difficult to practise mass marketing. As a result, many firms are embracing the concept of target marketing. Target marketing enables firms to focus on marketing opportunities more effectively. Instead of spreading their marketing effort too thinly, target marketing enables firms to produce product offerings, pricing, advertising and distribution strategies that can 'home in' on specific groups of buyers more efficiently.

To be effective, the overall process of target marketing needs to be carried out in a logical and systematic manner. The first, and perhaps the most important stage after suitably researching the market, is the process of market segmentation. The identification of commercially meaningful market segments forms the bedrock of the rest of the target marketing programme. The remaining two stages are market targeting and, finally, product positioning.

If the process of target marketing is carried out thoroughly and scientifically the firm should then be in a position to formulate a more meaningful strategy. Target marketing results in benefits for both the marketing firm and its customers. The firm should benefit in terms of a better competitive position for its products resulting in greater sales and profitability. The customer should derive greater satisfaction from the goods and services purchased. This is a particularly important point as the whole rationale of the marketing concept is increased business effectiveness through the provision of consumer satisfaction.

APPLICATION QUESTIONS

1. A micro-wave oven manufacturer wants to develop a benefit segmentation of the micro-wave oven market. Suggest some possible benefit segments.
2. In what circumstances might a marketing firm use a concentrated marketing strategy? Illustrate your answer with examples.
3. Marketing firms use certain criteria in evaluating the commercial attractiveness of market segments. Discuss the usefulness of such criteria for evaluating potential segments in the shampoo market.
4. Using the two primary dimensions of expensive/not expensive and serious/not serious, plot the product positioning of existing titles of national daily newspapers on a two-dimensional scale similar to that shown in Fig. 7.2. Discuss a possible product positioning for a new daily newspaper.
5. Show how the segmentation variables
   (a) service elasticity, and
   (b) market structure
   might be useful in determining a marketing strategy for a firm producing industrial valves.

REFERENCES

1. Stanton, W. J., M. S. Sommers and J. G. Barnes, *Fundamentals of Marketing*, McGraw-Hill, New York, 1977, p. 49.
2. Foster, D., *Mastering Marketing*, Macmillan, London, 1982, p. 151.
3. Kotler, P., *Marketing Management: Analysis, Planning and Control*, 5th edn, Prentice-Hall, Englewood Cliffs, NJ, 1984, p. 252.
4. Levitt, T., *Marketing for Business Growth*, McGraw-Hill, New York, 1974, p. 69.
5. Joint Industry Working Party, *An Evaluation of Social Grade Validity*, The Market Research Society, London, Jan. 1981.
6. Crimp, M., *The Market Research Process*, Prentice-Hall, London, 1985, p. 106.
7. Wofe, A. R. (ed.), *Standardised Questions, A Review for Market Research Executives*, The Market Research Society, London, 1973.
8. Haley, R. I., 'Benefit segmentation: A decision-oriented tool', *Journal of Marketing*, July 1968, pp. 30–35.
9. Bass, F. M., D. J. Tigert and D. T. Lonsdale, 'Market segmentation: Group verses individual behaviour', *Journal of Marketing Research*, **5**, August 1978, p. 276.
10. Frain, J., *Introduction to Marketing*, Macdonald and Evans, London, 1981, p. 103.
11. Kotler, P., op. cit., pp. 305–306.
12. Frank, R. E., W. F. Massy and Y. Wind, *Market Segmentation*, Prentice-Hall, Englewood Cliffs, NJ, 1972.
13. Hart, N. A. (ed.), *The Marketing of Industrial Products*, McGraw-Hill, London, 1984, pp. 11–23.
14. Buzby, S. L. and L. E. Heitger, 'Profit oriented reporting for marketing decision makers', *MSU Business Topics*, **24**(3), 1976.
15. Tull, D. A. and D. I. Hawkins, *Marketing Research, Measurement and Method*, 3rd edn, Macmillan Publishing Company, New York, 1984, p. 316.

THE MARKETING MIX

EIGHT
THE PRODUCT (OR SERVICE)

INTRODUCTION

People who are unfamiliar with marketing often hold the erroneous view that a 'product' is a physical object with readily identifiable and tangible attributes. They would not, for example, consider an insurance policy or a package holiday to be a 'product'. Marketing practitioners must, however, adopt a very much wider view of the product. In the first instance the definition must extend to the concept of the product as a 'service'. In a more abstract sense, products should be distinguished not only by their actual utilities, but also by the perceptions which consumers have of them. These can be real, imagined by the customer, or be the specific creations of the marketer. Thus, in the case of a frozen ready meal, the 'product' is not the physical food ingredients, but a convenience – a labour- and time-saving device. This is the basis for 'benefit segmentation', as explained in Chapter 7.

For the marketer, the product becomes any want-satisfying good or service which is considered together with its perceived tangible and intangible attributes. From the consumer's point of view, a product is a series or a group of satisfactions. It is important to realize that whatever we as marketers 'would like' our products to be, the real nature of the product is in the consumer's perception. This emphasizes the essence of marketing – a policy of customer orientation.

PRODUCT CLASSIFICATION

It should now be clear that the product is much more than the generic 'thing' or 'object'. We should now consider the product in its widest possible context so as to obtain a complete understanding of its nature. This final consideration has been described as the 'Total Product Concept' and its understanding lies at the heart of successful marketing. In his text, *Differentiation of Anything*, Levitt[1] proposes four concepts of the product which go to make up the 'total product'.

First, as we already know, we must consider the physical product or service. This is the generic bar of chocolate, machine tool or two-week package holiday. Without this there can be no sale – no offer or acceptance. The customer, however, expects more than this. The expected product is, of course, wider in scope than the generic but still only represents the consumer's minimum expectations. Such expectations would include price, delivery or availability, after sales service or packaging. A third dimension is the 'augmented product'; this is closely linked with the development of a policy of product differentiation, as opposed to customer originated 'expectations'. 'Augmentations' are the creations of the marketer. One photographic film manufacturer has, for example, recently included a film development service in the purchase price of the film itself. In the industrial sense, such things as a special 'tailor made' delivery or storage service would 'augment' the product from its original basic parameters. Over time, there may be a tendency for customers to regard attributes of the augmented product as standard items thus necessitating a further re-assessment of the product's nature. This leads us finally to the 'potential' product which encompasses all those things which 'could' be added to a product but which, as yet, have not been realized.

The product is, therefore, a complex idea, central to marketing and central to the consumer. It should never be viewed in the narrow terms of a physical object or service but in the context of what satisfactions it brings to the consumer. In addition to this, it cannot be considered in isolation. From both the buyer's and seller's viewpoint, the product is inextricable from the total approach which a firm has towards its market and customers.

We now have an insight into the scope and nature of a product. In order to aid market planning, products can be classified in a formal way. Such a classification system helps us to identify the way in which people view products, and thus why and how they subsequently purchase them.

A PRODUCT AND SERVICE CLASSIFICATION SYSTEM

Products can, in the first instance, be divided into two groups. 'Consumer goods' are purchased by the ultimate buyer while 'industrial goods' are used by all the firms in the manufacturing chain. Many industrial goods can, therefore, go to make up one retail or consumer product. In other words, industrial goods are purchased in order to make other products.

Consumer goods

Figure 8.1 sets out a formal classification for consumer goods.

Convenience goods The purchase of these goods requires very little effort and they are more often than not relatively inexpensive. Most of the contents of the average weekly shopping basket fall into this category and any planning is usually restricted to the preparation of a simple shopping list. The presence of brands may cause the shopper to prevaricate over purchases, but this does not detract from the fact that, in general, little effort is required from the shopper in order to make a profit.

Convenience goods can be subdivided into emergency, staple and impulse items. If sudden necessity is the motivator for a purchase, even less effort than usual will be required. Many small neighbourhood grocery shops owe their survival (faced with price competition from supermarkets) to our need for emergency convenience goods. Staple convenience goods form the bulk of everyday shopping. Items such as milk, bread, sugar or potatoes fall into this category, although it is true to say that nowadays many of these goods possess some sort of branding or other differentiation. Impulse items are self explanatory – pre-planning is obviously nil; these are goods which simply 'catch the eye' and price and price comparison play a minimum role.

Shopping goods This is the category of major, durable or semi-durable appliances. Due to the fact that they are usually more expensive than convenience goods, their purchase is characterized by a fair degree of pre-planning, information search and price comparison. This is not only due to their relative expense, but also because these purchases are made less frequently and the consumer is less knowledgeable about the respective merits of the products which are available. As

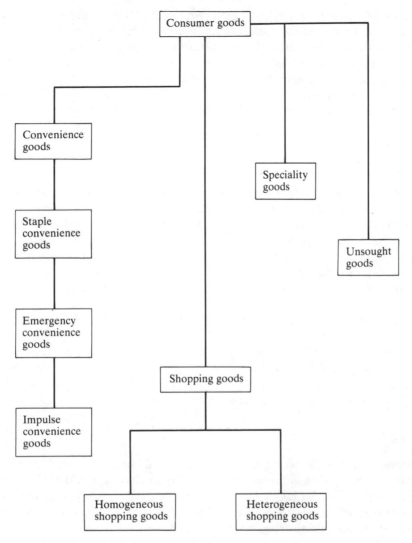

Figure 8.1   A formal classification system for consumer goods

well as price comparison, place of purchase, purchase terms, service and guarantees will all form part of the purchase decision equation.

Homogeneous shopping goods would include such products as 'white goods', prams and pushchairs or DIY equipment. Although these purchases can, in many ways, be 'special' to the consumer because of their relative infrequence of purchase, they are not classed as 'speciality' in marketing terms because the products themselves are not rare or exclusive, but are in fact almost necessities and form a part of everyday life.

Heterogeneous shopping goods are by definition 'non-standard', stylized and possess a degree of exclusivity. Price is usually of secondary importance – behavioural factors playing a more important role than for homogeneous goods. In the car market, the Porsche can be compared with the family saloon to illustrate this difference. Similarly, certain clothing labels can be classed as heterogeneous goods when compared with the more standardized ranges available from the high street multiples.

Speciality goods These are characterized by extensive search and an extreme reluctance to accept substitutes for the chosen product. Exclusivity is a prime purchase criterion. Certain 'long haul' holidays, designer clothing and jewellery, gourmet foods and Rolls Royce cars would fit into this category. While behavioural and life-style factors are important for all consumer purchases, it is likely that this category of goods provides the consumer with the greatest opportunity for self-actualization, ego-satisfaction and the satisfaction of esteem-oriented physical and psychological needs. The marketer also has the best opportunity for targeting and segmenting consumers with a 'tailor made' marketing effort. Although prices will usually be extremely high for such goods, we must remember that the number of consumers in a given population who will be able to afford speciality goods will always be relatively small.

Unsought goods By definition, these goods are those that the consumer does not actively seek out. Indeed the consumer may not even have been aware of them immediately prior to any purchase. New products are 'unsought' initially, but this category is also characterized by aggressive personal selling, direct mail and telephone campaigns. In this respect, unsought goods respresent that aspect of marketing which is most open to criticism. Typically, insurance policies which are solicited by the above means are classed as unsought. This is not to say that sales generated in this way do not uncover a genuine need within a previously unaware consumer.

Finally, we must be aware of the fact that while such a classification system has relevance for most consumers, there are, as always, 'grey areas' where a degree of overlap can take place. A television set may be a speciality good for some consumers, whereas Beluga caviare may, for some, represent a mere convenience item! The important implication for marketers is that for large groups of the population such a classification accurately reflects consumer behaviour and allows a firm to develop an optimum utilization of the marketing mix.

Industrial goods

Industrial goods tend to be characterized on a functional rather than on a behavioural basis. This is because the primary use of industrial goods is in the manufacture, directly or indirectly, of other goods. As with consumer goods, the purpose of a formal classification system is to enable a better understanding of the market by gaining knowledge of the use to which the goods are put and by gaining an insight into the reasons for their purchase.

A simple way to imagine the complex range of industrial goods is to imagine any company and think of all the things which that company will require in order to function efficiently. Obviously a manufacturing company will require machinery and raw materials to make the basic product, but it will also require all of the ancillary items which a company needs – cleaning materials, spare parts, stationery, typewriters, office furniture and so on. All of these items, while not being integral to the manufacturing process, are nevertheless essential to the running of the company. Figure 8.2 classifies these requirements into formal groups.

Installations These can be regarded as the 'speciality' goods of industrial markets. These are the major items of plant and machinery which a company requires for its production. Their purchase is critical and can determine the nature, scope and efficiency of the company. For a haulage company, the heavy goods vehicle would fall into this category.

Not surprisingly, final purchase is the culmination of extensive search and comparison because that decision is essentially long term and likely to be the single most important capital investment at any given time. Due to the long-term implications of purchase, price, while import-

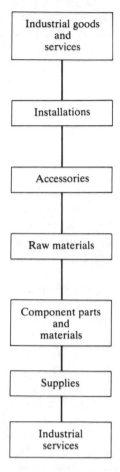

Figure 8.2   A formal classification system for industrial goods

ant, is almost never the single deciding factor. A heavy reliance is also placed on expert sales advice, technical support, availability of spare parts and the general level of after sales service.

Accessories   These comprise ancillary plant and maintenance and office equipment. A significant development of 'accessory' supply in recent years has, of course, been the increasing use of the microprocessor which permits computer controlled sales, production and accountancy information. Although still considered as capital items, accessories are less expensive and are depreciated over a fewer number of years. Fewer personnel are involved in the purchase decision, and this decision itself has less overall importance for the company. One only has to compare the often misguided purchase of office furniture with the implications of a similar decision involving a major piece of production machinery.

Raw materials   Unlike all the other goods in industrial product classification, these go to make up the final product. How close any particular manufacturer's output is to the final product will obviously depend on the position held in the manufacturing chain. It is also worth remembering that much industrial output is not necessarily destined for the consumer market, but goes to provide products for other industries so as to facilitate their manufacturing process.

The purchase of raw materials typically takes the largest share of the expenditure of the traditional 'buying department' of a company. Efficient purchasing is of the utmost importance, because the quality of the raw materials will have a direct bearing on the quality of the product to be produced. It is probably fair to say that the importance of price diminishes, the more the raw material forms part of a commodity market. Price is, however, by no means the only deciding factor of purchase, even in the most homogeneous of commodity markets: delivery, continuity of supply, quality and the general level of service all play a vital part in the decision to deal or not to deal with a particular raw material supplier.

Component parts and materials These are similar in nature to 'raw materials' in that they go to make up the end products. A vehicle manufacturer may purchase steel as a 'raw material' while engine parts would be classed as components. Similarly, a textile manufacturer might purchase natural or synthetic fibre as a raw material, but would also require chemical finishes, dyestuffs and so on as 'materials'. Machinery would also require replacement items: these too would be classified here, and should not be compared with 'accessories'. As with raw material supply, non-price considerations figure highly in reaching the purchase decision.

Supplies If we draw another parallel with the consumer market, supplies can be thought of as the 'convenience goods' of industrial supply. Supplies represent the multiplicity of items which most companies probably take for granted. These are cleaning items – soap, brooms, cloths, etc. In the office, stationery falls into this category as well as items for general maintenance (other than those required for plant) such as light bulbs, fuel oil and numerous 'repairs and renewals'. Purchase procedure is often routine and conducted through the medium of wholesalers. Due to the relatively homogeneous nature of supplies, and their wide availability, price is a major influencing factor of supply.

Industrial services The supply of industrial services has greatly increased in recent years. One only needs to think of the field of marketing itself where the opportunity to purchase the services of management consultants and market research agencies has increased many fold during the past decade. There has also been a similar increase in the use of contract cleaners and services such as 'express delivery' for urgent or fragile correspondence. The principal factor in deciding to use outside services rather than the firm's own personnel concerns the question of cost effectiveness. Frequently, when such services are not required on a continuous basis or when the long-term cost of employing expert personnel would exceed the cost of the required service, the use of outside agencies offers a convenient solution to the problem.

A classification of industrial products is an ideal aid and companion to the study of industrial buyer behaviour. Each category of products performs a different role for the firm and this knowledge can be used by suppliers in the design of their marketing and sales strategy. It should be uppermost in the minds of both buyer and seller that the finished products can only be as good as the machinery which makes them. The product classification system also permits emphasis of the fact that, just as consumers 'perceive' benefits other than the physical form a given product, industrial buyers are equally concerned with factors other than the immediate product and its price.

NEW PRODUCT DEVELOPMENT

The development of a new product is a component of overall marketing strategy. For most firms new products involve the effort and cooperation of the total management structure as well as a wide cross-section of the total workforce. New products involve large sums of money and higher than normal levels of risk when compared to many other major marketing decisions. It is for these reasons that it is thought worth while to highlight this subject as a separate element of product strategy.

What is a new product?

Most of us must be familiar with the bewildering selection of goods displayed in any supermarket. In industry, the professional buyer is consistently confronted with 'variations on themes' and occasionally with a product designed to 'revolutionize' a particular manufacturing process. Both in consumer markets and in industry, the purchaser has a tendency to adopt a 'blasé' attitude towards the latest offering from any given firm. From the manufacturer's point of view, the picture is very different – a new chocolate bar or machine part is the culmination of a vast commitment of resources, time and research. Before going on to examine in detail how this process is carried out, we should be aware of the variety of definitions which can be applied to a new product.

1. *Innovative products*: these are products which are truly 'new' to the consumer: they provide totally different alternatives to existing products which serve existing markets. Among such goods can be included the television, or the automobile which was made possible by the invention of the internal combustion engine. These new products provided an alternative to radio and cinema entertainment and to horse-drawn methods of transport. In more modern times, the microprocessor and robotic manufacturing methods would fall into this category. So too would a pharmaceutical cure to an illness which had been previously been thought incurable.
2. *Replacement products*: these are replacements for existing products which, while not being wholly 'innovative', do provide significant differentiations from those which are currently on offer. Using a previous example, one could say that a radically new design of car offers a 'replacement' product. Similarly, the Polaroid camera 'replaced' those cameras which required films to be developed independently from the taking of the picture. The compact disc, however technically innovative, is a replacement for the conventional hi-fi system, as was the hi-fi system a replacement for the original and truly 'innovative' (in the marketing sense) gramophone.
3. *Imitative products*: this final category involves all those products which are new to a company, but which are already well established in the marketplace. These follow on from the replacement and innovative products which have been developed initially by individual firms. Occasionally, imitative products are perhaps disparagingly described as 'me too' products because they imply a certain lack of imagination on the behalf of the firm launching them. It is also fair to say that all firms cannot be pioneers of product inventiveness, and thus the bulk of new products are imitative. Certainly, if a firm's financial resources and marketing expertise are strong, then it is advantageous to be an innovator rather than a follower, but in practice many firms appear content to let another take the risks of an innovative product launch, and then join the market when 'the dust has settled'. It also happens that a firm launches an innovative product and then quickly loses market share to a more powerful imitation.

    Imitative products are most often found when the technical development costs are low and are obviously launched before the initiator has had the opportunity to set up too many barriers to market entry. It is also with imitative products where the highest rate of product failure is likely to occur.

A final criterion for new product definition, irrespective of the above categories, lies in the consumer's perception. This is, of course, determined by the manner in which the product is presented to the marketplace. Thus, a relaunched product can appear 'new' if different benefits are promoted, whether or not these be tangible or intangible. Appearance or performance need not be radically altered. Provided the consumer perceives a product as being significantly different from that which already exists, then it is effectively a new product.

THE IMPORTANCE OF NEW PRODUCT DEVELOPMENT

In his famous article 'Marketing myopia',[2] Levitt emphasizes the absolute necessity of a 'total' commitment to new product development. This is the sole medium for adaptation to change and is, therefore, critical to the continued survival of the firm. This importance is mirrored and intensified by the fact that new products are the 'rocks on which many companies founder'.

The product (and its successors) is, therefore, central to the whole being of the firm. Any efficient sales manager will maintain that without customers there is no need for production. This perfectly valid standpoint can, however, be considered in a different way by stating that without a product, one has no need for a salesforce! Thus we move to the inevitable conclusion that the product is essential to the firm's physical existence, not only because a product is necessary for profit generation to take place, but also because the product is the medium through which a company fulfils the marketing concept. Taking the strictest interpretation of the marketing concept, the total ethos of the firm should be to produce goods which provide consumer satisfaction, profit being the reward of this if effectively carried out. Such a view, which may appear overly altruistic (and which is certainly complicated), is not, however, far removed from reality. Whatever company policies may be, competitive forces tend, over time, to militate against the firm whose products are not specifically aimed at fulfilling the marketing concept.

The marketing mix too is a meaningless tool without the product. It should be evident that all elements of the marketing mix are totally dependent on each other, but quite logically the core of the marketing mix is the product and new product developments. All marketing planning is based on, and must start from, the product. If that product is intrinsically weak, it will not ultimately survive, however skilfully the other elements of the mix are employed. This last factor underlines the importance of the product as the basic profit determinant of the firm. New products, moreover, should ensure that profit is sustained in the long term as well as providing the opportunity for growth and diversification.

Finally, from the strategic viewpoint, the firm must utilize new products as a means towards market leadership, rather than market imitation. The underlying trends towards a more affluent society in Western post-war history imply that the more basic of consumer needs are, to a great extent, fulfilled. The implications of this are that firms must be increasingly aware of the need to satisfy consumers on a higher plane than was previously necessary. This requires an even more dynamic and sophisticated approach to new product development.

STEPS IN THE DEVELOPMENT PROCESS

In view of the importance of new products, and of the high rate of product failure, it is axiomatic that any development programme should only be embarked upon with the utmost care. The ramifications of a new product are numerous, but the criteria for any developments and ultimate launch can be reduced to three basic questions; no undertakings should even be considered unless satisfactory answers to the following can be supplied:

1. Is there a real consumer need?

2. Does the company have the resources and technical ability to market and manufacture the product?
3. Is the potential market large enough to generate profit?

These are the key questions, but because new products do not just 'materialize', there must be a formal method for the generation of ideas, idea evaluation and for establishing practical feasibility. The following steps should provide answers to the three fundamental questions and establish a clearly defined cut-off point after which the company should feel confident in launching a new product.

Idea generation

These emanate from a variety of sources, but the source itself is less important than the system and attitude which the company has towards idea evaluation. The groundwork which leads to ideas can be described as 'opportunity exploration'. This process can be carried on by formal *research and development* departments. Here, care should be taken to avoid the syndrome of developing a product and then saying 'let's see if anyone wants it!' The *production department* can, in the course of manufacture, provide ideas for modifying and improving the existing product. The *sales team* is another source of valuable ideas: they are the people who receive direct customer feedback and who are often most able to say what competitors are providing which their firm is not. *Senior management*, if product-oriented, should be responsible for creating the correct attitude towards development within the firm and for organizing formal programmes which might include techniques such as brainstorming sessions and the organization of venture teams and planning committees. Finally, and irrespective of the firm's level of sophistication in the field of market intelligence, it is possible to draw heavily on *external sources* for inspiration and ideas. These would include: trade associations, published reports, governmental bodies, middlemen and foreign competitors.

Screening new ideas

Once equipped with a set of potentially viable ideas, it is necessary to devise a method of screening these ideas so as to reduce them to a manageable number which have real market prospects. Screening should also ensure that a good product is not eliminated at an early stage, which can be equally as damaging as having to bear the development cost of a product failure.

In order to develop a screening technique it is essential that the firm isolates a series of factors which research has shown are desirable to the consumer, and which are desirable to the firm in that they make the best use of existing marketing strengths. The product ideas can then be compared so as to establish a short list of those which fit most closely to these criteria. Typical factors under consideration might include: raw material availability, production, distribution and product line compatibility and the effect on sales of other products. Market research techniques such as brand mapping might provide a series of features which are thought desirable from the consumer's point of view.

The technique of screening is usually carried out by statistical weighting of the factors involved. A minimum rating score must, of course, be established and those ideas whose score is superior to this can then proceed to the next development stage. The use of 'Likert' type scales rather than numerical values is probably less effective because of the semantic difficulties in establishing what is, say, GOOD, POOR or FAIR.

Business analysis

This third step concerns the financial, rather than the practical, viability of the product idea. Research and forecasting techniques are used to establish demand. Cost analysis examines not only the basic cost of production, but should also include such factors as capital investment, marketing costs (perhaps advertising and new distribution channels) and in some cases the engagement of new personnel. Profitability can be established in terms of 'break-even' and 'rate-of-return' analysis.

Product development

Once it has been established by analytical methods that a product idea has market potential, it is necessary to develop some form of prototype in an effort to confirm this feasibility in physical terms. This confirmation must be related both to production and marketing. Marketing activities would include motivational research and concept testing. Physical testing of the prototype by the consumer would encompass performance, packaging and comparison with products where level of acceptance is already known.

It is also necessary at this stage to ensure that production and marketing departments are working in close harmony. The marketing responsibility is to communicate immediately any reaction which would suggest that the nature of the prototype should be altered, or if in fact the whole project should be seriously called into question. The production department must be as sure as possible that the prototype corresponds precisely with any production model which would subsequently be launched. If this was not the case, all marketing research would be a fruitless exercise.

At the end of the product development stage the firm faces a critical decision: whether to go ahead and market the new product or to 'cut its losses' by abandoning a project which appears to have an unlikely chance of success. Either decision requires considerable business competence, not to mention sheer courage! The 'go' decision involves the risk of product failure, while on the other hand the decision to abort requires that the firm must write off large expenditure and perhaps years of time spent in development. The decision must, however, be made because this is the whole reason for a 'planned' development programme.

Test marketing

Just as the prototype must correspond exactly to the final product, so it is vital that the 'test market' chosen for partial launch of the final product is highly representative of the total market.

Although, in practice, the test market and test marketing provide the firm with a final opportunity to withdraw the product before a full-scale launch, this is not the real purpose of the exercise. Test markets are not 'final screens'. At this stage the firm should have already made up its mind to commercialize the product. Test marketing objectives are: to predict the efficacy of the proposed marketing strategy (and refine this if needed) and to predict the effect of strategy in terms of market penetration.

The usual procedure for test marketing is to select an easily identifiable sector of the market which represents the total market in miniature and then to launch a product in the same way as a total market launch would be expected to take place, thus testing the feasibility of the full marketing programme. In the UK it is common to use ITV television areas as test marketing areas for consumer goods. As well as providing distinct geographical areas, television advertising can also be monitored area by area when experimenting with different campaigns, advertising frequency and so on. It is not uncommon to run more than one test market concurrently. In this way, different applications of the marketing mix can be experimented with, as can the attribution of marketing budgets. Market research agencies are increasingly active in test marketing, especially in the field of predictive analysis. As such predictive models increase in their level of sophistication, there is a tendency to reduce the scope of test markets in the physical sense by placing an increasing reliance on statistical hypotheses. This is less true in the industrial sense, but in consumer goods markets, 'mini' and 'micro' test markets are common.[3] For actual examples of UK test marketing procedure see Chapter 5.

Mini test markets provide one way of exercising greater control over the test itself. One danger of test marketing is that one is never completely sure that the test marketing accurately simulates the full-scale reality. This can be exacerbated by competitors who, aware that a test market is under way, can devise ways of creating artificial market conditions. An intense 'burst' of competitive advertising or a series of special offers would completely disrupt the effect of test marketing in a given area. A second danger is that while Company A is engaged in test marketing, Company B can 'leapfrog' the whole process by bringing a product to market without pre-testing it. For these reasons, as well as for good statistical practice, it is always advisable to operate a 'control' test market so as to estimate the impact of a number of control variables – including competitive action.

Commercialization

The stages of product development have 'filtered' commercially viable product ideas from a wide selection of original propositions. Furthermore, a product has been chosen *and* prepared for acceptability in the marketplace. Test marketing has fine-tuned the appropriate marketing strategy, and the firm is now sufficiently confident and knowledgeable to launch and commercialize the product on a full-scale basis. New product strategy to 'skim' or go for 'market penetration' is dealt with later in this chapter and in Chapter 13.

Figure 8.3 shows a schematic relationship between product development and expenditure. The relationship is inverse in that early stages cost relatively little. At the stages of product development and test marketing, potential products have been reduced to a few, yet these are the stages where cost is highest. This underlines the importance of effective screening and business analysis. Ruthless decisions must be made to eliminate those products thought unsuitable at each stage of the process. It is also worth while re-emphasizing that while development costs to the stage of a test market are high, the financial loss of launching a product 'full scale' which is a subsequent failure are always considerably higher. Typically, the development cost of a new model in the car industry is between £500 and £1000 million over a time span of 5–10 years. Imagine the cost of full production and market launch in addition to this, and the period of time required for break-even!

Despite the care and attention which goes into new product development, there exists an apparently endless list of product failures. In industrial markets, most go unnoticed by all but those who are directly involved. Consumers are, however, witness to a constant series of new products which are here today and gone tomorrow. Some estimates of failures versus successful products even go as high as 80 per cent, and evidence suggests that the figure is at least 50 per cent. Whatever the figure, failure is a feature of new products.[4] No guarantees are attached to a careful development plan and despite the best predictions, markets have a habit of being unpredictable. On the positive side, what we can be sure of is that like good marketing as a whole, the more thorough and professional is the development programme, the more this is likely to minimize the risk of product failure.

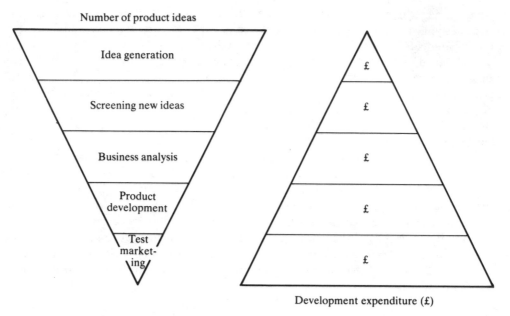

Figure 8.3   The relationship between cost and product development

THE PRODUCT LIFE CYCLE

The concept of the product life cycle (PLC) constitutes an important component of product strategy. The concept proposes that once the product or service reaches the market, it enters a 'life cycle' and will eventually fade from the market. We must remember that the PLC is meant to serve as a conceptual base for examining product growth and development and that every product does not necessarily fit neatly into all the elements of the theoretical curve (see Fig. 8.4). A study of business and economic history reveals that some predictable course of product development occurs sufficiently often for marketing planners to attach considerable credence to the concept. Thus, as well as providing a theoretical framework, the PLC can be used as a real managerial tool which is helpful in forecasting and, therefore, in strategic planning.

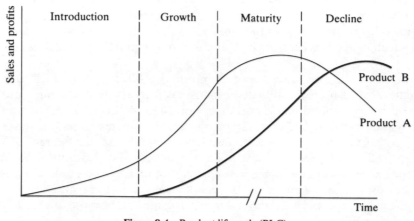

Figure 8.4   Product life cycle (PLC)

Figure 8.4 identifies four stages in the pattern of demand during the product's life. The cycles of two hypothetical products are shown to illustrate that the cycle concept is only a guide. The life cycles of different products will differ because they are a function of their intrinsic nature, their markets and their competitive environments.

Similarly, just as the shape of the curve is likely to differ according to the type of product, the time span of the cycle may vary from as little as a few days to as much as several decades.

Whatever the shape or time span of the life-cycle curve, the implications for the marketer are of equal importance and are as follows:

1. The appropriate strategy for each stage.
2. The identification of movement from one stage to another.
3. The likely shape of the total curve.

The definition of the points where different stages in the life cycle begin is somewhat arbitrary, but each stage has characteristic phenomena which suggest a specific reaction and mode of strategy formulation.

Introduction

Characteristics This stage is, of course, typified by conditions which relate to those of a new product launch.

1. A high product failure rate.
2. Relatively little competition.
3. Limited distribution.
4. Frequent product modification.
5. Company losses at least on that product because development costs have not yet been recouped, mass production economies are not possible and promotional expenditure is usually greater than profit returns on sales.

Money spent at the 'introduction' phase should be regarded as an investment in the future.

Introduction strategy Promotion is directed at creating product awareness. This may require extra effort in personal selling. For consumer goods, advertising is the most common method of promotion. In extreme cases, advertising expenditure can exceed not only profits but also sales revenue. In any case, introduction strategy requires that a firm's resources are deployed in larger than usual levels of marketing expenditure.

Pricing strategy will depend largely on the degree of distinctiveness of the product and on the length of time that this distinctiveness is likely to last. Two basic strategic options are open, either a 'skimming' or a 'penetration' strategy may be adopted. 'Skimming' involves the application of a high price to a small section of consumers (the early adopters). It is appropriate when the product is unusually distinctive and demand is inelastic. Depending upon the circumstances (a critical factor being the degree of competitive activity), potential new groups of adopters are encouraged to buy the product by a planned series of progressive price reductions.

'Penetration' is likely to be appropriate where demand is elastic and the level of competitive activity is high. This is a relatively low price strategy which aims to attract the largest number of new buyers early in the product's life.

Neither strategy has an immediate profit maximizing objective in the economic sense; rather these are 'marketing' strategies which are designed to ensure long-term profitability; that is, profitability during the subsequent stages of the life cycle. These pricing strategy notions are explored more fully in the next chapter.

The decision to pursue a policy of market share acquisition is a matter of corporate strategy and is a highly complicated subject. Suffice it to say here, that if market share is considered as being strategically advantageous, then it is most easily accomplished during introduction while the distinctiveness of the product remains intact.

In the sense of 'market evolution' or a life cycle for markets, Hofer and Schendel[5] have identified a 'shake out' stage between those of introduction and growth. This can be applied to individual products as well as to companies in a market because, in both cases, the numbers falling 'by the wayside' can have significant implications for those which survive into the growth stage.

Growth

Characteristics
1. More competitors – less product distinctiveness.
2. Rising sales.
3. Profitable returns.
4. Company or product acquisition by larger companies.

Growth strategy Although heavy promotion is a feature of the introduction stage, advertising and promotion also feature highly in the marketing budget during growth. However, there are two important differences: one is the promotional task itself which in growth centres its emphasis on promotion of the 'brand' or trade name, rather than on creating product awareness as this should already have been achieved. Second, the promotional budget, relative to sales, should allow room for a profit return, whereas in introduction it is not unusual for promotional expenditure to be grossly disproportionate to sales and profit. There are, however, exceptions to these guidelines. If, for example, a large company with an extensive product portfolio is determined to ensure market dominance for one of these products during maturity, then a promotional expenditure which continues to sap profits throughout the growth stage would not be unusual.

Distribution is also a major consideration during growth and manufacturers will fight strongly to acquire dealership and distribution outlets. Trends in the UK retail sector during the last 10–15 years emphasize this phenomenon. In many instances the key to whole markets lies within a small nucleus of retail groups. Similarly, owing to the pressure for profitable shelf space, retail groups, especially supermarkets, will rationalize the number of brands carried as soon as a hierarchy of leaders has established itself. For fast moving consumer goods, if a product fails to be stocked by even one of the major UK supermarket chains, a large section of that market will have been lost.

You will doubtless be already aware of the strongly 'interdependent' nature of the elements of the marketing mix: growth strategy ably demonstrates this. In growth, as indeed in the other stages of the PLC, the chosen strategy will fail if either one of the key elements (in the case of growth, promotion and place) is not efficiently effected.

The opportunity to achieve maximum profits usually peaks towards the end of the growth period. This is often because brand shares have stabilized to some extent and many companies are obliged to follow the leader. This last factor, coupled with the possible opportunity for economies of scale, sometimes leads to price decreases towards the end of this stage.

Finally, for the pessimistic as well as the cautious strategist, the end of growth also heralds the beginning of decline!

Maturity

The majority of products are in this stage of the life cycle. Much marketing activity is, therefore, directed at appropriate maturity strategies. This is also usually the longest stage of the life cycle.

Characteristics
1. Sales continue to increase, but at a greatly reduced rate.
2. Attempts are made to differentiate or re-differentiate the product, and the product line may be widened.
3. Prices begin to fall as manufacturers fight to retain market share.
4. Profits fall in line with falling prices and the continued need to promote the product.
5. Inventory and brand rationalization become common among retailers and dealers.
6. Marginal producers, faced with dwindling margins and severe competition, may drop out at this stage, although it is not impossible for new entrants to appear.

Maturity strategy Promotional strategy is directed at reinforcement of the 'message' so as to encourage re-buys. Subtle differences in brands are emphasized to attract new customers as well as to reinforce the loyalty of existing users. It must be remembered that at this stage, actual market growth has ceased, and companies can only increase their own market share at the expense of their competitors. Such a situation implies that promotional activity must be sustained merely to hold on to the existing market share.

Price reductions (as a means of achieving the above) are often a feature of the maturity stage, but care must be taken to avoid a 'pyrrhic' victory, because very often the net result of initiating price cuts is to decrease the revenue for all firms in the industry unless sufficient increased purchases can be induced so as to offset revenue losses.

Distribution strategy must be designed to retain existing dealerships and retail outlets, because once lost, they are unlikely to be regained at this stage. To achieve this, the emphasis of promotional effort may move from consumer to distributor.

Decline

Whether due to innovation or changes in consumer preferences, a continued fall in industry sales signifies the 'decline' of the product.

Characteristics
1. Falling sales for the total industry.
2. Price cutting may intensify.
3. Producers decide to abandon the market.

Decline strategy The major strategic decision here is whether to leave the market or not, and if the former decision is taken, when should this be? Many firms have successfully 'hung on' in a declining market by outliving their competitors and finding 'niches' or speciality areas to serve. Cost control, although always important, becomes critical in retaining profitability when the decision to remain in a declining market is made.

On the other hand, the decision to abandon a previously profitable product is a crucial one and is the source of much 'soul searching' on management's behalf. Many firms find it difficult to accept that a product (on which the very company may have made its name) must sooner or later be abandoned. Such decisions are, however, the essence of marketing management.

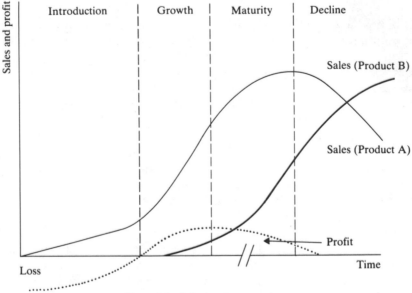

Figure 8.5   Sales/profit comparisons

USING THE PLC CONCEPT

The key to successful use of the PLC concept lies in the accurate identification of where each stage starts and ends. This calls for a high degree of marketing orientation by management and thus for extensive use of marketing research and intelligence.

If we assume the above to be possible, management then has the basic medium for long-term strategic planning. As well as providing a predictable pattern of product development (during which the appropriate strategies can be planned and budgeted for), the PLC is particularly useful for planning 'beyond the life' of the existing product.

Figure 8.5 shows the likely course of profits for Product A during its life cycle. Of particular importance, however, is the launch and overlap of Product B.

It is essential that planning is such that companies are already beginning to receive revenue from a new product before or while the previous product is in decline. Similarly, the funding of Product B must be derived from the profits of Product A – and so the cycle continues.

VARIATIONS OF THE CONCEPT

The value of the PLC as a strategic tool is undoubted, but as the student of marketing should now be aware, management should not be constrained by dogmatic adherence to a theoretical course of events. Success is determined by the ability to react and adapt to 'market conditions'. The PLC provides a 'framework' for planning rather than a rigid curve that must be followed. As has already been stated, the time span of the curve can vary enormously according to the product type, but the 'actual' life of the product can in practice be modified by management. Thus, faced with difficult trading conditions or with the opportunity for a better allocation of resources, management can prematurely end the life of a product, say, in early maturity. By the same token, the product's life can be extended and re-extended by finding new end-users for it, or by applying it to totally new markets. There is the possibility of some confusion in considering the extension of a product's life because in some cases, if the product has changed significantly, then it could be said that this is in reality a 'new product'. One must also distinguish here between the company product and the generic product. Using Levitt's example of Nylon,[6] we can see that the generic life of Nylon has been constantly extended by finding new end-uses for it. We must also be aware that some new end-users may themselves experience decline while the generic product lives on. The video recorder is a good example of a new product with which to study the PLC. Although a multitude of new brand videos may enter or leave the market at various stages, this will not affect the course of the video's cycle as a generic product. Provided that it remains popular with consumers, the video will not begin to decline until a radically new method of recording begins to supplant its use.

Finally, we must consider the views of those who criticize the use of the PLC as a basic concept. It is not the intention here to engage in full-scale debate but it is worth noting that critics of the PLC raise issues to which attention should be paid.[7]

A major point is the feeling that if used without imagination, the PLC can become a self-fulfilling prophecy. In other words, management may misinterpret market activity and think themselves into product decline and accept this as inevitable. One method of avoiding this is to extend or 'exploit' the PLC[8] by imaginative application of the product to new markets. Thus, although the product may decline in its existing form and market, this is not to say that it cannot be profitably employed elsewhere. Such a strategy does not imply that the life-cycle concept is being ignored – rather it is the recognition of the concept which permits such a strategy.

A further danger and cause for criticism is linked to that described in the preceding paragraph. This concerns the capacity of management to identify accurately the beginning and end of progressive life-cycle stages. This is, of course, no easy task, because each stage merges with another over a time span which may vary according to the product and its markets. In the case of a truly 'new' product, no empirical data will be available to aid decision making: such situations will, therefore, be 'unique'. Successful use of the PLC concept is not, however, an unattainable goal. It should be the result of a coherent and long-term marketing strategy. This in turn is supported and made possible by 'continuous' marketing and market research and the employment of a comprehensive marketing intelligence system.

THE PRODUCT ADOPTION PROCESS

It is important to consider product strategy and the PLC in conjunction with the reactions of consumers who are exposed to new products. The section on consumer behaviour in Chapter 3 deals in detail with this subject, but it is worth while here to consider briefly the PLC and the relationship this has with product adoption. By doing this, marketing management can appreciate the nature of the target market and its needs as the product moves through its life cycle.

Consumers can be grouped into five 'adopter categories', each of which has distinct characteristics and therefore requires that specific strategies are formulated which suit the individual needs of each group at a given time. The relationship between adoption theory and the PLC concept is shown in Fig. 8.6.

Figure 8.6 does, of course, present an extremely simple and logical relationship which is based on separate research studies. However, the implication is an essential ingredient of marketing strategy. This is that the marketing of a product should be seen in as many dimensions as possible. Marketing might say that the 'early majority' will require a specific approach to advertising, pricing and distribution. The fact that competitors will be employing the marketing mix in a similar way, will in turn create market conditions which require decisions and action of a strategic nature, which in this case should be relevant to the 'growth' stage of the life cycle.

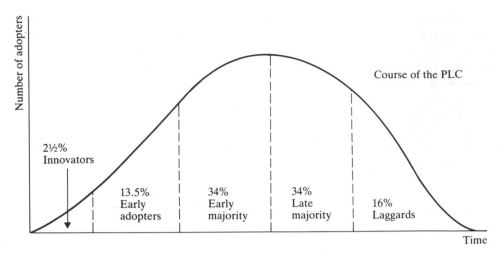

Figure 8.6   Adoption theory and the PLC
(*After*: E. M. Rogers, *Diffusion of Innovation*, The Free Press, New York, 1962, p. 162)

PRODUCT MANAGEMENT AND ORGANIZATIONAL STRUCTURE

This section is not concerned with the total study of organizational structure, rather, it is concerned with the subject as it relates to the product. As usual with marketing, the interdependent theme is strong as no one aspect of the firm can be considered in isolation. A striking aspect of product organization *vis-à-vis* the complete organizational picture is the indispensable, motivational involvement of top management.

It is the responsibility of senior executives to create the correct environment for innovation and forward thinking and thus to initiate and motivate the development of new products. The extent of their involvement is very often the only determinant of eventual product success. Vital though attitude is, this must be translated into some concrete form of organizational structure and procedure so that the communication of ideas 'top down' and 'bottom up' can flourish. One of the following formal sections is commonly found in those companies who enjoy consistent success in product innovation.

The new product section

The existence of such a section or department quite obviously implies a permanent commitment to product development. Typically, the section is small, perhaps four to six members, and it is their responsibility to set up a new product programme and to steer this through the stages of development which have already been described.

The new product function has the authority and credence of being a section or department in its own right and should have the ability to 'streamline' ideas, whereas a committee, for example, can have a tendency to operate in a manner rather abstract of the running of the rest of the firm. It is vital that the members of the team are drawn from a wide cross-section of other departments, thus ensuring that they have the necessary experience and expertise to cover *all* aspects of the product. Second, this experience should facilitate constructive communication with their peers throughout the firm. A real danger for new product sections is that this communication breaks down and it becomes a remote 'boffin-like' institution in the eyes of other employees.

Often the head of the section will report directly to the chief executive of the firm and will possess substantial authority. When the development stage is complete, the product will be turned over to the respective functional areas for test marketing and commercialization.

New product committees

In common with new product departments or sections, committee members are selected from key functional areas of the firm and in this case are usually senior managers in their respective fields. Their role is not as much in the actual conception of a product, but rather more in the approval and review of existing programmes. The strengths of committees are due to the authority of their members. Thus, if a particular plan is approved by, say, the production director, it is less likely that this will meet opposition later. On the other hand, there is a danger of the committee becoming remote from its purpose because members are often more anxious to concentrate on their own existing responsibilities. Moreover, decision making can be slow, compromising in nature, and have a tendency to impede rather than to accelerate the progress of promising developments.

In some companies, committees exist side by side with new product sections or departments and are the final arbiters of crucial stages of development.

The venture team

This is the newest organizational concept for product development. Its role is to manage the development of a specific product from conception to full-scale marketing. Again, members are multi-disciplinary, but unlike the two previous examples, the venture team operates outside the mainstream of the firm – almost like a 'mini-business' in itself. Its sole objective is to bring a new product to the market profitably. Most usually, team members are relieved of their existing responsibilities so as to concentrate fully on a given project. The life span of the team can run from a few months to several years – just as long as it takes to do the job.

The essence of the venture team is entrepreneurial spirit, and companies should endeavour to choose team members on this basis. How successful venture teams really are is uncertain. The 'entrepreneur' is often difficult to identify and it is extremely difficult to segregate a small team away from the firm and retain its effectiveness and to free such a team from 'bureaucratic' constraints and impediments, although this is the rationale on which the team is based.

Once a product reaches market launch, the team is usually disbanded and product management is then passed back to the mainstream of the firm and its functional departments.

Product managers

A product manager is an organizational unit in one person who has responsibility for the development of a new product and for the entire management of existing products. Functional marketing areas such as sales, marketing research and advertising exist on a 'company wide' basis, and it is up to the product manager to utilize these services as he thinks fit.

A major criticism of the use of product managers for new product development is that like committees, there is a tendency for them to become preoccupied with existing products and problems rather than new ideas. This is understandable, as their performance is usually assessed on the basis of established product success rather than idea generation, although the latter forms part of their remit in many firms. Similarly, it does not necessarily follow that the skills required for established product management coincide with those required for new product development. On balance, such role duality is likely to be neither fair nor efficient and much current thinking places the product manager's responsibility with the management of established products. For this reason, the product manager's role will be re-examined later.

There is no single 'best' method to organize for new product development. Like many other aspects of marketing, this organization is a function of the company's make-up – its managerial skils, financial resources and existing organizational structure. There are, however, distinct guidelines which, if followed, considerably increase the opportunity for success.

Whatever method is employed, development should not be harmed by bureaucratic constraints. This is the surest way to stifle progress and enthusiasm. Development should take place in an entrepreneurial atmosphere fostered by top management and permeated throughout the firm. Representatives from all functional areas should be involved in development. Finally, the importance and involvement of top management cannot be overemphasized. As long as 25 years ago E. J. McCarthy went so far as to say that 'new product development cannot be systemized'. Organizational plans can only 'facilitate' development whose key criterion for success is a 'dynamic, innovating attitude, instilled into and felt by the whole compnay'.[9]

THE PRODUCT MANAGER

The product manager as an organizational unit is not really a new or revolutionary breakthrough in marketing management. What is new is its rapid acceptance and adoption by most major companies during the past two decades. The principal reason for this can be ascribed to the emergence of multi-product organizations.

Where does the product manager 'fit in'?

The particular type of marketing organization which a company chooses is of course dependent on the products it markets and the markets within which it operates. The arrangements and solutions which a company decides upon are almost as numerous as the companies themselves. One major theme is common whatever the circumstances of the firm. They all must accommodate three basic dimensions of marketing activity, these being:

– functions;
– products; and
– markets.

The most common and least complicated approach to addressing the organizational problem is to organize the company around the marketing functions which must be performed. A marketing manager or marketing director is at the head of a function which coordinates and synchronizes the marketing operation in totality. This most simple structure is illustrated in Fig. 8.7. Advertising, sales and marketing research possess their own functional specialists, but work together under the unifying supervision of the marketing director. While the system is advantageous because of its simplicity, its appeal is considerably lessened as the number of products produced

Figure 8.7   A functional marketing organization

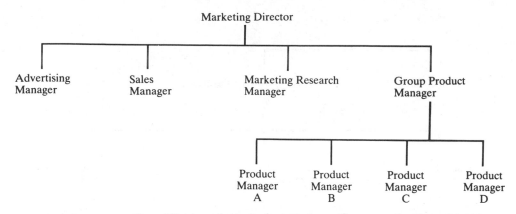

Figure 8.8 A product manager marketing organization

by a company begins to grow. When this happens, management becomes not only physically complicated, but more importantly, there is a risk that some products will become neglected at the expense of others.

The product manager type structure offers the solution of providing each product (or sometimes brand) with someone who is directly responsible for its success, allocation of functional support and general well-being. Figure 8.8 locates the product manager in relation to the rest of the firm's marketing activities. Each product manager draws on the functional areas for appropriate support and, because his or her activity is focused on one product only, the marketing of that product is uncluttered by dual roles and conflicting or confused product loyalties. Additionally, such a structure is highly flexible, as new managers who have very clearly defined objectives, can be added as product expansion takes place.

If the product range is sufficiently large and diverse the responsibilities can be broken down still further. A chemical company may have a manager for 'agricultural products'. Separate product managers may control 'insecticides', 'fertilizers', etc. These too can be broken down into individual 'brand managers', say, for brands within insecticides as in Fig. 8.9.

The role and responsibilities of the product manager

The product manager type company structure allows senior management to 'home in' on the progress and performance of any given product with relative ease and precision. As such, the system lends itself to marketing control and to marketing planning. Strategic planning and marketing 'audits' are, therefore, greatly improved by product manager feedback. Planning at the business level is also improved, because the product manager's primary role is to plan product objectives and strategy, ensure they are implemented, monitor their progress, take action if necessary and coordinate budget development and control.

The responsibilities are, therefore, erroneous – in reality the product manager runs a business within a business with direct responsibility for success or failure. Not only is the product manager a planner as well as an implementer, but a further burden is one of ensuring that the resources required to carry out a plan are readily available. In theory, as can be seen from Fig. 8.10, functional resources are shared and at the disposal of each product. Problems arise, however, if a functional area becomes overstretched and cannot share its resources equally. Here the product manager faces the task of negotiating, perhaps even fighting, for resources which are essential to carry out the job which senior management expects. In less difficult conditions, the least that is

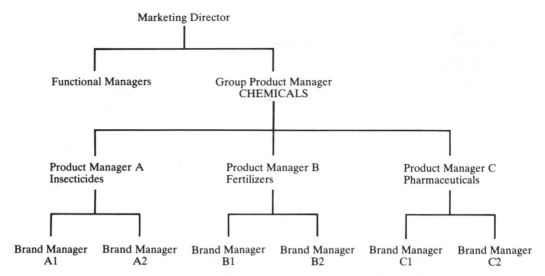

Figure 8.9 Expanded product manager organization

expected from a product manager (in addition to planning and implementation) is the ability to coordinate the functional resources at his or her disposal to the best advantage of the product plan.

The 'fundamental' tasks of the product manager have just been described. The remit is so wide that it is worth detailing the various involvements. The scope of product management is as follows:

1. Planning product strategy.
2. Sales forecasting.
3. Monitoring performance and gathering field intelligence.
4. Advertising.
5. Sales promotion.

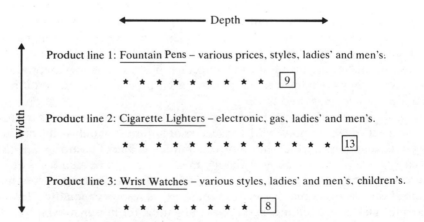

Figure 8.10 The consistency of the product mix

6. Marketing research.
7. Merchandising.
8. Packaging, branding, labelling.
9. New product development – product improvements.
10. Product line planning.
11. Pricing.
12. Inventories and warehousing.
13. Production planning.
14. Distribution.
15. Sales – stimulating interest and support among the salesforce.

Problems with product management

In view of the extent of the product manager's role, it is not surprising that certain problems are associated with this form of organization.

First, as has already been mentioned, the product manager, whose primary concern is the product, often extends much effort in vying for the functional resources which are shared with his or her peers. Time spent thus, dilutes the amount of effort spent on planning. Such 'in-house competition' also has a psychological effect in that the product manager is expected to be responsible for the results of, say, advertising decisions, but does not gain either personal expertise or the opportunity to be instrumental in the decision-making process. This syndrome can also be extended to profit accountability; the product manager is highly 'profit accountable', but rarely has the authority to make big profit decisions.

The product manager is, therefore, allocated great responsibility without the satisfaction of real control over the product's destiny. From the senior executives' viewpoints the product manager's decision-making abilities are restricted because of his exclusive involvement in one product. For the product manager, this is a good reason to be afforded more executive control!

A final problem concerns organizational policy itself. At one extreme, a strictly functional structure (Fig. 8.7) is not sufficiently flexible for the demands of multi-product companies. However, there is a real danger of carrying the product manager concept too far. The structure of Fig. 8.9 shows product managers and brand managers and here the difficulty for some companies is to know where to stop! If, for example, a product manager's time is being spent more and more on one aspect of management, an assistant may be appointed. So, in turn, a brand manager may request assistance. This process will in turn place increasing pressure on functional specialists. The end result may be an expensive and unwieldly 'superstructure' of personnel whose presence will defeat entirely the main object of product management – that of simplicity, direct responsibility and easy access to information.

Advantages of the product management structure

Much of the value of the product manager concept can be attributed to the direct responsibility and answerability which the system itself engenders. The product manager is a centre of information for planning. No single product is likely to be neglected because each manager has an obvious vested interest in obtaining the best possible level of resource support. With reference to overall product strategy, the product manager is uniquely placed as the firm's 'early warning system' giving information as to changes in the market which may require product adaptation, marketing mix modification or even the consideration of product deletion. Last, but not least, the job of the product or brand manager provides valuable experience and training to young men and women who aspire to higher managerial positions.

Despite these drawbacks the product management structure is popular and workable in companies whose product range is too diverse to be adequately serviced by a 'functional' type of marketing organization. Any risk can be further reduced if the company clearly delineates the product manager's responsibilities, is aware of potential areas of conflict and takes steps to reduce their number, and finally ensures that the methods used for assessment are consistent with the product manager's responsibilities and authority.

PRODUCT STRATEGY

Many companies, while not necessarily requiring brand and product managers, do market more than one product. This is especially true of firms operating in consumer goods markets. The fact that a company has more than one product necessitates that some method be devised for monitoring and comparing their respective performances, and for enabling decisions to be made about the future. The PLC concept illustrates that whatever the time span, the life of a product is temporary. With this in mind, the essence of product strategy is simple: the firm must manage the marketing of existing products, decide when products are of no further use and plan the development of new profit sources by providing new products to replace those that have been deleted.

In order that firms can organize for product planning, and that their products can be easily related to each other and to respective market areas, it is useful to consider products as a series of readily identifiable groups.

The first consideration is the *individual product*. This is any product considered as a separate entity irrespective of its relationship to other products and the type of market in which it is to be found. Provided that any product differs in some way from another, either through modification or market application, the firm can regard this as an individual product.

The sum total of the products offered for sale by a firm is referred to as the *product mix*.

Finally, those products that are related in some way to one another are classed as the *product line*. The relationship could be because they are simply different models of the same basic product, or because they have marketing similarities in that they are sold in similar outlets or serve the same customer groups.

It is common to attribute the product mix with 'width' and 'depth'. This enables an analysis of the consistency of the product mix to be made. The following example illustrates the idea of the product mix and product line, and forms the basic structure of analysis and selection of appropriate line strategies. A hypothetical example best illustrates this (Fig. 8.10).

A firm manufactures fountain pens, cigarette lighters and wrist watches. Each item is related in that they are marketed through similar channels and are targeted at approximately the same consumer segments.

The product mix represents the sum of the firm's products – in this case 30 products. The number of product lines is obviously three. 'Depth' refers to the number of products in each line – 9, 13 and 8 with the average depth being 10. 'Width' refers to the number of product lines which a company has to offer.

By looking at its products in this way, a company is able to begin to see where existing strengths and weaknesses lie. Is there scope for adding to the product line by adding, say, digital watches, to line 3? Do some products in the same line compete with each other? With respect to new products, will an addition to the line be consistent with its neighbours in terms of image, production, distribution and market segment? Conversely, is any one product so valuable in terms of image and reputation that its deletion will damage the product line or indeed the total mix? Finally, should the firm consider an addition to the width of the mix and will these be consistent with the existing product mix and compatible with the current long-term marketing strategy?

Mix analysis is also vital to a review of marketing strategy itself. The firm is merely a representation of its products and its marketing strategy. In the case of Personal Products Ltd the following are a few of the possible strategic options.

1. Augment product line by adding ball point pens. This would remove some measure of exclusivity and represent a strategy of being 'all things to people' – a bid to serve the whole market for ink-based writing implements.
2. Delete all but the most expensive men's lighters from line 2. This would have the effect of making the company a market specialist in men's lighters – aiming at an exclusive market segment.
3. Delete lines 1 and 2 and become a specialist in a single product line – wrist watches. In such a situation, options 1 and 2 would still be available to the company.
4. Delete all but one product and become expert in its marketing and production.
5. Add another product line. In the case of 'Personal Products Ltd' it could be that a new line of pens could be aimed at the designer or graphics market.

Some industrial companies become expert in supplying products for special situations, such as deep sea diving equipment. This represents a decision to reduce the product mix to its absolute minimum.

Given the existing product mix and the options available the company must begin to take product decisions which are in line with long-term strategy, and which are consistent with that mix. The introduction of ball point pens by Personal Products Ltd could influence the perception which the consumer has of the company as a whole. Cheaper disposable pens might not be consistent with the firm's reputation for high quality lighters. Similarly, the firm may be technically capable of producing an industrial line, but lacking in the marketing expertise required to serve this new market efficiently.

Analysis of the product mix thus questions every aspect of the company. Any decision has financial, technical, marketing and market connotations. The critical nature of product strategy becomes more apparent when one considers the consequences of failure and the necessity for success.

We must now consider ways in which the decision to choose any of the above options is made. First, we should remind ourselves of the absolute necessity of new products. If, at any time, the rate of new product development and launch is not equal or superior to the rate of product deletion or obsolescence, the company will lose profits rapidly and ultimately will be unable to survive. A long-term view of strategy must, therefore, be taken. Still keeping the product mix very much in mind, it is possible to look at the company's future from a more abstract viewpoint, which will stimulate and aid the long-term decision-making process.

The matrix shown in Fig. 8.11 presents all possible alternatives for fundamental product strategy. Of course, any decisions must be evaluated in relation to the company itself and to the market conditions which are prevalent and likely in the future. In the first case, a marketing audit is designed to establish whether the firm is currently making the best use of opportunities available in existing markets and for existing products. Market share and sales analysis should establish whether last year's objectives are being achieved, and a study of profitability by product, geographical area and market segment should be made. When an internal analysis has been completed, marketing research and intelligence systems should be brought to bear to examine whether or not any prepared action is feasible.

	Existing markets	New markets
Existing products	Improved performance Product performance Realignments of the marketing mix	New market segments Geographical expansion
New products	Same distribution channels, sales outlets and sales strategy	Diversification through innovation

Figure 8.11   A simple product strategy mix

Armed with knowledge of itself, and present and future markets, the company can address itself to the alternatives in Fig. 8.12 and go on to produce a plan for strategy realignment, new product development and possibly expansion.

Another variation of Fig. 8.11, ascribed to Ansoff, has already been provided in Chapter 4.

We now know that product strategy requires a thorough examination of the firm's own strengths and shortcomings, thorough market knowledge and an unequivocal commitment to new product development and thus long-term strategy. Product strategy must, logically, also involve methods for phasing out certain products to make way for new ones. Very often it is judicious to withdraw products from the mix long before the PLC has run its course, and such a decision is usually due to one or a combination of three reasons:

- A decrease in market share due to competitive pressure.
- A reduction in profitability which is deemed irreversible.
- A slowing down of sales growth which suggests that marketing resources might be better employed elsewhere.

Given available marketing information, both internal and external, and the existence of products in varying market conditions and stages of development, it is possible to classify the total product mix according to each product's potential usefulness to the company. Both the General Electric Company and the Boston Consulting Group (BCG) have devised a classification technique which does this by using a matrix which rates products according to sales growth and market

		Market share	
Market growth	High	1. Stars	3. Problem children (sometimes termed question marks)
	Low	2. Cash cows	4. Dogs
		High	Low

Figure 8.12   Product classification by sales growth and market share

share. Numerous variations on this theme exist and the matrix can easily be adapted to the needs of individual companies. Although the establishment of the rating scale can prove problematical, the concept itself is relatively simple, as can be seen from the explanation already provided in Chapter 4. To reiterate, the matrix is repeated in Fig. 8.12.

Similar matrices are also used in business portfolio analysis for multi-company corporations. The BCG's christening of each cell becomes apt as we examine the implications of the relative positions. In practice, each axis is sealed so that products can be precisely positioned according to the received marketing information.

Star products are highly profitable and the company should allocate sufficient resources so as to maintain market share.

Problem children may require a disproportionate amount of spending, relative to growth potential, in an effort to increase market share. Each case must be based on circumstances, but they are certainly candidates for divestment.

Cash cows, as the name suggests, are major sources of profit. Investment should equal that which is required to maintain market share: surplus profit can be used to finance 'stars'.

Dogs can either be 'profit milked' into decline, or deleted quickly so as to re-allocate resources.

Such techniques are designed to help optimize the product mix. The effect of deletion, for example, may be adverse to the consistency of the product mix. However, such matrices do offer formal procedures for considering deletion; a decision which should never be taken lightly, but which one should never hesitate to take after careful consideration.[10]

In summary, matrix analysis is a good method for organizing efficient resource allocation. It also helps to optimize the ratio of new product introduction to product deletion, and sets out objectives for each product.

CONCLUSIONS

This chapter has examined the product or service initially with a view to establishing what exactly the idea of a product or service is. The traditional, narrowly held belief, of a tangible item has been dispelled.

Product categorization has been investigated from the viewpoints of consumer and industrial goods and services.

New product development and its tactical and strategic implications have been viewed, followed by the product life-cycle concept and its practical use to marketing strategists. The adoption process was then explained as an idea to complement the PLC concept.

The management of products was posed through the 'product manager' organizational concept, as opposed to the traditional view of the organization of a marketing department.

Finally, the chapter examined product strategy matrices as vehicles through which product strategies could be formulated.

APPLICATION QUESTIONS

1. Define 'the product' in modern marketing terms. Give an example of a 'traditional' and 'modern' held view of a product (or service).
2. Explain and discuss the various product categorizations. What marketing approaches are normally associated with each?
3. Why is new product development so important to companies? Explain this with reference to the process of new product development.

4. How can the PLC concept be used as a tool for strategic marketing?
5. Explain the nature and role of product/brand management. Illustrate your answer with organizational structures most suited to different types of products and services.

REFERENCES

1. Levitt, T., *Differentiation of Anything. The Marketing Imagination*, Collier Macmillan, London, 1983, pp. 72–93.
2. Levitt, T., 'Marketing myopia', *Harvard Business Review*, **18**(1), July 1960.
3. Crimp, Margaret, *The Marketing Research Process*, Prentice-Hall, London, 1981.
4. 'Disastrous debuts – despite high hopes. Many new products flop in the market', *Wall Street Journal*, 23 March 1976.
5. Hofer, C. W. and D. Schendel, *Strategy Formulation – Analytical Concepts*, West Publishing Co, MN, 1978, p. 107.
6. Levitt, T., 'Exploit the product life cycle', *Harvard Business Review*, November–December 1965.
7. Dhalla, N. K. and S. Yspeh, 'Forget the product life cycle concept', *Harvard Business Review*, November–December 1965.
8. Levitt, T., 'Exploit the product life cycle', *Harvard Business Review*, November–December 1965.
9. McCarthy, E. J., 'Organization for new product development?', in: *Product Strategy and Management*, Thomas Libery and Abe Stuchman (eds), Holt, Rhinehart and Winston, New York, 1963, pp. 384–389.
10. Clayton, Henry, L., 'The pricing of sick products', *Management Accounting*, June 1966, pp. 17–18.

NINE
PRICING

INTRODUCTION

Following the discussion in Chapter 1 on the marketing concept, it is true to say that, in general, until the 1950s, price was considered to be one of the most important influences on buyer behaviour and choice. As a result of increasing competition, during the 1950s and 1960s non-price factors grew in importance with companies attempting to differentiate their products from competitors on the bases of branding, advertising and packaging. Increasing levels of inflation, particularly during the late 1970s, combined with decreased levels of real disposable income, have meant that competitive pricing has re-emerged as an extremely potent marketing tool. As a consequence many marketing managers are now of the opinion that price is, after the product, the most important element in the marketing mix.

This chapter covers the variety of approaches to making pricing decisions with an emphasis on the marketing approach to pricing. In order to understand and appreciate what represents this marketing approach to pricing, it is necessary to consider first the approach and contribution to pricing decisions of the economist and the accountant. In fact, in many companies, the final responsibility for making pricing decisions may, ultimately, rest outside of the marketing function. Of all the marketing mix decisions, pricing has the most obvious and clear-cut effect on company profit. Because of this, pricing is of central concern to all the managers in a company – not just marketing managers.

Given that it is logical to look first at the role which pricing plays in a company and in particular at the link between company and pricing objectives, against this background we can then consider the considerations or inputs to pricing decisions, including cost, demand and competitive considerations. Finally, we can consider pricing policies and procedures including the important aspects of quoting and changing prices.

THE ROLE OF PRICING

It is through pricing that a company covers the costs of separate elements of its various activities: research and development, raw materials, labour and administrative costs must, ultimately, all be recovered through the price charged to the customer. Marketing costs, too, must be covered by the final price of the product, including those costs incurred in promoting, selling and distributing the product. Last, but not least, the price charged for a product is required to generate additional funds in excess of those costs to meet company profit objectives. Thus pricing plays the following important roles:

1. Pricing fuses together the various elements of company activity necessary to fulfil customer requirements.
2. Pricing pays for their respective contributions to the final package offered to the customer.
3. To the extent that this package makes commercial sense in the marketplace, pricing generates residual profits in order to fulfil company objectives.

PRICING AS A STRATEGIC DECISION

It is sometimes asserted that compared to decisions about the other elements of the marketing mix – product, place and promotion – pricing decisions are relatively simple. For example, if we know the costs of producing and marketing a product, and, in addition, have specified a percentage amount which is to be added to these costs for profit we can 'easily' calculate the required selling price. Viewed in this way, pricing decisions become a matter of following simple rules or formulae. In addition, price is often viewed as being one of the most flexible elements of the marketing mix; that is, it can be readily changed to meet market conditions as and when required.

These notions about pricing are in fact based on a major misconception about pricing, namely that pricing decisions are tactical decisions. This is not to deny that short-term, tactical, price manoeuvres cannot – under certain conditions – be most effective, but pricing decisions are a strategic issue. This gives rise to the following implications:

1. Pricing decisions should be made in the context of overall marketing objectives and strategy.
2. Related to the above, pricing decisions should be related to, and be consistent with, the other elements of the marketing mix.
3. Care should be taken not to make price the overriding competitive factor. Alternatively, often more appropriate strategies for competing should not be neglected or ignored.
4. Pricing decisions should not become a matter of routine to be administered by the accounting department.
5. Pricing decisions should not place too much emphasis on cost inputs to the decision.

Some of these strategic implications of pricing are discussed more fully by Taylor and Wills, on pricing strategy[1] and in a recent text by Watkins.[2] It is useful to consider some of the basic approaches to pricing decisions before turning to its strategy and, in particular, the contributions of the economist and the accountant.

THE ECONOMIST AND PRICING DECISIONS

The classical economists have put forward a well-developed conceptual framework for the establishment of price levels. In fact for 150 years economists have regarded the price variable as being the most important factor in determining the level of demand. This strong, almost exclusive, emphasis on price has led to the economist neglecting the other elements of marketing effort such as advertising, product differentiation and selling efforts.

The classical economist suggests that prices should be set at that level which *maximizes short-term* profits. To maximize profit the notion of *marginal cost* and *marginal revenue* must be introduced.

– *Marginal cost* is the addition to total costs of producing one more unit of output.
– *Marginal revenue* is the addition to total revenue of selling one more unit of output.

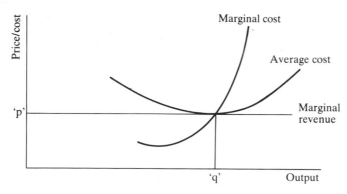

Figure 9.1 The economists' model of pricing in a competitive market

Using these concepts the following pricing rule can be derived from economists' models:

– Profits will be maximized when marginal revenue equals marginal cost.

This rule means that output should be set at a level which means a price where the marginal revenue from selling one more unit equals the addition to total cost of producing that unit. This position is illustrated in Fig. 9.1. At output 'q', marginal cost equals marginal revenue, the price required to sell this level of output is 'p'.

The marginal revenue curve is a function of the demand curve facing a company, which in turn is a function of the nature and extent of competition in the market. The revenue curve shown in Fig. 9.1 is that faced by a firm in a 'perfectly competitive' market structure and is a particular, and somewhat unrealistic, type of market structure where the nature of competition condemns the individual company to being a *price taker*. From this earliest model of market structure, economists have extended their analyses to take account of different, and more realistic, forms of market structure including markets which are characterized by product differentiation. Regardless of the type of market structure, however, the same decision rule for pricing decisions applies, i.e., prices or output are set so as to equate marginal cost with marginal revenue. For a fuller description of the economists' model, readers are advised to consult a good basic textbook on economics, for example R. G. Lipsey's *An Introduction to Positive Economics*.[3]

This model of price setting is appealing in that it suggests such a clear-cut decision rule for the price setter. Nevertheless, the economists' price maximizing theory has substantial shortcomings. In particular:

1. The assumption of the objective of profit maximizing: undoubtedly profits do figure very prominently in company objectives. Only by being profitable is the firm able to pay dividends to shareholders, generate the cash flow necessary to provide working capital and be attractive enough to potential investors when further capital is required. In practice, few, if any, companies set objectives in terms of profit maximization – much less do they even achieve it. Indeed, for most companies, profit objectives are couched in terms of a certain level of profitability, or return on investment (ROI). More specifically, the providers of the investment capital in a company are less interested in the absolute level of profit earned than in the percentage rate of return which they receive on their investment.
2. The assumption that price is the only factor determining the level of demand for a company's product: one only has to compare this assumption with what is known about the tools of marketing to see how restrictive this statement is.

3. The assumption that cost, and more particularly demand functions, can be measured with sufficient accuracy to be sure that the point of profit maximizing has been reached.
4. The implicit assumption that in making pricing decisions one can ignore the trade, i.e., channels of distribution.
5. The assumption that price is set independently of the other variables in the marketing mix.
6. The assumption that the customer attempts to maximize satisfaction with respect to price alone.

These shortcomings in the economist's model are sufficient to render it of little value to the marketing decision maker. Despite this, the model does point to one important consideration in practical price setting; namely, *the importance of demand*. We shall return to this important contribution of the economist later in this chapter.

THE ACCOUNTANT AND PRICING DECISIONS

In contrast to the economist's focus on demand, the accountant's approach to pricing is often one based essentially on costs. Such an emphasis on costs is perhaps not surprising coming from a function which often has responsibility for their determination and control. A variety of approaches to cost-based pricing have been developed by companies. For example, a simple, and, therefore, popular method of setting prices is to calculate the total costs of producing a product or service and add to this total cost a set percentage for profit. This *cost-plus*, or *full-cost* pricing as it is variously termed, is justified on a number of bases. First, as previously suggested, it is relatively simple. Second, it is argued that pricing in this way ensures that a known and pre-specified level of profit is attained, with all costs being covered. Finally, it is argued that cost-plus pricing is 'fair' both to trade and final customers. In fact, like the economist's profit maximizing model, this deceptively simple approach to pricing too has significant shortcomings. In particular:

1. Total costs are usually arrived at by calculating the variable cost per unit and adding to this an allocation of a proportion of the total fixed costs. Total fixed costs are calculated on an assumption of either a standard volume or a forecast level of output. Both the calculation of total fixed costs and the methods of allocating this total between products give rise to serious problems when using this method of pricing. For example, clearly the amount of fixed costs which will be added to each product, and consequently the price, depends upon the number of products produced. In turn, the number of products which a firm will produce will, ignoring stockholding, be a function of how many it can sell. How many will be sold, in turn, depends upon the price charged. Pricing in this way then is nonsensical; it means that for a given production capacity, if a company finds that it is selling less, and thus cuts its production, its market prices will need to increase. This, in turn, will probably lead to fewer sales, a further cut-back in production and even higher prices. To say the least, this is an unsatisfactory state of affairs.
2. A second major disadvantage with full-cost pricing is that strict adherence to a full-cost pricing policy can permit certain marketing opportunities to be passed by because the price which the customer is willing or able to pay does not cover the full cost.

Clearly then, there are problems if we base pricing decisions on total costs plus a margin for profit. In fact we can go further and say that costs generally should not be used to determine prices. This being the case, what role do costs play in pricing decisions and what contribution can cost information from the accountancy function play? Among the key roles which information on costs plays in pricing decisions are those which are concerned with the *evaluative* rather than decision-making role of such information; in particular it enables a company to:

– measure the profit contribution of individual selling transactions;
– determine the most profitable products, customers, or market segments;
– evaluate the effect on profits of changes in volume;
– determine if a product can be made and sold profitably at any price.

In order to fulfil these evaluative functions, it is important that the marketing manager has access to *accurate* and *relevant* information on costs.

Accurate cost information allows a company to identify costs on a very specific basis directly related to each product, activity, customer, etc. In this way management is able to make *informal* decisions about volume mix and pricing to target market segments.

Relevant cost information is information which is presented and analysed in such a way as to be pertinent and useful in decision making. In particular, the cost analysis should enable the marketer to distinguish between *fixed* and *variable* costs and the relationship between those and volume. Such a cost analysis and its usefulness is perhaps best illustrated in the use of *break-even analysis*. A simple break-even chart is shown in Fig. 9.2.

Fixed costs are those costs which do not vary with the level of output and are, therefore, represented by the horizontal fixed cost curve in Fig. 9.2. Variable costs, on the other hand, are those costs which are more or less directly related to production or sales. Increases in output or sales will lead to a proportional increase in those costs with any decrease leading to an overall reduction of variable costs. Taken together, of course, fixed and variable costs combine to give total costs as shown in Fig. 9.2. The remaining information contained in a break-even chart is the revenue curve. This shows the total revenue which will accrue to the company at a given price-quantity combination.

The break-even point is normally represented as that level of output where the total revenue from sales of a product or service matches exactly the total costs of its production and marketing (beq in Fig. 9.2). Such an analysis of cost/revenue relationships can be very useful to the pricing decision maker.

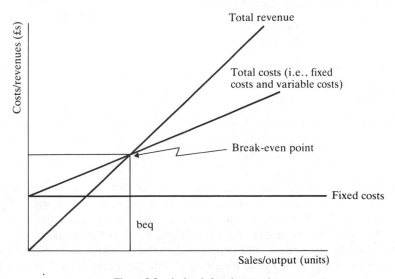

Figure 9.2   A simple break-even chart

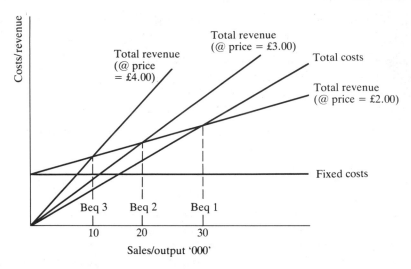

Figure 9.3   Break-even versus price (not to scale)

One use of break-even analysis is to compare the break-even points associated with different prices for a product. Again, a simplified example of this is shown in Fig. 9.3.

The effect of charging a higher price is to steepen the total revenue curve and as a consequence lower the break-even quantity. The pricing decision maker can then assess the effect of charging different prices in terms of what these different prices and break-even points mean to the company. Specifically, the information given by a break-even chart is:

– profit or losses at varying levels of output;
– break-even points at varying levels of price;
– effect on break-even point and profits or losses if costs change.

Break-even points can also be calculated using the following simple procedure:

Selling price − Variable cost = Contribution

$$\text{Break-even quantity} = \frac{\text{Fixed Costs}}{\text{Contribution}}$$

e.g.,   Selling price   = £10
        Variable cost   = £5
        Fixed costs   = £100 000

Contribution = £10 − £5 = £5
∴ Beq
$$= \frac{100\,000}{5} = 20\,000 \text{ units}$$

The notion of *contribution* is also a valuable addition to the price maker's armoury. It illustrates that, in the short run at least, it may pay a company to sell a product at a price which is *less than the full cost* of producing it. Remember that fixed costs are those costs which do not vary with the level of output. If a company produces and sells nothing it will still incur these costs. At any price over and above the variable cost of producing each product, then, the company is receiving a contribution to those fixed costs. In the long run, of course, a company must cover all its costs through the price it sets on its products.

There is no doubt that break-even analysis, and the distinction between fixed and variable costs (and therefore contribution) on which it is based, is of much greater relevance to the price setter than is the simple provision of total costs implied by the cost-plus approach. Nevertheless, one should note that once again its relevance is still more of an evaluative rather than prescriptive one in terms of price setting. This is because it is still cost, rather than demand based. The total revenue curve in the break-even chart illustrates only the total revenue which would be received if we sell any given price/quantity combination. It is not, however, a demand curve. That is to say, it does not indicate the actual quantity which will be sold at any given price.

It is clear that neither the economist's model of price setting, nor the accountant's contribution of cost information, is in itself a sufficient basis on which to determine prices. Nevertheless, taken together, they do point to a clear-cut and universal presumption for delineating pricing decisions which can be incorporated into a more realistic and marketing-oriented approach to pricing.

THE MARKETER AND PRICING DECISIONS

Notwithstanding the shortcomings of their approach to pricing, both the economist and the accountant have provided useful, if partial, insights into this area of the marketing mix. Specifically, we can take the economist's notion of demand, and the accountant's emphasis on costs and incorporate them into the following prescription:

– The upper limit to the price of a product (or service) is determined by *demand*. Therefore, this price should not exceed what the market will bear. Put another way, the price of a product (or service) should not exceed the value of its benefit to the buyer.
– In the long run the price should not fall below the costs of making and distributing the product (or service).

Demand and costs, then, can be likened to the two blades of a pair of scissors as shown in Fig. 9.4.

This notion of demand and costs as determinants of upper and lower limits is important in a wider context than that of simply pricing decisions. You will note that the gap between the blades in Fig. 9.4 gives the marketing decision maker some discretion on pricing decisions. If there is no gap, then there is no profit and hence no discretion. A company can widen the gap between the blades in two ways:

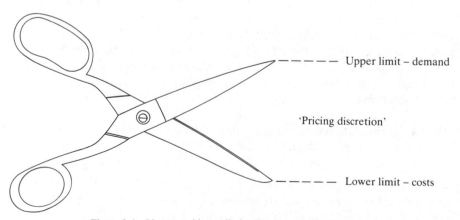

Upper limit – demand

'Pricing discretion'

Lower limit – costs

Figure 9.4   Upper and lower limits to price: pricing discretion

1. It can reduce its costs, through improved manufacturing, greater efficiency, etc.
2. It can increase the perceived value of the benefits of its market offerings to the buyer.

The greater part of a company's marketing efforts is, or should be, aimed at the second of these. As far as is possible, effective marketing should 'desensitize' the customer to price. Unless the company is able and prepared to weather losses, price competition is the lowest form of competition. In order to be effective, competing primarily on price requires that rather stringent conditions be met, namely:

– Sales volume must be much more sensitive to price changes than to changes in other elements of the marketing mix, e.g., advertising, salesforce, products, etc.
– Price advantages should be based on definite cost advantages that will not be easily lost over a period of time: for example, when based on new and superior (patented) technology, or where barriers to entry are high.

In addition to cost and demand considerations the marketing manager must consider the other elements of the marketing mix and the company's generic marketing strategy when considering pricing decisions. Similarly, the marketer's approach to pricing is characterized by a recognition of the need to consider a wide range of factors which will affect the pricing discretion and the eventual choice of a price level. Some of the more important of these factors are summarized below.

Input to, and considerations in, marketing pricing decisions

– Costs.
– Demand.
– Company and marketing objectives/resources.
– Competition/market structure.
– Social/legal aspects.
– Distribution/trade.
– Other factors.

Each of these is considered in turn.

Costs We have already seen how costs play an important role in pricing decisions. In addition, we have counselled against using costs alone to set prices. Nevertheless, costs do constitute the lower blade of the pricing decision and the cost structure of the firm must be considered when setting prices. With respect to pricing generally, it is useful to consider three measures of the cost structure of the firm: the ratio of fixed to variable costs; the relationship between costs and volume; and the costs of a firm relative to its competitors. Techniques such as break-even analysis, outlined earlier, and accurate and relevant cost information are extremely useful in the delineation and evaluation of price decisions.

Demand We have stressed that demand constitutes the upper blade of the scissors of pricing decisions. We cannot charge prices higher than those which the market will bear. Ideally, the price maker would like information bearing in mind the following two interrelated questions:

– What will be the quantity demanded at any given price?
– What will be the effect on sales volume of changes in price?

What we are discussing here can perhaps best be explained with the help of a simple diagram.

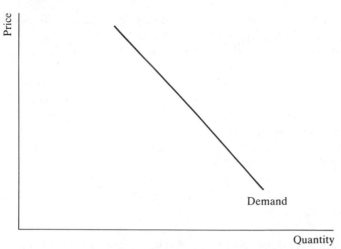

Figure 9.5   A simple demand curve

Figure 9.5 shows a simple demand curve. Even this simple demand curve contains a substantial amount of information which is extremely useful for pricing decisions. In particular, it allows the company to ascertain the relation between the price charged and the resulting level of demand. As Kotler suggests,[4] normally demand and price are inversely related, i.e., the lower the price, the greater the demand.

The slope of the curve in Fig. 9.5 also indicates how sensitive demand is to price changes, i.e., it indicates what the effect on quantity demanded will be for any given change in price. We normally refer to this as *price elasticity* of demand. It is important to distinguish between the demand curve for the industry as a whole and that faced by the individual company. Ideally we would like information on both.

Formally, price elasticity of demand can be calculated as follows:

$$\text{Price elasticity of demand} = \frac{\text{Percentage change in quantity demanded}}{\text{Percentage change in price}}$$

Measures of price elasticity commonly range through:

$e < 1$ – *Relatively price inelastic* – a change in price results in a less than proportionate change in quantity demanded.

$e = 1$ – *Unit price elasticity* – a given change in price results in an equal proportionate change in quantity demanded.

$e > 1$ – *Relatively price elastic* – a change in price results in a more than proportionate change in quantity demanded.

Useful though this information may be, in practice the relationship between demand and price, and, therefore, estimates of price elasticity, are difficult to ascertain and interpret. In particular, you should note the following considerations.

In markets where suppliers are able to *differentiate* their products from those of competitors, sales volume for the individual company is a function of:

– the total marketing effort of that company, i.e., marketing mix; and
– the marketing efforts of competitors.

It is difficult to appraise the impact of our price policy upon sales without analysing the entire marketing mix relative to the marketing mix of our competitors.

Price sensitivity may be expected to differ between individual customers and/or groups of customers.

Taken together, differentiated 'products' and differences in price sensitivity mean that the price sensitivity of demand confronting a company is influenced by the choice of market segment and the extent to which prices are congruent with the *total marketing effort* to these segments.

In analysing demand it is necessary to examine the *buyer's perception of value* as the key to pricing decisions. Essentially, that involves appraising the benefits sought by customers, these benefits being reflected in their buying criteria.

This enables a company to select the most appropriate market targets and then to develop a marketing mix for those targets with a particular marketing positioning in mind with respect to price, quality, service, etc.

Company and marketing objectives/resources We have already stressed that all marketing decisions, including pricing decisions, need to reflect and be consistent with overall company and marketing objectives. A company with an objective of a minimum of 20 per cent return on investment based on rapid market penetration may well require a different pricing strategy to that which is seeking only a 10 per cent ROI and a relatively small rate of market growth. Effectively, therefore, the selection of company objectives, market targets and the formulation of a marketing mix, serve to constrain or delimit the range of appropriate pricing strategies and specific price levels. A particularly good illustration of this delineating of price decisions is contained in Oxenfeldt's 'Multi-stage' approach to pricing.[5] The essence of Oxenfeldt's approach is as follows:

1. The selection of market targets The company's size, location, existing distributional arrangements, contracts with suppliers, customers and creditors, its reputation and past history will influence to a large extent the type of product the company can make, the service it can offer, and its probable costs, and will determine the market that the company can command, and the segments of that market that it should attempt to cultivate. It must identify where its strengths and weaknesses lie.

2. The selection of a brand image The image of a company or brand can have considerable bearing on the price that the company can charge, and will influence the type of customer that the company can attract. Most companies will be constrained by the image they have already built up. Thus to a large extent, steps 1 and 2 are totally interdependent.

3. The formulation of a marketing mix The marketing mix (of advertising, promotion, selling, distribution, product, etc.) must be selected that can help to reinforce the desired brand image. The direction or emphasis of this marketing mix will be limited by the target market and the brand image.

4. The selection of a pricing policy Oxenfeldt uses the term 'policy' to refer to overall pricing strategy, and suggests that the company should establish in advance a policy for dealing with general pricing conditions, answering such questions as:

- 'Do we price above or below the market average?'
- 'Who are our competitors on price?'
- 'Should we change price to meet competitors' price changes, and how quickly?'

– 'Do we vary prices or aim for stability?'
– 'Do we run price promotions?'

Thus pricing policy deals with recurring pricing problems, and tries to anticipate answers in advance.

5. Establish a pricing strategy Oxenfeldt uses the term 'strategy' to refer to the tactics that would be used to cope with unusual or irregular market conditions, such as:

– a change in legislation;
– a massive price reduction by a competitor;
– a radical fall-off in demand;
– a new entrant to the market.

All of which might call for some pricing action as a counter-measure.

6. The selection of a specific price The previous five steps will have narrowed down the choice of a final price to a fairly small price zone. The cost and revenue implications of various prices within this restricted range can be compared, elasticity within the range studied, etc. If the five steps leave no freedom of choice, then break-even analysis can be used to determine whether the demand that could be generated by that price would be profitable or not.

Company resources too, and particularly cash resources, must be considered in setting prices. For example, a decision to undercut competitors' prices is often a substantial drain on cash resources and should only be considered if a company can afford to sustain such a pricing approach.

Competition/market structure Companies in differing product markets find themselves faced with varying degrees of competition. Some markets are characterized by large numbers of competitors, whereas others may comprise of relatively few companies competing for the same customers. The number of competitors affects pricing decisions in the following ways:

– Where there are many competitors selling similar or identical products, competition on price will be severe.
– When there is only one supplier that supplier can establish his own price, within the constraints of government legislation.

Between these two extremes are those market structures which more often characterize the market economy. The first of these is a market structure where there are relatively few competitors and where often one or two dominant firms emerge which set the lead in determining prices in the industry. In turn, smaller less dominant firms in the industry determine their price levels in relation to those determined by these price leaders. The second type of market structure frequently encountered, is one in which although there is a large number of competitors, firms in the industry attempt to escape from severe competition on price by differentiating their market offerings through advertising, quality and product features.

In addition to current competitors the company must also consider the relative ease with which *new competitors* are able to enter the market.

Social/legal aspects Legal and social considerations are also inputs to the pricing decision. Much of the legislation which pertains to trading practices and consumer protection relates to price setting and pricing practices. Very few marketing managers are legal experts in this area, nor indeed can they be expected to be. Nevertheless, the variety of legal and social issues confronting the marketing manager today means that they must be treated as an additional input in the pricing decision.

Distribution/trade We must not forget that most companies market their products via middlemen in the channels of distribution. For this reason marketing management must consider how this will affect pricing decisions. For example, do we set prices with the final consumer in mind or do we set them with distributors in mind? What control, if any, do we have over the final price which our distributor, perhaps a retailer, will eventually put on our products? What quantity discounts and what credit terms are we willing to extend to our distributors? . . . etc. Such considerations may serve to complicate what is already a difficult decision area, but they are considerations with which the price setter must contend whenever he is dealing with distributors or the trade.

Other factors The above are some of the main considerations in pricing decisions. In addition, the decision maker may have to consider many other factors in setting prices. Some of these factors might be company specific. For example, a supplier of products to the National Health Service may be involved in a system of tendering prices and may need to consider the policies and procedures of local authorities. Other factors may become important to the pricing decision as a result of unexpected changes in the company's market environment. For example, a major supplier might suddenly increase the prices of his raw materials; political events may cause commodity or energy prices to change as currency exchange rates fluctuate.

Psychology can also play a part in pricing, particularly at retail levels. This accounts for prices like 99 pence, £1.99, £9.99 and so on, because one penny more represents a psychological barrier. There are also psychological price brackets at work in which consumers are 'conditioned' to realize that goods falling within such brackets represent 'value for money'. Prices outside such brackets may infer that the goods are inferior or over-priced. It is well known that pricing goods or services cheaply, perhaps through mechanistic cost-plus procedures, can often be as bad as pricing too expensively.

PRICING METHODS, PRICING POLICIES AND PROCEDURES

Because of the wide range of possible factors which need to be taken into account in pricing, and because of the fact that their relative importance will vary from company to company, the marketing manager needs to be wary of adopting admittedly much simpler but possibly less effective heuristic pricing methods. Full cost, or cost-plus pricing is one example of such a pricing method but there are many others, for example, 'going-rate' pricing or 'target pricing'. Whatever the specific method used to set prices, it helps reduce the complexity of pricing decisions considerably if a company establishes a framework of pricing policy and procedures after due consideration of some of the factors outlined above.

A policy framework for pricing decisions should include processes and procedures covering the following areas:

1. *Pricing and company objectives*: this should cover the role of pricing in relation to company objectives viewed as a set of targets with respect to, e.g., return on investment, market share, etc.
2. *The role of price in marketing strategy*: this should delineate the major policy objectives for pricing in terms of its role in marketing. The policy should cover the extent to which price will

be used to compete in the marketplace *vis-à-vis* the other element of the mix and market targets.

3. *Procedures and methods for determining specific pricing levels*: this should specify how specific prices shall be set on products and services and the considerations in such decisions, e.g., costs, demand, competition, etc. This part of pricing policy should also allocate responsibilities, i.e., who is to be involved in pricing decisions and on what basis.

4. *The administration of price changes*: in addition to setting prices, a company must also consider its procedures and policies with respect to administering and implementing price changes. The need to change prices may, of course, result from a number of factors including increased costs, changed demand, etc. It is important that a system be established such that price changes are implemented effectively and efficiently. Also, care needs to be taken that frequent, short-term, price changes are not detracting from the long-run overall pricing objectives determined earlier.

5. *Policies and procedures on credit, discounts, etc.*: in addition to pricing levels and price changes, we should not forget that credit policies and procedures for offering discounts for quantity and/or early payments are important facets of pricing policy.

SPECIAL ISSUES IN PRICING DECISIONS

So far in this chapter we have outlined and discussed the factors which need to be considered in making any pricing decision. Having said this some categories of pricing decisions do give rise to certain problems and issues which deserve special attention. Two of the more important of these categories are: 'product-line pricing', and pricing to account for stages in the product life cycle.

Product-line pricing

The majority of companies produce and market not one but a variety of products and services. Provided that neither the costs nor the demand for a range of products are interrelated, decisions on the price of each product may be made independently. Where, as is usual, this is not the case we must, at the very least, consider the possible effect of these interrelationships on our pricing decisions. In particular we must consider establishing product-line pricing strategies. The meaning of interrelated demand and costs plus an outline of possible alternative product-line pricing strategies are detailed below.

Interrelated demand Products are interrelated in demand when the price (or some other element of the marketing mix) of one affects the demand for the other, in either a positive or negative way.

Interrelated costs Two products are interrelated in cost when a change in the production of one affects the cost of the other.

Alternative product-line pricing strategies
1. Prices proportional to full cost, i.e., same net profit margin for all products.
2. Prices proportional to marginal cost, i.e., same percentage profit margin over marginal cost (contribution).
3. Prices proportional to conversion cost or 'value added'. Conversion cost is found by subtracting purchased material costs from the allocated full costs.
4. Prices that produce the same degree of contribution margins dependent upon conditions of demand in differing segments.

5. Prices related to target market requirements such as to yield an overall required rate of return from the product mix.

1, 2 and 3 are dependent upon cost and ignore demand; 4 and 5 are more adequate. These are based on the criterion that prices should reflect the demand relationships existing between products in the line to yield the required return on average assets employed.

Pricing and the product life cycle

As we have seen pricing decisions are not once-and-for-all decisions; they need to reflect changing competitive and market factors.

One of the factors that is suggested to affect the pricing decision is the stage of a product in its life cycle. In Chapter 8 we classified these stages as:

– Introduction
– Growth
– Maturity, and
– Decline.

The suggestion is that each stage may require, or be best fitted to, a particular set of marketing strategies and marketing mix combinations, including, of course, price. For example, in the case of pricing *new products* at the introduction stage of the life cycle we may distinguish between, for example:

– *Selective penetration strategy* High price/low promotion often referred to as market skimming, with the price being lowered at successive stages in time as the product achieves larger sales; and
– *Pre-emptive penetration strategy* Low price/heavy promotion.

The strategy selected at this stage then has clear implications for pricing.

Similarly, research indicates that market response to the different elements of the marketing mix may change over the life cycle of a product.[6]

Clearly, then, we must reflect these considerations in a dynamic pricing policy.

CONCLUSIONS

In this chapter we have considered the role of pricing decisions in overall company and marketing strategies. We started by exploring a number of popular misconceptions about pricing: misconceptions which mitigate against effective strategic pricing.

Before considering how the marketing manager might approach pricing decisions we looked at the approaches of the economist and the accountant. Despite limitations in each of their approaches we saw that both contribute a number of useful concepts and techniques. In particular, the economist helps by stressing the importance of demand – the upper limit to pricing discretion, and the accountant contributes to our knowledge and recognition of the importance of cost – the lower limit. With these upper and lower limits in mind we then examined a variety of other important inputs to the pricing decision, inputs which the marketer must include if he is to arrive at sensible pricing strategies. In addition to demand and cost inputs, the marketer must also consider, in particular, company and marketing objectives, company resources, competition and market structure, social and legal aspects, and middlemen, in addition to a number of other factors according to the circumstances.

The need to consider this number of factors makes it important that a company should establish a framework of pricing policies and procedures to include, for example, pricing and company objectives, pricing and marketing strategy, procedures and methods for setting specific prices, price changes, credit and discount policy.

Finally, we looked at special issues in pricing decisions and, in particular, at the additional problems posed when pricing in a multi-product company and when considering setting prices for products in the different stages of their life cycle.

APPLICATION QUESTIONS

1. Why are pricing decisions strategic and what misconceptions detract from this strategic role for pricing?
2. (a) What does the economist contribute to the pricing decision?
   (b) What does the accountant contribute to the pricing decision?
3. How does the marketer's approach to pricing differ from both that of the economist and the accountant?
4. What factors should be encompassed in a system of pricing policies and procedures?
5. What special pricing problems are posed
   (a) in product-line pricing?
   (b) in pricing to take account of the stage a product is at in its life cycle?

REFERENCES

1. Taylor, B. and G. Wills, *Pricing Strategy*, Staples Press, 1969.
2. Watkins, T., *The Economics of the Brand*, McGraw-Hill, London, 1986, pp. 41–85.
3. Lipsey, R. G., *An Introduction to Positive Economics*, 6th edn, Weidenfeld & Nicolson, London, 1983.
4. Kotler, P., *Marketing Management: Analysis, Planning and Control*, 5th edn, Prentice-Hall, London, 1984, pp. 508–509.
5. Oxenfeldt, A. R., 'A decision making structure for price decisions', *Journal of Marketing*, **37**, January 1973.
6. Kotler, P., op cit., pp. 362–372.

TEN

CHANNELS OF DISTRIBUTION

INTRODUCTION

In this chapter we shall be examining the routes by which the marketer of products and services can ensure that these reach his intended market. We normally refer to these routes as *marketing channels* which include those intermediaries through which products and services pass from the point of production to point of intermediate and final use.

In the first part of the chapter we shall concentrate on the development and structure of marketing channels; we shall find that this area of marketing is in fact among the most dynamic, being characterized by increasingly rapid technological and market change. Within marketing channels in the United Kingdom this change is particularly marked in the area of retailing. Not only is the structure of retailing in the UK undergoing a period of rapid evolution but increasingly this is being accompanied by innovations in technology which threaten to change the face of shopping as we know it. The modern marketer must adapt to and plan for these changes. Increasingly, the company which fails to take account of this changing structure will find itself at a disadvantage in the marketplace.

This first part of the chapter also explains the place of marketing channels in the marketing mix. The marketing manager needs to appreciate the various types of channel intermediaries, their role and function. Here, again, we shall find that these roles and functions are themselves changing. Against this background of evolving and changing channels of distribution we shall examine the use and limitations of the once much vaunted 'wheel of retailing' hypothesis in order to assess the extent to which the hypothesis is relevant to marketing decision making in this important area of the mix. With this as a background the second part of the chapter looks at the management of channels from the point of view of the marketing decision maker. Here we shall find that channel decisions are among the most important of the marketing decisions made by a company and are therefore strategic rather than tactical.

If channel design and choice are strategic considerations the manager must also devote sufficient attention to the implementation and control of these strategies. Individual middlemen must be encouraged to act for the company and their activities must be monitored and assessed. Thought needs to be given to the minimizing of possible channel conflict and the achievement of maximum cooperation both within and between the variety of channel members.

Finally, in this chapter we shall look at how the concept of what constitutes the 'place' element of marketing has widened in recent years to include the management of physical distribution and logistics.

THE DEVELOPMENT OF CHANNELS OF DISTRIBUTION

It is a fact that today most producers do not sell directly to the final users. Instead, the majority of goods and services move from producer to user through a series of intermediaries or 'middlemen' who perform a variety of functions. Collectively, these intermediaries and the institution of which they form a part, are variously referred to as trade, marketing, or as we shall term them here, *distribution channels*. Bucklin[1] offers the following definition of a channel of distribution:

> A channel of distribution comprises a set of institutions which performs all of the activities utilized to move a product and its title from production to consumption.

In discussing the development of channels, a basic question must be why are they used at all? Or, put another way, why don't all producers themselves sell directly to the consumer? Some, of course, do, but as we have seen the majority do not. There are a variety of reasons for this.

One reason is simply that many producers lack the necessary skills and resources to perform all the activities referred to in Bucklin's definition. Figures 10.1 and 10.2, together, illustrate this.

Figure 10.1 would seem to indicate that the exchange relationship between producer and user is essentially very simple. Goods and services are provided to the final user who in return for them passes back money to the provider. In fact, as shown in Fig. 10.2, today's business transactions are often characterized by a diverse range of complex and interacting activities which are required in order to facilitate the process of exchange. As McGarry[2] points out, a number of

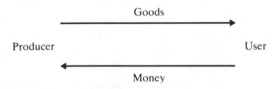

Figure 10.1   A simple system of exchange

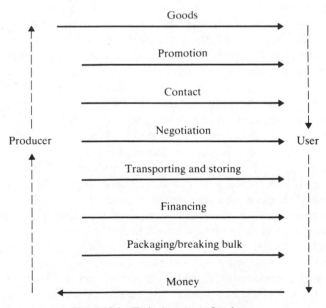

Figure 10.2   Today's system of exchange

functions are necessary to bridge the time, place and possession gaps that separate producer and user. For example, a consumer may require to see the product before he commits himself to purchase. This may require that adequate display facilities are made available for the potential end-user. An individual producer may lack the necessary financial and skill resources to make such a facility available on a national basis.

Similarly, the end-user may require that a variety of products be made available to him at one geographical location. Imagine, for a moment, how much more complex, time consuming and frustrating it would be if the shopper had to purchase sugar at one retail outlet, jam at another, soap at another and so on. It has long been a key function of middlemen to transform what Alderson[3] has referred to as 'heterogeneous mixtures' (of products) into 'meaningful assortments'.

A further, if connected, reason for the function of channels of distribution has been the increasing separation of the producer from his end-users. The households which purchase goods and services are not only separated geographically from producers, but the households themselves are often geographically dispersed. This dispersion, both at a national and an international level, has led to the growth of intermediaries who can bridge this spatial gap between producer and user.

Finally, the growth of channels of distribution is linked to the growth in complexity in industry itself, and in particular the increase in specialization. For example, the mining company extracts bauxite and from it produces aluminium. This aluminium is sold to a can manufacturer. The can manufacturer sells his product to the food processing company. The food processing company sells its canned products to the wholesaler who in turn sells to the retailer. Finally, the retailer sells the food in aluminium cans made from the bauxite to the housewife. Industry, today, is comprised of a vertical chain of extractive, manufacturing and service companies often each specializing in one part of the conversion process. This specialization gives rise to what might be referred to as 'breaks' in the industrial conversion process, and it is these break points that the institutions and individuals that comprise channels of distribution have stepped in to bridge.

We can see from these reasons for the growth of channels of distribution, that they play a very important role not only in the marketing mix of the individual company but in an economy as a whole. In fact at this second, macro level, channels of distribution can be said to form part of the marketing system of a country and, therefore, of the individual firm. As Howard points out,[4] a marketing system is for a total economy, it being the *means* by which all of the goods and services flow to the end-user from the different stages of manufacture and all of the funds flow in the reverse direction. An effective and efficient system of distribution, therefore, is essential to the well-being of an economy and the individual units which comprise it. Having said this, and notwithstanding the reason discussed for the development of distribution channels, there is no *a priori* reason why the functions performed by channels of distribution should not be performed by individual companies. In fact, the only economic justification for a company or a society entrusting these functions, or at least some of them, to middlemen is if they perform them more effectively and efficiently than would otherwise be achieved. Figure 10.3 illustrates more specifically how using intermediaries can contribute in this respect.

Without a middleman each producer must contact all four customers. Therefore, 12 contacts are required for every producer's product to reach every customer. Including a retailer cuts the number of contacts down to only seven, and in fact each producer need only make one contact to the retailer in order to reach all the prospective customers. Even this much simplified example illustrates how channel intermediaries can bring economic benefits both to the individual company and to the economic system as a whole. The example should also serve to dispel a widely held, but frequently misplaced, view that middlemen are economic 'parasites'. This view stems

(a) No middleman

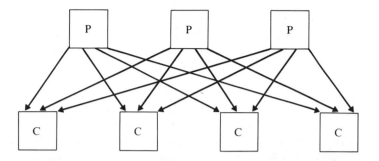

P = Producer
C = Customer
Number of contacts = 3 × 4 = 12

(b) With a middleman

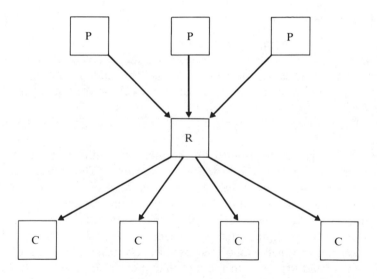

P = Producer
C = Customer
R = Retailer
Number of contacts = 3 + 4 = 7

Figure 10.3   How the middleman can contribute to efficiency

from the misconception that middlemen add nothing to benefit, but serve only to increase costs. Not only can middlemen substantially reduce the final cost to the consumer but, in addition, they add to the utility which the customer derives from products by means of, for example, variety, convenience, after-sales service, information, etc.

ELEMENTS OF CHANNELS OF DISTRIBUTION

It has already been shown in Chapter 4 that channel decisions constitute the 'place' element of the marketing mix. In ensuring that his or her products and services are available at the right time, in the right place and in the right quantities, the marketing manager is making decisions about distribution. Specifically, a company must decide the type of channel it will use to reach its target markets; it must select, recruit and organize channel intermediaries, and it must decide on stock levels, delivery modes and times. These aspects of decision making, channel strategies, channel choice and logistics, are considered in more detail later in this chapter. In order to make these decisions the marketing manager must understand the elements of channels of distribution. For example, the marketing manager must understand the various *dimensions* of channel structure, and, in particular, the *variety of channel types* which these dimensions give rise to. He or she should also be familiar with the *different sorts of channel intermediaries* or *middlemen*; their roles and relative advantages and disadvantages. Finally, the marketing manager must understand and appreciate the implication of the *dynamic and changing nature* of marketing channels.

Dimensions of channel structure

Channels of distribution are extremely complex marketing structures and we can examine their components in a variety of ways and from a variety of angles. Nevertheless, one or two key characteristics of channel structure are associated with the 'personality' of a particular channel and are therefore associated with differences between various channels. One of these key characteristics is *channel length*.

Figure 10.4 illustrates several alternative channels of distribution distinguished primarily by channel length.

Clearly, channel length is determined by the number of different intermediaries through which a product passes *en route* from producer to consumer. The shortest channels are those where no intermediaries are involved, i.e., the producer deals directly with the final consumer. One might be tempted to suppose that the most effective channels are those which involve fewer intermediaries and preferably none at all, i.e., direct marketing. Certainly, as we shall shortly see, direct marketing has grown in importance and there are distinct advantages to both producer and consumer of keeping channels as short as possible. Nevertheless, our discussion of why intermediaries are used, should alert one to the fact that shorter channels are not invariably more effective and efficient. Remember that the justification for using intermediaries is that they can perform certain functions more efficiently than can the producer. In the long run, and certainly in a free market economy, competitive forces and the profit incentive will tend to lead towards that

1. Producer→Consumer

2. Producer→Wholesaler→Consumer

3. Producer→Wholesaler→Retailer→Consumer

Figure 10.4   Channel length

length of channel which is most efficient under the circumstances. Circumstances here would include, for example, factors such as type of product, number of customers, geographical dispersion of customers, variety required by customer, type and range of services required, etc. Of course, this is not to say that the length of marketing channels for established product markets has arrived at the optimum: the optimum length is likely to change, and as we shall see, the role of some intermediaries has diminished considerably in marketing certain products. Nor should we assume that what is the appropriate length of channel for one company is identical for another company in the same industry. As with all other marketing decisions, decisions about channel length are company specific.

A second key aspect of channel structure concerns the *relationship between channel members* and, in particular, the relationships which pertain to the locus of power and decision making in the channel structure. This, again, is an area of channel structure which has seen significant changes over the past few years. Today, three broad types of channel structure can be identified on the basis of different relationships: free flow or conventional marketing channels; single transaction channels; and vertical marketing systems.

The first of these, *free flow or conventional marketing channels*, is what many people have come to think of when they consider the relationship between different channel members. In this type of channel essentially each member in the channel, producer, wholesaler, retailer, etc., operates as an autonomous business unit. Each level operates with its own aims and objectives in mind and no one level of the channel has any degree of substantial control over the remaining levels. The primary force keeping the channel intact is a mutually beneficial trading arrangement which can be ended by either party should the arrangement become less beneficial. Although no formalized or contractual arrangement exists between the different levels in the channel (other, that is, than those pertaining to each business transaction), such channels do tend to establish trading practices with respect to the expected behaviour of each channel member. Such behaviour would include, for example, services or functions to be performed, consumers to be served, mark-ups and prices, etc.

The second type of channel based on this aspect of structure is what Bowersox *et al.* refer to as *single transaction channels*.[5] In fact this type of channel is not really a channel at all in the sense of its duration, although a substantial amount of transactions are executed in this way. A single transaction channel is a channel which is brought into being or use specifically for each transaction. After the transaction is completed the channel has fulfilled its role and the business arrangement in the channel ceases to exist. Examples of transactions which require and use this form of channel relationship would include financial stock and bond purchases, sales and purchases of houses, etc.

The third type of channel structure, based on different relationships between channel members, is what has come to be termed the *vertical marketing system* (VMS).[6] A vertical marketing system is where each level in the distribution channel acts in a planned and unified way so as to achieve maximum efficiency for the channel as a whole. Unlike the conventional marketing channel, therefore, each level in the channel acknowledges and functions on the basis of interdependence.

The concept of vertical marketing may be split into three distinct approaches according to how and on what basis coordination and cooperation are achieved in the system. These three approaches to VMSs are: the *corporate VMS*; the *administered VMS*; and the *contractual VMS*.[7]

The corporate vertical marketing system, is one in which one of the channel members *owns* preceding and/or subsequent levels in the channel. So, for example, a manufacturer who moves forward into retailing or a retailer acquiring production facilities would constitute a corporate VMS.

An administered vertical marketing system is one in which channel cooperation and co-ordination at the various levels are achieved through the dominance and power of one of the channel members. This has been perhaps one of the most significant developments in channel structure in the United Kingdom. Increasingly, power in channels has shifted to the retail end of the distribution network. As we shall see shortly, the trend in UK retailing has been towards larger and much more powerful retailing organizations. This concentration of power has meant that the larger retailing organizations are able to secure strong cooperation and support from suppliers. Retailers now play a very prominent role in determining, for example, pricing levels, product specifications and features, displays and promotional and branding policies, on the part of their suppliers.

A contractual vertical marketing system is one in which coordination and cooperation in the channel are achieved through a formal contractual arrangement. There are many forms of such contractual channel arrangements including, for example, exclusive dealerships, cooperative and voluntary groups, and, the rapidly growing area of franchising. Again, some of these developments in contractual VMSs, and particularly franchising, are considered later in this chapter. At this stage, however, one should note that the key difference between contractual and corporate VMSs is the absence of ownership.

There are many reasons for the growth of vertical marketing systems but the prime reason has been to improve overall effectiveness in the channel through increased cooperation and control. As we shall see, one of the important factors in channel design is the minimization of conflicting interests in the channel. Vertical marketing systems may not eliminate potential sources of conflict in channels: indeed they can give rise to such conflict. Nevertheless VMSs do bring with them a variety of tools and arrangements for dealing with conflicting interests.

Together, channel length and channel relationships constitute the most important elements of channel structure. A related aspect to structure, however, are the channel intermediaries themselves and, in particular, their role and functions in the channel. It is to these considerations that we now turn our attention.

Channel intermediaries

We have seen that the reason for using intermediaries to move products and services from producer to consumer rests on their superior efficiency in the performance of basic tasks. We have also seen that the range and nature of these tasks which an intermediary is required to perform would include, for example, providing an assortment, breaking down bulk, promoting and merchandising products, etc. As in other areas of industry and business, over time, specialization has arisen in the intermediaries' industry. Because of this, the range of functions which a particular type of intermediary is customarily expected to perform can be broadly delineated for each of the major categories or types of marketing channel members. Some examples of these major types are briefly outlined and discussed below, although one should note that the tasks and responsibilities of a particular type of intermediary can vary considerably from company to company. It should also be noted that within each broad category of intermediary, a variety of specific or specialized formats can operate. For example, in wholesale trading we can distinguish between wholesalers, who deliver to their customers and often extend credit terms, and cash and carry wholesalers where the purchaser selects and collects the goods from the wholesaler's warehouse with no credit being given.

Wholesalers The primary function of the wholesaler was, and still is, the breaking down of bulk. The wholesale trader buys in bulk from one or more producers and sells in smaller quantities *to* *the retailer.* In performing this key function, however, the wholesaler often provides the following services in addition:

- The provision of storage facilities thereby reducing the need for the retailer and producer to carry extensive stocks.
- A reduction of the contact costs between manufacturers and retailers.
- The reduction of marketing risks for the producer – the wholesaler shoulders some of the risks involved in interpreting and forecasting consumer demand.

Recent trends and patterns in the distribution system of the United Kingdom have led to a significant reduction in this type of channel intermediary.

Agents In many markets, in particular in export markets, the agent is a widely used type of intermediary. Agents are of two basic types:

1. A *commission agent* who secures orders from customers but does not, under normal circumstances, take title to the goods, and is not responsible for obtaining payment.
2. A *stockist agent* who carries a stock of the manufacturer's products. He may either have purchased these stocks or hold them on consignment. Often such agents will determine the mark-up on products and the discount which will be offered to dealers.

Retailers As Pitfield points out,[8] the traditional functions of the retailer in the channel of distribution stem from the personal relationship with the customer. Among the functions of the retailer in the channel can be included:

- The provision of variety (reducing shopping times and costs).
- Where appropriate, individual packing.
- Customer and credit facilities.
- Delivery and credit facilities.
- Promotion and merchandising.
- Final product pricing.

This relatively brief discussion of types of channel members and their functions illustrates that in channel decisions the marketer must consider not only the length and relationships aspects of channel design, but must also be aware of the variety of channel intermediaries and the function which they are best able to perform. In addition, the producer must also take account of the trends and changes in channels and reflect these in channel decisions. It is to this dynamic aspect of channel management that we now turn our attention, with particular emphasis on one of the most rapidly evolving elements of channel structure in the United Kingdom – retailing.

Changing channels of distribution: the structure of retailing in the United Kingdom

Channels of distribution represent possibly one of the most rapidly evolving and dynamic areas of marketing. Nowhere is this more the case than in the area of retailing in the United Kingdom. Not only have these changes led to the growth of new types of intermediaries and the subsequent decline of more traditional ones but, in addition, these changes have led to the growth of completely new channels for distributing products and services. Accompanying, and often underpinning, these changes in overall structure have been equally important changes in the relationship between retailers and manufacturers and, in particular, in the locus of power in channels.

Some of the more important of these changes and trends in UK retailing are summarized below:

- Retailing has become, and is continuing to become, progressively more concentrated, i.e., a few very large retailers now account for a significant proportion of the retail market. Nowhere is this trend towards increased concentration in retailing more pronounced than in the area of grocery retailing where the large multiples have grown to dominate this sector of the market. This growth has been achieved largely at the expense of the smaller independents and the co-operative societies. By the early 1980s large multiples accounted for some 67 per cent of all food sales in the United Kingdom, and nearly 37 per cent of sales of drink, confectionery and tobacco.
- The statistics illustrate that the number of retail outlets is declining.
- The trend has been towards much larger retail stores.
- Employment has fallen in retailing but productivity has increased.
- Competition in UK retailing is severe with a large number of retailing companies competing for a share of consumer expenditure.

Some of the statistics on which these conclusions are based are shown in Tables 10.1 and 10.2.

These broad structural changes in retailing are the result of a number of factors. For example, as car ownership has increased, more and more consumers have required 'one-stop' shopping, i.e., stores with adequate car parking facilities and with a range of merchandise which allows the customer to purchase all or most of the household needs from the one store. Overall, the changes have occurred as a result of retailers, in search of higher profits, having adapted themselves to changing circumstances.

This description of broad changes, too, tends to mask some quite significant and more specific developments in retailing which will continue to affect the producer's marketing policies. Some of the more important of these are detailed below.

- A continuing growth of trade towards large multiples.
- A continuing trend towards edge of town, one-stop shopping in larger stores, for example, superstores and hypermarkets.
- A continuing shift of power from the producer to the retailing end of the distribution channel.
- Linked to the above factors, an increase in administered vertical marketing systems, with implications in particular for own branding and specification buying.

Table 10.1   Percentage shares of components of consumers' expenditure (current prices)

Year	Total	Durable goods	Non-durable goods					Services	
			Food	Alcoholic drink and tobacco	Clothing and footwear	Energy products	Other non-durable goods	Rent, rates, etc.	Other services
1952	100	6	26	15	10	4	10	7	22
1961	100	8	24	13	10	6	10	8	22
1971	100	9	20	12	8	7	10	11	23
1979	100	11	17	11	8	7	11	11	24
1984 (p)	100	10	14	11	7	9	10	13	26

(p) = provisional
Source: Economic Trends Annual Supplement, 1985, CSO.

Table 10.2   Sales, outlets and employment for all retailing

1980 = 100

	1961	1966	1971	1976	1980	1982
Retail sales volume (at 1980 prices)	72	80	88	93	100	102
Number of outlets	149	139	130	112	100	96
Total engaged (employees and self-employed)	118	119	118	105	100	93
Total manpower (full-time equivalents)	137	131	124	111	100	93
Sales volume per outlet	48	57	68	83	100	106
Sales volume per full-time equivalent	53	61	71	84	100	109

Source: NEDO estimates based on results of Annual Retail Inquiries. Not comparable with Department of Employment data.

– A continuing decline in both the numbers of independents and cooperatives, and the proportion of retail sales for which these types of outlets account.
– The continued growth of contractual vertical marketing systems, e.g., franchising.

These factors represent changes which have taken place in UK retailing over the past 10 to 15 years, and they are trends which are likely to continue. They are also changes which are of considerable marketing significance to the various levels of the marketing channel from producers to the retailers themselves. Some of them are discussed in more detail below.

The growth and success of the multiples A multiple is a retail company which operates a number of retail branches with common ownership and a high degree of centralized control. It could be said that any retail organization which owns and operates more than one branch is a multiple. In fact, initially, the term was only applied to retail organizations with five or more branches. The success of the multiples in UK retailing (and the relative lack of success of independents and cooperatives) is indicated in Table 10.3.

In recent years it has become common to distinguish between small multiples (operating between two and nine branches) and large multiples (operating 10 or more branches). It is the second of these, the large multiples, which have dominated UK retailing in recent years. The extent of this domination, particularly in food, clothing, mixed retail and hire and repair is shown in Table 10.4

The success of the multiples is due to a number of factors, in particular:

– A very marketing-oriented approach based on responding to changes in consumer shopping and spending habits.

Table 10.3   The multiples in UK retailing: share of retail trade 1961–86 (%)

	1961	1966	1971	1978	1986
Cooperatives	10.9	9.1	7.1	6.8	6.5
Multiples	29.2	34.5	38.5	46.5	55.0
Independents	59.9	56.4	54.4	46.7	38.5

Sources: Census of Distribution 1971; Retail Inquiry 1977; Retail Inquiry 1978 (provisional results); 1986 Estimated.

Table 10.4   Large multiples and sector dominance

	1978 (%)	1979 (%)	1980 (%)	1982 (%)
Total retail trade:	100.0	100.0	100.0	100.0
(cooperative societies)	(6.8)	(6.6)	(6.5)	(5.8)
single outlets	32.0	31.8	31.6	30.2
small multiples*	14.7	14.2	14.6	13.8
large multiples†	53.4	54.0	53.7	56.0
Food:	100.0	100.0	100.0	100.0
single outlets	26.5	25.2	24.7	23.1
small multiples	9.9	9.9	10.6	9.6
large multiples	63.5	65.0	64.8	67.2
Drink, confectionery and tobacco:	100.0	100.0	100.0	100.0
single outlets	53.3	52.3	51.3	49.9
small multiples	12.2	11.6	13.1	13.4
large multiples	34.5	36.1	35.7	36.7
Clothing, footwear and leather goods:	100.0	100.0	100.0	100.0
single outlets	28.3	27.9	27.8	24.8
small multiples	20.4	20.4	21.3	22.0
large multiples	51.3	51.7	50.9	53.2
Household goods:	100.0	100.0	100.0	100.0
single outlets	39.1	36.8	38.4	38.0
small multiples	22.3	23.7	23.4	23.0
large multiples	38.7	39.4	38.2	39.0
Other non-food:	100.0	100.0	100.0	100.0
single outlets	53.5	54.6	52.8	51.0
small multiples	27.3	27.3	28.8	30.2
large multiples	19.2	18.1	18.4	18.8
Mixed retail:	100.0	100.0	100.0	100.0
single outlets	20.8	24.5	24.2	22.5
small multiples	12.6	9.4	8.9	5.4
large multiples	66.7	66.3	67.0	72.2
Hire and repair:	100.0	100.0	100.0	100.0
single outlets	13.9	13.6	14.9	12.2
small multiples	11.0	7.0	6.3	7.7
large multiples	75.0	79.3	78.6	80.1

*Small multiple: 2–9 outlets.
†Large multiple: 10 or more outlets.
Source: Annual Retail Inquiries.

- Their willingness and ability to introduce new innovations in retailing.
- As they have grown in size, their ability and power to bulk buy from manufacturers, coupled with centralized control, has made them very cost competitive. They are in a position to specify precisely what they want in the products supplied to them by manufacturers and will often have products produced for them by a manufacturer and market those products using the multiple's own brand name.

The growth of supermarkets/hypermarkets and superstores The trend towards larger, one-stop, retail outlets in the UK began in the early 1960s with the supermarket. Supermarkets began the trend for one-stop shopping. Previously this had involved visiting a small number of small specialist shops often located in different areas. This trend towards larger, one-shop outlets has continued with hypermarkets and superstores.

Definitions vary, but a hypermarket is said to be a retail outlet having over 50 000 sq. feet (4645 sq. metres) of selling space with at least 15 checkouts. The number of hypermarkets in the United Kingdom continues to grow. More recently we have seen the growth of superstores which have in excess of 60 000 sq. feet (5574 sq. metres) of selling space.

Both hypermarkets and superstores are likely to take an increased proportion of retail business in the UK based on the competitive advantages of economy and convenience.

The decline of the independents and cooperatives Accompanying these trends towards multiples and superstores, and in fact as a direct result of these, the independent and cooperative sectors of UK retailing have declined (see Table 10.3). Again, this trend is likely to continue. A knock-on effect of this decline has been the reduced importance of the trade wholesaler whose principal customers are the independents. Independents, cooperatives and wholesalers have each fought against this decline by, for example, forming voluntary groups (sometimes called 'symbol' shops), improving marketing and merchandising and by switching to cash and carry.

Technology and retailing: the wheel of retailing There is little doubt that the broad structural changes which have occurred in retailing, and the more specific events on which these are based, have resulted in changes in the marketing and distribution policies of channel members. Technology, too, is now beginning to change the face of UK retailing and, in particular, the application of the ubiquitous micro-chip. Computerized stock control and order processing, often linked through computerized, laser-aided checkouts are becoming commonplace in retailing. Similarly, a number of schemes are currently in operation which enable the 'shopper' to order products direct from the home via a computer terminal/television link. Such schemes will probably become more widespread in the future as the technology improves and the banking system becomes able to cope with electronic funds transfer. These and other developments pose questions as to the future shape of retailing in the United Kingdom.

In the 1960s McNair[9] suggested a hypothesis to explain and help predict changes in retailing structure – the so-called 'wheel of retailing' hypothesis. Essentially this hypothesis suggests that new forms of retailing operation begin as low-price, utility operations, established to challenge the higher margin and, by comparison, luxurious established outlets. These low-cost, low-margin operations attract price conscious customers. Their success leads to expansion with an upgrading of facilities, services and eventually prices. They, in turn, become susceptible to newer low-cost/low-price operations. The 'wheel' has turned full circle.

There is no doubt that at least some of the structural changes which have taken place in UK retailing do in fact accord with this hypothesis. More recently, however, McNair[10] himself has concluded that the term is too narrow and limited to explain adequately the changes which have taken place. Nevertheless, what McNair's hypothesis does point to is the fact that retailing institutions, much like products, have life cycles. Moreover, a marked trend in retailing is the shortening of the life cycle for a particular type of institution and for each successive retailing innovation. It took, say, 50 years for department stores to achieve maturity, only 25 years for supermarkets, and hypermarkets will probably reach it in 10.

Only one thing is certain about the shape of UK retailing in 10 years' time and that is that it will be different from that which exists today. These, then, are some of the major facets of channels and intermediaries, together with some of the major structural changes which are taking place in this important area of marketing. In the next part of this chapter we turn our attention to the design of channels and the important aspects of channel strategy.

CHANNEL STRATEGY

It is now recognized that channel decisions are strategic decisions in a company. There are two major reasons for this:

1. Channel decisions generally involve a company in long-term commitments – often to other organizations. Once established a company's channels of distribution can be difficult to change, at least in the short run. Of course, as we have seen, the dynamic nature of marketing channels inevitably means that at some stage a company will need to re-assess the extent to which its channel strategy is optimum and may have to make changes. Few companies, however, change channels at the same frequency or with the same relative degree of ease which they might and can change their advertising or their prices.
2. Channel decisions intimately affect, and are affected by, virtually all of a company's marketing and operating activities. For example, the selection of target markets is affected by, and in turn affects, channel design and choice. Similarly, decisions about the individual marketing mix elements, for example, pricing, product and promotion, must reflect a company's channel choice.

The four major strategic elements of channel choice and design are as follows:

– *The delineation and selection of basic channel structure* Included under this element would be considerations as to channel length, types of intermediaries and functions of intermediaries.
– *The determination of required market exposure* Included under this element would be the decisions concerning the number of intermediaries to be used and their geographical dispersion.
– *Systems and procedures for ensuring maximum cooperation in the channel and the minimum of channel conflict* This would include, for example, the specification of territorial rights, franchising conditions, etc.
– *Marketing and channel support strategies* In particular under this heading would be the relative emphasis and focus for marketing efforts in the channel.

These key elements are considered in more detail below.

Basic channel structure

We saw earlier that one of the principal differences between channel types is in the number and types of intermediaries used. At one extreme the manufacturer may opt for the shortest channel available, i.e., direct distribution with no intermediaries being used. On the other hand, some channel structures incorporate several distinct levels with a variety of intermediaries being involved in many products from producer to final user. Because of the variety of basic channel alternatives in this respect, we should be careful not to suggest what Stanton[11] refers to as an 'orthodoxy which does not exist'. Nevertheless, some of the basic channel structures ranging from the most direct and shortest channel, to one involving several levels, are illustrated in Fig. 10.5.

You should also note that channels with the same degree of directness (or indirectness), i.e., number of intermediaries, may differ in terms of the types of intermediaries used. An example of this is shown in Fig. 10.6.

To reiterate, the choice of basic channel structure involves both the choice of number and types of intermediaries that will be used. Very many factors will influence the basic range of channel alternatives and the choice between them by the marketer. At this stage, one should recall why channel intermediaries are used at all – namely that their use is justified when they per-

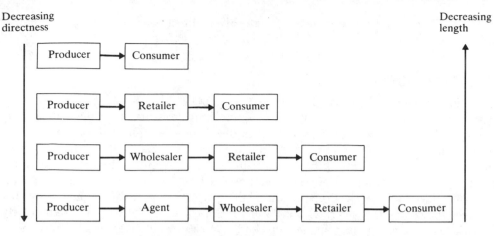

Figure 10.5 Some basic channel alternatives

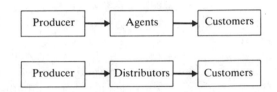

Figure 10.6 Channel variations based on different intermediaries

form functions more effectively and efficiently that would be the case if they were not used. Both the number and types of intermediaries that will be used depends upon the range and nature of the tasks involved in moving products and services from producer to final consumer and the extent to which one particular channel alternative is superior to another. Against this general consideration, and again at the risk of over-simplifying this aspect of strategic channel choice, some of the factors influencing the choice between direct and more indirect channels of distribution are shown below.

More Direct (shorter)	*Less Direct* (larger)
Industrial products	→ Consumer products
Services	→ Tangible products
Few, more-concentrated customer groupings	→ Larger numbers of customers: geographically dispersed
More control required, e.g., quality, after-sales service, etc.	→ Control less important
Customer purchase in large amounts at infrequent intervals	→ Customers purchase frequently but in small amounts
Products which are bulky/expensive to handle, custom-built, high unit value, or perishable	→ Less bulky, cheaper, standardized, non-perishable products

One is counselled to treat these facts affecting choice of channel length and types of inter-mediaries with caution. For example, many tangible consumer products of a non-perishable, low value, standardized nature are distributed very effectively direct from producer to final consumer through mail-order.

Required market exposure

A second key element of strategic channel decision making is the decision concerning the required degree of market exposure. This is underpinned by decisions about the number of intermediaries which will be used at each level and their degree of geographical dispersion.

If a company wishes to have its product available through as many intermediaries as possible then it must design an *intensive* system of distribution. For example, it will seek to recruit or encourage as many different types of retailers as possible to stock and sell its products. Further, it may seek as wide a geographical dispersion of these stockists as it can. Again, many factors would affect choice of channel strategy, including the marketing objectives and particularly the target markets envisaged by the company. One of the most influential factors in determining this element of distribution strategy is the extent to which the customer is likely to require a place and/or convenience utility from the distributor. For example, few buyers of razor blades would welcome having to travel long distances to purchase this relatively simple, inexpensive, and frequently purchased product from one of a relatively few specialist retailers of this product.

In contrast to this form of intensive distribution the marketer may instead opt for a system of *selective* or *exclusive* distribution.

Whereas intensive distribution involves the sale of company products or services through as many outlets as possible, selective and exclusive distribution refer to the distribution of those products and services through a deliberately restricted number of intermediaries.

In fact there are two dimensions to the 'selective'/'exclusive' decision. The first relates to the earlier decision as to type of intermediaries to be used. For example, the marketer may determine that his products will only be made available through multiple retail outlets and not, say, through mail-order. The second dimension relates to the possible choice of certain intermediaries within a particular type. For example, the marketer may determine that only a few selected multiples, or dealers or agents will be encouraged to handle his or her products. The extreme form of this aspect of channel strategy is exclusive distribution where only a few, or possibly only one, intermediary is given exclusive rights to distribute the company's products.

Since, by implication, a selective or exclusive system of distribution provides less 'convenience' and 'place utility' than an intensive distribution system, there must be other reasons for selecting those systems. Some of the factors which would tend towards a company selecting a more exclusive system of distribution would include, for example:

- where the product and/or service is such that the customer expects and/or requires specialist advice, service facilities, etc.;
- where the marketer and distributor would benefit from the possibly enhanced image associated with more selective distribution;
- where the potential volume of market/territorial sales would not warrant more intensive distribution;
- where the marketer wishes to retain more control of the intermediaries' marketing of the product, including, for example, pricing, promotion, credit, etc.;
- where more intensive distribution may give rise to problems associated with channel conflict between intermediaries at the same level in the channel, e.g., between different agents, different retailers, etc.

This last aspect of this element of channel strategy illustrates an important consideration in our discussion so far on this topic; namely that the elements themselves overlap. Decisions between intensive and selective or exclusive distribution have implications for the third element of channel strategy, i.e., channel cooperation and conflict.

Channel cooperation and conflict

Earlier in this chapter vertical marketing systems were outlined and discussed. We saw that channel relationships constitute an important dimension of channel structure. We also saw that the growth of various types of VMSs is in part explained by the need to achieve coordination throughout the full length of the channel. An important strategic element of channel decisions, therefore, are those decisions which relate to channel cooperation and conflict.

Essentially it is in the interests of all the members of a channel for there to be a substantial degree of cooperation. After all, a marketing channel is, or should be, a set of interlocking and mutually dependent elements which combine with a complete system for achieving a given set of tasks. Having said this, an almost inevitable feature of marketing channels is the potential for conflict between channel members. This should be considered by the marketer in the strategic design of his channels.

Stern and El-Ansary[12] point to two distinct types of conflict in channels based on the level in a channel at which such conflict may arise.

The first of these is *horizontal* channel conflict. This is conflict which occurs between intermediaries at the same level in the channel. This type of conflict is primarily competitive conflict and may occur between similar intermediaries (e.g., multiple v. multiple) or between dissimilar intermediaries (e.g., discount store v. multiple). Horizontal conflict may also arise between the members of a company's own channel. An example would be where conflict arises, say, between two of a company's own distributors, possibly concerning trading rights and practices.

The second, and much more prevalent type of conflict, is *vertical* channel conflict. This is conflict which occurs between different levels of the same channel, e.g., between producer, wholesaler and retailer. This type of conflict is primarily power conflict between channel members.

Clearly, some types of channel conflict are natural and healthy. For example, it is to be expected that in a competitive market environment, channel intermediaries at the same level will lock in competitive conflict. As we have seen, at the retailing level in the United Kingdom, the multiples appear to have emerged victorious from this competitive struggle. Nevertheless, we can expect both more traditional and newer forms of retailing institutions to continue to challenge this supremacy.

If this type of conflict is healthy and even functional, then potentially at least, conflict between channel members may be very damaging indeed to one side and/or the other. For example, the producer may come into conflict with his retailers about the way they are merchandising and promoting his product. Retailers, on the other hand, may come into conflict with their suppliers about, say, the issue of own-label brands. The issue is not so much of totally eliminating such conflict, but is rather one of designing channel structures and relationships in such a way that the potential for conflict is reduced, and where some conflict is inevitable, it should be better managed. Examples of mechanisms for achieving this, and thereby increasing cooperation in the channel, would include clear and enforceable dealer and franchising policies, arbitration procedures, producer/distributor councils, and as we have seen, the use of vertical marketing systems. Regardless of the mechanisms, or administrative and contractual procedures for improving cooperation in the channel, one issue will be as to which level or type of organization should act as channel leader and exercise control over the channel. In practice, the resolution of this issue comes down to where the power lies in the channel. Various views have been put forward as to where this power is, or should be, concentrated in the channel. For example, some argue that the power and, therefore, the leadership in a channel should rest with the manufacturer who is best suited to translate consumer needs and wants, and scarce economic resources, into marketable products and services.

Others argue that this type of argument is 'vague' and 'subjective',[13] or that today the retailer is uniquely placed in the channel system to interpret end-user or consumer needs.[14] Again, as we have seen, there is no doubt that the developments in UK retailing have, in fact, led to channel power increasingly being vested at this end of the distribution system and this fact must be taken into account in strategic channel decision making. But why should any one channel level or intermediary exercise channel power? The hypothesis appears to be that without channel leadership there is a substantial possibility of conflicting dynamics destroying the channel. If leadership exists, on whatever basis and however it is exercised, there is less chance of this occurring. An alternative hypothesis is that the exercise of channel leadership in fact creates increased instability in the channel since controlled cooperation is in effect only subdued conflict.

These contrary arguments illustrate that the study of the cooperation and conflict aspects of distribution decisions, and the concepts of leadership and power on which they are based, is still very much in its infancy. The decision maker will need to exercise his knowledge, experience and simple common sense. Simply to suggest or argue for a particular arrangement of channel leadership and power ignores the complexity of markets, products and channel relationships. In general terms, in order to fulfil the primary objective of the marketing channel, channel leadership and power should devolve, or preferably be arranged to devolve, to the channel members who are best able to fulfil this objective.

Marketing and channel support strategies

The fourth major element of strategic channel decisions concerns the relative emphasis and focus for marketing efforts in the channel. Of particular importance in this respect would be the choice between *push* and *pull* marketing strategies.

In some companies marketing efforts and tactics are aimed primarily at 'the trade', i.e., wholesalers, distributors, retailers, etc. For example, advertising and sales promotion, selling effort and pricing strategies are aimed at generating trade interest and demand for the company's products. This focus of company marketing effort is designed to 'push' a product or service into the distribution pipeline by increasing salesforce and/or dealer interest and motivation to stock and sell the products.

A 'pull' marketing strategy on the other hand, is one where the primary focus of company marketing efforts is concentrated on the final consumer. The objective with this strategy is to generate sufficient consumer interest and demand for the company's products to be 'pulled' through the distribution pipeline. The distinction between 'push' and 'pull' strategies in relation to channels of distribution is shown in Fig. 10.7.

Examples of marketing efforts within each category of channel strategy include:

1. Push strategies:
   (a) Cash discounts and increased margins for dealers.
   (b) Direct mail shots to dealers.
   (c) Dealer competitions, free gifts or premiums.
   (d) Merchandising and dealer points of sale display material.
   (e) Salespeople's incentive schemes: competitions, bonuses, sales rallies, etc.

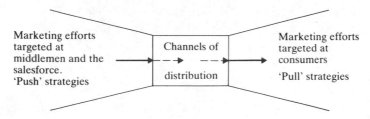

Figure 10.7 Push versus pull strategies

(f) Trade advertising.
(g) Trade exhibitions.

2. Pull strategies:

(a) Consumer advertising.
(b) Reduced price offers to consumers.
(c) Consumer sales promotion.

In fact there are many more tools available to a company to implement 'push' or 'pull' activities. However, it is usually not a case of deciding between one or other of these strategies, but more one of determining where the balance should lie, towards push or towards pull.

Again, many factors will influence the choice of an appropriate balance, for example, types of product, target market, marketing objectives, etc. What is important, in terms of strategic channel decisions, is that this relative balance should be determined in advance of, or at least in conjunction with, the strategic channel decisions which it so intimately affects.

In summary, we have looked at some of the key elements of strategic channel decision making. In doing so we have also touched on some of the factors which will affect what would be an appropriate choice of channels for a company and their design. In the next section we will consider further some of the major factors that will serve to constrain and affect the channel decision. We shall also examine some of the specific criteria against which the variety of channel alternatives may be evaluated.

IDENTIFYING AND EVALUATING CHANNEL ALTERNATIVES

Bearing in mind the four key elements of channel strategy outlined earlier, the marketing decision maker will need to delineate the major alternatives available to him or her in channel choice and design. In delineating these alternatives he or she needs to consider a number of factors which effectively serve to constrain the channel choice. Some of the more important of these considerations are outlined below.

Company and marketing objectives and resources

A key factor in delineating options for channel decisions is the company itself and, in particular, overall company and marketing objectives and company resources. For example, a company with long-run growth objectives based on increasing market share may have to look towards extending the breadth and depth of its distribution channels. Similarly, companies wishing to become market leaders in the grocery market have little option but to consider distributing through the multiples. The smaller company with fewer financial and staff resources may be forced into using more indirect channels for its products and will certainly have little power in the administration of the channel as a whole. Remember, as with other marketing mix decisions, distribution decisions should be consistent with and reflect overall company objectives and marketing strategy.

Target markets/customers

The design of channels of distribution is greatly influenced by the choice of target markets and the nature of customer characteristics within this market.

Before a company begins to consider the alternatives for channel choice and design it should, ideally, have determined its target markets. In particular the choice of target markets and channel alternatives may be interdependent. A company may discover that it cannot reach its preferred target market with the channel alternatives available, or it may find that this target market can only be served profitably with a particular system of distribution. In either case target market selection and channel decisions must be made together. In addition, the company must take account of customer characteristics in the target market(s). Examples of possibly important customer characteristics would include:

1. *The number of customers*: as we saw earlier large numbers of customers for a product tend to favour a more indirect channel of distribution, particularly where this is associated with a second key customer characteristic (see 2 below).
2. *Their geographical dispersion.*
3. *Customer needs, habits and preferences*: together these probably represent one of the most important considerations in channel design. It is pointless selecting a particular channel design which satisfies the company but does not satisfy the needs of the customer. For example, customers in the target market may have a preference for a particular type of channel intermediary or they may have particular needs in purchasing the product which certain channel arrangements cannot provide. Sometimes consumer preferences may be based on custom and habit. Although it does not pay to ignore such preferences, where they are based only on habit a company should consider the possibility of developing other and possibly innovative channels of distribution for its products.

Product

The influence of product characteristics on channel decisions was outlined earlier in this chapter. For example, it was suggested that generally, bulkier perishable, non-standard products will tend towards a more direct system of distribution. It must also be remembered that there are no rules here. We often find that essentially the same types of product are distributed in very different ways by different companies.

Competition

Channel decisions must, like other aspects of marketing, reflect competitive considerations. Again, one should be careful to note that we are not suggesting that a company should utilize the same or even similar channels to those used by its competitors. Indeed, a company may seek to examine the practices of its competitors in order to devise alternative methods.

Together, these considerations will constrain the range of appropriate channels and systems available to a company. It is likely that the decision maker will still be faced with a range of channel alternatives including a range of possible intermediaries for which he or she must make the final choice. At this point each of the remaining alternatives needs to be assessed against a set of additional and more specific criteria. Kotler[15] suggests that among the more important of these criteria are those which relate to *control, adaptive,* and *economic* factors; to these we would add an additional element – that of *coverage.*

In terms of control criteria and channel choice a company must consider carefully the extent to which its channel design will allow the company to exercise control over the marketing effort. As a general rule a company has more control where it uses more direct channels for its products. Of course, it is often the case that the producer determines to relinquish some degree of control over how his or her products are marketed. After all he or she may not have the necessary resources to, say, promote the product extensively. There is no 'recipe' as to what constitutes an appropriate degree of control but it is important that this aspect be considered in the channel decision.

Adaptability in channel choice relates to the extent to which a company is able to change its distribution policy to accord with changed conditions. We know that today's marketer operates in a dynamic environment. Further, we have seen that channels themselves represent one of the most turbulent components of this environment. In this context adaptability in channels relates to two important factors. First, the marketer must consider how easily he or she can change to an entirely new system of distribution, but it must be remembered that often channel decisions commit the marketer to long-term contractual relationships with channel intermediaries. A company can find itself at a serious disadvantage in the market if a long-term channel arrangement becomes inappropriate. A second aspect of channel adaptability relates to the relative ease with which a company can adapt its marketing effort *within* existing channels. This aspect is related to the control issue discussed earlier. For example, selling through multiples may afford the producer little option as to how his products are marketed to the final customer to take account of changed market and competitive conditions.

In terms of coverage citeria, again there are two related aspects. The first relates to the extent to which a particular channel arrangement affords the marketer access to sufficient numbers of customers and/or market segments. The second aspect of coverage relates to the extent to which the channel alternatives will lead to the required degree of coverage for the entire product range. For example, it is often the case that intermediaries will stock only the more profitable (for them) product lines and will refuse to have, or neglect, other less profitable products in the product range.

The final criterion for assessing specific channel alternatives is possibly the most important. After all, controllability, adaptability and coverage are only important in that they affect long-term profits. Economic criteria, then, are predominant in the assessment procedure. Selection of channel structures and individual middlemen should be based on a careful assessment of the costs and revenues associated with each. On the basis of this assessment the marketer should choose those channel arrangements which meet both the company's requirements – including that of profit – and customer requirements at the lowest possible cost.

FURTHER CONSIDERATIONS IN CHANNEL DECISIONS

So far we have outlined the key elements of strategic channel decisions and some of the considerations and constraints which will affect these. Having arrived at a strategic channel choice a company must act to implement, evaluate and control this strategy. Individual intermediaries must be encouraged and/or recruited to suggest the channel choice. Marketing efforts and resources must be swung into operation; sales teams organized, merchandising and promotional material developed, delivery and warehousing systems developed, etc. Further, channels, and the intermediaries which comprise them, should be subjected to continuous and rigorous evaluation and control procedures with regard to both effectiveness and efficiency. These additional considerations point to the fact that the management of distribution in a company involves wider issues than those associated only with overall channel design. Increasingly, this is being recognized and has given rise to the growth of a total systems approach to distribution. We shall conclude this chapter by examining this systems approach. Before we do so, two further considerations about channel decisions should be noted.

Throughout this chapter we have discussed channel design and choice from the point of view of the producer. Remember, intermediaries themselves, from wholesalers to agents, distributors and retailers, are marketers too, and have their own marketing decisions to make including distribution. Finally, you should note that increasingly the question for the producer in channel decisions is not so much: 'What channels should we choose?', as 'Which channels will choose us?'

THE TOTAL SYSTEMS APPROACH TO DISTRIBUTION: LOGISTICS

In recent years, views on what constitute the elements of distribution management have increasingly taken into account additional elements over and above those associated only with the channel itself. It is now recognized that the effective management of the total system of distribution can contribute significantly to overall company success and profits. This total systems approach is variously referred to as *physical distribution* or *logistics* management. The more encompassing nature of the total systems approach to distribution is illustrated in the following definition of physical distribution offered by Arbury[16] as long ago as 1967.

> By 'physical distribution' we mean the interrelationship of all the factors which affect the flow of both goods and orders necessary to fill orders. This flow starts when the customer decides to place an order and ends when the order is delivered to the customer. Physical distribution involves not only the action required to fill a particular order, but also the action necessary to prepare oneself to meet customer needs.

The term 'logistics' is essentially a military one and was applied originally to the science and practice of moving, lodging and supplying troops. Some authors in fact make a distinction between marketing logistics and physical distribution, suggesting for example that the management of physical distribution is more concerned with the planning and control of distribution activities in order to minimize costs, whereas logistics broadens this to include the notion of customer and market needs. For our purpose the terms 'physical distribution', 'logistics' and 'total distribution' systems are used interchangeably. Two vital considerations, however, will guide our discussion of this aspect of distribution:

1. The design of the total distribution should begin with customer needs and wants.
2. The total system should be designed so as to provide the required level of customer service or utility at the minimum system cost.

Before we discuss these considerations further it is useful to explain the reasons for the growth in importance of this area of company operations and also some of the more important elements in the system. We shall start by examining the background to marketing logistics.

Two related factors explain the growth of marketing logistics. The first of these is the increasing awareness of the potential cost savings to be derived from the more effective management of physical distribution. In some companies the total cost of all the activities implied in Arbury's (op. cit.) definition can represent the most significant simple element of cost on the organization. Important though this may be, it does not ask itself why companies have only comparatively recently turned their attention to these costs. A clue to this recent interest is given by Drucker[17] when in an article in *Fortune* magazine he referred to physical distribution as 'The economy's dark continent'. What he was highlighting in the use of this colourful phrase was the fact that, unlike so many other areas of company activity with well-developed systems of monitoring effectiveness and well-established costs, physical distribution activities represent a broadly uncharted area in this respect. Together, high costs and relatively underdeveloped cost control mean that in many companies physical distribution represents one of the last remaining areas for potentially substantial cost savings. The second factor which has given rise to growth in the application of marketing logistics is the recognition that properly managed, effective marketing logistics represents a powerful competitive tool in the marketplace. Cost savings in physical distribution can be passed on to customers in the form of reduced prices. Alternatively, the same improved efficiency can be used to improve the service level to the customer while maintaining competitive price levels.

The components and related activities of a company's total system of distribution will vary from company to company, but will broadly encompass some of the following factors:

- Materials procurement.
- Raw material inventories.
- Sales forecasting and production planning.
- Packaging.
- Warehousing and delivery.
- Order processing.
- Customer service.

You will note from this list that marketing logistics involves the total system of inputting, transferring and outputting materials, goods and services in a company. The idea is that the system as a whole be designed to provide the required level of customer service at minimum total cost. Again, you will note that we did not suggest that the system be designed to offer maximum customer service at minimum cost. This is because the total system concept of distribution incorporates the relationship between the total cost of distribution and the cost of lost sales due to decreased levels of customer service. A simple example will serve to illustrate.

Company A undertakes to deliver its products to customers in a maximum of five days from receipt of order. In order to achieve this it has a regional network of distribution depots in which stocks are held.

Company B, on the other hand, cannot guarantee delivery in less than 10 days to its customers. However, its distribution costs are lower than Company A because it distributes from one central depot.

Which system is best from the point of view of the companies involved?

Of course, we can't answer this question unless we know *both* the precise level of distribution costs in each company *and* the sales revenue associated with each different level of service (in this case delivery times) offered by the companies. Company B, for example, has lower costs of distribution, but how much is the inferior delivery service costing the company in terms of lost revenue? The answers to both the questions raised here are illustrated in Fig. 10.8. Figure 10.8 shows that Company A's marketing logistics system is the most desirable. The increased costs of distributing Company A's products are more than offset by the cost of lost sales suffered by Company B due to its inferior system of distribution. It also illustrates that spending more on distribution can lead to increased profitability.

This simplified example of the application of the concept of marketing logistics illustrates

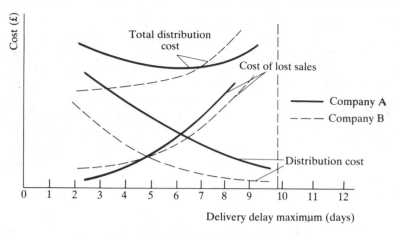

Figure 10.8 Applying the total distribution concept

many of the potentially useful contributions of the total systems approach to distribution decisions. The techniques and ideas in this area of marketing are increasingly being developed and refined and it is likely that their use in companies will continue to grow.

CONCLUSIONS

In this chapter we have looked at the means by which products and services are channelled from producer to final customer. A channel of distribution is made up of institutions and middlemen where activities centre on the activities required to achieve this. The question is not, should we perform these activities? It is more, who should perform them? The reason for utilizing the services of intermediaries is that often they perform these activities much more effectively and efficiently than can the producer alone.

In order to make decisions about channels the marketing manager must understand the elements of these channels. In particular he or she must understand the key dimensions of channel structure: length, and relationships; the role, function, and types of intermediaries; and, finally, the dynamic and changing nature of marketing channels.

Against this background we looked briefly at the changing nature of retailing in the United Kingdom. We have seen that the face of retailing is changing with recent trends being towards larger, more concentrated retail institutions. The multiples, in particular, have dominated UK retailing over the past 10 years. Finally, we have looked at the wheel of retailing hypothesis in order to gauge the extent to which this explains the changes we have seen; it does not. What we have noted, however, is that the pace of retail change is increasing, a factor which the marketing manager will undoubtedly need to take account of in planning for the future.

In addition, we have seen that channel decisions and management are among the most important decisions which a company faces. In fact channel design and selection is a strategic consideration. Among the key elements of this strategic decision are the delineation and selection of the basic channel structure, the determination of required market exposure, systems and procedures for ensuring maximum cooperation and minimum conflict, and marketing and channel support efforts.

Channel design and operating decisions are company and situation specific – in short there is no one superior method for distributing products and services. Important considerations in identifying channel alternatives in a company would include: company and marketing objectives and resources, target markets and customers, products and competitive factors. The final choice of specific channel(s) needs to be assessed against control, adaptive, economic and coverage criteria.

Finally, we have seen that, increasingly, companies are assessing their distribution activities from a marketing logistics or total systems viewpoint. Not only does this approach offer potentially large cost savings in the often high cost area of distribution, but in addition, it can help a company become more marketing oriented in the design of its system of physical distribution.

APPLICATION QUESTIONS

1. What reasons account for the development of channels of distribution?
2. Explain the importance of 'channel length' and 'channel relationships' in channel structure.
3. Outline some of the more significant changes in UK retailing over the past 10 years. To what extent are these changes indicative of a life cycle for retailing institutions?
4. (a) Outline the major strategic elements of channel choice indicating the significance of each to channel design.
   (b) Outline and discuss the criteria which you would use in selecting a particular channel structure.
5. What are the key concepts in marketing logistics and what do these mean in terms of designing the total distribution system in a company?

REFERENCES

1. Bucklin, L. P., *A Theory of Distribution Channel Structure*, Institute of Business and Economic Research, University of California, Berkeley, 1966, p. 5.
2. McGarry, E. D., 'Some functions of marketing reconsidered', in: *Theory in Marketing*, R. Cox and W. Alderson (eds), R. D. Irwin, Homewood, IL, 1950.
3. Alderson, W., *Marketing Behaviour and Executive Action: A Functionalist Approach to Marketing Theory*, R. D. Irwin, Homewood, IL, 1957.
4. Howard, J. A., *Marketing Management: Operating, Strategic, and Administrative*, 3rd edn, R. D. Irwin, Homewood, IL, 1973, pp. 4–5.
5. Bowersox, D. J. *et al.*, *Management in Marketing Channels*, Macmillan, London, 1968, p. 69.
6. Bucklin, L. P. (ed.), *Vertical Marketing Systems*, Scott, Foresman, Glenview, IL, 1970.
7. Kotler, P., *Marketing Management, Analysis, Planning and Control*, 5th edn, Prentice–Hall, Englewood Cliffs, NJ, 1984, pp. 546–548.
8. Pitfield, R., *Business Organization*, Macdonald and Evans, London, 1982.
9. McNair, M. P., 'Significant trends and development in the postwar period', in: *Competitive Distribution in a Free, High Level Economy and Its Implications for the University*, A. B. Smith (ed.), University of Pittsburgh Press, Pittsburgh, 1958, pp. 1–25.
10. McNair, M. P. and E. G. May, The Evolution of Retail Institutions in the United States, Report 76–100, Marketing Science Institute, Cambridge, MA, April 1976.
11. Stanton, W. J., *Fundamentals of Marketing*, 5th edn, McGraw–Hill, London, 1978, pp. 364–365.
12. Stern, L. W. and A. I. El-Ansary, *Marketing Channels*, 2nd edn, Prentice–Hall, Englewood Cliffs, NJ, 1982, Chapter 7.
13. Wilkinson, I. F. 'Power and influence structures in distribution channels', *European Journal of Marketing*, 7(2), 1973.
14. Mallen, B., 'Conflict and co-operation in marketing channels', in: *Reflections on Progress in Marketing*, L. G. Smith (ed.), American Marketing Association, Chicago, IL, 1965, pp. 74–7.
15. Kotler, P., op. cit., pp. 556–557.
16. Arbury, J. N., *A New Approach to Physical Distribution*, Dryden Press, Hinsdale, IL, 1967.
17. Drucker, P., 'The economy's dark continent', *Fortune*, April 1962, p. 103.

ELEVEN

MARKETING COMMUNICATIONS

INTRODUCTION

Marketing communications is one of the most developing elements within the marketing mix, although many companies continue to ignore its importance. Despite the fact that above-the-line (direct advertising) expenditures currently account for about £3000 million per annum in the UK, with below-the-line (indirect promotional) expenditures at an even higher level, the application of management in these areas is subject to much criticism.

The purpose of this chapter and Chapter 12 is to examine the scope of the marketing communications mix in some detail – advertising, sales promotion, public relations and personal selling – and to discuss the nature, role and principles of these communication tools. The basic purpose of these tools is to communicate with consumers in order to persuade them to buy the company's products. As we shall see, this is by no means the only objective of this variety of communication methods open to marketing practitioners. To view them as being only sales oriented, is to underestimate the complexity of modern marketing communications.

COMMUNICATION EXPLAINED

H. Lasswell[1] puts forward the proposition that five basic questions form the basis of analysis in communications.

1. Who is the communicator? In this, the *control analysis*, the main task is to discover the purpose of the sender so that his message can be correctly interpreted.
2. What is the content of his message? *Content analysis* very often revolves around the question of informative and persuasive messages – while D. Ogilvy[2] claims that informative advertising is the most profitable – quoting the example of how effective it would be at emptying a building simply to inform people there was a fire. To try to persuade them, could lead to arguments and delays.
3. Who is the audience for which the message is intended? *Audience analysis* is concerned with the identifying of prospects, the target audiences and the segmentation of markets.
4. What information media or means of transmitting the message are employed? *Media analysis* can be viewed as discovering where audiences are located and selecting the media and media vehicles which reach them most effectively.

5. What behaviour follows the receipt of the message? *Effect analysis* is concerned with the relationship between message content and the subsequent behaviour of the audience.

These five basic analyses will be a recurring theme in this chapter and in Chapter 12.

A communication process can thus be summarized as who says what, in what channel, to whom, and with what effect. The four basic components of the process are:

- the communicator (the encoder);
- the message (the symbols);
- the channel (method of communication); and
- the audience (the decoder).

Figure 11.1 is a very simplistic analysis, and the process of marketing communications calls for countless problems to be considered. For the communications to be effective, these problems must be researched and then overcome.

One of the major problem areas is *channel noise*. This is a term used to describe anything which interferes with the message during its time in the selected channel. We may view it as a variety of distractions between the communicator and his audience. With reference to marketing communications, the advertisement might be subjected to poor reproduction in the mass media in some way, or the salesperson might have to put up with a variety of interruptions while in the middle of his or her presentation. Not all of these can be planned for in advance, but some ways in which channel noise might be overcome are:

- *The use of attention-getting devices* – highlighting the need for good, effective creative ideas and using methods of communication which secure the attention of the audience. This applies in all areas of marketing communications, whether it is the memorable jingle used in the advertising campaign, or the tactics employed in below-the-line and personal selling efforts.
- *Repetition of the key part of the message* – in an effort to try to ensure that this is received and remembered by the audience, even if other parts of the message are lost.

Another interference which presents problems for the communicator is that of *semantic noise*. Even though the message is received exactly as it was transmitted by the encoder, for some reason it is misunderstood. Each person in the decoder group aimed at by the marketing communicator will have his or her own frame of reference. Any words, for example, which are unknown to the audience, or which mean different things to the audience from what the communicator intended, may very well result in misinterpretation taking place. A need for the perceptions of the encoder and decoder to be common is thus highlighted, since any disparity between what the communicator perceives and what his audience perceives can result in severe problems, and ineffective

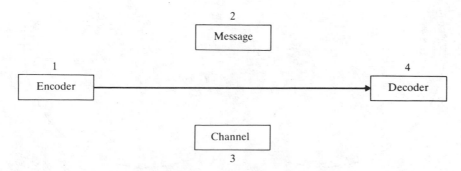

Figure 11.1 Components of communication

communications. Advertisers are often criticized for being out of touch with their audiences' tastes and attitudes, while salespeople may not possess the technical know-how and expertise to be able to relate to prospects.

Frye[3] argues that this problem, while being a key one for marketing management to contend with, may be less harmful in the early stages of the product life cycle when the target audience (the innovators) may tend to be on a similar social and economic scale as the marketing communicator. This may be true in some instances, but equally untrue in many others. For example, in industrial markets there may be little difference between the various decision-making units in potential buying companies, or at least the differences may exist among groups of buyers at all stages.

The need for commonality of perceptions between communicator and audience is illustrated by Frye as a Venn diagram (see Fig. 11.2).

The marketing communications management team must, therefore, identify the possible problem areas. Where perceptions are not shared they must try to reduce the problem areas by careful definition of terms used and by the adjustment of vocabulary used.

It must also be realized that the context in which words appear may affect interpretation, and also that material which is deemed to be too complex or too simplistic by the audience may then be dismissed. Audiences might then turn to competitors' communications in their search for more rewarding material.

A further problem area which the marketing communicator may face is a result of the *beliefs* and *attitudes* held by the various people in his audience. As already stated, interpretation of the message may depend upon the terms of the frame of reference. Each person has certain beliefs and attitudes, which may be individual (ego-related) or they may stem from reference groups which affect him or her (family, friends, etc.). A message which challenges these may lead the audience to distort, misinterpret or reject the communication. Many authors believe that it is easier to try to redirect attitudes in some way, rather than meet them in a head-on clash.

Related to this, is the concept of *cognitive dissonance* put forward by Festinger.[4] When a person takes action which is inconsistent with what he or she believes, then the cognitive elements are in conflict. This provides the marketing communicator with a most useful analysis framework, in both the pre- and post-purchase situations. The underlying principle is that new in-

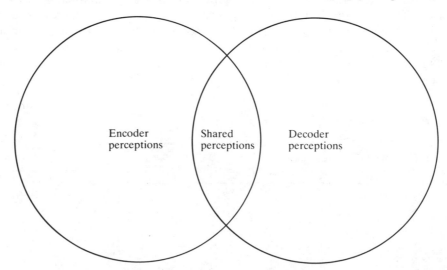

Figure 11.2   Encoder/decoder perceptions

formation must be in harmony with existing knowledge if dissonance is to be avoided. This is discussed in greater detail in Chapter 12, suffice it to say here that marketing communicators must realize that audiences will attempt to reduce dissonance by exposing themselves to further messages in order to reduce the conflict. They will turn again to the advertisements, the sales literature and the salespeople in their attempts to seek reassurance.

The final problem area facing the marketing communicator is that of *feedback*. These are reactions which take place along the communication process, but which are transmitted backwards – from audience to communicator. This flow might, of course, not be a direct one, but rather pass through a number of intermediary stages before it is received by the communicator. The obtaining of feedback is vital to communications management, if campaigns are to be correctly evaluated and controlled and the question 'why were we successful or otherwise?' answered. Within the area of marketing communications, feedback is one of the principal differences between the various activities. For example, in personal selling it can be instantaneous, whereas in advertising it is often slow, difficult and expensive to obtain.

COMMUNICATION STRATEGIES

All of these problems mean that the tasks facing marketing communications management are not as simple as the process initially outlined in Fig. 11.1. There are many potential problems which may have to be surmounted, but at least the recognition of these problems provides a useful starting point in the formulation of communication strategies. Marketers must recognize that even the most effective communication strategy is unlikely to lead to effective communication with all the consumers at which it is aimed.

Once the scope and limitations of various communication strategies have been recognized, a strategy adapted to particular needs may be formulated.

Questions which now should be asked are as follows:

1. To which consumer group should the communications be directed?
2. What information will these consumer groups seek from our communications when deciding whether or not to buy?
3. What objectives should be set in order to communicate effectively with these groups?
4. How much will it cost to achieve these objectives? What size should the total budget be?
5. How should this total budget be apportioned among the various marketing communication activities available?
6. How much responsibility is to be assumed by the manufacturers and by the channel intermediaries?
7. How might the effectiveness of the campaign be evaluated and controlled?

CAMPAIGN PLANNING

This campaign planning process highlights the major decision areas faced by management. In order to provide insights into these, the rest of this chapter and Chapter 12 are devoted to close examination of many of the more important aspects of campaign planning. A marketing communications campaign planning process is put forward in Fig. 11.3.

By planning and implementing their communication campaigns in this structured way, it is suggested that a more professional approach can be adopted by communications management teams. Many authors have criticized the lack of management application in the area of marketing communications. Wills[5] asserts that it is not surprising that not many companies can truthfully

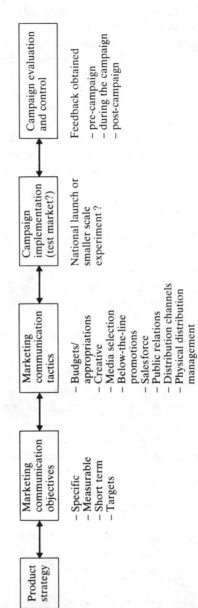

Figure 11.3   A marketing communications campaign planning framework

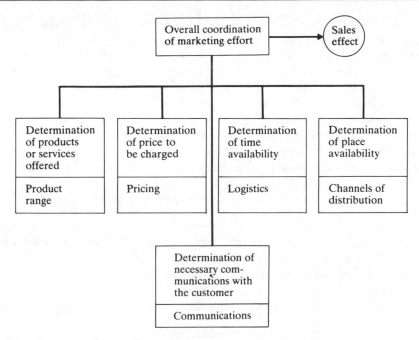

Figure 11.4 Marketing communications coordination

answer the question of how good or bad their marketing communication efforts are. Wills puts forward the following reasons for this being the case:

- The inertia of existing organizational structures.
- The lack of realization about the potential benefits of adopting a more professional approach to marketing communications.

There appears to be far more attention paid to other areas of the marketing mix, most notably product and pricing policies, while marketing communications tends to be ignored.

The organizational solution proposed is, as Wills points out, relatively simple (Fig. 11.4).

Here, we see the need to raise marketing communications in the hierarchy of management thinking. Referring back to Fig. 11.3 we find that the prime need in the planning and implementation of marketing communication campaigns is for management to be objective oriented.

Product strategy, as has been pointed out in Chapter 8, is seen as providing the initial sense of direction for the campaign. It acts as the key between the consumer, product and market analyses which form the basis of strategy formulation and the determination of the marketing communication programmes. The purpose of product strategy is to provide a single, unified direction for *all* of an organization's marketing programmes – including marketing communications. In this way, all the efforts are coordinated, and the product is moved towards the same goal by all of the organization's marketing efforts.

Product strategy receives inputs, and in turn provides guidance not just for marketing efforts. All of the organization's functional areas – production, financial, legal, personnel, etc., – are likewise coordinated by means of the overall product strategy, so that all of these efforts are directed towards a single, unified goal. There should only be one direction for a product, and the marketing communication activities should be coordinated with all of the other efforts in this way.

The strategy decision is long term, first decided upon before the product is even produced or marketed; it will only be adjusted when major events happen – such as changes in the product itself or a change in consumer tastes.

Marketing communication objectives have now to be determined. These are, of course, more specific and short term, and must be in line with the overall product strategy. The determination of these objectives is a key area in the planning of campaigns, and forms the corner-stone of the analysis. If good objectives are developed and clearly stated at the beginning of the process, then all the planners involved in the marketing communications process can attack their particular problem areas with good purpose and with their tasks having been eased. Copy specialists can prepare messages which are directed at achieving a specific purpose; personal selling, advertising and below-the-line promotional activities can all be coordinated, and the experts in media planning can use their expertise more effectively.

As Majaro[6] points out, the setting of clear, precise and measurable objectives can help in the following ways:

1. To integrate the marketing communications campaign with other marketing activities.
2. To improve the liaison with external agencies.
3. To determine communication budgets and appropriations.
4. To secure appraisal of the plans by top management.
5. To measure the results of the communication efforts.

Too often, communication objectives are set which are too general, are confused with overall marketing objectives, or are non-existent. In a major survey of campaigns planned and implemented by advertising agencies in the US, Britt[7] examined two major aspects of each campaign:

– Were specific objectives set well enough for subsequent measurement to be made?
– Did the agency attempt to measure effectiveness by clearly stating how the campaign fulfilled any previously stated objectives?

Only two of the campaigns met Britt's criteria for adequate objective setting, and most failed to specify what criteria were to be used for evaluation.

Under the circumstances discovered by Majaro and Britt, everyone concerned with the campaign building process lacks direction, with the inevitable reduction in the utilization of skills. Unless valid objectives are set, then the tendency will be for each manager in sales, advertising, sales promotions and public relations to set his or her own targets. These might be good objectives viewed individually, but because they are not coordinated, then these must be sub-optimal. Optimization can only be sought by there being a common goal, with all of the marketing communications activities being coordinated in the pursuit of this.

COMMUNICATION OBJECTIVES

It may prove useful to list here some of the common objectives of communication campaigns:

1. Consumer communications
   (a) To inform about a new product.
   (b) To correct misconceptions about a product.
   (c) To increase frequency of use.
   (d) To remind.
   (e) To present special offers.
   (f) To educate consumers in how to use a product.

(g) To build an image for the product/company.
(h) To built up consumer loyalty.
2. Trade communications
   (a) To provide information.
   (b) To inform about promotional programmes.
   (c) To present special trade offers.
   (d) To avoid stockpiling.
   (e) To educate the trade on product usage.
   (f) To build patronage motives.

These are not, however, all-inclusive, and when used as the basis of a specific campaign, they must be expressed in precise, measurable terms. The fact, however, that consumers and trade will receive not only commercial information via the organization's communication campaigns, but also information from non-commercial sources, presents major problems to the communications manager. Editorial comments from the various media, and word of mouth are both examples of communications which are not under the control of the marketer, and which may contradict the messages he is conveying. Marketers must, therefore, recognize that even the most effective communications strategy is unlikely to lead to effective communication with all of the prospects all of the time. The recognition of these limitations puts the marketer in a position to formulate a strategy adapted to his own needs. The identification of problems to be surmounted is the first vital step in the formulation of any strategy.

    Having specified the objectives of the campaign, the next step facing the marketer is the selection of the tools to disseminate the necessary information to the target audience. The nature of the programme objectives will obviously play a large part in establishing some guidelines for the overall communications budget. For example, the task of creating awareness for a product may require a smaller budget than say the task of instilling consumer loyalty for the product. Here communications management must try to achieve the following:

1. Identify and satisfy the target audience's interests in information.
2. Maximize the expenditure, so that the marginal cost of disseminating the information does not exceed the marginal revenue which is brought about.
3. Identify the extent to which the informational needs of the prospects can be resolved by promotional elements of the marketing mix, or by non-promotional elements.

There are many considerations to be taken into account:

- The level of competitive promotional spending in the target markets. Here, smaller producers tend to take their cue from larger manufacturers and adjust their budgets in line with the market leader.
- The level of sales generated by promotional activities.
- The objectives sought (called the 'objective and task' method). This calls for an ascertainment of advertising expenditure needed to reach marketing objectives that have been laid down in the marketing plan.
- The affordability of the proposals. Here, the philosophy is that after other cost centres have received their budgets, what is left over goes to advertising.

Each of these may be used as the basis of determining the budget. On an individual level, they may only provide limited insights. For example, if competitive spending is the only variable which is taken into account, then one major problem may be that the budget fails to take account of the fact that the problems/opportunities faced by the company may be very different from those of its competitors.

Equally, if sales is the sole determinant of the budget total (whether this is a last year's, per unit or an adjusted sales figure), then a major criticism of this approach is that it regards the sales as the stimulus with the communications as the response. It is obvious that this is wrong, and that the stimulus should be communications – leading to the response of sales. Taken further, the notion of sales determining the promotional budget implies that falling sales means a decreased budget and conversely, increasing sales generates a larger budget. Logic must dictate that the opposite should be the case!

The whole area of budget determinaton within the field of marketing communications is one full of controversy and criticism. A paper presented by Roberts[8] warns management of what he calls planning blight, and points out that advertising budgets are some of the last budgets to be set and the first to be slashed! The danger is one of the spiral decay.

A method of budget allocation is probably the most logical one. It assumes that advertising is a tangible item that extends beyond the budget period and looks at it as a long-term investment and attempts to ascertain the return on such expenditures. The 'incremental method' is its corollary and this assumes that the least unit of money spent on advertising should bring in an equal amount of revenue.

Much support from many academic sources comes for the 'task approach'. This involves the marketer, once an objective has been specified, in costing out the various promotional tasks which are necessary to achieve this objective. Once again, we see the need for valid objective setting within the area of marketing communications. The best guideline to management must be to realize the importance of all these factors – sales, competitors, objectives and affordability, etc. – and to take account of them all when determining the budget. Adequate returns on investment will enable the marketer to command the resources necessary to continue satisfying consumers' interests.

COMMUNICATIONS PRACTICE

The marketer, when deciding which promotional tools to use, is faced with a wide range of alternatives. Sometimes it is mistakenly assumed that advertising and personal selling are the only marketing tools to disseminate information. This view is far too narrow, since through publicity and public relations activities, short- and long-term sales promotions and by means such as packaging, information can be conveyed most effectively by the marketer.

Determining which combination of these tools to use in particular situations is a very complex operation involving many considerations. One of the most important of these is determining how many and which decisions are made at the possible locations. For example, is the decision made chiefly in the home, at the office or in the store? When decision making occurs mainly in the store, for example, then the emphasis should be placed on point-of-sale and personal selling activities.

The nature of the product is also important in this respect. Although there are many dangers in putting forward rigid guidelines here, it would appear that advertising may be most effective when the information needs are not overly complex, as may be the case with convenience goods. Personal selling, on the other hand, with its obvious advantages of face-to-face exchanges, maybe most suitable in disseminating information about more technical, specialist goods where the individual needs of particular customers have to be taken into account. The kinds of information to be disseminated must have a bearing on the selection of the marketing communication tools. It is the function of the creative programme to specify what message is to be communicated to the audience. The creative programme provides direction for the creative people, who will implement the campaign when the plan is completed and approved.

The basic direction for creative ideas is provided by the product strategy, since the market position which is to be aimed for must be the starting point. The more specific communication objectives specify the steps to be taken to solve immediate problems facing the product, and the consumer, product and market analyses will have provided information upon which the creative programme should be based. In particular, the nature of the target audience and the problems which consumers are trying to solve will form the basis of the creative programme.

The three essential steps in building this programme for a product are:

1. The determination of the content of the message, aiming for consistency of information from various sources.
2. The presentation of the message. Identifying a central idea and the way in which it is to be expressed and creating the advertisements and sales approaches.
3. Determining how the communication effort will be produced, for example, estimates of the production costs and production time schedules of advertisements, point-of-sale material and sales literature.

Communications management delegates much of the work involved in this process, since it involves very specialized skills. In most instances there is clearly a need to employ the services of the creative specialists to be found in the agencies. Responsibilities still remain for providing information and directions to the creative team and for evaluating the output in terms of specific, pre-determined criteria.

Advertising agencies are examined in more detail later in the chapter, together with other detailed examinations of various aspects of advertising. Personal selling is considered in Chapter 12. The next sections are devoted to the remaining aspects of the communication campaign plan – below-the-line promotions and public relations – in order to assess their applications in campaign planning and implementation.

BELOW-THE-LINE PROMOTIONS

Below-the-line promotions have been defined by Christopher[9] as 'all non-media promotion'. Engel et al.[10] define it as 'the supplementary selling activity which coordinates personal selling and advertising into an effective persuasive force'. There are, however, many problems of definition, since the 'line' is an artificial concept, used originally by advertising agencies to distinguish between promotional expenditures which were commissionable, and those which were not. 'The implication of the line is that there is some radical difference between the purpose and effect of expenditures above and below the line.'[11] To some extent any definition of below the line assumes a false dichotomy, since many promotions are dependent on media advertising, for example, when reduced offers are backed by national press advertising.

Within the context of communication planning the marketer should be more concerned with adopting a total approach, whereby above the line and below the line are integrated to complement and support each other in the total communication process. A useful distinction has been drawn between those promotions which aim to move products from the marketing channel intermediary, and those aimed at moving the product from the manufacturers into the channels of distribution. These have been referred to as 'pull' and 'push' promotional techniques, which have already been detailed in Chapter 10.

Some promotional methods have already been detailed, but more specifically in the communications context, the marketer can use 'push' and/or 'pull' techniques. The methods

employed must depend upon the objectives sought, the nature of the product, the type of distribution channel employed and the target audience.

The range of 'pull' (consumer incentives) includes the following:

– Price reductions – by the manufacturer, or by the retailer in the form of store price cuts.
– Coupons – a form of price reduction.
– Self-liquidators – where profits made on the merchandise offered (in return for money and 'box
  tops') covers the cost of the promotional effort.
– Premiums given free in/on/off the pack.
– Personality promotions.
– Consumer competitions.
– Free samples – either offered by post or in-store demonstrations.
– Merchandising and point-of-sale displays, and advertising in the stores.
– Packaging.
– Sponsorship.
– Purchase privilege plans (buy one, get one free).
– Container premiums – where the container can be used after the contents have been consumed.
– Trade-in facilities.
– Credit facilities.
– Training schemes.
– Guarantees.
– Direct mail 'shots'.
– Saving schemes.
– Banded and twin packs.

Over the past 20 years, there has been tremendous growth in expenditure on these consumer incentives, to such an extent that it is estimated that the level of expenditure in the UK today
exceeds that of above the line, running in excess of £3000 million per annum. Most of the increase
has been on price-based promotions, with the economic recession being a prime reason for this.

The range of 'push' (trade and salesforce incentives) includes the following:

– Cash discounts.
– Increased margins.
– Competitions – trade and salesforce.
– Dealer premiums.
– Salesforce cash incentives.
– Exhibitions.
– Demonstrations.
– Direct mail 'shots'.
– Training schemes.
– Credit facilities.

The marketer may be faced with a number of problems, which offer him the opportunity to utilize
some of these 'push' and 'pull' techniques. Spillard[12] states that the main advantages of these
below-the-line techniques stem from their being:

– very flexible and adaptable;
– capable of specific action;
– wide ranging in applicability;

– economical and cost saving;
– swift in action.

The marketing situations in which sales promotion may make a valuable contribution can range from payment problems to the need for advertising to have more 'punch', from consumer purchase to dealers not stocking the product, from the need to motivate the salesforce to blockages in the distribution channel, from the need for expert advice to the need for additional market information.

The decision whether or not to use sales promotion, and which particular techniques, is summed up by Ann Morgan[13] who suggests the following: ✓

1. Determine, in order of priority, the problems faced by the product/brand.
2. Determine the money available to solve these problems.
3. List and cost all the possible alternative solutions to the problem, e.g., theme advertising, pricing or product strategy, consumer promotions, etc.
4. Estimate the effectiveness of each solution.
5. If the answers to (3) and (4) suggest that a promotion is the most efficient answer to the problem, and if there is enough money available in (2), then a promotion is indicated.

PUBLIC RELATIONS

Defined by the Institute of Public Relations[14] as 'the deliberate, planned and sustained effort to establish and maintain mutual understanding between an organisation and its public', this is a key element in the discussion of communication tools. Public relations is concerned with the behaviour of the organization, its products, services and individuals which give rise to publicity. Unlike publicity, which is a result of information being made known, the results of public relations are controllable.

Control will only result from public relations activities if, as F. Jenkins[15] states, 'the communications with various publics are planned with the purpose of achieving specific objectives'. Here again, we see the need for providing our marketing communications activities with a clear meaning and purpose.

The 'publics' which should provide the direction for an organization's public relations activities are as follows:

1. *The community*: where the clear need is for the organization to act as if it were a member – just like a private citizen. Involvement in community activities and the development of a community relations programme are the ways to achieve this goal.
2. *Employees*: this internal aspect of public relations is often a reflected area in many organizations, but there are obvious benefits in involving the workforce in organizational goals and establishing mutual understanding.
3. *Government*: both local and national politicians are important sources of information for an organization, for example, proposed legislative changes affecting the business. The lobbying of politicians is not without criticism, but should be recognized as an acceptable procedure in industrial/government relations.
4. *The financial community*: commercial and merchant banks, investors and share analysts and city journalists provide a 'public' with whom an organization should communicate if it is to be seen as financially credible. The recent spate of mergers in the UK has highlighted the need to establish consistent relations over a period of time.
5. *Distributors*: all types of middlemen in a company's channel of distribution – wholesalers,

retailers, brokers, agents and dealerships, etc. – need information about products and services if they are to have the knowledge and confidence necessary to become effective re-sellers.

6. *Consumers*: often thought to be the only 'public' which concerns public relations. Here, as with distributors, there is a need for a company's public relations activities to be coordinated with other areas of marketing communications: advertising, sales promotion and personal selling. The education of consumers and creating and maintaining interest among target audiences can lead to favourable attitudes being generated towards a company's products and services.

7. *Opinion leaders*: for example trade associations and pressure groups. Public relations must attempt to understand the position of all important external groups, even if the group is opposed to them, if effective communications with them are to take place. It is far better for factual information to be the basis of discussion, not hearsay and exaggeration.

8. *Media*: public relations has a role to play in the development of relationships with the press. By aiming to achieve maximum publication and broadcasting of information, a company may create understanding in many target markets. Press relations is, therefore, seen as part of a well-organized public relations campaign.

There is a variety of techniques available to secure effective communications with the above 'publics'. These are discussed in detail by Haywood[16] who also discusses the specific tactics to be employed. Such techniques include:

– Visits to the workplace.
– Open days.
– Sponsorship.
– Community projects.
– In-house publications.
– Annual reports.
– Video films.
– Training courses.
– Press releases.

Public relations has come a long way from its origins. No longer should it be viewed as merely 'free advertising', 'propaganda' or 'publicity'. It has a key role to play in the planning and implementation of marketing communications campaigns. A 'personality' must be developed by an organization with a clear need for true and full information.

ADVERTISING

The dictionary defines advertising as 'make known: to inform'. All advertisements can be seen to offer information, and can be regarded as communications about products, services and organizations. Viewed in this way, advertising's purpose can be seen as communication, but since all advertisements contain persuasive elements directed at the ultimate purpose of a sale, advertising must also provide motives. Consumers must be moved towards purchase; ideas must be communicated. These ideas might sometimes be generated by the creative people; at other times the ideas might be in the product, the service or the organization itself. A business definition of advertising would include this origination of ideas and the subsequent communication of these ideas with the purpose being to motivate consumers along the path to purchase.

Advertising is concerned with the identification and presentation of desirable and believable benefits to the target audience in the most cost effective manner. Most advertising expenditure is devoted to the promotion of brands by manufacturers. Currently, in the UK this area of advertising accounts for approximately 40 per cent of the total advertising 'spend'.

Advertising thrives on product differentiation, and an essential element here is the strategy of branding. Brand names are the vehicles through which manufacturers can establish an identity for their product; consumers relate to brands and form images of them. Whether the company aims for the same brand name for all its products, or whether it brands each of its products separately is a question of policy and there are many promotional advantages available for each alternative. 'Family' brands might make the introduction of new products into the marketplace a comparatively easy task. Of course, there is always the danger that if the new product fails, then damage might have been done to the whole of the product range. Consumers might begin to perceive all of the company's products as being inferior. Individual branding of various products produced by a company, where different brand names are used for each, might offer more segmentation possibilities. Different varieties of a fast-moving consumer good might be individually branded and aimed at different segments of the market.

The defensive role of advertising should not be ignored, and it is often the case in situations of heavy branding, that manufacturers advertise merely to preserve the *status quo*, knowing that their advertising efforts will be cancelled out by competitors.

It is not only with consumers that we find advantages of branding. Promotional effectiveness might also be increased in the case of trade advertising. Channel intermediaries might want to take on new brands from a manufacturer whose previous successes indicate that the new brand will also succeed. Indeed, in many cases where the middlemen find that they cannot refuse a new brand, the power within the distribution channel is often in the hands of manufacturers – strong, effective branding having put them in this powerful position.

In the case of private branding by the retailers, not only does a manufacturer stand to increase output with possible resultant economies of scale, but also the promotional onus is on the retailer. These possible advantages must be carefully weighed against any possible disadvantages which may accrue from distributional power having been sacrificed.

Imagery is concerned with personality. Brand image is what consumers will see and feel when the brand name is called to their attention by means of advertising. The task of the advertiser is to ensure that consumer reactions are favourable when the brand name is mentioned. Advertising is seen as being an important determinant of brand image, along with the physical characteristics of the brand, the price charged, the satisfaction which it provides and the retailers who stock it.

Consumer knowledge about a brand is often quite high, particularly when the decision-making process has involved a lot of fact finding and comparisons between alternatives – often the case when purchasing a speciality good, but such consumers do not always know so much about the company itself.

Corporate image

To establish, maintain and improve a corporate image, institutional advertising can be utilized. Corporate advertising, as practised today, is a relatively new phenomenon, but is very often misunderstood. Critics accuse it of being:

- self-indulgent;
- a waste of money;
- too general, since it has no specific targets.

Companies should, however, regard it as being a valuable public relations tool which may be directed at consumers, middlemen, financiers, employees, pressure groups, etc., in order to build up goodwill and confidence in the firm, create identity and publicize the firm's strengths. It is a long-term activity, requiring careful planning in order that the company is not faced with sudden crises which threaten its perceived standing. Not all events can be catered for, but corporate advertising – although it does involve the costs of buying the media time and space – is more controllable than public relations. The timing and content of the messages are no longer subject to the whims of editors, sub-editors and journalists.

Generic advertising

Advertising may be used to stimulate primary demand for a type of product or service, for example, the promotion of wool by the International Wool Secretariat. The aims of generic advertising are to increase primary demand by promoting new uses, securing new users and persuading current users to buy more. A group of sellers often sponsor these programmes, these sellers being an association of manufacturers, service firms, agricultural producers, etc., all with a similar product to sell.

Seldom does a single producer use generic appeals in advertising, but an interesting example was the 'Put Mustard On It' campaign run by Colman's. A dominant market position and research findings indicated that the problem was one of frequency of usage, and this led Colman's to put forward this generic appeal rather than use a specific brand message. Primary demand determines the total market, with the commodity being pitched against a competing commodity (e.g., tea versus coffee) compared to brand competition which is the basis of selective demand.

Sales effects

The ultimate purpose of all advertising is to generate sales. Direct, immediate responses are sometimes the objectives of advertising campaigns, as in the case of mail-order firms who aim for consumers to buy at once through the post. For instance, producers of records use television to generate as many sales as possible in the minimum amount of time. The objectives here are usually short term in nature, and consumers are urged to act upon needs of which they are already aware.

To view sales as being the only valid objective of advertising is, however, too narrow a viewpoint. Modern advertising is far more complex than this. Indirect actions are also aimed for, although the ultimate purpose remains that of sales. In order that sales might eventually be brought about, the advertiser might direct his advertising campaign at other objectives, for example:

– Influencing attitudes.
– Creating awareness about products and services.
– Increasing knowledge of brands and companies.
– Acting as a reminder.
– Motivating enquiries.
– Providing leads for the salesforce.

Here, advertising is often used to make buyers aware of needs they feel.

Sequential models

In order to determine *what* to say in advertisements, the advertiser must understand the advertising process in his target markets. Advertising works in a myriad of different ways: it varies according to many factors, including the following:

- The product or service being advertised.
- The organization doing the advertising.
- The target markets aimed at.
- The competitive environment.
- The time period in which the advertising is done.
- The media being used.
- The message content of the advertisement.
- The level of advertising being employed.

In order that specific, measurable objectives may be set for the advertising campaign, marketing must familiarize itself with current knowledge about how advertising works. Theories can only put forward general perspectives; the task for marketing is to analyse how these may be applied in the specific task under consideration.

The behavioural scientists have formulated a number of sequential models, attempting to shed light on the process which consumers pass through on their way to action (purchase). In the 1920s the AIDA approach was put forward stating that consumers pass through the successive stages of: attention – interest – desire – action. Criticism of this approach mainly centres around the fact that there is no allowance for 'build-up' and that the emphasis is far too much on the message with little consideration of the role of the prospect.[17]

Daniel Starch[18] wrote in 1925:

> An advertisement, to be successful:
> (a) must be seen;
> (b) must be read;
> (c) must be believed;
> (d) must be remembered;
> (e) must be acted upon.

Again, the assumptions are focused on the advertisement itself, rather than the consumer and there is far too much emphasis on the stimulus. There is too little analysis of the responses of the potential customer. There is also no allowance for 'build-up' in the model, with the implication being that successive exposures to the same advertisement will not interact. In practice it is far more likely that there will be increasing (or diminishing) returns from additional advertising efforts.

In 1961 Colley[19] put forward the DAGMAR treatise – Defining Advertising Goals for Measured Advertising Results.

This is an attempt to identify the steps in the consumer decision-making process in order to allow for more precise definitions of advertising objectives and their measurement. Goals should be set in order to move prospects through the various levels; progression through the sequence increasing the likelihood of purchase (see Fig. 11.5). Colley drew attention to the fact that often the people concerned with implementing the advertising decisions may not have a common understanding of the purpose of the advertising effort: a point also commented on by D. Bernstein.[20]

In 1961, Lavidge and Steiner[21] proposed that consumers pass through the sequence shown in Fig. 11.6. As consumers perceive advertisements, they move along the hierarchical sequence of effects towards purchase.

Evaluation of the sequential models These sequential models have been used extensively by adver-

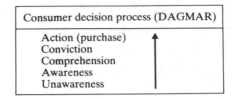

Figure 11.5   Consumer decision process (DAGMAR)

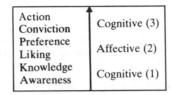

Stage (1) is concerned with knowledge and the process of thinking.

Stage (2) is concerned with attitudes, feeling or emotion.

Stage (3) is concerned with motives and the desire for action.

Figure 11.6   Hierarchy of effects

tising researchers, but they are put forward not on the basis of empirical evidence but on the basis of common sense. In fact, Colley, when putting forward the DAGMAR model, stated: 'The concept of the Marketing Communications Spectrum is applied common sense'. The implications of these models are that the objectives of advertising are to get the consumer to learn something; to present persuasive messages which appeal to rational decision making; and to turn non-buyers into buyers.

Palda,[22] in a critique of the models, draws attention to the following:

— Consumers may not always have favourable attitudes before purchasing a product.
— The models may be operationally weak because of the lack of dependable measurement devices.
— Consumers may not move through the sequence in a forward manner: they may also move backwards (from, say, 'conviction' back to 'liking' a product).

Sequential models are thus more theoretical than practical and clearly work needs to be done in this area before actionable models can be put forward as active advertising tools.

Practical theories

Reeves[23] states: 'the consumer tends to remember just one thing from an advertisement – one strong claim, or one strong concept'. This theory of the unique selling proposition (USP) proposes that because of the problems of memory and credibility, if an advertisement tries to tell consumers too much it may fail. Effective advertising is secured by making a single, strong and motivating proposition to 'pull over new customers to your product'.

An alternative approach to the USP theory is that of 'brand image', often associated with David Ogilvy.[24] The claim here is that the purpose of advertising is 'to give a brand a first-class ticket through life'. This approach seems to be concerned with non-verbal methods of communication. By the evocation of moods, it is proposed that emotions will be generated which will lead to effective advertising. If consumers purchase on an emotional basis, then this approach may well prove to be effective, and rationality may not be necessary. Consider for a moment how the Martini advertisements successfully put forward the 'jet set image' and how the consumers would react *if* the 'voice over' finished by saying 'and only £2.89 a bottle'!

Emotion is also proposed by Martineau.[25] His opinion is that all human behaviour is a form of self-expression and that 'user images' are important. However, since people need to think of themselves as being rational, a rationalization is required by the consumer to justify his or her decision. The ideal advertisement proposed here is a combination of emotion and rationality, in line with the needs, perceptions and attitudes of the target audiences.

Joyce[26] states that the advertising/purchasing system is a rather complex system of inter-acting variables. The question of *what* to say is a key question for all advertisers, and it is proposed that the discussion of the various theories has shed some light on the question of how advertising works. The general perspectives provide insights. Joyce states 'the model itself is tentative, but this general conclusion seems unlikely to be overthrown'.

ADVERTISING RESEARCH

Claims that advertising efforts have been successful must often be viewed with a good deal of uncertainty. There are many variables over which the advertiser cannot hope to have complete control (e.g., competitors' actions, economic factors and prices), all of which may affect the advertising/sales relationship. The sequential models of the advertising process are used extensively in practice as a means to establish objectives for the measurement of advertising success or failure.

The amount of marketing communications research done is a frequent source of criticism – including the level of advertising research (see Table 11.1). It appears that research into advertising and other marketing communication efforts is far less than research into other areas of marketing.

P. Hodgson[27] surveyed the types of marketing research undertaken in the UK, and discovered that research into marketing communication was only a minor part of the total.

One reason often quoted to explain the lack of advertising research activity, is the amount of confidence which marketing managers have in the available techniques.

Table 11.1 Marketing communications research

Turnover of research agency	Advertising research (%)	Sales promotion research (%)	Other marketing research (%)
£500 000 +	9½	1½	89
£150 000–499 000	16½	1½	82
Under £150 000	23	3	74
Total average	13	2	85

(Based on 28 UK agencies, including 18 of the 23 major UK research companies represented in the Association of Market Survey Organizations (AMSO).)

Advertising research techniques

Although marketing research has already been covered in Chapter 5, this discussion centres more specifically upon research into advertising. A fuller discussion of this subject is also provided by Chisnall.[28] Generally, the tools of advertising research are referred to as 'pre-measurement' or 'pre-testing' and 'post-measurement' or 'post-testing'. In other words, the probable effectiveness of advertising may be assessed before the campaign is implemented and evaluation of an advertising effort, once it has been run, may also take place. The measurements provided by both types of advertising research are potentially of immense value to advertising management. Indications of the ability of advertising to communicate messages effectively to target audiences will enable operational principles and guidelines to be developed.

Pre-testing advertisements

Advertising management may feel that an advertisement appears to be promising, but it is vital that the likely reactions of the potential buyers are first assessed. Advertisers must decide what responses will constitute effectiveness in line with pre-stated objectives, and then set out to see how likely it is that consumers will react accordingly to proposed advertisements. The effectiveness of the creative elements of individual advertisements – headlines, body copy, illustrations, slogans, etc. – may be tested, or the entire advertisement may be tested.

The major techniques employed in pre-testing are as follows:

1. *Checklists*: a form of internal assessment by the advertiser, who picks the elements which he or she considers should be in an advertisement to enable the systematic review of proposed advertisements to take place, point by point, against this list. The weakness of this approach is that a company is dependent upon the validity of the points which are contained in the list, and some important ones may also be omitted or overlooked when the checklist is compiled.

2. *Consumer juries*: a sample of prospects independently visited or contacted by mail, or interviewed on a group basis, is used to test advertisements. Simple or complex responses from jury members are sought in order to gain insights into how well an audience has understood an advertisement just seen or heard by them. The major weakness of this technique is that assessment is on the basis of what people *say*, and this may not always reflect their behaviour in the market.

3. *Enquiry tests*: alternative advertisements, published independently or together on a split-run basis (where different advertisements appear in the same issue of a magazine), are coded and the levels of enquiries generated are measured. In order to elicit enquiries, the advertiser must offer some reason for the audience to reply (e.g., a free sample of the product or an information brochure). The major weakness of this technique is that the advertiser has to assess the quality of the enquiry (some people write in just to receive mail!) and to assess further how effective the advertisement would be in communicating messages of a less direct nature (when offers are not made).

4. *Laboratory measurement devices*: sample consumers are placed in a controlled setting, shown proposed advertisements and their physical responses then measured. Sweat gland activity is measured by means of the psycho-galvanometer; pupil dilation can be recorded by a perceptoscope; images are flashed on a screen for a fraction of a second by the tachistoscope; the movement of an individual's eyes across the printed page is traced by an eye movement camera. These devices have the advantage of being apparently objective, of being conceptually simple and distortion is limited since involuntary responses are measured (except in the case of the

tachistoscope). Major shortcomings are that the laboratory setting may affect responses, and the relative sales effectiveness is not being measured.

5. *Experimentation*: where representative areas are chosen to test advertising ideas. Different advertisements may be evaluated in this way, by publishing them in different parts of the market, and sales data obtained to enable measurement to take place.

There are many managerial problems in conducting these experiments summarized under three main headings:

− The setting of valid objectives.
− The control aspects when designing and running the test.
− The interpretation of the data.

Post-testing advertisements

1. *Enquiry tests*: may be used to post-evaluate advertising efforts, when offers are made to which the potential buyer can be expected to reply. In the case of mail-order selling, the yardstick used to measure the level of effectiveness may consist of sales generated as well as enquiries for further information.

    By varying the advertisements used over time, and by maintaining detailed records, the advertiser is able to discover significant variations which can then be attributed to the differences in the advertisements.

2. *Recall/recognition tests*: attempts to measure the number of people who have actually read a particular advertisement. The readership levels of various magazines are measured on a regular basis by the Starch Message Report Service, whereby readers 'recognize' advertisements or parts of them. A more rigorous version of recall testing does not involve showing advertisements to respondents, and advertisements must be recalled from memory (e.g., Gallup and Robinson's Impact Service).

    Recall testing may also involve 'dummy' magazines, where the respondent has advertisements in a scrapbook left for a few days. He or she is then tested by questions being asked about the various advertisements contained in the portfolio.

    Recognition studies may be subject to biased or distorted responses by consumers, in that sample members may tend to exaggerate their actual readership. Recall tests attempt to control this by more vigorous screening of sample members and by counting only recall. A major criticism is that simple ideas and facts are favoured. The communication of complex ideas − which may be necessary for technical or novel products − may score low in recall tests.

3. *Consumer audits*: a random group of consumers are asked if they have bought a product, how often they have bought it and what they have on hand − prior to the advertising being launched. Re-interviewing of these consumers then takes place after the advertising has been conducted in order to assess the percentage increase or decrease in the sales of the advertiser's product.

4. *Retail audits*: similar to consumer audits except that the retailer's stocks are measured before and after the advertising. The major problems with measuring the sales effects of advertising in these ways is that it is difficult to conclude that advertising has been responsible for the sales.

The pre-testing and post-testing of individual advertisements in the above ways can provide some insight into the overall effectiveness of advertising, but one is seldom able to measure all of its effects. At times, because the results of advertising may not happen immediately, it is difficult to relate the response to a particular stimulus. A lot depends on what other selling efforts are employed by the company and its competitors, how fast the turnover of the product is and how important advertising is to the sale of the product. Specific, measurable goals must be clearly defined in line with the DAGMAR treatise.

MEDIA SELECTION

In using media, the objective of management is to plan a media schedule which consists of the combination of media, and media vehicles which most efficiently reach the target audience while still meeting various constraints (e.g., creative and budget). The first task for marketing is to identify and define the prospects (i.e., buyers and potential buyers of the product or service). In this way, various media alternatives will be seen to have more potential than others and the range of choice will become narrower. For example, if the campaign is to be directed to a group of potential female buyers, then magazines which are read predominantly by males are clearly ruled out.

More specific requirements of the media programme may be obtained by analysing the following:

1. *Budget constraints*: aiming to fulfil the audience requirements in the most cost effective manner. The usual measure used here is 'cost per thousand', provided by the formula:

$$\frac{Cost\ of\ the\ insertion\ of\ the\ advertisement}{Number\ of\ prospects} \times 1000$$

$$\text{e.g.,} \frac{£30\,000\ \text{for TV spot}}{15\,\text{million audience}} \times 1000 = £2 \text{ to reach every 1000 viewers}$$

The major weaknesses of this approach are:

   – It assumes that *all* of the audience are prospects.
   – It makes no allowances for effectiveness, i.e., to evaluate on a purely cost basis overlooks the fact that a medium alternative which has a more expensive 'cost per 1000' could be far more effective in getting the message across.

2. *Creative constraints*: the media must also comply with creative requirements, and various messages may lend themselves to words/pictures, colour/black and white, prestigious/dominating medium, etc. The media planner must analyse these features of the various media alternatives closely.

   Each of the various mass media has its attributes and shortcomings as shown in Table 11.2.

3. *'Reach' v. 'frequency'*: whether the message should be distributed very widely among the prospects (termed 'reach') or whether to concentrate on a smaller number of prospects ('frequency'). Where all potential buyers are estimated to be of equal value, it may be better for the advertiser to reach as many of them as possible; in cases where there are better prospects (heavier users of the product for example) it may be better to build up frequency by providing them with many opportunities to see (OTS).

4. *Other constraints*: these may be important depending upon the product, its strategy and objectives. For example, there may be a need for the quick production and insertion of advertisements in dynamic markets.

Matching prospects with media

A profile of the prospects should already have been obtained. The remaining alternatives still

Table 11.2   Media comparisons for advertisers

Media	Advantages/disadvantages
Television	Large audiences; demonstration of product in use (sound and vision); compulsiveness; viewed at home in a relaxed manner. Commercial breaks may be seen as irritating; a transient medium.
Cinema	Has many of the above advantages, but problem is the size of the audiences which do, however, still retain segmentation possibilities.
Newspapers	Great flexibility in terms of timing – booked at short notice; illustrations can be used; regularly purchased by large numbers of people. Do have short life spans; may be difficult to get people to notice the advertising content.
Magazines	Have 'editorial' facilities with which to integrate advertising content; advertisements are expected by readers; magazines have long life spans; read at leisure; high 'readership' compared to circulation. May have 'desert' areas which are seldom noted by readers, e.g., front and back pages.
Commercial radio	May be perceived as an 'intimate companion'; use of sound; segmentation possibilities. Has disadvantages of small audience size; transient medium – how well are the messages perceived or retained?
Outdoor and transportation	Many people have an OTS (opportunity to see) – most of the population spend some time outdoors; relatively low costs; short- and long-term possibilities; national campaigns are possible; segmentation possibilities. May be subject to effects of the weather; how eye-catching and noticeable are they? Sites are subject to environmental criticism.
Newspaper supplements	Offer vast circulations at relatively low cost; opportunity to expose message at concentrated times; Sundays are a day of rest and family gatherings. Not passed around as much as magazines; have 'desert' areas.

under consideration should now be profiled in more detail. The audience characteristics (the total size of audiences; the demographic, the geographical, the psychographic details of the audience); the production requirements of the medium/vehicle; the size of insertions and potential effects on salesforce and trade must now be analysed.

A decision must also be taken on the number of media to be used. Many large advertisers do use a single medium, and television is used particularly because it is so dominating. In cases where the advertiser dominates a medium relative to competitors, it may be expected that the audience is more familiar with the advertiser's brand and preference may result. There are, however, many advertisers who spread their budgets among the media. The potential advantages of this strategy are:

– Synergism – the '2 + 2 = 5' idea of media working in combination to product a greater output than the sum of the individual parts. Primary media may be chosen by the advertiser, with supportive media being used to back these up.
– Coverage may be extended beyond what could be achieved via a single medium.
– Greater segmentation capabilities – different messages attracting different market segments through different media.

Timing of campaigns

The two decisions to be taken now are:

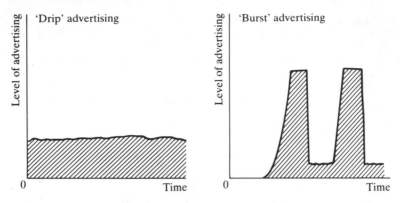

Figure 11.7   Advertising expenditure strategies

1. The duration of the media schedule (i.e., when the campaign is to start and when it is to stop). Concentration should be placed when prospects feel most need for the product, or when they feel the particular need which is the key part of the message.
2. The spread of activity over this time period.

Advertisers may choose between spreading the messages fairly evenly over the time period, and alternating between heavy and light periods of activity within the time period (see Fig. 11.7).

The media schedule

The media requirements, and the reasoning that leads to the selection of final media choices, should now be stated in full. This has meant that the advertiser has reached this stage by a gradual process of elimination, and the listing of the purchases to be made. Such purchases include: the size/length of insertion; insertion dates and times; the anticipated costs and the projected reach. Frequency and cost efficiency of the insertions provide the benchmark against which actual performance may be compared.

ADVERTISING AGENCIES

Most advertisers use the services of an advertising agency for major parts of their advertising programmes. The selection of the agency is a key decision area, since the success of the advertising depends to a large extent upon the contribution of these specialists. The 'full service' agency offers a wide range of services – creative, media planning, marketing research; sales promotions and public relations; account planning and customer contact. It should be noted that a client may use such an agency over some or all of this wide range. Perhaps because of a feeling that the temptation exists to use more services than originally anticipated, or because of a feeling that the 'specialists' are better, there has been a growth of specialist 'hot shops'. These media and creative specialists offer their specialism and nothing more.

There is a lot of industrial concentration in the world of advertising agencies, with a large percentage of total advertising expenditure being handled by a relatively small number of agencies. The 'billings' (the amount of money handled) by the ten largest agencies in the UK are listed in Table 11.3.

Using an agency

The first question to be asked is: 'Do we need to use an agency at all?' A major consideration here

Table 11.3   Agency billings

1983 Ranking	1984 Ranking	Agency	1983 Billing (£m)	1984 Billing (£m)
1	1	Saatchi and Saatchi	134.00	162.00
2	2	J. Walter Thompson	131.50	142.60
4	3	Ogilvy and Mather	95.00	110.00
3	4	D'arcy MacManus Masius	98.00	107.00
11	5	Dorland Advertising	60.40	102.00
7	6	Leo Burnett	72.30	82.40
9	7	Foote Cone and Belding	62.50	81.96
6	8	McCann Erickson	72.60	78.70
10	9	Boase Massimi Pollitt	61.50	76.90
8	10	Young and Rubicam	66.50	76.72

Source: Campaign 11/1/85.

is the likely costs of the deal – in financial terms agencies derive most of their incomes from the *commission system*. This tripartite arrangement is the subject of much criticism (i.e., who is the agency working for?) but it does continue despite various threats that it should be modified.

Under the system agencies pay the media owner for mass media time/space purchases, minus a commission usually in the 10–15 per cent range, and then collect the full amount from the client. In the UK income from commission currently accounts for 70 per cent of all advertising agency incomes. In addition, 'service fees' are charged by advertising agencies and account for the remaining 30 per cent of income.

Advantages for the advertiser in using an agency

1. Administrative economies – high salaries of full-time staff may be avoided.
2. Provision of monthly invoices – no 'hidden' costs, better recording of the costs and monitoring of budgets.
3. Commission system may 'subsidize' the specialized services provided by the agency.
4. Agencies have more power in cases of disputes with the media owners.
5. Specialist services provided by the agency – particularly creative and media expertise – may make advertising more effective.

Disadvantages in using an agency

1. Service fees may make the work expensive – particularly if a lot of creative work is undertaken.
2. If the client is a relatively small customer, then work may be delayed or handled by agency juniors.
3. Possible security leaks – agency personnel, particularly account executives (the agency contact men) must work very closely with and within the client's organization.

Advantages to the media owner

1. Contact with fewer people – costs reduced and operations simplified.
2. Agency acts as a 'salesforce', getting orders for the media owner.

3. Agencies act as a 'principal' in law, i.e., the media owner collects from the agencies, who in turn stand any bad debts from clients.
4. Agencies possess specialist knowledge which may be of use to the media owner in improving the quality of reproduction of the advertisement and other content of the media.
5. The specialist skills provided by agencies may improve the effectiveness of advertising, and indirectly help to bring in more clients and advertising revenue.

Client/agency relations

Corkindale and Kennedy[29] put forward the following recommendations:

- Client and agency should agree a written advertising brief specifically on advertising objectives.
- Someone in the company must be responsible for coordinating the activities undertaken in the agency.
- Someone in the company must be able to justify the work being done in the agency.

The client must develop selection criteria once it has decided to use an advertising agency. The initial screening process will narrow down the range of alternatives, and hopefully lead to a more effective relationship. Factors to be taken account of here are:

- Size of proposed agency.
- Specialist skills offered by the agency.
- Range of services to be used.
- Skills of existing marketing/advertising personnel in the company.
- Agencies used by competitors.
- 'Track record' of agencies.
- Location of agencies.
- The need for establishing *rapport*, and the likelihood of a long-term working relationship.

CONCLUSIONS

This chapter has shown the place of communications in the marketing mix. Communication strategies have been examined followed by an explanation of the purpose of advertising from the viewpoint of a company marketing its products or services. It further explored brand image and corporate image. Generic advertising was then discussed and the potential effect of advertising was summarized in terms of its effect on sales.

Theoretical models of advertising were considered and their usefulness assessed followed by a practical assessment of advertising effectiveness through the medium of advertising research.

The selection of agencies and media is an important consideration in communication strategy, and criteria surrounding such selection were considered.

Chapter 12 considers the more personal elements of promotion in the form of selling and sales management.

APPLICATION QUESTIONS

1. With examples of your choice, show the usefulness of the following:
   (a) Brand advertising.
   (b) Corporate advertising.
   (c) Generic advertising.

2. Why are the sequential models of the advertising process so called? What insights may be gained by studying these?
3. Give three examples of each of the following:
   (a) Advertisements using the USP.
   (b) Advertisements based on 'imagery'.
   (c) Advertisements using rationality as the main motivator.
4. To what extent do you believe that below-the-line promotions are particularly useful in encouraging impulse purchases?
5. What do you understand by the terms internal and external publics in the context of public relations?

REFERENCES

1. Lasswell, H., in: *Communication of Ideas*, L. Bryson (ed.), Institute for Religious and Social Studies, 1975.
2. Ogilvy, D., *Confessions of an Advertising Man*, Atheneum, New York, 1963.
3. Frye, J., *Introduction to the Marketing Systems*, Stanford University Press, Stanford, CA, 1973.
4. Festinger, L. *A Theory of Cognitive Dissonance*, Row, Peterson & Co., 1957.
5. Wills, G., How Good or Bad are Your Marketing Communications? MEG Conference, 1976.
6. Majaro, S., 'Advertising by objectives', *Management Today*, January 1970.
7. Britt, S. H., *Marketing Management and Administrative Action*, McGraw-Hill, London, 1973.
8. Roberts, A., *Selling Advertising Budgets*, Advertising Association, London, 1986.
9. Christopher, M., *Marketing Below-the-Line*, George Allen & Unwin, London, 1969.
10. Engel, J. F., H. G. Wales and M. R. Warshaw, *Promotional Strategy*, R. D. Irwin, Homewood, IL, 1975.
11. Schlackman, W., *Some Psychological Aspects of Dealing*. MRS Papers, 1964.
12. Spillard, P., *Sales Promotion – Its Place in Marketing Strategy*, Business Publications, Plano, TX, 1966.
13. Morgan, A., *A Guide to Consumer Promotions*, Ogilvy and Mather, 1980.
14. Institute of Public Relations London, Public Relations Definition, 1986.
15. Jenkins, F., *Public Relations*, 2nd edn, International Ideas, Philadelphia, PA, 1983, pp. 1–11.
16. Haywood, R., *All about PR*, McGraw-Hill, London, 1984, pp. 141–244.
17. Corkindale, D. and S. H. Kennedy, *Processes of Advertising*, MCB Publications, Bradford, 1978.
18. Starch, D., *Principles of Advertising*, 1925.
19. Colley, R. H., *Defining Advertising Goals for Measured Advertising Results*, Association of National Advertisers, New York, 1961 and 1983.
20. Bernstein, D., 'Advertising: inexact science – bastard art', *Business Graduate*, Summer 1975.
21. Lavidge, R. T. and G. A. Steiner, 'A model for predictive measurement of advertising effectiveness', *Journal of Marketing*, October 1962.
22. Palda, K. S., 'The hypothesis of a hierarchy of effects – a partial evaluation', *Journal of Marketing Research*, **3** (1), February 1966.
23. Reeves, R., *Reality of Advertising*, A. A. Knopf Inc, New York, 1961.
24. Ogilvy, D., op. cit.
25. Martineau, P., *Reality in Advertising*, McGraw-Hill, London, 1961.
26. Joyce, T., 'What do we know about how advertising works', *Advertising Age*, 1967.
27. Hodgson, P., 'What happened to sales promotion research?', *Marketing*, April 1977, pp. 71–74.
28. Chisnall, P., *Marketing Research*, McGraw-Hill, London, 1986, pp. 204–40.
29. Corkindale, D. and S. H. Kennedy, op. cit.

TWELVE

SELLING AND SALES MANAGEMENT

INTRODUCTION

Personal selling is one element in a company's marketing mix. It is in fact classed within the 'promotion' (or communication) element of the '4 Ps', but it warrants a separate treatment in its own right. In industrial marketing, personal selling is likely to be the main communicational tool with expenditure in this area very much higher than for non-personal communications such as advertising or public relations. Highly technical products require a talk to prospective customers about their merits and to answer questions about their use. Consumer goods companies also use salespersons, primarily to sell into the trade but in this area expenditure is likely to be higher for advertising than personal selling.

Personal selling must, therefore, be integrated with the whole marketing programme and not seen as a distinct activity divorced from the other elements of the communications and marketing mixes. Selling and sales management within a marketing-oriented firm are concerned with the analysis of customers' needs and wants and, through the company's total marketing efforts, with the provision of benefits to satisfy these needs and wants. Although the selling process might seem to be simple at first sight, a body of theory surrounds the subject which has been documented by Saunders et al.[1]

THE SELLING PROCESS

Although no sales interview follows a rigid pattern it is useful to distinguish six elements in the sales process.

1. The opening.
2. Need identification and stimulation.
3. Presentation.
4. Dealing with objections.
5. Negotiation.
6. Closing the sale.

The fragmentation of the selling process into these phases is helpful when training salespeople since development of skills within each area can be worked upon until proficiency is achieved.

The opening

Experienced salespeople know the importance of initial impressions. Consequently, they pay great attention to their appearance, manner and opening remarks. Buyers expect salespeople to be businesslike in their personal appearance and behaviour. Untidy hair and unbuttoned shirts with loose ties can create a lack of confidence in the salesman. Further, the salesperson who does not respect the fact that the buyer is likely to be a busy person, with many demands on his or her time, may cause irritation on the part of the buyer.

Opening remarks are important since they set the tone for the rest of the sales interview. Normally they should be business related since this is the purpose of the visit; they should show the buyer that the salesperson is not about to waste time. Where the buyer is well known to the salesperson and where, by his or her own remarks, the buyer indicates a willingness to talk about a more social matter, the salesperson will obviously follow. This can generate close *rapport* with the buyer, but the salesperson must be aware of the reason for being there, and not be excessively diverted from talking business.

Need identification and stimulation

Customers buy products to meet needs and solve problems. Consequently, key factors in sales success are to identify customer needs and problems, and in certain circumstances stimulate the recognition of a need or problem on the part of the buyer.

This 'needs analysis' approach suggests that early in the sales process the salesperson should adopt a question-and-listen posture. In order to encourage the buyer to discuss his problems and needs, salespeople tend to use 'open' rather than 'closed' questions. An open question is one which requires more than a one word or one phrase answer.

- 'Why do you believe that a computer system is inappropriate for your business?'
- 'What were the main reasons for buying the XYZ photocopier?'

A closed question, on the other hand, invites a one word or one phrase answer. These can be used to obtain purely factual information, but excessive use can hinder *rapport* and lead to an abrupt type of conversation which lacks flow. Examples of closed questions are:

- 'Would you tell me the name of the equipment you currently use?'
- 'Does your company manufacture 1000cc marine engines?'

Salespeople should avoid the temptation of making a sales presentation without finding out the needs of their customers. It is all too easy to start a sales presentation in the same rigid way, perhaps by highlighting the current bargain of the week, without first questioning the customer as to his or her needs.

Need and problem stimulation are necessary when a prospect is happy with the *status quo* and does not recognize that the purchase of the salesperson's product or service could, for example, improve productivity, lower costs, or give greater financial security. In these cases, the sales task may involve the process of 'disturbing' whereby the salesperson disturbs the buyer's perception of life by showing, for example, how present methods are inefficient, and costly, or how present insurance cover is inadequate.

The presentation

The advantages conferred by carrying out a 'needs analysis' are realized during the presentation.

The salesperson knows which product or brand from the range of products or brands he or she is selling best fits the customer's requirements, and is also aware of which benefits to stress.

The key to this task is to recognize that buyers purchase benefits and are only interested in product features in as much as they provide the benefits that the customer is looking for. Training programmes and personal preparation of salespeople should pay particular attention to deriving the customer benefits their products bestow.

Benefits should be analysed at two levels: those benefits that can be obtained by purchase of a particular type of product; and those that can be obtained by purchasing that product from a particular supplier. For example, automatic washing machine salespeople need to consider the benefits of an automatic washing machine compared with a twin-tub, as well as the benefits that their company's automatic washing machines have over competitors' models. This proffers maximum flexibility for the salesperson in meeting various sales situations.

Dealing with objections

Objections should not always be viewed with dismay by salespeople. Many objections are simply expressions of interest by the buyer. What the buyer is asking for is further information because he or she is interested in what the salesperson is saying. The problem is that he or she is not, as yet, convinced. Objections highlight the issues which are important to the buyer.

An example will illustrate these points. Suppose an industrial salesperson working for an adhesives manufacturer is faced with the following objection: 'Why should I buy your new adhesive gun when my present method of applying adhesive – direct from the tube – is perfectly satisfactory?' This type of objection is clearly an expression of a desire for additional information. The salesperson's task is to provide it in a manner which does not antagonize the buyer and, yet, is convincing. It is a fact of human personality that the argument which is supported by the greater weight of evidence does not always win the day; people do not like to be proved wrong. The very act of changing a supplier may be resisted because it may imply criticism of a past decision on the part of the buyer. For a salesperson to disregard the emotional aspects of dealing with objections is to court disaster. The situation to be avoided is where the buyer 'digs his heels in' on principle, because of the attitude of the salesperson.

The effective approach for dealing with objections involves two areas: the preparation of convincing answers; and the development of a range of techniques for answering objections in a manner which permits the acceptance of these answers without loss of face on the part of the buyer. Two commonly used methods for dealing with objections are the 'agree and counter' and the 'forestalling' techniques:

Agree and counter This approach maintains the respect the salesperson shows to the buyer. The salesperson first agrees that what the buyer is saying is sensible and reasonable, before then putting forward an alternative point of view. It takes the edge off the objection and creates a climate of agreement rather than conflict. For example:

Buyer: The problem with your tractor is that it costs more than your competition.
Salesperson: Yes, the initial cost of the tractor is a little higher than competitors' models, but I should like to show you how, over the life time of the machine, ours works out to be far more economical.

Forestall the objection Perhaps buyers are continually raising the objection that the salesperson is working for one of the smallest companies in the industry. One way of dealing with this objection is to forestall it. The salesperson raises the objection himself as part of the sales presentation. This allows it to be dealt with effectively by changing the objection into a benefit. Thus the salesperson may say, 'My company is smaller than most in the industry which means that we respond quicker to our customers' needs and try that bit harder to make sure our customers are happy.'

Negotiation

Many salespeople are given some discretion regarding the terms of the sale. They may negotiate price, credit terms, trade-in values and delivery times. It is a fact of much commercial life that the profit realized from a transaction will be dependent upon the outcome of negotiations. Success in negotiating derives from two factors: preparation and the application of negotiating skills.

Preparation Before the parties to the negotiation meet, each should make careful preparations. This involves four factors: (i) assessment of the balance of power; (ii) determination of objectives; (iii) concession analysis; and (iv) proposal analysis.

A seller's position will be strengthened if the buyer has very few options available to him or her, if the salesperson's products offer better solutions to the buyer's problems than the competition, and the problem is of high importance and visibility to the buying organization. The salesperson should assess his or her position so that objectives can be set and the level of concessions he or she is willing to give can be planned.

When setting objectives it is useful to consider two types: 'must have' and 'would like' objectives. 'Must have' objectives are the minimum requirements of the deal, e.g., the lowest price at which a seller is willing to trade. 'Would like' objectives are the maximum a negotiator can realistically achieve. They define the opening positions of buyers and sellers.

Concession analysis is vital to negotiating success as it allows calm consideration at what can be traded. A skilful negotiator will attempt to trade concession for concession so that ultimately an agreement which satisfies both parties is reached.

Proposal analysis involves determining the likely demands of the buyer, and the reactions to them. By this kind of anticipation, the seller can plan the kinds of counter-proposals he or she wishes to make, and thus avoid making mistakes in the heat of the negotiating battle.

Application at negotiating skills Two basic principles of negotiation are to start high but be realistic, and to trade concession for concession. Making the opening stance high has two benefits. First, the buyer might agree to it. Second, it provides room for negotiation if he or she does not agree. Indeed, a buyer may have become accustomed to concessions from the seller in return for purchasing. Trading concession for concession can be achieved by means of the 'if . . . then' technique.[2] For example, the seller might say, 'if you are willing to collect these goods at our premises, then I am prepared to reduce the price by £10'. This is a valuable tool at the disposal of the negotiator since it promotes movement towards agreement and yet ensures that proposals to give the buyer something are matched by proposals for a concession in return.

Closing the sale

Some salespeople are reluctant to close the sale because they fear rejection. Yet in many sales situations failure to close will mean the order being placed with a competitor. In other situations, often industrial, it is inappropriate to attempt to close the sale since the buying process is lengthy.

However, when the time has come for the close to be made there are a number of techniques available. Two methods are the summary close and the concession close.

Summarize and then ask for order This technique allows the salesperson to remind the buyer of the main points in the sales argument in a manner which implies that the moment for decision has come and that buying is the natural extension of the proceedings.

> Well, Mr Smith, we have agreed that the ZDXL4 model meets your requirements of low noise, high productivity and driver comfort at a cost which you can afford. May I go ahead and place an order for this model?

The concession close This involves keeping one concession in reserve to use as the final push towards agreement: 'If you are willing to place an order now, I'm willing to offer an extra $2\frac{1}{2}$ per cent discount'.

SALES MANAGEMENT

The sales manager's job is particularly difficult because subordinates are usually geographically separated from him or her. This can produce problems of communication and control not experienced by a purchasing or financial manager whose staff are located within the same building as himself or herself. However, the key responsibilities of sales management are similar to other managerial positions namely:

1. Setting sales objectives and strategies.
2. Recruitment and selection of salespeople.
3. Motivation.
4. Organization.
5. Training.
6. Control.

Setting sales objectives and strategies

The sales manager is unlikely to be the only person involved in setting corporate sales objectives. Top management, marketing personnel and statisticians as well as sales managers may influence the level of the sales target for the forthcoming year. Once agreed, the performance targets for individual salespeople are likely to be set by sales management after consultation with the salespeople themselves. Performance targets may be set in terms of sales volume, call rates, profit margin achieved, numbers of new customers, etc. Sales strategy is the method by which objectives are achieved. For example, an increase in target sales may be achieved by the strategy of increasing calls to new customers, spending more time with existing customers or setting up a telesales team to give increased service to small customers. Sales management plays a key role in determining the most effective strategy to achieve corporate sales objectives.

Recruitment and selection of salespeople

The selection of salespeople, while of obvious importance to the long-term future of the business, is a task which does not always receive the attention it should from sales managers. All too often, the 'man profile' is ill-defined and the selection procedure designed for maximum convenience rather than optimal choice. The assumption is that the right person should emerge whatever procedure is used. Consequently, the interview is poorly handled, the smooth talker gets the job and another mediocre salesperson emerges.

Two key aspects of recruitment and selection are the preparation of the job description and personal specification and interviewing. A job description usually covers the following factors:

- The title of the job.
- Duties and responsibilities – the tasks which will be expected of the new recruit, e.g., selling, after-sales service, information feedback, and the range of products/markets/type of consumer with which he or she will be associated.
- To whom he or she will report.
- Technical requirements, e.g., the degree to which the salesperson needs to understand the technical aspects of the products he or she is selling.
- Location and geographical area to be covered.
- Degree of autonomy – the degree to which the salesperson will be able to control his or her own work programme.

Once generated, the job description will act as the blueprint for the personnel specification which outlines the type of applicant the company is seeking. The technical requirements of the job, for example, and the nature of the customers which the salespeople will meet, will be factors which influence the level of education and, possibly, the age of the required salesperson. A personnel specification may contain all or some of the following factors:

- Physical requirements, e.g., speech, appearance.
- Attainments, e.g., standard of education and qualifications, experience and successes.
- Aptitudes and qualities, e.g., ability to communicate, self-motivation.
- Disposition, e.g., maturity, sense of responsibility.
- Interests, e.g., degree to which interests are social, active or inactive.
- Personal circumstances, e.g., married, single, etc.

The factors chosen to define the personnel specification will be used as criteria of selection in the interview itself.

The objective of the interview is to enable interviewers to form a clear impression of the strengths and weaknesses of the candidates with respect to the selection criteria. Candidates should be encouraged to talk openly about themselves but interviewers should take care to control the interview so that all relevant areas are covered. Otherwise a candidate may be allowed to talk about his strengths without due consideration of his weaknesses.

What happens at the beginning of the interview is crucial to subsequent events. The objective at this stage is to set the candidate at ease. Most interviewees are naturally anxious before the interview and when they first enter the interview setting. They may feel embarrassed or be worried about exposing weaknesses; they may feel inadequate and lack confidence; and above all they may feel worried about rejection. This anxiety is compounded by the fact that the candidate may never have met his interviewers before and may thus be uncertain about how aggressive they will be, the degree of pressure which will be applied and the type of questions they are likely to ask. Some sales managers may argue that the salesperson is likely to meet this situation out in the field and therefore needs to be able to deal with it without the use of anxiety-reducing techniques on the part of the interviewers. A valid response to this viewpoint is that the objective of the interview is to get to know the candidate in terms of the criteria laid down in the personal specification, or 'man profile' as it is sometimes called. In order to do this the interviewee must be encouraged to talk about himself or herself. If sales ability under stress is to be tested, role playing can be employed as part of the selection procedure.

Motivation

Motivation in theory Although motivation is dependent on each salesperson's individual needs and desires, a sales manager can influence motivation both positively and negatively by his or her actions and policies. Some people have the opinion that salespeople are motivated solely by money and indeed the type of compensation plan a firm adopts can be a factor in achieving enhanced performance. However, there are other job-related factors which can influence motivation. A major contribution in this area was made by Herzberg *et al.*[3]

Herzberg distinguished between factors which can cause dissatisfaction but cannot motivate (hygiene factors) and factors which can cause positive motivation. Hygiene factors included physical working conditions, security, salary and interpersonal relationships. Directing managerial attention to these factors, postulated Herzberg, would bring motivation up to a 'theoretical zero' but would not result in positive motivation. If this was to be achieved, attention would have to be given to true motivators. These included the nature of the work itself which allows the person to make some concrete achievement, recognition of achievement, the responsibility exercised by the person, and the interest value of the work itself.

The inclusion of salary as a hygiene factor rather than as a motivator was subject to criticisms from sales managers whose experience led them to believe that commission paid to their salespeople was a powerful motivator in practice. Herzberg accommodated their view to some extent by arguing that increased salary through higher commission was a motivator through the automatic recognition it gave to sales achievement.

The salesperson is fortunate that achievement is directly observable in terms of higher sales (except in missionary selling, where orders are not taken, e.g., pharmaceuticals, beer and selling to specifiers). However, the degree of responsibility afforded to salespeople varies a great deal. Opportunities for giving a greater degree of responsibility to (and hence motivating) salespersons include giving authority to grant credit (up to a certain value), discretion to offer discounts, and handing over responsibility for calling frequencies to the salespeople.

Herzberg's theory has been well received, in general, by practitioners, although academics have criticized it in terms of methodology and over-simplification, especially Dessler.[4] The theory has undoubtedly made a substantial contribution to the understanding of motivation at work, particularly in highlighting the importance of job content factors which had hitherto been badly neglected.

Other theorists such as Maslow,[5] Vroom[6] and Likert[7] have worked within the area of motivation. For an evaluation of their contribution, see Lancaster and Jobber[8] who have given a detailed review.

Motivation in practice Three key elements in motivating salespeople in practice are the type of compensation plan adopted, the setting of sales targets, and manager–salesperson relationships.

Type of compensation plan There are, basically, three types of compensation plan:

– Fixed salary.
– Commission only.
– Salary plus commission.

Each will now be evaluated in terms of benefits and drawbacks to management and salespeople, with particular reference to motivation.

Fixed salary This method of payment encourages sales personnel to consider all aspects of the selling function rather than just those which lead to a quick sales return. Salespeople who are paid on fixed salary are likely to be more willing to provide technical service, complete information feedback reports and carry out prospecting than if they were paid solely by commission. The system provides security to the salesperson who knows how much income he or she will receive each month and it is relatively cheap to administer since calculation of commissions and bonuses is not required.

The system also overcomes the problem of deciding how much commission to give to each salesperson when a complex buying decision is made by a number of DMU members who have been influenced by different salespeople, perhaps in different parts of the country. Wilson[9] cites the case of a sale of building materials to a local authority in Lancashire being the result of one salesman influencing an architect in London, another calling on the contractor in Norwich and a third persuading the local authority itself.

However, the method does have a number of drawbacks. First, no direct financial incentive is provided for increasing sales (no profits). Second, high-performing salespeople may not be attracted, and holding on to them may be difficult using fixed salary since they may perceive the system as being unfair and may be tempted to apply for jobs where financial rewards are high for outstanding performers. Third, selling costs remain static in the short term when sales decrease; thus the system does not provide the in-built flexibility provided by the other compensation systems.

Because of its inherent characteristics, this system is used primarily in industrial selling where technical service is an important element in the selling task and the time necessary to conclude a sale may be long. It is particularly appropriate when the salesperson sells very high-value products at very low volumes. Under these conditions a commission-based compensation scheme would lead to widely varying monthly income levels depending on when orders were placed.

Commission only The commission-only system of payment provides an obvious incentive to sell. However, since income is dependent on sales results, salespeople will be reluctant to spend time on tasks which they do not perceive as being directly related to sales. The result is that salespeople may pursue short-term goals, to the detriment of activities which may have an effect in the longer term; salespeople may be reluctant to write reports providing market information to management and spend time out of the field to attend sales training courses, for example.

The system provides little security for salespeople whose earnings may suffer through no fault of their own, and the pressure to sell may damage customer–salesperson relationships. This is particularly relevant to industrial selling, where the decision-making process may be long and pressure applied by the salesperson to close the sale prematurely may be detrimental.

From management's perspective the system not only has the advantage of directly financing costs automatically, but also allows some control over salespeople's activities through the use of higher commission rates on products and accounts in which management is particularly interested.

It is most often used in situations where there are a large number of potential customers, the buying process is relatively short and technical assistance and service are not required. Insurance selling is an example where commission-only payments are often used.

Salary plus commission This system attempts to combine the benefits of both of the previous methods in order to provide financial incentives with a level of security. Since income is not solely dependent upon commission, management gains a greater degree of control over the salesperson's time than under the commission only system, and sales costs are, to some extent, related to revenue generated. The method is attractive to ambitious salespeople who wish to combine security with the capability of earning more by greater effort and ability.

Clearly, managers who wish to use the incentive of extra money for good performance are going to choose commission only or salary plus commission as their method of compensation.

However, fixed salary schemes may be used where it is difficult to tie performance to individual salespeople's achievements and to do so may cause resentment and feelings of unfairness which may lead to demotivation.

Setting sales targets A key feature of the commission-only or salary plus commission payment plan may be the determination of each salesperson's sales target or quota. If a sales target or quota is to be effective in motivating a salesperson it must be regarded as fair and attainable and yet offer a challenge. Because the salesperson should regard the quota as fair, it is usually sensible to allow him or her to participate in the setting of the quota. However, the establishment of the quotas is ultimately the sales manager's responsibility and he or she will inevitably be constrained by overall company objectives. If sales are planned to increase by 10 per cent, then salespeople's quotas must be consistent with this. Variations around this average figure will arise through the sales manager's knowledge of individual salespeople and changes in commercial activity within each territory; for example, the liquidation of a key customer in a territory may be reflected in a reduced quota. The attainment of a sales target usually results in some form of extra payment to the salesperson.

Sales manager/salesperson meetings There are a number of ways in which meetings between the sales manager and his salespeople can lead to better motivation. First, they allow the sales manager to understand the personality, needs and problems of each salesperson. The manager can then better understand the causes of demotivation in individual salespeople and respond in a manner which takes into account the needs, problems and personality of the salesperson. Second, meetings in the field, which may form part of an evaluation and training programme, can also provide an opportunity to motivate. Sales technique can be improved and confidence boosted, both of which may motivate by restoring in the salesperson the belief that performance will improve through extra effort. Third, group meetings can motivate, according to Likert, when the sales manager encourages an 'open' style of meeting. Salespeople are encouraged to discuss their sales problems and opportunities so that the entire sales team benefits from the experience of each salesperson. This leads to a greater sense of group loyalty and improved performance. Finally, meetings between manager and salespeople provide the opportunity for performance feedback where weaknesses are identified and recognition for good work is given.

Organization

A major aspect of organizing a sales team is the decision regarding organizational structure. There are three basic alternatives – geographically-, product- and customer-based structures.

Geographical structure An advantage of this form of organization is its simplicity. Each salesperson is assigned a territory over which he has sole responsibility for sales achievement. His close geographical proximity to customers encourages the development of personal friendships which aids sales effectiveness. Also, compared with other organization forms, for example, product or market specialization, travelling expenses are likely to be lower.

A potential weakness of the geographical structure is that the salesperson is required to sell the full range of the company's products. They may be very different technically and sell into a number of diverse markets. In such a situation it may be unreasonable to expect the salesperson to have the required depth of technical knowledge for each product and be conversant with the full range of potential applications within each market. This expertise can only be developed if the salesperson is given a more specialized role.

Product-based structure One method of specialization is along product lines. Conditions which are conducive to this form of organization are where the company sells a wide range of technically complex and diverse products, and where key members of the decision-making unit of the buying organizations are different for each product group. However, if the company's products sell essentially to the same customers, problems of route duplication (and hence higher travel costs) and customer annoyance can arise. Inappropriate use of this method can lead to a customer being called upon by different salespersons representing the same company on the same day. When a company contemplates a move from the geographically-based to a product-based structure, some customer overlap is inevitable, but, if only of a limited extent, the problem should be manageable.

Customer-based structures Three customer-based methods of organization are the market centred, account size and the new/existing account structures.

Market-centred structure Another method of specialization is by the type of market served. Often, in industrial selling, the market is defined by industry type. Thus, although the range of products sold is essentially the same, it might be sensible for a computer firm to allocate its salespeople on the basis of the industry served, e.g., banking, manufacturing companies, retailers, given that different industry groups have widely varying needs, problems and potential applications. Specialization by market served allows a salesperson to gain greater insights into these factors for his or her particular industry, as well as to monitor changes and trends within the industry which might affect demand for his or her products. The cost of increased customer knowledge is increased travel expenses compared with geographically determined territories.

Account size structure Some companies structure their salesforce by account size. The importance of a few large customers in many trade and industrial markets has given rise to the establishment of a 'key account' salesforce. The team comprises senior salespeople who specialize in dealing with large customers who may have different buying habits and may demand more sophisticated sales arguments than smaller companies. The team will be conversant with negotiation skills since they are likely to be given a certain amount of discretion in terms of discounts, credit terms, etc., in order to secure large orders. The range of selling skills required is, therefore, wider than for the rest of the salesforce, who deal with the smaller accounts. Some organizations adopt a three-tier system with senior salespeople negotiating with national accounts, ordinary salespeople selling to medium-sized accounts, and a telephone sales team dealing with small accounts.

New/existing account structure A further method of sales organization is to create two teams of salespeople. The first team services existing accounts, while the second concentrates upon seeking new accounts. This structure recognizes that gaining new customers is a specialized activity, demanding prospecting skills, patience, the ability to accept higher rejection rates than when calling upon existing customers, and the time to cultivate new relationships. Placing this function in the hands of the regular salesforce may result in its neglect since the salespeople may view it as time which could be better spent with existing customers. Pioneer salespeople were used successfully by trading stamp companies to prospect new customers. Once an account was obtained it was handed over to a maintenance salesperson who serviced the account.

Training

Training should not be confined to new salespeople. Experienced salespeople also require refresher training which has the benefit of sharpening skills and stimulating thought on new ways of selling. A training programme usually has five components:

– The company – objectives, policies and organization.
– Its products.
– Its competitors and their products.
– Selling procedure and techniques.
– Work organization and report preparation.

The first three components are essentially communicating the required level of knowledge to the salesperson. The first component will probably include a brief history of the company, how it has grown and where it intends to go in the future. Policies relevant to the selling function, for example, how salespeople are evaluated, and the nature of the compensation system will be explained. The way in which the company is organized will be described and the relationship between sales and the marketing function, including advertising and market research, will be described so that the salesperson has an appreciation of the support he or she is receiving from headquarters.

The second component, product knowledge, will include a description of how the products are made and the implications for product quality and reliability, the features of the product and the benefits they confer on the consumer. Salespeople will be encouraged to carry out their own product analysis so that they will be able to identify key features and benefits of new products as they are launched. Competitors will be identified and competitors' products will also be analysed to spotlight differences betwee them and the company's products.

Some training programmes, particularly within the industrial selling area, stop here, neglecting a major component of a training programme – selling procedures and techniques. This component will include practical sessions where trainees develop skills through role-playing exercises. For experienced salespeople, sales skills will be developed by on-the-job training. They will be accompanied on sales visits by their sales manager who will highlight strengths and weakness and provide guidance as to improved performance.

The final component of the programme – work organization and report writing – will endeavour to establish good habits among the trainees in areas which, because of day-to-day pressures, may be neglected. The importance of these activities on a salesperson's performance and, hence, earnings will be stressed.

Evaluation and control

The prime reason for evaluation is to attempt to attain company objectives. By measuring actual performance against objectives, shortfalls can be identified and appropriate action taken to improve performance. However, evaluation has other benefits. Evaluation can help improve individual salespeople's motivation and skills. Motivation is affected since an evaluation programme will identify what is expected of the individual, and what is considered good performance. Second, it provides the opportunity for the recognition of above average standards of work performance, which improves confidence and motivation. Skills are affected since carefully constructed evaluation allows areas of weakness to be identified, and effort to be directed to the improvement of skills in those areas.

Although sales managers are primarily interested in sales as a percentage of quota or target, in practice a whole range of measures may be used – often for diagnostic purposes. Table 12.1 gives a summary of the more common quantitative measures.

Table 12.1   Quantitative measures of performance

Sales	Orders
Sales revenue	Number of orders taken
Sales revenue as a percentage of quota	Order per call ratio
Sales revenue per order	Average order value
Sales revenue per call	Average profit contribution per order
Sales revenue from new accounts	
Accounts	*Calls*
Number of new accounts	Number of calls per period
Number of accounts lost	Calls on potential new accounts
Total number of accounts	Call on existing accounts
Profit	*Expenses*
Gross profit	Sales expenses to sales revenue ratio
Net profit	Average expenses per call
Return on investment	Expenses per square mile of territory
Profit per call ratio	

In addition, salespeople may be evaluated on a number of qualitative dimensions. The most usual ones are:

- Sales skills.
- Customer relationships.
- Self-organization.
- Product knowledge.
- Cooperation and attitudes.

For an evaluation and control system to work efficiently, it is important for the sales team to understand its purpose. For them to view it simply as a means for management to catch them out and criticize performance is likely to breed resentment. It should be used, and be perceived, as a means for assistant salespeople to improve performance, through integration with the company's sales training programme. Indeed, the quantitative output measures themselves can be used as a basis for rewarding performance when targets are met. This chapter has provided a checklist of measurements from which individual sales managers can select the most appropriate one for their particular situation. They are summarized in Table 12.1. Such improvements in the sales evaluation and control system should result in enhanced effectiveness in the marketplace.

CONCLUSIONS

This chapter has reviewed the selling and managerial skills necessary for efficient personal selling. The modern marketplace requires sales teams who can not only sell but also negotiate terms and conditions which result in profitable orders. Sales managers must recognize the full extent of their managerial responsibilities which include setting objectives and strategy recruitment and selection, motivation, organization, training and control.

The chapter has been written from the viewpoint of a company selling to customers, rather than buyers seeking out sellers. Particularly in industrial markets, the latter is often the case. Chapter 3 was concerned with 'Marketing and customers', and buyer behaviour (consumer and organizational) was discussed there in some depth. It can, therefore, be appreciated that a study of buyer behaviour is an essential prerequisite to good selling, because the seller can then focus appropriate selling points on to the avowed and unavowed needs of buyers.

APPLICATION QUESTIONS

1. Discuss the importance of 'needs analysis' within personal selling.
2. Outline the main stages in personal selling and discuss the techniques which can be used to achieve a sale.
3. What are the major functions of sales management? Discuss how the achievement of any *two* functions may be accomplished.
4. How can the links between motivation, training and evaluation lead to better sales performance?
5. It is not possible to motivate, only to demotivate. Discuss.

REFERENCES

1. Saunders, J., T. Hong-Chung and G. Lancaster, 'Traditional and modern views of personal selling', *Journal of Sales Management* (Monograph), **2**(1), 1985.
2. Kennedy, G., J. Benson and J. MacMillan, *Managing Negotiations*, Business Books, London, 1980.
3. Herzberg, F., B. Mausner and B. Block Snydeman, *The Motivation to Work*, Wiley, New York, 1959.
4. Dessler, G., *Human Behaviour: Improving Performance at Work*, Prentice-Hall, Englewood Cliffs, NJ, 1979.
5. Maslow, A. H., 'A theory of human motivation', *Psychological Review*, July 1943.
6. Vroom, V. H., *Work and Motivation*, Wiley, 1964.
7. Likert, R., *New Patterns of Sales Management*, McGraw-Hill, London, 1961.
8. Lancaster, G. and D. Jobber, *Sales Technique and Management*, Macdonald and Evans, 1985.
9. Wilson, M., *Managing a Sales Force*, Gower Publishing, Aldershot, 1983.

THIRTEEN
MANAGING THE MARKETING MIX

INTRODUCTION

In this chapter we shall examine the functions of marketing personnel in their role as managers.

All managers, irrespective of the functional specialism in which they spend their working lives, share common duties and activities. In particular, managers, including marketing managers, are responsible for *planning*, *organizing*, *directing* and *controlling* within their own function. Underpinning these control tasks of management is the manager's role as a maker of decisions. In Chapter 4 we examined the key decision areas of marketing management, including those which were referred to collectively, as the marketing mix decisions. We also examined how marketing management relates to, and interacts with, the other functional areas in the business and in particular its role in the overall planning and decision-making process.

With this as a background, this chapter traces the planning, organizing, directing and controlling aspects of marketing management. We shall start with the formulation of marketing plans and the strategies and tactics which accompany them. We shall then examine how scarce marketing and company resources need to be allocated and organized to support these marketing plans and the need for marketing efforts to be evaluated and controlled.

The chapter concludes with a necessarily brief account of the important 'people managing' aspects of marketing management. Marketing managers, like other managers, normally rely on 'getting things done through people'. To be effective, the marketing manager must be aware of the importance of managing the human assets under his or her control. This involves careful selection, training, motivation, and above all, leadership of marketing personnel.

THE NATURE OF MANAGEMENT

Most people have a notion of what managers do. In fact it has proved extremely difficult to define what a manager is or does. There are many so-called 'theories of management' often offering different and personalized views on the nature of management. Before examining some of the most practical of these views it is useful to explain briefly why the form and content of managerial work has attracted so much attention.

Since the early 1900s attention has focused on the nature and function of managerial work. The prime concern of this attention has been to analyse the necessary managerial skills and behaviour with a view to improving effective managerial performance. A substantial part of the early attention in this field was in fact aimed at developing a 'science' of management or at least a set of prescriptive guidelines or principles that could be applied in all managerial functions. This desire to establish a body of management theory and principles was in turn prompted by the increasingly rapid industrialization which many countries experienced at the turn of the century, with its accompanying growth of large-scale organizations and mass production on a factory system. As industrialization progressed scientific principles and practice were applied increasingly to the manufacturing and production processes. No such body of knowledge was available, however, to the practising manager of the time. Most managers learned how to manage the hard way; through a process of trial and error built upon experience. Not only was this felt by many to be an unsatisfactory situation, but the separation of ownership from control, which the growth of large-scale organization prompted, gave rise, for the first time, to the professional manager: a 'professional manager' none the less unsupported by the underpinning body of knowledge or learning necessary to any profession. Thus management tended to be by 'hunch' or 'rule of thumb'.

Some of the easiest attempts to professionalize the management function came from practising managers, who on the basis of their experience suggested basic principles of management in order to aid others in their work. For the purposes of this book we do not need to be concerned with the variety of principles which were suggested, nor indeed with the controversy surrounding which of the individual viewpoints is most appropriate; there are many excellent texts available for the reader who is interested in an in-depth discussion of these issues including that of Albors.[1] For our purposes it is sufficient to note that despite the 'unscientific' nature of many of these early approaches, the fact that they represent the collective wisdom extant some eighty or more years ago and the differences between the viewpoints offered, a picture did emerge of what comprised the essential elements of the management process. Moreover, these basic elements are still propounded as being relevant to the manager of today. These basic elements of management are *planning*, *organizing*, *directing* and *controlling*. We shall examine how each of these relates to the task of marketing management.

PLANNING AND MARKETING MANAGEMENT

Planning is now recognized as being an essential feature of the manager's job. We have seen, in Chapter 4, how planning applies at the corporate or overall business level and the interrelationships which this gives rise to between strategic planners and marketing management. In addition to the marketers' input to development of corporate plans, marketing managers must, in the light of these plans, prepare plans for their own functional activities. As in corporate planning, marketing planning involves a series of iterative steps which require marketing management to set *objectives* ('where do we want to go?'), *formulate strategies and tactics* ('how do we intend to get there?'), and *prescribe time scales* for the implementation and achievement of these plans ('when do we want to get there?'). This 'where', 'how' and 'when' content of all plans is encompassed in our definition of the planning role of marketing management which can be summarized as follows:

The planning role of marketing management comprises the determination of marketing objectives together with the choice of strategies and tactics to achieve these objectives and a time scale for their implementation and achievement.

Each of the steps in this process is considered further below.

Setting marketing objectives

The determination of marketing objectives involves much the same procedure as that outlined for the setting of those at the corporate level. The process begins with an analysis of current and past performance in existing product markets together with a review of potential marketing opportunities and threats. Together with overall corporate objectives and strategies this analysis provides the backcloth against which marketing objectives are set. Given that planning is concerned with the future, it might seem strong to suggest that setting marketing objectives should start with the past. In fact historical data are essential if marketing objectives are to have that necessary characteristic of all objectives – realism. To set marketing objectives without regard to past performance is akin to planning a journey into unknown territory without consulting a map. For this reason, the start of the planning elements – setting objectives – is limited to the first basic element of all management – controlling. In fact, as we shall see, all four basic elements of marketing management are interlinked one with another.

In addition to the analysis of current and past performance it was suggested that the determination of marketing objectives requires a review of potential marketing opportunities and threats. This stage of the objective setting process requires a careful analysis of the marketing environment of the company. Of particular concern here will be those opportunities and threats posed by trends and changes related to *markets*, *customers*, *competitors* and *distributors*. At best, failure to consider these factors is likely to result, again, in unrealistic objectives; at worst it can lead to company failure.

The outcome of these analyses should be clearly defined, preferably in quantitative terms, and realistic objectives set for the marketing function. Multiple objectives for marketing should be consistent one with another and with overall corporate objectives and strategies. Finally, marketing objectives should be communicated to, and agreed by, those responsible for achieving them.

Determining and selecting marketing strategies and tactics

Having determined our marketing objectives the second step is marketing management's planning role in the determination and selection of the routes by which these objectives will be achieved.

Increasingly, planning texts have drawn from the ideas and terminology of the military strategists with terms such as 'encirclement', 'flanking', and 'bypass' strategies being used. Irrespective of the term used to describe a particular strategy it is important to understand what the term 'strategy' means and the distinction between marketing strategies and marketing tactics.

Marketing strategies relate to the overall, broad patterns of marketing actions which a company might take to achieve marketing objectives. For example, a company with a marketing objective of increasing sales revenue by X per cent must select from a variety of different routes to achieve this objective. Among the marketing decisions which might be involved in this selection process, Kotler[2] identifies the following:

– Selection of market targets.
– Choice of market positioning strategies.
– Selection of an appropriate marketing mix.

A statement of the company's overall marketing objectives and strategy in our example, therefore, might run as follows:

To increase sales revenue X per cent in the business micro-computer market based on increased sales to the small business user via product improvement and penetration pricing.

Once again the choice of marketing strategies must reflect both company strengths and weaknesses and a careful analysis of customer/market needs.

Within this broad framework of marketing strategies, marketing management must also specify *marketing tactics*. If strategies represent the 'grand plan' – the overall route to achieving marketing objectives – then tactics represent the 'fine tuning': the details necessary to undertake and complete the journey successfully.

The importance of marketing tactics to the successful achievement of objectives should not be underestimated. Many excellent strategies have failed because of lack of attention, or an inappropriate tactic. On the other hand, although rare, even ill-conceived strategies can succeed because of clever tactical decisions.

Both conceptually and in practice, the lines of demarcation between marketing strategies and tactics are blurred. Tactics are derived from strategies, but these tactics in turn may be considered as sub-strategies which themselves require further tactics for execution. One principal factor which gives rise to this blurring between strategies and tactics, is the existence of a *hierarchy of different planning levels* within a company. What at one level in the planning hierarchy is considered tactics is, at another level, considered strategy. For example, what can be considered tactical decisions at the corporate or overall business planning level become strategies at the functional level. Furthermore, within a function what is one manager's strategy may, for another manager, represent tactics. For example, the sales manager may have a strategy of opening a given number of new accounts. He proceeds to develop the appropriate tactics for his salesforce in order to achieve this. However, the strategy of opening new accounts may itself represent a tactical move as part of an overall marketing strategy. Having said this, we may broadly distinguish marketing tactics from marketing strategies in terms of the following general characteristics.

1. As stated previously, generally, tactics are *more detailed* than strategies.
2. Tactics generally encompass a *shorter period of time* than do strategies.
3. Tactics are *more flexible* than strategies and can be more readily changed to acommodate to new or changed circumstances. This element of flexibility is one of the most important aspects in the imaginative use of tactics in marketing and can add substantially to the effectiveness of marketing efforts. However, great care needs to be exercised in the use of tactics in this way. For example, it is possible that in using tactics to meet changing markets and competitive conditions, a company gradually drifts off course with respect to planned marketing strategies.
4. Finally, tactics differ from strategies in that the *range* of tactics available to the marketer is normally *far wider* than the range of strategies at the disposal of marketing management.

Collectively, these characteristics of marketing tactics mean that the imaginative use of them is particularly beneficial when faced with particular marketing problems. Some examples from the wide range of possible situations favouring the use of effective marketing tactics are shown below:

– When it is necessary to increase stock levels in channels of distribution.
– When competitive activity becomes particularly marked in certain products and/or geographical areas.
– When a company requires to quickly establish demand for a new product.
– When the motivation of the salesforce is waning.

The overall relationship between marketing objectives, strategies and tactics is shown in Fig.

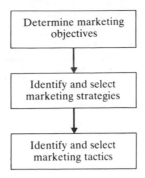

Figure 13.1   The relationship between marketing objectives, strategies and tactics

13.1. The final issue in the marketing manager's role as planner is the determination of time scales for marketing activities.

Prescribing time scales for marketing plans

The final element of marketing planning is specifying time scales for marketing activities. This involves not only prescribing a time scale for the achievement of objectives, but also the timing and scheduling of activities required to meet them.

Time scales for the achievement of marketing objectives may vary to encompass anything from one month ahead to 10 years ahead and more. It is conventional to refer to marketing objectives and plans as being either short, medium or long range in nature. For example, a company may have a long-range marketing objective to become market leader which might involve a sequence of marketing activities covering some five years or more. On the other hand, the same company might have short-term marketing objectives and plans covering, say, the next six months. What constitutes an appropriate time span for marketing activities and, therefore, the distinction between long-, medium- and short-term plans will vary from company to company. Steiner[3] suggests that what constitutes an appropriate 'planning horizon' for a company is related to the length of time to which the planning decision commits the resources of the company. In terms of marketing management, however, one of the most important planning tasks is the preparation of the annual marketing plan.

PREPARING THE ANNUAL MARKETING PLAN

Although the precise format of the annual marketing plan and its contents will vary between companies, the steps involved in its preparation will be broadly similar for any marketing manager, and will mirror the steps already outlined for the planning process.

In most companies preparation of the annual marketing plan will start with an analysis of the current situation with regard to present product markets. This forms the background to developing annual marketing plans and might include, for example, information on some of the following factors:

- Company sales and profit trends: by product/customer.
- Total market size: volume/value.
- Competitor and market share analysis.
- Factors likely to affect company marketing activity over the next 12 months.

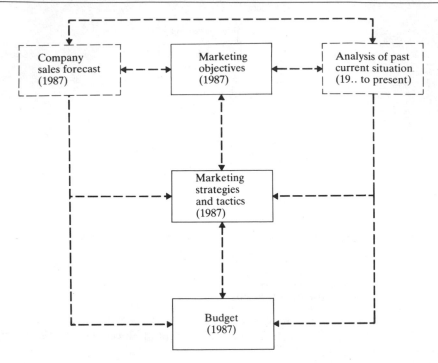

Figure 13.2 Preparing the annual marketing plan

The second step in annual marketing planning includes the preparation of company sales and profit projections. Of central importance here is the preparation of the annual sales forecast. We have examined both the purpose and techniques of sales forecasting in Chapter 6.

In some companies the forecast level of company sales for the forthcoming year often becomes the central objective around which annual marketing strategies and tactics, including the annual budget, for these activities are based. Again it should be noted that the iterative nature of marketing planning is important in this respect. It is vital to remember that the level of company sales forecast for the coming year is a function of company marketing effort and not a basis for determining the extent and nature of that effort. In practice, then, annual marketing object-ives, annual marketing strategies and tactics, and annual sales forecasts and budgets are inter-related. This is illustrated in Fig. 13.2.

PLANNING AND THE REMAINING MANAGEMENT FUNCTIONS

Once the marketing manager has arrived at a satisfactory set of objectives, strategies and tactics his next tasks include the allocation of resources, activities and responsibilities required to im-plement the plan. This involves marketing management in the tasks of ensuring that the annual plan is put into action and that the efforts of those involved in actioning the plan are effectively marketed. In order to gauge the effectiveness of these efforts, and indeed of the planning process itself, the marketing manager must also undertake a systematic appraisal of marketing activities. This leads us on to the three remaining essential elements of the marketing manager's task, namely: organizing, directing and controlling. We shall consider first the essentials of the organ-izing role of marketing management followed by an overview of the nature of marketing control. Finally, we shall conclude by examining the implications of the directing element of marketing.

ORGANIZING AND MARKETING MANAGEMENT

While the marketing manager is heavily involved with marketing mix decisions, and as we have seen, in planning for these, another range of duties are principally organizational in nature.

The organizational element of marketing management is concerned with allocating the resources at management's disposal in a manner which facilitates the achievement of objectives. This, in turn, requires that the marketing manager makes decisions in areas such as the following:

1. *The structuring of authority and responsibility*: tasks which derive from the marketing plan need to be allocated to individuals. An individual must know not only with what responsibilities he or she is charged but also the marketing manager must ensure that the individual is endowed with the necessary authority to discharge that responsibility.

2. *The establishment of lines of communication*: the organizing aspects of marketing management require the marketing manager to ensure that adequate and efficient systems of reporting and communication exist. It is essential that both he or she and the staff under his or her control are kept in touch one with another and with developments outside the functional boundary which might affect its operation. The establishment of satisfactory lines of communication can range from the organization of regular staff meetings, through to systems of reporting from the salesforce, or sophisticated management information systems.

3. *The delineation of line and staff functions within the marketing department*: the marketing manager must also organize the various activities of the department into those which contribute directly to the department's output (line functions) and those activities which are of a support or advising nature (staff functions). He must ensure that those staff positions which exist are still relevant and effective and that they have not grown unwieldy or time consuming.

4. *The grouping of activities into units*: the marketing manager must determine the most appropriate and effective grouping of marketing activities in his or her department. For example, he or she must determine if advertising, sales promotion and public relations will form one unit or whether, alternatively, it is advisable to have public relations separate.

5. *The choice between internal (company) marketing staff and outside agencies*: the marketing manager must also determine on what basis, and under what circumstances, he or she will utilize the services of outside agencies, for example, marketing research agencies, specialist public relations consultants, etc.

6. *The determination of the overall structure of the marketing department and its relationship with other functions*: a final example of the marketing manager's organizational tasks is his or her role in the overall structuring of the marketing department, how it is to figure in company structure as a whole, and in its relationship with other functions. Many of these particular aspects of organizing for marketing were considered in Chapter 3, and it is strongly advised to consider the issues raised there again. It should be noted, however, that decisions about how to structure the marketing organization are a key duty of the marketing manager and should not be neglected in favour of the more 'exciting' aspects of marketing decision making.

CONTROL AND MARKETING MANAGEMENT

The third basic element of management is that which relates to control. We have seen that the marketing manager must ensure that he or she secures the necessary resources to implement marketing plans. In any company, resources – be they financial, human or whatever – are scarce. Any manager, therefore, must not only ensure that the department is effective, but also that the activities for which he or she is responsible are carried out efficiently. This requires that the marketing manager ensures that there be an adequate system of evaluation and control.

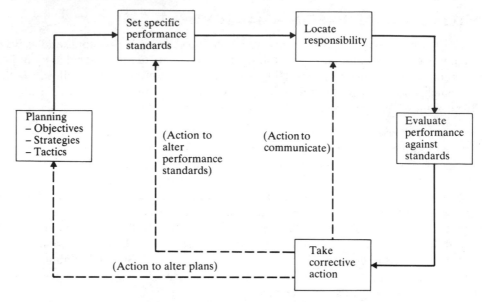

Figure 13.3   The control sequence in marketing

The essentials of a system of evaluation and control are shown in Fig. 13.3. Once again it should be noted how this, the third basic function of marketing management, is related to the functions of planning and organizing. In fact this control sequence is applicable at any level and for any management function in a company. Its essentials are:

- Setting standards for performance.
- Evaluating performance against these standards.
- Taking action to correct any deviations from standards.

As we have already discussed the importance of setting specific and preferably quantifiable standards of performance for marketing, we shall concentrate here on the important evaluative and corrective action elements of this process.

Essentially, in evaluating the department's marketing efforts the marketing manager needs to consider the following questions:

- What has happened?
- How does this compare with the standards of performance?
- What explains any differences between standards and actual performance?
- What action needs to be taken and by whom?

In fact, although the control process and the questions which relate to it are common to any control problem, as Kotler[4] points out, four types of marketing control may be distinguished, as follows:

- Control of the annual marketing plan.
- Control of profitability.
- Control of efficiency.
- Strategic control.

The marketing manager is interested in all four types of control, but the prime concern is with the first and last of these, namely: control of the annual plan, and strategic control. We shall examine both the purpose of these two control areas and some of the control techniques or approaches which are associated with each.

Annual plan control

The purpose of annual plan control is to determine the extent to which marketing efforts over the year have been successful. Among the most frequently used control techniques in this evaluation are likely to be *sales analysis* and *analysis of market share.*

Sales analysis Despite exhortations to be marketing rather than sales oriented in our approach to customers overall marketing standards of performance and, therefore, techniques of evaluation and control are often geared to the analysis of sales.

Normally sales analysis will commence with a comparison of budgeted sales revenue against actual sales revenue. Any variations may be due to volume and/or price variances. For example, an unfavourable sales variance may be due to having had to cut prices. The manager must now examine closely the possible reasons for this. Further detailed analysis may be by individual products, territories, customers, etc., in order to determine more precise information on the nature and extent of price cutting. It should be recognized that these analyses may not lead directly to action. Frequently, data from sales analysis will be used to formulate hypotheses that will form the basis for experimentation. The results of these experiments are actionable. Sevin[5] has referred to the combination of analysis and experiment as *productivity analysis.*

Analysis of market share Of all the approaches to controlling annual marketing operations, analysis of market share represents one of the most useful and, therefore, widely used techniques. The principal reason for measuring and evaluating market share performance is that it allows a company to assess how well it is doing *vis-à-vis* competitors. For example, a company might find that while its sales volume has declined over the year, its market share has increased. Clearly, declining sales volume would still represent a cause for concern; nevertheless, an increase in market share would indicate that a company is faring better than competitors in a market which has declined overall. The importance of this conclusion would suggest a very different course of action on the part of marketing management than that suggested by a simple analysis of sales.

A second reason for using market share analysis in marketing control stems from the fact that often overall marketing objectives are couched in terms of market share. Certainly, to some extent, market share does indeed represent an overall indication of the efficiency of total marketing efforts compared with competitors. However, as we have seen in Chapter 5 with portfolio analysis perhaps a more pressing reason for stating objectives in terms of market share is the newly recognized strong link between relative market share and profitability. The general nature of this relationship is shown in Fig. 13.4.

As with sales analysis, measurement of market share alone is not sufficient to determine what actions should be taken. The evaluation process requires that marketing management determines the reasons for observed levels of company market share and any significant differences and trends. On the basis of this, the marketing manager must then determine what actions are required and by whom. Results and conclusions of the evaluation of the annual marketing plan must be discussed with those responsible, and a future plan of action agreed.

Strategic control: the marketing audit

More often than not, annual plan control will result in a re-evaluation of objectives, strategies and tactics with a view to preparing a plan of action for the subsequent year. From time to time,

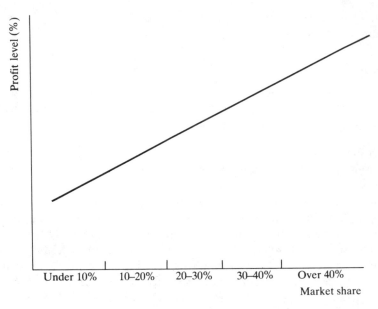

Figure 13.4   Generalized relationship between market share and profitability

however, a more comprehensive and far-reaching evaluation of total marketing activities needs to be undertaken. One approach to such an evaluation is the marketing audit.

A marketing audit is a systematic, critical and preferably impartial appraisal of the total marketing operation: it would include an appraisal of basic objectives and policies, marketing methods and procedures, marketing personnel and marketing organization.

The primary concern of the marketing audit is not only with marketing performance but also, equally importantly, with the overall marketing philosophy in the company. It is more an appraisal of effectiveness rather than efficiency. In part, because of this, it is suggested that the full marketing audit be conducted not by marketing management but by an 'outsider', if not to the company then at least to the marketing function. The use of the full marketing audit is at present rather restricted – only a handful of UK companies have this as part of marketing control. Nevertheless, the usefulness of the marketing audit in a rapidly changing environment will no doubt lead to an increase in the number of companies incorporating this procedure.

DIRECTING AND MARKETING MANAGEMENT

The final, basic, and therefore essential, function of marketing management relates to the marketing department's human element. The marketing manager like any other manager relies upon people to get things done. Sophisticated marketing techniques, effective marketing plans and substantial financial resources in a company do not in themselves guarantee success. In the final analysis a key factor in the determining of success or failure is the effective management of people. This is as true in marketing as in any other functional area of business. To some extent this aspect of marketing management is sadly neglected in marketing tests: perhaps surprising when one considers just how many 'failures' in marketing can be traced to the ineffective management of the human asset. The marketing manager must, therefore, give careful thought to the direction of these assets such that they contribute as much as possible towards desired results. Effective direction of marketing staff involves recruiting and selecting, training and developing,

Figure 13.5 Effective performance and aspects of directing

and leading and motivating, marketing personnel. The relationship between these elements and effective performance is shown in Fig. 13.5. In addition, it must also be realized that managerial influences will subjectively affect the planning process – a topic explored in detail by Greenley.[6]

Abilities

Every manager will find it difficult to secure maximum performance from the staff if they lack the necessary abilities to function effectively in their duties. Ability, however, is in turn a function of a combination of effective recruitment and selection, plus effective training and development of marketing staff. Normally these aspects of human asset management are seen as being the prerogative of the personnel manager. The marketing manager, however, must not abrogate his duties in this area. The personnel function must be kept informed of the essential qualities and skills which they are required to look for in job applicants for sales and marketing posts. This, in turn, will require a careful job analysis and the preparation of job descriptions. Marketing managers need to be involved in this process; indeed there is a wider value to a company of conducting regular job analyses and preparing up-to-date job descriptions. This wider value lies in the fact that determining manpower requirements makes it necessary for the marketing manager to think carefully about the tasks which he requires his marketing staff to perform and the extent to which these tasks are still relevant to the effective performance of his function. Job analyses and descriptions also form the basis for assessing performance and organizing development and training programmes.

Having selected the best available staff for the marketing function individual potential must be developed and refined; this applies equally to both new entrants and existing staff. The marketing manager should ensure that all his staff are adequately trained. In the case of new staff this may involve induction training and the development of the basic skills required to do the job. Existing staff too, may from time to time be required to acquire new skills and patterns of behaviour. The marketing manager should ensure that there is an adequate system of career planning for the human assets in his function. Once again it is recognized that training and development are specialist areas requiring specialist staff, specialist knowledge, and a specialist text.[7] Every marketing manager, however, is directly responsible for ensuring that his or her staff are given adequate leadership and are motivated.

Effort

Motivation and leadership together constitute the second major element of human asset performance. Surprisingly, the first of these – motivation of marketing staff – is given very little attention in conventional texts on marketing management. Surprisingly, because as we have seen in Chapter 3, an understanding of human motivation is essential for effective marketing decision making. This understanding should be applied to the motivation of marketing staff. Marketing management should look beyond the simplistic view that what motivates individuals at work is financial inducement: money. In the same way that consumers may be motivated by a variety of complex and often hierarchical factors, so too research has shown that many of the higher order needs in Maslow's hierarchy[8] can be fulfilled if the work is designed so as to give marketing staff a real feeling of responsibility and achievement.

Finally, in the role of managing the human asset, the marketer must fulfil his or her leadership function. As Handy points out[9] the 'leadership problem' has attracted countless theories and spawned endless research. The evidence and the theories remain ambiguous and inconclusive. In practice, effective leadership in marketing management requires that the manager achieves a balance between supporting and encouraging his or her staff, and ensuring that objectives are successfully met. Above all the effective leader must constantly strive to win the trust and respect of subordinates.

CONCLUSIONS

All managers, regardless of their functional specialism, have certain basic tasks to perform. Key among these tasks are the managerial elements of planning, organizing, directing and controlling. We have seen how each of these tasks applies to marketing management, from the planning of annual marketing activities through to their evaluation and control. Finally, we have examined briefly the often neglected but vitally important area of managing marketing personnel. If marketing management is to be effective careful consideration should be given to selection, training, leadership and motivation of staff.

APPLICATION QUESTIONS

1. Outline the key steps in the development of the annual marketing plan.
2. Distinguish between marketing strategies and marketing tactics. Under what circumstances is the effective use of marketing tactics particularly beneficial?
3. What is involved in the organizing element of marketing management?
4. Discuss the use of 'annual plan control' and the 'marketing audit' in the evaluation of marketing activities.
5. Why is it important for marketing management to make the most effective use of its human assets?

REFERENCES

1. Albors, H. H., *Principles of Management: A Modern Approach*, 4th edn, Wiley, New York, 1974.
2. Kotler, P., *Marketing Management: Analysis, Planning and Control*, 3rd edn, Prentice-Hall, Englewood Cliffs, NJ, 1976, pp. 57–61.
3. Steiner, G. A., *Top Management Planning*, Collier Macmillan, London, 1969, p. 24.
4. Kotler, P., *Marketing Management: Analysis, Planning and Control*, 5th edn, Prentice-Hall, Englewood Cliffs, NJ, 1984, pp. 744–745.
5. Sevin, C. H., *Marketing Productivity Analysis*, McGraw-Hill, New York, 1965.
6. Greenley, G. E., *The Strategic and Operational Planning of Marketing*, McGraw-Hill, London, 1986, pp. 143–164.
7. Markwell, D. S. and T. J. Roberts, *Organisation of Management Development Programmes*, Gower Press, 1970.
8. Maslow, A. H., 'A theory of human motivation', *Psychological Review*, **50**, 1943, pp. 370–396.
9. Handy, C. B., *Understanding Organisations*, Penguin, Harmondsworth, 1976, pp. 87–104.

FOUR

MARKETING'S WIDER ISSUES

FOURTEEN
INTERNATIONAL MARKETING

INTRODUCTION

The aim of this chapter is to give an insight into the complex area of international marketing. There is no suggestion that, having read this, you will have become an expert in marketing overseas or in export procedures, but you should at least be aware of some of the additional implications.

INTERNATIONAL MARKETING DEFINED

Marketers are not agreed that international marketing can be considered a subject separate from marketing on a domestic scale and this is perhaps one reason why it has been difficult to arrive at a comprehensive yet succinct definition. For the purposes of this chapter it is proposed to accept the definition put forward by Walsh.[1] International marketing is:

(a) the marketing of goods and services across national frontiers
(b) the marketing operations of an organisation that sells and/or produces within a given country when:
  (i) that organisation is part of, or associated with, an enterprise which also operates in other countries; *and*
  (ii) there is some degree of influence on or control of that organisation's marketing activities from outside the country in which it sells and/or produces.

In other words, the term 'international marketing' can be applied to the activities of the exporter and any organization which has some international concern. A small manufacturing company can be an international marketer to a limited degree simply by distributing its products in foreign markets. Companies with overseas sales subsidiaries, overseas manufacturing plant (whether wholly or partly owned, or operating independently and manufacturing under licence) and the multinational corporation are all included in the definition.

From the point of view of the United Kingdom, export activity continues to be a significant factor in international marketing activities. As an industrialized nation lacking valuable raw materials, the UK is particularly dependent on international trade. It differs, therefore, from the US, for example, from whose viewpoint many texts on international marketing have been written, since the latter's domestic market is not large enough to absorb its production. Succeeding sections reflect the importance of engaging in international marketing.

MULTINATIONAL CORPORATIONS

The term 'multinational corporation' is widely used and has been variously defined. Once again Walsh[2] provides a useful working definition. The multinational corporation is a company:

(a) which has a direct investment base in several countries;
(b) which generally derives 20–50 per cent or more of its net profits from foreign operations; and
(c) whose management makes policy decisions based on the alternatives available anywhere in the world.

The key factor is that the company should have a global outlook, making its business decisions with regard to the options available worldwide. It is not, therefore, a domestically based US or Swiss or Dutch company (although many multinational corporations have their origins in single domestic markets) but is a company whose operations span the globe. Manufacturing occurs simultaneously in several different countries and goods are sold worldwide.

Multinational corporations have become increasingly large over time, several having annual sales which equal the GNP of the smaller European nations. They are, therefore, an extremely significant force. For a more detailed discussion the reader is directed to Tugendhat's work.[3]

It is useful at this point to distinguish between international marketing and international trade. While trade between nations will inevitably impinge on the activities of international marketing, the terms are not synonymous. World trade is often a simple exchange of goods. In the Eastern Bloc, for example, goods are seen as methods of payment rather than being designed to meet market needs and hence much trade is by barter.

While some of the activities of marketing may be involved in the exporting process (for example distribution activities), there may well be no marketing management. Terpstra[4] suggests a useful table of comparison (Table 14.1).

STAGES OF ECONOMIC DEVELOPMENT OF EXPORT MARKETS

The environment within which marketing operates is continually dynamic and largely uncontrollable. For international marketing this difficulty is magnified; not only are the uncontrollable

Table 14.1   Comparison of international trade and international marketing

Dimension	International trade	International marketing
Actors	Nations	Firms
Goods move across frontiers	Yes	Not necessarily
Impetus	Comparative advantage	Company decisions (usually profit motivated)
Information source	Nation's balance of payments	Company records
Marketing activities:		
Buy and sell	Yes	Yes
Physical distribution	Yes	Yes
Pricing	Yes	Yes
Market research	Generally not	Yes
Product development	Generally not	Yes
Promotion	Generally not	Yes
Distribution channel management	No	Yes

Source: V. Terpstra, *International Marketing*.[4]

elements of the environment different from country to country, but the controllable elements of the marketing mix must be adapted to these differing environments. Particularly significant is the diversity which exists between levels of economic activity among nations.

W. W. Rostow[5] has provided a description of economies which suggests that all nations are in or are passing through one of the following stages:

- Traditional society.
- Preconditions for take-off.
- Take-off.
- Drive to maturity.
- Age of high mass consumption.

More common terms are now in use, and while these may change over time (for example, the term 'less developed country' has given way to 'developing country') they provide a more current classification.

1. *Subsistence economies*: this category consists of those nations dependent on primitive agriculture, with a limited infrastructure and high dependence on foreign aid. Examples include much of Africa (Ethiopia, Burkina Faso) and parts of Asia (Bangladesh).
2. *Developing countries*: there is increasing industrialization and a developing infrastructure. Such economies are usually reliant on raw-material exports, often based on the extractive industries, including oil (Nigeria, Mexico and the Middle East).
3. *Industrializing countries*: the rapidly industrializing economies of many South American countries (e.g., Brazil) and countries such as Spain, Portugal and Greece can be considered under this heading.
4. *Industrialized countries*: this includes the major Western industrial countries of Europe, North America and Japan.

An additional sub-grouping, *affluent countries*, usually includes the US, Sweden and West Germany, with their demand for high quality, sophisticated consumer goods.

Note While the oil-exporting countries of the Middle East have a high GNP *per capita*, the development of their infrastructure is still limited and there is a wide disparity between rich and poor. Consequently, they cannot be considered as being truly affluent countries, but perhaps merit a separate category for the purposes of international marketing.

While the above classification is useful, it must be remembered that as with all environmental factors, it is constantly subject to change. Equally, it may be difficult to place a nation in a particular category.

For the marketer, therefore, the stage in economic development may be a starting point for researching opportunities overseas, but in itself will provide limited guidance.

IDENTIFYING EXPORT OPPORTUNITIES

Information for marketing decisions was considered in some detail in Part Two of this text. Quantitative and qualitative techniques previously discussed are equally relevant when attempting to identify overseas opportunities. In general, however, the backcloth against which these opportunities are seen is broader.

The number of possible markets is large – some 240 political states are listed in the *United States Statistical Yearbook*; of these some 150 are members of the United Nations. The number of nations that will provide viable market opportunities will, of course, differ from firm to firm and from product to product, and the arguments for concentration of marketing activity within a small group of markets versus spreading to a large number of overseas markets can also be seen to follow this pattern. Be that as it may, a framework for analysing overseas markets is a useful starting point in a programme of marketing research. The aim of such a programme is to produce a ranked list of overseas markets for future marketing research in depth on the basis of likely potential for the company and its product(s) and to do it in the most cost effective way. A suggested step-by-step approach is reproduced in Fig. 14.1.

The first step is to consider market accessibility. This is more than determining how close a country is to the UK or other domestic market. It will include an assessment of both tariff and non-tariff barriers to trade.

A *tariff* can be simply defined as a tax on products crossing a frontier. Tariffs are often imposed by governments to protect local industry from overseas competition. The General Agreement on Tariffs and Trade (GATT) is an institution established to provide a worldwide forum for discussion in an attempt to reduce the need for tariffs.

Non-tariff barriers include other forms of government action to restrict imports, for example, quotas. A *quota* is where a specific limit is placed by volume or value on the amount of goods exported to a specific market and is usually applied to a specific nation or group of nations. For example, the Multi-Fibre Arrangement (MFA) limits exports of textile products from developing countries to the UK and other European nations. Other non-tariff barriers include discriminatory exchange rate policies, restrictive customs procedures and restrictive administrative and technical regulations. For example, the technical regulations for electrical appliances differ between the UK and West Germany, despite common membership of the European Community (EC). France introduced a regulation whereby all video-cassette recorders imported from Japan were cleared through customs in a limited number of inland towns, effectively reducing the number of imports since only a relatively small number of products could be cleared per day. Non-tariff barriers also include geographic and climatic barriers.

Despite these problems, finding such information is relatively easy when using government sources such as the British Overseas Trade Board (BOTB). This first stage will reduce the number of potential markets literally from three figures to two, at least as far as direct export is concerned. It may well identify a group of countries for potential joint venture agreements which are discussed later. Further research can then be considered under the following headings:

1. *Economic*: GNP/GDP; population figures; wage levels and distribution; price levels; inflation; resources.
2. *Market*: size; stage in product life cycle; market penetration level or average consumption level per annum; competition; market segmentation; availability of media, services, distribution.
3. *Cultural*: material culture (e.g., role of women); social structure and family relationships; social relationships; religion(s); aesthetics; language(s).
4. *Political environment*: *incentives* for joint venture/wholly owned manufacture, e.g., tax exemptions, protection against competitive imports (tariffs and quotas). *Risks* of appropriation or domestication of foreign owned manufacturing plant.
5. *Legal*: there is no true international law, although attempts to reconcile different legal practice have been made. The Madrid Convention, for example, protects trade marks of signatories in all member countries (limited to some 20 states).

Much of the information needed can be obtained from secondary sources, an outline list of which is given in Table 14.2 in addition to the information given in Chapter 5.

Note Market information is more difficult to obtain for goods sold to industrial/organizational buyers, but this applies equally to domestic market research.

It is worth pointing out at this stage that while desk research is relatively cheap and easy to

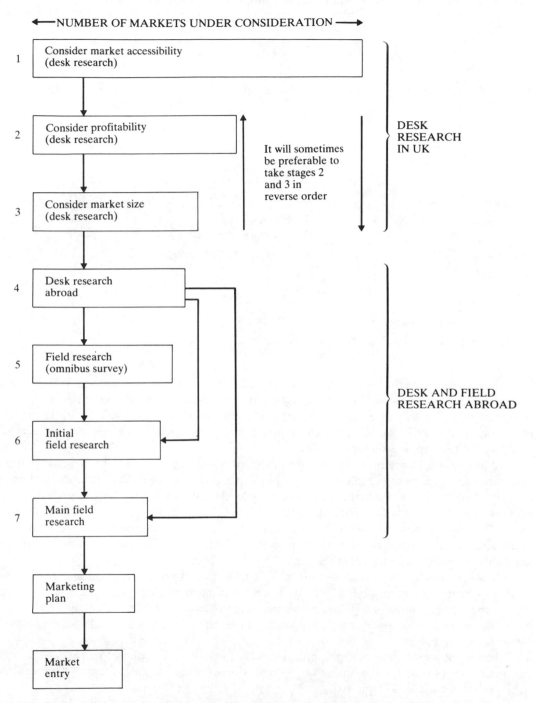

Figure 14.1 International research strategy: a stage-by-stage approach aimed at selection of the markets of greatest potential at the lowest possible research cost

Source: L. S. Walsh, *International Marketing*, Macdonald and Evans, London, 1981, p. 18

Table 14.2   Some sources of secondary data for international market research

1. Government	—	Department of Trade and Industry
		British Overseas Trade Board
		Central Office of Information
		HMSO
2. International institutions	—	Organization for Economic Cooperation and Development
		International Monetary Fund
		General Agreement on Tariffs and Trade
		European Economic Community
3. Trade associations		
4. Professional bodies	—	Institute of Marketing
		Institute of Export
5. Chambers of commerce		
6. Commercial organizations	—	Market research agencies
		Advertising agencies
7. Consultants	—	e.g. Economist Intelligence Agency
8. Service industries	—	Banks
		Airlines
		Freight forwarders
9. European Society for Opinion and Market Research (ESOMAR)		
10. Other published sources, e.g., Axel Springer Publishing Group (W. Germany)		

carry out there are problems in the international environment not encountered with domestic marketing research. Availability of information may be limited in certain countries, e.g., census information readily available in the industrialized countries is not easily available in the developing world. Where information is available it may be unreliable, out of date and may not compare easily with information gathered elsewhere.

Additional problems are encountered where field research is required. Any questionnaire or interview technique readily employed in the domestic market may be difficult to employ overseas. Cultural differences such as language and literacy levels exist; there may be an unwillingness to respond, e.g., as in the Middle East where housewives may not be interviewed except in the company of their husbands, a fact which limits the timing of any such interviews. Nevertheless, many market research agencies do offer their services, and the BOTB provides significant financial assistance to would-be exporters in the UK.

Finally, it should be said that for some producers to view the world as a collection of separate markets, and to follow through a step-by-step marketing research programe for each, as suggested above, may be inappropriate. Examples of products which have been successful on an international scale to a specific market segment can be cited, e.g., Coca Cola and Levi jeans for the world youth market.

The aim of a marketing research programme is to arrive at a group of markets which offer potential for export and where similarities with the domestic market, rather than differences from it, can be emphasized and exploited.

THE MARKETING MIX APPLIED TO INTERNATIONAL MARKETING

The term 'marketing mix' was introduced in Chapter 4 and its major elements discussed in some detail in Part Three of this text. Again, it must be said that the issues raised are as important to marketing internationally as they are to marketing in the domestic environment. Certain aspects of the mix hold special significance for international marketing.

Distribution

A detailed discussion on channels of distribution has already been provided in Chapter 10, but distribution for international marketing includes not only the structure of channels within a range of overseas markets, but perhaps more fundamentally must address the strategic problem of market entry.

The options available fall into the following broad categories:

– Export.
– Manufacture and assembly overseas.

These can be further subdivided as shown in Figs 14.2 and 14.3.

Any or all of these alternatives may be in use in one company and for a full discussion of all the options listed the reader is directed again to Walsh's[6] work. Certain alternatives have been selected for brief consideration here.

Agency This may be defined as the legal relationship that exists when one person or company (the agent) is employed by another person or company (the principal) to bring that principal into

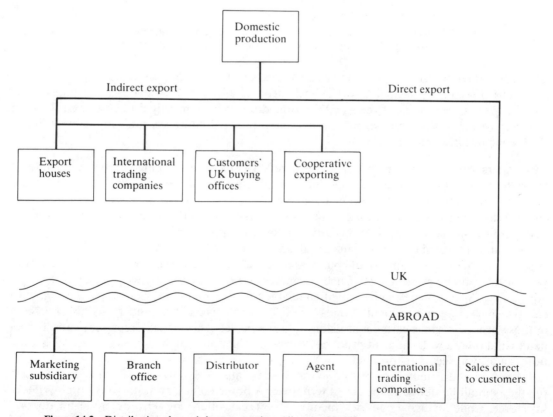

Figure 14.2   Distribution channels between nations (direct and indirect export): principal alternatives

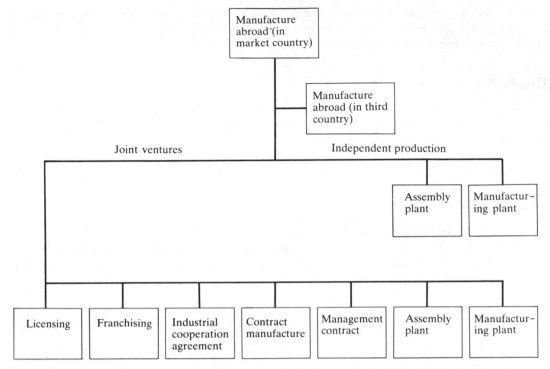

Figure 14.3 Distribution channels between nations (manufacture abroad): principal alternative channels
Source: L. S. Walsh, *International Marketing*, Macdonald and Evans, 1982

a contractual relationship with third parties. A sales agent is thus employed to bring about a sales contract between his principal and the third party. The legal title to goods never passes to an agent; it passes, as a result of the agent's efforts, directly from principal to customer, the agent receiving a commission as payment. In marketing practice, however, the expression is loosely used to include distributors.

Distributors These have been defined as customers who have been granted exclusive or preferential rights to purchase and re-sell a specific range of products in specified geographical areas or markets. The distributor is, therefore, a wholesaler, who is 'paid' by the difference between purchase price and re-sale price (and *not* from any commission from the suppliers). As such his role is as defined for similar channel intermediaries in domestic operations.

Agents and distributors offer similar advantages to the would-be exporter. They have local experience of market conditions and business practice, valuable to the new exporter, and they involve little or no investment costs. Such advantages should be carefully weighed against the disadvantages. Agents, in particular, are often unable to take a long-term view which is essential for effective marketing management. Agents have a living to make and are understandably interested in those products which earn commission from the outset. They usually represent various companies and offer a wide range of products. A new product thus might not receive as much attention as a proven successful product.

Agents and distributors are only two options available to exporters, and while often successful, they should be viewed against the alternatives. A branch office, and company-employed local salesforce, while involving considerable investment, can offer long-term potential for development.

As far as *overseas assembly and manufacture* are concerned, joint ventures require some attention. It would be impossible to consider all the alternatives in a chapter of this length, but the major advantage common to all options is that of market access (where this may be impossible as a result of tariff or quota restrictions). The degree of risk varies – it is relatively low where licensing is concerned and substantial in the case of jointly owned manufacturing facilities, where the possibility of expropriation by the national government adds to the problem of financial outlay.

For purposes of clarification, some attention is now given to two joint venture options, licensing and franchising.

Licensing This is the term used to cover a wide range of agreements relating to the sale or leasing of industrial or commercial expertise. This may include a patent covering a product or process, manufacturing 'know-how', and the use of a trade mark or brand name. In return the licensee pays a sum, often a minimum amount annually, or an agreed percentage of turnover annually. Licensing can, therefore, be said to involve the sale of intangibles.

Franchising This, on the other hand, is a form of licensing, but the franchiser provides a standard package of components or ingredients together with management and marketing services and advice. Since franchising involves the transfer of tangibles, it can enable greater control of the operation for the originating manufacturer than licensing. Examples of successful franchising operations include Pepsi Cola which sells its concentrate to franchises who own bottling plants, employ local staff and control their own promotional budgets. Other examples are Benetton, an Italian knitwear manufacturer, whose franchised shops are now a common feature of European high streets.

The selection of a channel for market entry is vital to the success of distribution within each overseas market. The shorter the overall channel of distribution the greater the control. In terms of international marketing a greater cost is the financial involvement. For smaller firms, some sacrifice of control is thus inevitable in many instances and a balance between these two issues must be achieved.

Finally, no section on distribution can ignore physical distribution or logistics. The importance of physical distribution for exporting in particular is such that a short section is devoted to this topic at the end of the chapter.

Product

Perhaps the most significant decisions for international marketing are those of product standardization and variety reduction. Examples of the need to meet individual national requirements, in particular where consumer goods are concerned, abound. One particularly descriptive example of the modifications needed to the BL Mini for successful exporting to Japan is given by Whymant.[7] In addition to overcoming the emission requirements a wide range of other specifications had to be met:

1. The tyre must not protrude, so on Minis 'eye-brows' have to be fastened on the two front wings.
2. An audible warning device at 110 kph.
3. A red band on the speedometer to show when this speed is reached.
4. A heat shield above the catalyst to stop occupants of the car cooking, and a grass shield underneath so that all the grass you see in Tokyo doesn't catch fire!

5. Special low wattage headlamps.
6. Overheat catalyst warning.
7. Special regulation number plate bracket.
8. Torch for use in breakdown.
9. Modification of emergency parking system for use in breakdown.
10. Side-wing repeater flashers to show when back indicator is on.
11. Reflectors on rear must be a different size and at a different angle from the British ones.

While a standard product to meet a global need is attractive to the marketer, not least in terms of economies of scale, it may be impossible in practice. Legal, technical or climatic requirements may make modification mandatory. In addition, local tastes may make it desirable. Certainly, in view of the differing stages of economic development reached by different nations discussed above, a similar need may be met by a variety of products. The following section on a product life cycle for international trade highlights this problem.

The eventual result of product modification can lead to an over-full range of products, and while the review and elimination procedures presented in Chapter 8 remain valid for international marketing, the scale of the problem is often much greater. International product elimination is, therefore, an area of great importance. In certain circumstances where domestic production costs or small-scale production runs make a product unprofitable, alternative options such as licensing (see above) may enable the marketer to improve profits while retaining market position.

Keegan[8] has identified five possible strategies (Fig. 14.4) for international marketing which encompass the mix elements of product and promotion. These are discussed in brief prior to considering the promotional element in the next section:

1. *Straight extension*: this is the introduction of the product in the same form and with the same communications in use at home. This is a tempting strategy as it involves no additional manufacturing or marketing costs. Examples of successful products include Pepsi Cola.
2. *Communication adaptation*: this is where a company modifies its promotional theme but retains an unchanged product. This strategy has a relatively low cost of implementation since major manufacturing costs are not incurred. The example quoted by Keegan is that of bicycles, which are a product designed to meet leisure needs in the US and other developed countries, but which are a basic mode of transport in many developing nations.
3. *Product adaptation*: this involves the modification of a product for reasons discussed earlier, e.g., preferences, while retaining the communications theme. Products which are particularly susceptible to taste, e.g., food and clothing products are such examples.

		Products		
		No change	Adapted	New product
Marketing communications	No change	Straight extension	Product adaptation	
	Adapt	Communication adaptation	Dual adaptation	Product invention

Figure 14.4   Keegan's strategies for international marketing

4. *Dual adaptation*: this involves modifying both product and communications to meet the needs of specific markets. Keegan cites the introduction of instant coffee into the United Kingdom, where tastes differed from other European nations where there is a longer coffee-drinking tradition and where the initial launch was to a different market segment, the young, who were less traditional and for whom a specific communications message was required.

5. *Product inventions*: where product needs and market conditions are similar to those in the home market, the first four strategies are effective options. In other countries, such as the developing nations, this may not be the case. Product invention, or the development of a new product to meet consumer needs at an affordable price, may be the only alternative. The invention 'backwards' from modern technology of a better manual washing machine for those countries where washing is still done by hand is a good example.

There is no best strategy for a firm – the optimum choice will depend on the specific product–market–company mix.

Promotion

The elements of the communications mix discussed in Chapter 11 are as relevant for international marketing as they are for domestic marketing. For an established company marketing its products overseas the decisions to be taken hinge on whether or not a standardized promotional campaign can be contemplated or whether promotion should be adapted to individual national needs.

Complete standardization of all aspects of a campaign is rarely possible – language differences alone ensure this. It is possible, however, for a *common creative idea and message* to be used – the Esso Tiger is a classic example – using similar media and a common advertising strategy.

The organization of advertising on an international scale is modelled on the US pattern, with branches of many US advertising agencies throughout the world. The environmental differences, discussed above in relation to international marketing research, play a very significant role in international advertising decisions: cultural differences, government attitudes to advertising, and in particular, availability of advertising media are of particular relevance. Even among industrialized nations, commercial television is not always available to the advertiser, as is shown in Table 14.3. Where it is offered, advertising flexibility (by channels in the UK for example) can be lacking with lead times of a year being common.

In addition to the national media available within each overseas market, an additional category, international media, can be added to the list of means of promotion for the international marketer. These are publications which aim, as a matter of policy, at coverage in several different countries. They include consumer magazines, such as *Readers' Digest*, *Time*, the various airline publications, trade and technical magazines, international commercial radio (for example Radio Luxembourg) and international commercial television which is becoming increasingly significant with the growth of cable television. Such developments make the prospect of a standardized campaign attractive, particularly in view of cost savings in the production of creative promotional material.

Exhibitions, often considered as an element of below-the-line advertising, are probably of more importance to the international marketer than they are in domestic business. They allow buyer, intermediary and seller to come together, minimizing the costs and time involved for each. Exhibitions range from the giant international trade fairs covering all products and industries such as Leipzig and Hanover, to the highly specialized international exhibitions specific to a particular product category, for example Pret-à-Porter and the London Boat Show. For a detailed

Table 14.3   Media availability

	Newspapers		Magazines		Radio		Television		Cinema	
	Daily	Non-daily/free sheets*	Consumer	Trade/Tech.	No. of sets (millions)	No. of commercial channels	No. of TV sets (millions)	No. of commercial channels	Commercial minutage per day	No. of screens
Austria	29	175/65	67	268	2.5	2	2.3	2	20	540
Belgium	35	167/460	110	1196	4.6	650	3.6	NC†	†	353
Denmark	51	3/330	50	600	2.0	NC	2.0	NC	NC	310
Finland	94	152/74	151	913	3.3	NC	2.2	2	25	368
France	91	26/250	350	400	57.2	950	22.3	3	46	3034
Greece	500	n/a	250	200	6.5	2	3.0	2	100	470
Ireland	7	49/10	30	59	1.1	2	0.79	2	83	168
Italy	9	1850/n/a	89	5000	18.3	2000	17.8	350	149(1)	5200
Netherlands	47	145/580	94	299(2)	14.9	3	6.4	2	30	545
Norway	65	98/50	40	450	2.7	NC	1.97	NC	NC	353
Portugal	31	307/n/a	901(4)		8.9	2	2.9	2	135	448
Spain	135	400/n/a	60	320	30.0	300	11.2	2(3)	100	2621
Sweden	68	46/5	50	300	7.0	NC	3.9	NC	NC	590
Switzerland	124	170/160	70	2000	2.4	21	2.1	3	60	466
United Kingdom	120	1301/668	1533	2789	55.6	46	30.2	2	180	1301
West Germany	195	195/676	2500	2400	65.0	12	30.0	2	40	3590

Notes
1. Three state-owned channels only listed (excludes networks and local stations).
2. Only includes titles that carry advertising.
3. Excludes the Canary Islands.
4. 901 is combined figure for both magazine categories.
* Weekly and bi-weekly.
†RTL is received from Luxembourg.
NC = Non-commercial.

list of international exhibitions, the reader is advised to consult the DTI's *Trade Promotions Guide*.

Agents and distributors have been considered above as intermediaries in the distribution channel. They should also be viewed as an integral part of a company's promotional activities. The representative overseas (and this will include a company employee whether based locally or in the domestic market) is the first point of contact for the potential buyer. The representative's attitude to the buyer, his or her knowledge of the company and its products, and freedom to negotiate terms have an important (and sometimes adverse) influence. The position of the overseas sales representative is one of isolation from head office and it is essential to foster *two-way communication* links.

Note The Central Office of Information (COI) offers a substantial public relations/publicity service to exporters of new or improved products or services. A professional news release is prepared and distributed to media in a variety of countries, including radio and television in certain countries where the COI has regular spots. The service is *entirely free* and is, according to the COI, often little known to would-be exporters.

Pricing

The methods of pricing detailed in Chapter 9 should be used as a basis for any pricing decision in international marketing. However, additional factors must be taken into consideration. Not least of these is the relationship between domestic and overseas pricing.

The true marketer will expect to price the product or service according to the needs and requirements of the market. This may or may not be a similar price to that at which goods are sold at home. In practice, various constraints may prevent this, such as inadequate market information (which may not always be the fault of the marketing researcher, but rather a result of the market's stage of development as a whole), a prevailing world price, the proximity of other markets where the same product is sold. Legal reasons may also be of relevance, where the recent decision of the European Court to ban price differentials for motor cars sold in different member states of the EC was such an example.

The terms of payment under which goods are sold to export markets will add a further dimension to the price. Costs of packing, insurance and freight between buyer and seller all have to be borne and will determine the real selling price of goods. It is beyond the scope of this chapter to consider terms of trade in detail, but your attention is drawn to Walker's work[9] which includes definitions of accepted terms of trade (Incoterms).

Finally, the question of which currency is to be used as a basis for quoting prices overseas is significant. Following the marketing view, the aim of meeting consumers' or industrial buyers' needs would suggest that goods sold in the local currency to intermediaries would be more acceptable. Clearly, such a policy would simplify the buyer's position and would provide a significant competitive advantage in many instances. It must be stated, however, that pricing in the currency of the market may be inappropriate or impossible where developing or Eastern Bloc countries are concerned. Since these currencies may not be freely convertible on the international money market, the decision is then to trade in either the domestic market currency or the currency of a third country (for example US dollars or Swiss francs).

Two final comments will be made before leaving this topic. First, although a price to meet the needs of the market must be desirable to achieve an optimum level of sales, it is undoubtedly simpler to base overseas prices on one of the techniques of cost-based pricing. In some instances, however, this may lose a market for the company, since the initial price may be too high for any significant sales to result; in others, it may cause the company concerned to price a product too low in relation to the established competition, thereby reducing potential profit and perhaps adversely affecting the image of the product in the eyes of the consumer.

Second, there have been allegations of 'dumping' of products overseas by a variety of nations. Dumping can be described as the sale of goods in foreign markets at a price lower than the production cost. This appears to contradict the theory of market pricing, but it is true that industrialized countries tend to penalize such imports. How far a price set to meet market demands can, or should, be viewed as dumping is open to debate. It is a question of degree and will, in many instances, depend on the product or industry concerned. In any event the practice of true dumping, often at marginal prices, can be a high risk strategy in international marketing. Goods sold at artificially low prices to an overseas buyer can (and often do) return to compete as competitively priced imports in the domestic market.

Pricing is a complex area that, in common with the other elements of the marketing mix, cannot be viewed in isolation. An integrated approach to all '4Ps' is an essential for international marketing as for domestic marketing.

PRODUCT LIFE CYCLE FOR INTERNATIONAL TRADE

The product life cycle theory, as discussed in Chapter 8, has proved useful in identifying future strategies for products and services. By applying it to international trade Wells[10] has shown the relevance of the theory to importing and exporting a product.

It is contended that it would assist exporters if they had methods of analysing the export potential of their products and had predictors of which products were most likely to be threatened by import competition.

Exporters have traditionally relied upon economic theories which concluded that each country will export those products that use the country's most abundant production factors. However, when such theories are applied to the detailed problems facing business people they become of limited value.

The trade cycle model has been proposed as an aid to exporters and this is closely related to the product life cycle concept in marketing. Wells first proposed a theory that combined both, and in order that we might attempt to modify his model, a summary of his proposal is given below.

According to the trade cycle concept, many products follow a pattern which can be divided into four stages:

Phase 1: US export strength.
Phase 2: foreign production starts.
Phase 3: foreign production competitive in export markets.
Phase 4: import competition begins.

A brief look at the reasoning underlying each of these stages will give some clues which might help the business person to identify the stage at which particular products may be. The concept can then be of assistance in predicting the future product trade performance, and in understanding what actions the manager can take to modify the pattern for certain products and to profit from different stages of the cycle.

Phase 1: US export strength

The US market is special because it has a large body of very high-income consumers, and products which satisfy the special demands of these consumers are likely to be introduced in the

United States. Moreover, due to the monopolistic position of the United States as a supplier of such new products which satisfy these special demands, they offer the best opportunities for export.

There is no simple relationship between demand and invention, but nevertheless there can be little doubt that certain products are simply more likely to be developed initially in America. Although labour is cheaper abroad and production costs would be lower, it is more sensible to manufacture in the US because production is closer to the market and near to specialist supplies. This is because at the early stages of a product's life, design is often in a constant state of flux, and demands for design changes must be rapidly translated into more suitable products which require the availability of close communication with specialized suppliers. The existence of a monopoly, or significant product differentiation at the early stages of the product life cycle, reduces the importance of costs to the manufacturer.

At this point, the American manufacturer has a virtual monopoly for the new product in the world market. US exports start as a trickle and develop into a steady stream as active export programmes are established by the American firms.

Phase 2: Foreign production

Product familiarity abroad increases, causing overseas markets to become so large that the product which once appealed primarily to the US consumer has a broad appeal in more prosperous foreign countries. Not only does a potential foreign producer now have a market close at hand but also some of his costs will be lower than those of the US producer. Imports from America have to bear duty and overseas freight charges – costs which local products will not carry. Moreover, the potential foreign producer may have to invest less in product development, the US manufacturer having done part of this for him. Some measure of the size of his potential market has been demonstrated by the successful sale of imports. Favourable profit projections based upon a demonstrated market and an ability to underprice imports will eventually induce an entrepreneur in a more prosperous foreign market to commence manufacture.

During this second stage, American exports will still supply most of the world's markets. However, as foreign producers begin to manufacture, US exports to certain markets will decline. The patten will probably be manifested in a slow-down in the rate of growth of US exports.

Phase 3: Foreign production competitive in export markets

As the early foreign manufacturers become larger and more experienced their costs should fall. They will begin to reap the advantages of scale economies previously available only to US manufacturers, but, in addition, they will have lower labour costs. Hence, their costs may be such that foreign products become competitive with American goods in third markets where goods from both countries have to carry similar freight and duty charges.

During this stage, US producers will be protected from imports in their domestic market where they are not faced with duty and overseas transportation costs. However, foreign goods will gradually take over the markets abroad which were previously held by American exports. The rate of growth of US exports will continue to decline.

Phase 4: Import competition begins

As the foreign manufacturer reaches mass production based on the home and export markets, the lower labour rates and perhaps new plant may enable him or her to produce at lower costs than an American manufacturer. The cost savings may be sufficient to pay freight and American duty and still compete with Americans in their own market. This stage will be reached earlier if the foreign producer begins to think in terms of marginal costs for export pricing. If he or she believes that selling can be done above full costs in the home market and excess capacity can be used up by 'dumping' abroad, US producers, who are pricing on full costs, may very quickly be undercut. During this final stage, US exports will be reduced to almost zero, while import competition becomes severe.

Thus the cycle is complete, from the United States as a strong producer and exporter, to the stage where imports may capture a significant share of the American market.

The early foreign producers (usually Western Europeans) will face a cycle similar to that of the US manufacturer. As still lower-income markets become large enough, producers in these countries will eventually become competitive, displacing the dominance of the early foreign manufacturers. The manufacture of products moves from country to country in what Hufbauer[11] has called a 'pecking order'.

Clearly, no simple model can explain the behaviour of all products in international trade. However, this model does appear to be useful for understanding trade patterns in manufactured goods. Although no such model should be used by the business person, without careful examination of individual products, it does provide some useful hints as to which products might be exportable and which might suffer import competition. The concept can also give clues as to the potential success of various product policies.

To extend the market for a product at home and abroad, the business person may practise a strategy of market segmentation making design changes in the product to appeal to different types of consumers, but there comes a point where design changes can no longer make a product competitive abroad or safe from imports. Firms may follow two strategies for survival: a continual product roll-over, shifting resources to new products more suited to the unique demands of the market; and/or manufacturing abroad to take advantage of lower production costs and to save tariffs and transportation charges.

LANCASTER'S MODIFICATION AND EXTENSION TO THE THEORY[12]

According to Wells's theory, as a product moves down the 'pecking order' over time, a series of curves with similar amplitudes will result. However, Lancaster suggests that the further down the pecking order a product goes, the higher will be its consumption over time. Thus each product life-cycle curve will have a progressively higher amplitude. This is explained diagrammatically in Fig. 14.5.

Curve (1) represents Band 1 and we can see that (a) represents (Band 1) production of a product for the (Band 1) market. It is appropriate that the first curve should be the US as most new products commence their life there. As this market becomes saturated, the American producers seek export opportunities in developed European markets (Band 2), shown in (b). The American production of the product continues to supply one market in decline in (c) as European producers begin to market the same product in their home market (d). At this stage European production grows as rapidly as American production declines, and eventually European producers are meeting their home market demand by themselves (e). In stage (f) the developed European producers have reached the pinnacle of production, providing their home market, the American market and next band developing countries (Band 3) with the product. However, in section (g) sales of the product decline in the European and developing country markets now being supplied, as the developing countries themselves begin to produce the product (h). Now developing

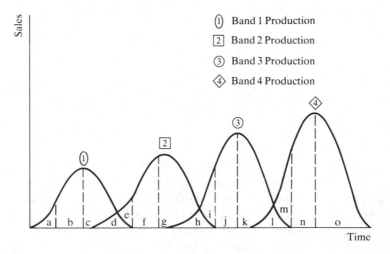

Stage	Production	Consumption
a	①	①
b	①	① + ②
c	①	① + ②
d	① + ②	① + ②
e	②	① + ②
f	②	① + ② + ③
g	②	① + ② + ③
h	② + ③	① + ② + ③
i	③	① + ② + ③
j	③	① + ② + ③ + ④
k	③	① + ② + ③ + ④
l	③ + ④	① + ② + ③ + ④
m	④	① + ② + ③ + ④
n	④	① + ② + ③ + ④
o	④	① + ② + ③ + ④

Figure 14.5   Lancaster's modification to Wells's theory

country production grows as rapidly as European production declines and eventually developing country producers are meeting their home market demand by themselves (i). Now the developing countries have reached the height of their production (j), supplying America, Europe, their home market, and less developed countries (Band 4), and then move into decline (k) as less developed country production increases (1). This cycle of trade from one group of countries to another can continue as long as there are countries less developed than the previous ones.

It should be noticed that each curve is higher than the previous one because production increases in relation to the increased demand. This is because the movement of the product from one curve to the next creates active consumers who did not exist before, primarily due to product development and experience gained in production, but also due to increased demand as less-developed countries become more affluent.

To give examples of the type of countries involved in the above model, 'Europe' denotes Western Europe – those countries which are technically advanced second only to the United States. Such countries would typically be Great Britain, West Germany or France. By developing countries, we mean some European countries and some Far Eastern countries – Portugal, Yugoslavia, Hong Kong and South Korea would be good examples. Less-developed countries would follow economically and technically after these developing countries, but may be split into various degrees of development. Such countries would typically be Thailand, Indonesia, Sri Lanka and Nigeria.

Looking at the model cumulatively we can see a gradual progression in sales of the product. By adding the total consumption levels at each point in time (i.e., by inverting sections d, h and l) we find a straight line of cumulative consumption (see Fig. 14.6). The different stages in each curve can still be identified on this straight line.

In fact, the descriptions given more or less neatly match the definitions given earlier in this chapter with the US being an example of an 'affluent country' and so on down the scale to 'subsistence economies'.

LOGISTICS OF EXPORTING

Physical distribution or logistics is an activity often neglected in texts on international marketing. It is, however, an extremely important subject, particularly for the export marketer; it is one of the major cost elements in international marketing and has been identified as a crucial factor in non-price competitiveness. Research by Steuer et al.[13] showed that in the case of machine tools a rise in waiting time of one month will reduce export orders by approximately 10 per cent.

Logistics includes the three areas of warehousing, inventory control and transport (and in the case of export marketing, the associated documentation). As far as consumers are concerned, these factors are represented by:

(a) the speed with which orders are filled;
(b) the ability to meet emergency orders;
(c) the delivery of goods in acceptable condition;
(d) the policy on returned goods;
(e) the options offered on minimum order sizes and transport modes;
(f) the charges for services (if any).

The concept of total distribution cost has been discussed in Chapter 10. Nowhere is this concept of more importance than in international marketing. The methods of transport potentially available to the export marketer are varied: seafreight, road, rail, canal and airfreight, and it is well known that on a unit weight or volume rate, the costs of airfreight, for example, are significantly

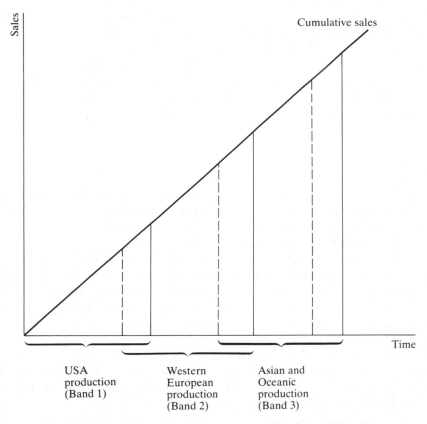

Figure 14.6   Cumulative sales, per Lancaster's modification to Wells's theory

greater than seafreight. This simplistic comparison ignores cost saving in other areas of logistics that can be achieved by airfreight. Greater speed of delivery has a positive effect on cash flow – a company's money is tied up in goods for a shorter period of time; lower safety stock levels reduce the costs of stockholding; cost of insurance packaging, handling and customs clearance can be significantly reduced. This is not to say that airfreight should be the preferred mode of transport – bulk items are clearly excluded – but serves as an example that it is unrealistic to consider the freight rate alone in physical distribution decisions. In general terms, however, it can be said that on a regular basis, low-bulk, high-value items are carried by air, while high-bulk, low-value products (e.g., coal) are more effectively moved by sea.

This generalization tends to ignore the other modes of transport already mentioned. Road transport as a means of transporting goods from place of manufacture to place of consumption is highly developed throughout Western Europe, and the use of roll-on roll-off (ro-ro) ferries is extremely important in trade between the UK and her EC partners. On mainland Europe the canal and river system is commercially viable. The important factor is, therefore, to consider what is available to reach a specific overseas destination and to place this in the context of total distribution cost.

Few export marketers have the knowledge or experience to make all logistics decisions. Traditionally, a freight forwarder has been used to bridge the gap between seller and shipper. His role has included the booking space on a particular transport mode, documentation and customs procedures and, in many cases, export packaging. Control of logistics was, therefore, fragmented. Most companies have now replaced at least a part of the international freight forwarder's role by an in-house function. Developments in aligned documentation under the auspices of the Simplification of International Trade Procedures Board (SITPRO) mean that international documents can be produced as easily as companies' commercial invoices.

The management of international logistics has all the problems of domestic physical distribution, but is complicated by its needs to operate across a wider spectrum of transport modes and accepted practice in differing countries. For a full discussion of this topic you are recommended to consult Davies's text on export distribution.[14]

CONCLUSIONS

Any chapter of this length on a topic as wide as international marketing must by its very nature be selective. An attempt has been made to concentrate on those aspects of international marketing which are different from similar areas of activity in domestic marketing by posing additional issues and problems faced by the international marketer.

The chapter has, therefore, covered the international economic environment, the identification of export opportunities and international physical distribution. A large portion of the chapter has been devoted to the elements of the marketing mix on an international scale and, in particular, strategies for entering the overseas market, product and communication alternatives, the concept of the international product life cycle and aspects of pricing as related to overseas marketing.

The principles of marketing are as true for international as for home markets. Customers' needs have to be analysed and understood, objectives must be set and performance must be controlled and measured. Special knowledge is, however, required and special training is necessary, both in the practicalities of export marketing and in the linguistic sense.

APPLICATION QUESTIONS

1. How does the international marketing environment differ from the environment in the domestic market?
2. What are the major difficulties likely to be encountered in carrying out research (both desk and field) for international marketing?
3. What alternative product and communication strategies are open to the international marketer?
4. What are the additional issues to be considered in pricing a product for overseas markets?
5. What are the major alternative market entry strategies, and what benefits and disadvantages do they have?

REFERENCES

1. Walsh, L. S., *International Marketing*, Macdonald and Evans, London, 1981, Chapter 1, p. 4.
2. Walsh, L. S., op. cit., pp. 5–6.
3. Tugendhat, C., *The Multinationals*, Penguin, Harmondsworth, 1984.
4. Terpstra, V., *International Marketing*, 3rd edn, Dryden Press, Hinsdale, IL, 1983.
5. Rostow, W. W., *The Stage of Economic Growth*, Cambridge University Press, Cambridge, 1960.
6. Walsh, L. S., op. cit.
7. Whymant, R., 'Why Britain is bamboozled by a bamboo curtain', *Guardian*, 21 October 1980, p. 19.
8. Keegan, W. J., 'Multinational product planning: strategic alternatives', *Journal of Marketing*, **33**, January 1969, pp. 58–62.

9. Walker, A. G., *Export Practice Documentation*, Newnes-Butterworth, London, 1977, pp. 22–26.
10. Wells, L. T., Jr, 'A product life cycle for international trade', *Journal of Marketing*, **32**, 1968, pp. 1–6.
11. Hufbauer, G. C., *Synthetic Materials and the Theory of International Trade*, Harvard University Press, Cambridge, MA, 1966.
12. Lancaster, G. A. and I. Wesenlund, 'A product life cycle theory for international trade: an empirical investigation', *European Journal of Marketing*, **18** (6/7), 1984, pp. 72–89.
13. Steuer, M. D., R. J. Ball and J. R. Eaton, 'The effect of waiting time on foreign orders for machine tools', *Economica*, **33**, pp. 387–403.
14. Davies, G., *Managing Export Distribution*, Heinemann, London, 1984.

FIFTEEN

SOCIAL, LEGAL AND ENVIRONMENTAL ASPECTS OF MARKETING

INTRODUCTION

Much of marketing literature is concerned with the functional activities of marketing management, this being applied to the concept or philosophy of marketing, which holds that its basic purpose is the satisfaction of consumers' wants and needs. This chapter examines marketing from a wider 'social' perspective and suggests that management responsibilities involve more than the company/consumer interface. A recognition is, therefore, made of the increasing complexity of marketing. The satisfaction of one consumer group may create considerable conflict in another group. The existence of the consumer movement is evidence of this conflict and on a broader scale, ecological and social issues must also be incorporated into a marketing equation whose original variables were restricted to sales, growth and profit.

In an increasingly competitive business environment, it is not suggested that the need for profit should in any way be relegated. Similarly, this chapter does not criticize the basic tenets of the marketing concept. Rather, the objective is to make the reader aware of marketing's obligations to society as well as to specific consumer groups. Society is made up of individual consumers; a marketing approach which considers society will, therefore, ultimately fulfil the requirements of the marketing concept.

MAJOR CRITICISMS OF MARKETING

Micro dimensions

As consumer markets have become more complex and marketing more sophisticated, its practice has become the subject of increasing controversy and criticism. This is due, to some extent, to media and organized consumer misuse and misunderstanding of the word 'marketing' itself. 'Marketing' as discussed today in the media often becomes the generic term which describes a multitude of malpractice ranging from actual dishonest trading to over-exaggerated advertising claims. A company which describes itself as 'marketing oriented' can run the risk of being grouped with those firms that do not practise marketing at all in the real sense. This is one explanation for the poor image which marketing has in the minds of many consumers and media controllers.

However, it must be recognized that even among those companies that adhere to the marketing concept, some criticism as to its functions is justified. Typical criticisms are outlined in the following list.

- Poor product quality.
- Deceptive packaging and labelling.
- Advertising is misleading.
- Advertising exploits children and makes people dissatisfied.
- Delivery is unreliable.
- After-sales service is inefficient.
- Market research invades privacy.

The existence of such a list is not excusable and there is obviously much room for improvement. It must be remembered that in a competitive environment firms do not set out to antagonize customers if they wish to remain in business. Moreover, consumers usually have the sanction of spending their money where levels of service are more acceptable. The onus here is on marketing practitioners to recognize and remedy their areas of weakness and to promote themselves and their activities so as to be distinguished from the less savoury and often purely sales-oriented approaches that some companies employ.

Macro dimensions

There is a more intellectual and more fundamental basis from which marketing can be criticized. This concerns marketing's economic and ethical role in the way in which needs are satisfied and resources are allocated. The fundamental debate as to the validity of respective political systems and their approach to resource allocation is beyond the scope of this text; the intention is to consider the problem within the context of 'market' economies. Within such a framework it is perhaps inevitable that the marketing manager has, in his professional role, typically viewed the problems of society from a different viewpoint from that of the external or public observer. The former has tended to emphasize the success and contribution which business in general has made to society, while the latter looks beyond the individual firm and highlights the negative aspects of marketing in society. A subsequent section of this chapter examines how differing ideals in the way marketing is viewed can be reconciled. This section deals with criticisms which call into question marketing's impact on society and which are, therefore, 'macro' in nature.

Although it is difficult to classify such criticisms conveniently because of their wide variety, they can be roughly divided into 'economic' and 'ethical' sub-groups. Economic criticism centres around the theme that marketing is inefficient and chiefly concerns the following proposals.

Marketing creates monopoly and limits consumer choice The possibility of a company becoming so powerful that it will decide what the consumer will buy and at what price is a denial of the marketing concept and one of the chief fears of the consumer movement. In the private sectors of the developed world, although the development of even larger and more powerful companies is recognized, true monopolies rarely exist. As well as government regulation (in the form of the Monopolies and Mergers Commission in the UK and Anti-trust Legislation in the USA) the buying public is rarely sufficiently homogeneous to permit exclusive control by a monopolistic power.

Part of the opposition to monopoly is rooted in the economist's notion that perfect competition among sellers is the fairest way in which business can serve society and that a state of monopoly will allow the worst fears of marketing critics to materialize. It is true that monopoly is the antithesis of perfect competition but these represent extremes of economic theory: the reality lies somewhere between the two. Marketing is in fact characterized by many economic business conditions. Some markets are supplied by numerous small to medium-sized companies, while others are represented by the state of oligopoly.

We should remember that good marketing strategy should centre around a distinctive competence of the firm.[1] In this way the most successful companies become something of a monopolist in their field. For the consumer, the most important factor is that such a firm's competitors will continually strive to emulate such success. Thus, the current leader has little room for complacency. Such competition acknowledges the idea of consumer sovereignty and is the best safeguard that consumers have against exploitation by powerful companies.

The reality that increased market share leads to a disproportionate increase in market advantages, profits and thus in power has led many markets to a state of oligopoly.[2] The existence of such power has caused marketing's critics to prophesy that such firms will eventually dictate as to what, where and when consumers will buy. Certainly there are instances of the abuse of power, most notably among some multinational companies in the Third World, and such activities must be deplored. In Western markets such power is tempered by competition as well as the ability of the consumer to remove his or her custom. In the UK in the early 1970s, genuine fears were expressed about the power of large bakeries and breweries to 'impose' white sliced bread and gas filled beer upon the nation. Although these markets were in fact oligopolistic, it seemed that they were in possession of monopoly-like powers, supplying only what was profitable and convenient for them to produce. The resurgence of more traditional products was testimony to consumer power and a timely reminder to those firms that had neglected the marketing concept. Currently, Britain's 'Big Four' banks are shaking off any complacency that they may have had in the 1970s. Competition has not only increased between themselves but also they are realizing that they have no 'divine right' to exclusivity in the marketing of their services.

Similar examples are not difficult to find; they usually reveal that successful companies gain power so long as they efficiently satisfy demand, while at the same time, the standards of other companies are raised in their efforts to emulate the leader. Such a lead is constantly under threat from potential competition, differentiated and substitute products and changes in the nature of consumer demand. Critics of marketing play a valuable social role – it would be naive to bestow complete altruism on all the business world, or indeed to overlook genuine mistakes. It is proposed that the nature of markets themselves will militate against monopoly and that if situations approaching monopoly exist, these will only remain while they efficiently satisfy consumer needs and wants.

Marketing involves too much competitive promotion The major criticisms of competitive promotion are directed at the advertising industry. Indeed, advertising is criticized by business itself because of the notorious difficulties involved in evaluating its effectiveness. Our main concern is with external critics who contend that purely competitive advertising is wasteful and that the consumers' real need is for advertising to be informative. If advertising was reduced or did not exist (so the argument runs) manufacturers' overheads would decrease and this would result in cheaper goods. The argument is extended to question the need for the multiplicity of apparently similar products which advertising is engaged in promoting.

The desire of consumers to have brand choice is well known, but marketers should not reject such criticism out of hand. When the US government banned cigarette advertising, it was interesting to note that sales did not fall significantly and that the relative market share of the cigarette manufacturers (all of whom were heavy advertising spenders) did not change. Cigarettes may, of course, present a special case, but the event certainly caused large spenders of advertising money to stop and think.

More usually marketers are able to provide economic justification for their promotional expenditure. So as to maintain profitability, manufacturers place great reliance on their ability to achieve an optimum production/overhead ratio. Advertising can help to achieve and maintain such a position, but it must be remembered that if sales which exceed the optimum are induced, such effort may become counter-productive.

Marketing is wasteful The 'middleman' is often the butt of marketing criticism. A long and complicated channel system is seen as wasteful and unnecessary. Students of channel structure should be able to present cogent reasons which justify the need for middlemen – that is from the manufacturer's point of view. There is no doubt that some channel systems are less than efficient. In the macro sense, critics bemoan the transportation around the country of apparently identical goods which are produced by different manufacturers. Frequently these goods are in fact highly differentiated with respect to style, design and brand name. There is moreover an important movement towards the simplification of channel systems which is discernible in the rise of discount stores and hypermarkets.

Despite the inefficiencies of marketing it is logical to assume that companies will endeavour to reduce costs whenever possible. Efficiency is, of course, necessary for profit, and profit is essential for survival, but the implication for the consumer is that it allows the company to increase competitiveness and so reduce prices or improve service.

From the social perspective, critics question social values which it is claimed marketing is largely responsible for creating.

Marketing promotes materialism and creates artificial needs and values The economist and social philosopher J. K. Galbraith described, as early as 1952, the creation of wants as the 'dependence effect'. He criticized the processes of production and marketing for satisfying wants that were not 'original' within the consumer, but which were actually created by marketing in the first place.[3] Much of the blame for the so-called stimulation of wants is laid at the door of advertising. Whether the source of our desire to acquire products and life styles which we could physically live without is inherent in ourselves, or is imposed upon us by phenomena such as advertising, is the subject of major philosophical debate. Some psychologists maintain that our wants are not really concerned with the acquisition of, say, an expensive hi-fi system but rather that such an act realizes an inner psychological need. If this is the case, then marketing plays the valuable social role of want fulfilment, satisfying wants which otherwise, it could be argued, the consumer would search to fulfil in some other way. To this extent, if blame is to be attached, it must be shared by the buyer and the seller.

Questions as to the power of marketing and advertising to distort values and create artificial wants cannot be easily resolved. Is marketing to be blamed for the general rise in living standards which has facilitated the style of spending which is itself the source of so much criticism? It may be that some critics underestimate the ability of consumers to discriminate and choose for themselves. The existence of social inequality has led to the comment that advertising dissatisfies the poor by portraying a world which is beyond their means. This is a socio-political comment as much as a direct criticism of marketing.

Advertising is offensive and deceptive Fraudulent and deliberately deceptive advertising is infrequent as it is controlled by legislation. It is relatively rare because it is the advertiser's job to gain confidence among the target market and not to destroy it.

Much of the advertising deemed 'questionable' involves sins of omission as well as commission. The existence of advertising control is testimony to the fact that some advertising has presented half truths which, although not necessarily making blatantly false claims, have in reality set out to deceive. The socially responsible advertiser aims to communicate genuine product features to the public, and while the need for regulatory bodies to control the less ethical is reprehensible, its existence appears to have raised the standards of advertising in general. In the US, the Federal Trade Commission now reports that 97 per cent of advertisements checked each year, satisfactorily adhere to its code of conduct.[4]

Marketing is unethical Often the individual marketer's own personal standards may be compromised in the business situation. This problem of ethics is aggravated by the confusion which exists as to what the ethical obligations of marketing are. In recent years we have witnessed numerous examples of 'leaks' and revelations from individual employees of large organizations. If, for example, in detriment of his or her own career and financial security, an executive publicly discloses that the company has deceived or endangered its customers, the employee's corporate allegiance has then been overruled by his or her personal ethical code. For the average individual, the dilemma is unlikely to reach such critical proportions, but an ethical problem nevertheless remains.

Clearly the solution lies with higher management, who could obviate the causes of ethical conflict. The power of the media and of consumerism has developed to such an extent, that management is in any case under considerable pressure to adopt an increasingly responsible stance. Major initiatives have indeed been taken by enlightened companies that see valid marketing opportunities in such an approach. The question of social responsibility in marketing will be dealt with in a later section of this chapter.

THE CONSUMER MOVEMENT

The phenomenon of consumerism is central to the theme of this chapter. Its existence is testimony to the failures of marketing while, at the same time, consumerism has been responsible for marketing's increasingly important social dimension. Much of this process of change is due to legal and governmental action which has obliged companies to pay heed to consumerist activity. A potentially more important outcome is that responsible companies view consumerism not as coercive or threatening, but as a definite opportunity to serve their markets better.

Development of the consumer movement

The origins of the consumer movement are firmly based in the US. This is not to say that the need for consumerism did not exist in Europe and the UK. Rather, factors such as mass production and mass marketing were quicker to develop in the US. Here, organized consumers successfully achieved their aims both at the turn of the century and in the 1930s. However, these were isolated movements which were directed at specific targets. Once successful, there appeared to be no need to continue with further organized action. It was not until the late 1950s and early 1960s that the consumer movement as we know it today began to materialize. Social commentators such as J. K. Galbraith, Vance Packard and Rachel Carson began to alert the American nation, not to specific cases, but to the whole philosophy and social rationale on which society (as it related to the business world) was based. The Second World War probably developed the birth of such a movement because the austerity of the immediate post-war environment made consumers more likely to be grateful for the luxury of being able to acquire goods which had previously been scarce, than to complain about their quality or the marketing methods associated with them. Moreover, during the war period itself, organized groups of dissatisfied consumers were not conducive to the spirit of patriotism which prevailed. By the early 1960s definite challenges to the *status quo* which business had enjoyed were emerging.

The Second World War notwithstanding, it is likely that consumerism was an inevitable development of our economic system and it is equally likely that the movement will endure.[5] In America, the 'champion' of consumerism was Ralph Nader whose book, *Unsafe at Any Speed*, was a challenge to, and a formidable indictment of, the American automobile industry – and in particular General Motors. Nader was an influential figure of the 1960s who was responsible for a number of Federal Laws such as the Meat Inspection Bill and the Fire Research and Safety Law, but his influence was far wider than in these specific spheres. His greatest impact was that he engendered in the public the idea that monolithic business institutions could in fact be challenged and those who were at fault could no longer act with impunity. This notion spread through America via the mass media and was transferred (albeit more slowly) to the UK.

Within the UK itself, an important parallel to Ralph Nader (in terms of influence on the public attitude) was the development of the consumer magazine *Which*. From very humble beginnings in a garage in South London, circulation experienced a dramatic rise, such that within a very short time *Which* became a household name. *Which* selects a series of consumer goods for each publication, objectively tests them on a variety of counts and then publishes its conclusions. The result is that products and their companies are classified according to their relative performance. Such a concept was hitherto undreamed of. Like Nader, *Which* has not only achieved a specific task, but has also contributed to the feeling, or notion, that consumers need no longer accept the offerings of big and small businesses alike without voicing their opinions.

The meaning of consumerism

Consumerism is well defined as 'a social movement seeking to augment the rights and power of buyers in relation to sellers'.

To understand the full implications of such a definition it is worth while examining what these rights have traditionally been held to be.

Sellers have the following rights:

1. To introduce any product in any style or size provided that it is not injurious to health and safety and provided that potentially hazardous products are supplied together with appropriate warnings.
2. To price products at any level provided that there is no discrimination among similar classes of buyers.
3. To say what they like in promotion of their products provided that any message is not dishonest or misleading in content or execution.
4. To spend any amount of money they wish, to promote their product and to introduce any buying incentive schemes provided that these cannot be defined as unfair competition.

Buyers in their turn have their own rights and the right to expect certain things from sellers and their products.

Buyers have the following rights:

1. Not to buy products offered to them.
2. To expect the product to be safe.
3. To expect that the product is in fact essentially the same as the seller has represented.

An appreciation and a knowledge of the respective rights of the buyer and seller help to put the consumer problem into perspective.

The biggest weapon of the consumer has traditionally been held to be that of the 'silent vote', that is the right not to buy unsatisfactory goods; this is the concept of consumer sovereignty. Logically, therefore, companies who mis-serve the market will usually run out of customers. This is indeed a powerful sanction and has been cited earlier when discussing major criticisms of marketing. Consumerists argue that the onus is not on the consumer to veto unsatisfactory goods after having first been disappointed, rather that it is up to the sellers of goods to take all reasonable steps to ensure satisfacton before offering goods for sale. They further argue that such a step will be greatly facilitated if certain basic consumer 'rights' are recognized.

What should consumer rights be?

In 1962 President John F. Kennedy clearly delineated four basic consumer rights. His declaration was probably the most important single step in the advancement of consumerism. He proposed the following 'consumer rights':

1. *The right to safety*: consumers have the right to expect that products do not possess hidden dangers. This was the basis of Nader's campaign against the automobile industry. In the UK, the aftermath of the thalidomide affair forced attention to turn on food and drugs. Occasionally, such attention has led to allegations of alarmist activity by consumerists. In the US the use of cyclamates in artificial sweeteners was alleged to have a carcinogenic effect. Subsequent investigations held that such products were harmless in the quantities normally consumed by human beings.
2. *The right to be informed*: consumers should be protected from inadequate and misleading product information and from deceptions in advertising, guarantees and product labelling. Possibly the most extreme example is that of cigarette advertising and the introduction of government health warnings. Other examples are less controversial, but the idea remains the same: consumers should be responsible for their purchase decisions only after having been in receipt of adequate product information.
3. *The right to choose*: consumers have the right to real competition among sellers and should not be subjected to confusing promotion and product labelling. An experiment in California showed that such was the variety and complexity of labelling, that supermarket shoppers were incapable of relating quantity to cost when making purchases.[6]
4. *The right to be heard*: consumers have the right to express their dissatisfactions in a manner which will attract attention and so achieve positive results. Consumerists argue that individual consumers, apart from having no 'voice', do not necessarily have the time or the skills to make complex choice decisions or to absorb product information when it is preferred. Organized bodies should, therefore, be established to speak for them. A further argument is that modern shopping methods have distanced the seller from the buyer so that dissatisfactions are difficult to voice with any degree of success.

Consumerism today

A great deal of the demands which the consumer movement originally made have now been met. This is not to say that the need for consumer protection has diminished, or that it is likely to do so. There is also the danger that after several years of success, those responsible for administering and improving consumer protection will become complacent, less dynamic and less responsive to change. Consumerists are also becoming involved with protection at the macro level. The progress already made must not be allowed to slide, but it is likely that future consumerist interest will focus more on macro price levels (such as lobbying the EEC on food prices) and on multinational business, rather than the day-to-day problems of the high street. Increasing attention is also paid to environmental and ecological issues and it must also be remembered that as society is confronted by new social and economic problems, so the consumer movement must respond by adapting to the ensuing challenges.

The undoubted success of the consumer movement cannot be wholly ascribed to a positive response on behalf of the business world. During the 1960s and 1970s in particular, mistrust, misunderstanding and complacency were typical corporate responses to the consumerist phenomenon. Just as few motorists are likely to consider themselves as being bad drivers, few firms are able to appreciate or be willing to admit that the consumer movement has been aimed against them. It is not suggested that companies have decided to persevere with a policy of deception or poor service; the real answer is that until consumer issues began to take on national importance, most companies genuinely believed that they were fulfilling their consumer responsibilities.

Despite the initial reluctance of firms to respond to the consumer movement, the 1980s have witnessed definite progress in the attitudes and actions of business organizations. That this has been due to enlightenment and altruism is the subject of debate. What is more certain is that governmental and legal action has obliged companies not only to initiate change but also has permitted the realization that consumerism has become a fixture of society which, if properly approached, can provide positive opportunities for marketing management. The creation of a Ministry for Consumer Affairs testifies to the government's commitment to consumer protection. The following section details the extent of remedies in law and sources of advice which are available to consumers. It is, therefore, perhaps lamentable that statutes and official bodies have had to be the instrument of change, but what is important for the consumer is the fact that change has taken place. It is significant that major companies in the retail sector have adopted unit pricing voluntarily or have insisted on explicit labelling details. Other businesses have published true rates of interest (annual percentage rates) for credit deals or have used the fact that their products adhere to the respective regulations as a major theme of their promotional campaigns. Whether this is altruism or a response to legislation is not really relevant; the important thing is that these initiatives have been taken.

MARKETING AND CONSUMERISM

Marketing's ethical issues are, of course, inextricably bound up with consumerism, and the implications for both reach beyond the boundaries of 'marketing management' in the commonly accepted sense of the term. The response of marketing to consumerism presents us with philosophical as well as practical questions. Kotler's call for a 'revised marketing concept'[7] would take into account the long-term moral and social issues with which marketing should now concern itself. Before examining further such a concept, we should recognize certain practicalities which complicate the issue.

The essence of marketing strategy is to think and plan for the long term. This strategic approach is also essential if a firm wishes to adopt an increased social orientation and respond positively to consumerism. The economies of business life on the other hand, tend to invoke short-term concern, and while the evidence of successful long-term strategy is all around us, this is never easily achieved. It is likely that such difficulties will be accentuated by the addition of a consumerist/social dimension to long-range planning.

The second important consideration is that of the social/economic environment itself. Consumerism, taken to its logical and ultimate conclusion, implies a major redistribution of wealth and power. By how much the business world is willing, or able, to subscribe to such a movement is an important subject of debate. This in turn is closely linked to the attitudes of government which may vary according to the social and economic conditions which prevail. In theory, pro-consumer government action should benefit the government (in terms of popularity) plus business, if a positive response is made then consumers themselves will react favourably. Major initiatives have already been taken by various governments and such a sequence of benefits has already occurred. However, it is important that we do not underestimate the complexity of this process.

Having taken into account the above considerations, we can now examine how marketing should react to consumerism. It is apparent that the consumer movement has graduated beyond the realms of 'micro' issues, although it has been suggested that the need for vigilance in this respect will continue. The future concerns of marketing should involve the long-term and broader issues of consumerism. This is the theme of the following 'Social marketing' section. The immediate realization must be that consumerism must be seen as an opportunity, and that the suspicion previously associated with it should be abandoned. Many firms have already proved this to be a viable and profitable approach. In many respects, consumerism has done the work of the marketer by identifying a whole range of previously unsatisfied needs and wants. These opportunities concern such items as unit pricing, honesty in labelling and credit agreements. They extend into the satisfaction of psychological needs. The manufacturer who, for example, produces a prduct and includes and conceals a hazardous component in order to save costs, will suffer in the long term at the hands of a competitor who treats safety as a 'feature' and builds this into marketing strategy and tactics. Consumerism, properly viewed, does not challenge the marketing concept but is a major reinforcement of it.

CONSUMER LAW AND PROTECTION

The consumer movement has had a profound effect upon the British legal system. The rate of change in consumer marketing since the early 1960s has brought with it equivalent change in the law which has been considerably modified to protect the consumer from unfair practices. The law relating to consumer protection is not a clearly defined code; it is made up of extensions and amendments to contract law. Its basis is in legislation (such as the Factors Act 1889)[8] which was designed to define the law as to contractual relationships between traders. In Britain there is no such thing as a 'consumer law' as a single entity, nor is there a comprehensive code of consumer protection. There are, nevertheless, a wealth of statutory instruments which have been introduced during the last 20 years designed to effect specific control over potential injustices and exploit actions of the consumer. There is also the existing contract law which has a high degree of relevance to current situations in which the consumer may be at a disadvantage.

The following is a list of statutes which have particular importance for the consumer. It is not meant to be exhaustive, but is included so as to provide an insight into the legal development of consumer protection.

1. Aerosol Dispensers (EEC Requirements) Regulations 1977.
2. Babies Dummies (Safety) Regulations 1978.
3. Business Advertisements (Disclosure) Order 1977.
4. Consumer Credit (Credit Reference Agency) Regulations 1977.
5. Cooking Utensils (Safety) Regulations 1972.
6. Cosmetic Products Regulations 1978.
7. Electric Blankets (Safety) Regulations 1971.
8. Mail Order Transactions (Information) Order 1976.
9. Nightdresses (Safety) Regulations 1967.

10. Price Marking (Bargain Offers) Order 1979.
11. Pyramid Selling Schemes Regulations 1973.
12. Toys (Safety) Regulations 1974.

Further remedies in law for the consumer are to be found in contract law. Although it has already been stated that there is no such thing as 'consumer law', and although existing legislation is somewhat hybrid in nature, it is possible to place the law as it relates to the consumer into two broad categories. First, remedies exist under private law and second, remedies have been created by administrative and governmental action. These latter remedies are backed up by criminal law and come under the jurisdiction of the Director General of Fair Trading.

Before continuing, it is important that one should understand the nature of a 'contract'. To be binding in law, a contract need not necessarily be formally drawn up by solicitors and signed by both parties. All that is necessary is that an 'offer' be made which is 'accepted' and that the exchange takes place for some 'consideration': in most cases this is financial. The implication for consumers is that such a contract takes place every time a purchase is made.

Remedies available under private law Sale of Goods Act 1979

The original Sale of Goods Act was passed in 1893 and has been constantly amended since then. The Act defines the statutory rights of the buyer (and seller) with respect to the transfer of property in goods for a money consideration (the price). The 'inalienable' rights of the consumer are set out by the Act. These concern the transference of title from the seller to the buyer, the description and the quality of the goods.

An important component of the Act concerns the question of 'merchantable quality'. The definition of merchantable quality is the cause of some debate. The question is covered by the implied terms of the Act and should not be equated with mere 'description' of the goods. The definition which currently applies can be paraphrased as follows:

> Goods of any kind are of merchantable quality ... if they are as fit for the purpose for which goods of that kind are commonly bought and which it is reasonable to expect them to be having regard to the description, price and circumstances of purchase.

Linked to the idea of merchantable quality is the 'fitness for purpose' for which goods are bought and the 'availability' of those goods which are also implied terms of the Act.

The supply of services

As marketing is concerned with the provision of both goods and services, we should also consider consumer rights when the product is a service rather than a tangible good. Separate, and perhaps less exhaustive, legislation covers this area, but there are well-established precedents which refer to contracts for services. The Unfair Contract Terms Act 1977 is particularly concerned with the application of exemption clauses by the supplier of services. The 'reasonableness test' affords protection for both buyer and seller when such clauses are included in a contract.

The more recent Supply of Goods and Services Act 1982 has furnished the consumer with further specific attention. Services must be carried out with 'reasonable care and skill', 'within a reasonable time' and at 'a reasonable charge'. Of course, what is 'reasonable', is dependent on the facts and circumstances of the case and how these are interpreted by the judge.

Misrepresentation and false trade descriptions of goods

Perhaps the most often quoted piece of consumer legislation is the Trade Descriptions Act of

1968 and 1972 (TDA). It is also likely that while the seller should be aware of all consumer legislation, the TDA has the widest scope of application. The Act overlaps to some extent with other legal remedies, but it is specific in that it applies only where a trader has made a claim about the goods offered for sale. This is of particular relevance to the consumer nowadays when advertising, promotion and direct mail campaigns have reached an intensive level. Test cases in the courts have tended to concern malpractices in second-hand car trading, but the precedents which have been set, have equal applications in all manner of consumer transactions.

The TDA is clearly of particular relevance to advertising practice. While the TDA does not specifically deal with claims as to 'value' and 'worth' (such claims are controlled by the Price Marking (Bargain Offers) Order 1979), the creative jargon of the advertiser's copy may lead to the making of intentional or unintentional false claims about a good or service. This leads us to an important legal point on the subject of advertising – that of the traders' 'puff'. Claims made about a brand of perfume or beer, or the hackneyed 'desirable residence' of the estate agent's jargon are not likely to be construed as being legally binding. If, however, the advertiser uses a phrase such as 'results guaranteed', such a promise is sufficiently definite as to be legally enforceable. If a company makes a claim about its product, it is up to the courts to decide whether the statement is legally enforceable or merely a 'puff' of creative imagination.

The subject of false trade descriptions is linked to that of misrepresentation, which is dealt with separately under the Misrepresentation Act of 1967. The easiest way to understand misrepresentation is to remember that it must relate to a question of fact and that any representation only becomes legally significant if it turns out to be false. The categories of misrepresentation should also be appreciated. These are: fraudulent, negligent or innocent. In the latter case, damages are not usually available to the consumer, although costs and expenses arising from the trader's action may be awarded.

Consumer credit

The Consumer Credit Act 1974 is an example of direct response to consumer protection as the purchase transaction becomes more complicated and open to abuse.

The Act controls the advertising of credit and canvassing where dishonesty is concerned, and it requires the company which offers credit to disclose fully all information about the agreement, including the rights of cancellation. The consumer also has the 'right to a remedy' if a so-called 'credit bargain' is subsequently found to be extortionate. More recently a 'cooling off' period has been introduced during which the consumer may reflect on a purchase, and decide whether or not to go ahead with the responsibilities of a credit agreement.

The proliferation of credit facilities which now exist has led to a whole series of legislation on the subject. The principal intention here is to bring attention to the significance of this legislation, rather than to expand upon the individual statutes.

Product liability

The consumer usually makes a contract of sale with a retailer. Under the terms of the Sale of Goods Act, the usual recourse to justice in the event of complaint is made to the retailer and not to the manufacturer. There are, however, occasions when the consumer has the right to bring a case against the manufacturer of defective goods. Such liability with respect to safety is set out in the Consumer Safety Act 1978 and the Consumer Protection Act 1961. Similarly, where a guarantee is offered by the manufacturer, the offer for sale is deemed to have been made by that party and not the retailer.

In civil law, a consumer has the right to sue in the 'tort' of negligence, because a manufacturer has the legal duty of care to ensure that his goods are not dangerous (this being subject to a series of limitations). Although remedies in fact existed long before the consumer movement, such an action is nevertheless a powerful weapon in the modern consumer's armoury in cases of negligence.

Remedies available due to administrative and governmental action

The failure of traders and manufacturers to comply with government regulations may result in civil or criminal action being taken against them. The rationale behind the establishment of the various consumer bodies is not to facilitate a flood of legal actions. The principal idea is to create a system whereby the existence of such bodies performs a self-regulatory function on behalf of manufacturers, advertisers and similar business practitioners. Before 'going to law' the consumer has (in the event of complaint) various sources of advice, plus the opportunity to take advantage of official assistance which will bring pressure to bear upon the offending party. The Gas Consumers' Council is a good example of such an institution, although in this case it is a monopolistic-type industry which is involved.

In addition to, and in conjunction with, legal remedies, the consumer is protected by the following bodies that 'supervise' the law.

The Director General of Fair Trading The post of Director General of Fair Trading was created by the Fair Trading Act 1973. This Act was also responsible for setting up the Consumer Protection Advisory Committee. The role of Director is essentially supervisory. He must monitor the activities of the business world and investigate potential causes for concern and publish the findings if necessary. Such information is available from the Government Office of Fair Trading. He should also encourage trade associations to prepare codes of practice and thus encourage self-regulatory activities. An example of the influence of the Director was in the creation of the Price Marking (Bargain Offers) Order 1979. This was introduced after recommendations for action against misleading bargain offers were made.

Self-regulation by manufacturers The setting up of voluntary codes of practice by various industries is valuable for consumer protection in that it is beneficial for companies to be seen to be adhering to the code. Moreover, a company will usually support the elements of the code because miscreants will damage the image of the industry as a whole. Voluntary codes will not, however, protect consumers from companies who are determined not to take part in such schemes. Such industry codes do, in many cases, obviate the need for legislative action. The Office of Fair Trading is a useful arbitrator in consumer/trade disputes. The duties of the office are also to approve, monitor and revise codes which are not functioning satisfactorily.

The advertising industry set up the British Code of Advertising Practice as early as 1962. Consumer complaints are brought before the Advertising Standards Authority whose duty it is to see that advertisements are 'legal, decent, honest and truthful' and that they are prepared with 'a sense of responsibility to the consumer'.

Sources of advice and assistance for the consumer Consumer activism has identified the fact that, for a large proportion of the population, legal remedies, however comprehensive, are beyond their financial reach. Similarly, many consumers are not able to articulate their complaints in the manner which the law often requires. To compensate for this, a conscious effort has been made by volunteers (often from within the legal profession) and by local authorities, to establish advice centres. With one exception, these centres do not deal exclusively with consumer problems, but provide a wide range of legal advice and consumer information. Legal Advice Centres and Neighbourhood Law Centres provide an advice service in the largest UK cities. In the latter case this extends to representation in courts, although this is normally only available to those who could qualify under the Legal Aid Scheme.

All local authorities have a Trading Standards Department which exists expressly for the protection of the consumer. This was originally established to ensure the proper execution of the Weights and Measures and Food and Drugs Acts. While this is still the case, the remit of the department now encompasses an advisory role in the event of consumer disputes. Since 1972, such assistance has been augmented by the creation of Consumer Advice Centres. These also publish a wide range of informative leaflets which help consumers to know what is available and what their rights are.

Finally, Citizens Advice Bureaux are run on a volunteer basis in most UK cities. As with law centres, the work of the bureaux is not exclusively concerned with 'consumer affairs'. They are particularly involved with social issues such as housing and payment of social security.

Although the range of legal remedies, and the scope of advice sources, may seem daunting to a prospective business person, it must be remembered that they are merely designed to uphold the law and ensure fair treatment of the consumer. A business which is seriously engaged in satisfying consumer 'wants' and 'needs' need not feel threatened or treat the protectors of consumers as adversaries. Indeed, as has already been suggested, consumerism should be viewed as a marketing opportunity rather than a threat.

SOCIAL MARKETING

The term 'social marketing' has yet to acquire a universal definition as to its nature, and the extent of its boundaries has yet to be agreed. However, it is clear that the satisfaction of business management needs is no longer an exclusive sphere for marketing. It is also accepted that marketing should act in conjunction with the public interest by serving the goals of society as well as those of business. Social marketing is, therefore, a broader concept than that expressed by the management system's definition. Social marketing 'refers to the study of markets and marketing activities within a total social system'.[9]

Development of social marketing

Marketing management has been exceptionally efficient in satisfying the material wants and needs of consumers. With this in mind, many economists and sociologists alike believe that for large sections of the Western world, the needs of consumers now centre on the 'quality' rather than the quantity of life, and that this shift of attention is a feature of the post-industrial society. Of course, the high demand for consumer goods and services is unlikely to abate, but a change in the priority of needs is likely to accelerate. A. H. Maslow has called these new priorities the 'meta-needs' of society. This change is undoubtedly the result of affluence. Related to this, but not as easily explained, are marked value changes. These have also contributed to the emergence of the social marketing concept.

Certainly consumerism has shifted its emphasis from what might be termed 'micro' to societal issues, these being social costs, social values, social products and social benefits. Some progressive companies have been quick to recognize this and they in turn have heightened this level of social awareness.

A further feature of 'post-industrial' values[10] concerns the issue of environmentalism.

Marketing's success in providing for our material needs and wants has also created widespread pollution (both cultural and physical), congestion, waste and ecological imbalance. Marketing is in fact only partly responsible for these phenomena, but it must share the burden of finding products and methods which reduce or eliminate their harmful effects.

Whatever the precise reasons for the development of a social marketing system, it is clear that there remains vast scope for further development, and that like consumerism, this movement will endure.

Boundaries of social marketing

The traditional viewpoint of marketing would hold that the principal responsibility of marketing is to provide products which satisfy consumers' needs efficiently and profitably. Provided that this is done in a socially responsible way (so runs the argument) the socio-economic *status quo* will be maintained to the mutual benefit of consumers and producers. The difficult question is in the definition of social responsibility. Is this fulfilled by the production of safe products, the publication of honest advertising or the reduction of pollution?

Proponents of 'social marketing' would greatly extend this responsibility. They see marketing as a social force which transmits not only a standard of living, but also serves as a force which reflects and influences cultural values and norms. Thus the boundaries of marketing extend far beyond purely economic criteria. This would concern those areas where there are clearly recognizable links between marketing and its social effects, e.g., cars – pollution and congestion; foodstuffs – pesticides and preservatives; manufacturing – atmospheric pollution, noise and safety. If business is so efficient in satisfying the most detailed wants of consumers, surely this expertise could, and should, be used in finding ways of providing this satisfaction at a reduced social cost. This would have the effect of creating markets as well as making individual firms and whole industries more attractive to the consumer.

Some regard marketing as being so powerful and intrinsic to society that it should concern itself with welfare issues such as poverty, education and health care. It is not in fact uncommon for businesses, both large and small, to involve themselves with such issues. The cynical may regard this as sophisticated image building. Whatever the motives may be, the fact remains that business and marketing expertise is beginning to develop and exhibit social, as well as economic roles.

It is not clear where the boundaries of social marketing should be erected, but it does appear that there are clear advantages both to society and business if a social orientation were to be incorporated into marketing strategy.

The transition from 'managerial' to 'social' marketing does not imply a replacement of the traditional marketing concept, but its extension so as to recognize and encompass the wider needs of society. This added dimension suggests that profit need no longer be marketing's sole goal. The need for profit undoubtedly remains the most essential element of a company's survival, and even the most enlightened firm cannot begin to implement a social programme without sufficient funds to initiate and perpetuate its actions.

The role of the government

Early moves towards consumer awareness were more the results of consumerist pressure than action which was initiated by business. This pressure was in turn supported and strengthened by government in the form of legislation and advisory bodies. The issues raised by social marketing in the 1980s require solutions by business, by government or by both. Social progress is likely to be more successful and beneficial for all concerned if business initiates social change rather than having this enforced upon it by an external agent.

Already the decision whether or not to adopt socially oriented measures is in some cases no longer an option, but a question of legislative enforcement. It is vital, therefore, that marketing becomes a socially oriented method of management as a result of its own efforts. Governments and their policies change quickly relative to the life span of companies. Moreover, they are not necessarily the best equipped to ensure that changing social needs are met. Marketing is already a social activity, and changes which it is involved in are likely to be enduring and closely related to society. This is not to say that governments have enacted bad legislation, or that they do not have an important role to play in social development. There obviously exist many companies that would have ignored their social responsibilities had not government forced them to recognize them. The important factor is that marketing executives and corporate bodies react before coercion takes place, and that this reaction has a beneficial effect.

Social orientation

By how far government will be instrumental in social development is unclear. The pragmatic view is that consumers would benefit from, say, pollution control no matter who the initiator is to be. It is suggested that consumers will receive better long-term benefits if the greater part of this responsibility is adopted by marketing.

A positive response to the requirements of fair trading or product reliability is relatively simple. Here the actions of the firm have a direct and immediate effect on its customers. The results of social marketing may have little immediate benefit for the individual, but profound significance for society as a whole. If a company re-formulated its packaging so that it was less wasteful and did not pollute, the immediate customers might prefer the original formula of packaging and the company would lose custom. Similarly, added safety features in cars and modified engines that reduced pollution would inevitably cost more and thus be unpopular with car buyers. In the long term, however, such moves would be beneficial to society. There is, therefore, a severe conflict between the long- and short-run interests of consumers and business. The social marketing concept holds that if non-consumers suffer in the course of immediate user satisfacton, then the marketing concept is not ultimately being fulfilled.

This is a difficult, ambitious and long-term proposal which will require re-education on behalf of consumers, the business community and society as a whole. The role of marketing is to adopt a social orientation which, while generating long-term profitability for the firm, satisfies immediate consumers and those parts of society which are affected by the firm's activities.

MARKETING AND NON-PROFIT ORGANIZATIONS

The previous section has distinguished between managerial or systems marketing and the broader based societal approach to marketing. In order to evolve from the purely business oriented to the social concept of marketing, companies will have to undergo substantial changes in their approach to strategy. This transition has a mirror image when one considers the role of organizations whose function it is to cater for the public, rather than the commercial needs of society. Just as the business world has in the past tended to ignore the social dimension, public services have tended not to apply a marketing management approach to their activities.

Such an attitude towards the management of public services has been fostered by the 'market economy' common to most Western countries which suggests that 'marketing' is the exclusive domain of the business world. Public bodies, on the other hand, because they have not been in the business of attracting customers, but of providing services which consumers have considered as their right, have often not thought it necessary either to make themselves attractive, or to be sensitive to the needs of those whom it is their duty to serve. This section presents the marketing concept as equally applicable to non-profit as well as commercial organizations. This is true because non-profit organizations also have 'products' and 'consumers', but in particular because marketing should be seen as a social activity which goes 'beyond the selling of toothpaste, soap and steel'.[11]

Non-profit organizations have 'marketing' problems

Non-profit organizations, whether inside or outside the mainstream of the public service, are frequently the subject of criticism for having top-heavy bureaucratic structures, an apathetic attitude to their consumers and poor and wasteful management which is characterized by a reluctance to innovate. Such criticisms can be summed up as unresponsiveness and lack of communication. These are classic marketing problems and it is not, therefore, unreasonable to assume that marketing can contribute to their solution.

Due to the fact that most public services are (a) virtual monopolies and (b) funded by government, it is not possible to draw significant parallels between such organizations and the commercial sector other than to recognize that both groups have 'marketing' problems. The essential difference is that for non-profit organizations the principle of consumer sovereignty has no, or at least reduced, significance. For the most part it not been possible for consumers to exercise the utimate sanction – the withdrawal of patronage. This is not to say that all public bodies have failed to respond effectively to their consumers. It is, however, true, that where such failure has taken place, had the rules of the commercial sector been applicable, the guilty organizations would probably have been forced to change or go out of existence.

Since the period immediately after the Second World War, the UK has witnessed a dramatic growth in the number of non-profit organizations dedicated to the service of the public. At the outset, the level of altruism and the immediate job in hand were probably such, that a conscious marketing effort was not thought necessary. Over time the same changes which have necessitated changes in commercial marketing have also affected the public sector. Changes in life style, levels of affluence and the economy have altered attitudes to institutions which were once considered to be major social benefits. These changes have not been restricted to amenities such as libraries and other public recreational facilities, but also extend to charities, the police force and the health authorities. It could be argued that the public have little choice but to accept the public services with which they are provided. To accede to such a proposition would, however, be to deny the fundamentals of the marketing concept. While a city library may lose custom because it is not a pleasant place to visit, the only equivalent to such a sanction with respect to more immediately essential services is an unresponsiveness which engenders apathy and eventually hostility. When such a situation occurs an organization becomes inefficient, not only from an internal viewpoint, but quite clearly from the viewpoint of consumer satisfaction.

The missing element in organizations which have had experiences as described above is 'communication'. Quite simply, the organization has lost touch with its consumers. During the last decade non-profit organizations have begun to adopt a 'marketing orientation' which is designed to remedy this, not only in what is physically being offered, but also in terms of image and customer impressions. Like the business sector, there has been a transitional period during which organizations have moved from a 'selling' to a 'marketing' orientation. The providers of public amenities, for example, have recognized that it is not sufficient merely to offer short-term incentives and promotional campaigns, rather they have come to terms with deciding 'what business they are in'! Libraries or public swimming baths are more than what they seem to be if one considers them as satisfying the 'leisure' needs of the community, rather than providing a lending service or a space of water in which to swim.

That non-profit organizations can have marketing problems has not always been recognized. This recognition is the first and principal step of re-adjustment to the changing needs of society and to better serving those needs which have always existed. The second step is to adopt a marketing approach to management. This can be achieved by viewing the non-profit organization as the marketer views the firm and its markets.

Non-profit organizations have marketing structures

The principles of marketing are no different for non-profit organizations than they are for any commercial enterprise. The concept of the marketing mix has equal application: just as different companies employ a mix which is appropriate to their markets, the optimum marketing mix for public bodies will depend on the type of organization and the market conditions which prevail.

Applying marketing to non-profit organizations is made easier by regarding their marketing structures first as one would regard that of any commercial enterprise.

Non-profit organizations are made up of the following components:

1. *Production*: this may seem unusual at first sight, but makes sense if one considers production as an input/output system, whatever the 'product' might be. Input may simply involve the generation of ideas or the acquisition of the means to produce a service. However, this should be subject to the same degree of impetus and control that is applied to any production line of physical goods.
2. *Personnel*: the labour force is an integral part of the total marketing system; the appointment, training and reward structure should be implemented with this 'total' system in mind.
3. *Purchasing*: just as in business, this should be conducted with cost and finished product in mind.
4. *Marketing*: marketing is responsible for thinking in terms of the 'product' whether this be a good or a service. Marketing's role should also concern image, the environment and the optimization of the individual components which make up the organization. An actual marketing director is an increasingly evident feature of progressive organizations.
5. *Consumers*: whatever the degree of choice which consumers have as to their usage of an organization, it should be uppermost in the minds of managers that, although custom may not be lost by inefficiency and poor communication (as in the case of a hospital), these defects imply that the marketing concept is not being successfully implemented. All the factors listed above should, therefore, be focused on the consumers.
6. *Publics*: in addition to the immediate consumer/supplier interface, the list of miscellaneous publics common to any organization should be considered so as to measure and improve goodwill and to afford a monitor on the changing environment.

This is an extended view which takes us beyond the limited definition of marketing as being solely a business activity. The extended view is that marketing is a socially useful activity essentially concerned with the satisfaction of human needs. This is the 'customer' rather than the 'marketing' concept; it embodies the real meaning of marketing and as such is ideally suited to the management of non-profit organizations.

CONCLUSIONS

This chapter has looked at marketing from a social viewpoint and has discussed how this is sometimes at odds with, and sometimes complementary to, the managerial view. More to the point, it has demonstrated that the social view can have positive connotations in terms of marketing.

Major criticisms of marketing have been cited together with a discussion of the causes of these criticisms. The consumer movement has been charted from its roots in the US to the up-to-date situation as it now pertains in the UK. The legal situation has also been discussed from the viewpoint of consumers and a discussion has been undertaken as to how this can have beneficial effects for marketing. Social marketing has been considered together with the need for modern non-profit organizations to adopt the marketing concept.

APPLICATION QUESTIONS

1. By how much do you feel that management has failed to fulfil the marketing concept? What arguments would you offer in defence of marketing?
2. Why should management consider consumerism to be more of an opportunity than a threat?
3. Discuss the role of government activity in the consumer/marketing interface.
4. What do you consider to be the realistic boundaries of social marketing? List ways in which a social orientation has become evident in the marketing activities of companies in the 1980s.
5. In what way do you think that marketing management and the marketing concept has relevance for non-profit organizations? Illustrate you answer with actual examples of non-profit organizations that have adopted a marketing approach.

REFERENCES

1. Hofer, C. W. and D. Schendel, *Strategy Formulation: Analytical Concepts*, Southwest American Publishing, Edmond, OK, 1978, p. 151.
2. Buzzel, R. D. *et al.*, 'Market share – a key to profitability', *Harvard Business Review*, January/February 1975.
3. Galbraith, J. K., *The Affluent Society*, Houghton Mifflin, Boston, 1952, pp. 124–125.
4. Dunn, S. W. and A. W. Barban, *Advertising – Its Role in Modern Marketing*, Dryden Press, Hinsdale, IL, 1978.
5. Kotler, P., 'What consumerism means for marketers', *Harvard Business Review*, May–June 1972, pp. 48–57.
6. Bell, M. L., *Marketing Concepts and Strategy*, 2nd edn, Houghton Mifflin, Boston, 1972.
7. Kotler, P., 'What consumerism means for marketers', *Harvard Business Review*, **50**, May–June 1972, pp. 48–57.
8. For those students who seek precise information as to the law relating to consumer protection see: *Consumer Law Statutes*, 4th edn, Monitor Press, Sudbury, Suffolk, 1984.
9. Lazer W. and E. J. Kelley, *Social Marketing – Perspectives and Viewpoints*, R. D. Irwin, Homewood, IL, 1973, p. 4.
10. Lazer W. and E. J. Kelley, 'Redeploying market resources towards new priorities: the new "consumer demand"'. Reprinted in: *Social Marketing*, pp. 246–248.
11. Kotler, P. and S. L. Levy, 'Broadening the concept of marketing', *Journal of Marketing*, **33**, January 1969, pp. 10–15.

FIVE

CASE STUDIES

SIXTEEN
AN INTRODUCTION TO CASE STUDIES

INTRODUCTION

Case studies deal with real situations and, by providing an opportunity for the student to make decisions under similar constraints as the actual decision later in the real world, have real significance in marketing and business education.

It is to be recognized and appreciated that the organizations which provide for a case study scenario may be disguised to prevent company identification.

The implicit question to be answered in every marketing case is: 'What is wrong and what should be done to put things right?' This does *not* mean that there is necessarily any known or uniquely correct solution to the marketing situation discussed in the case. In many case studies the outcome of the situation is not known, and even if it were, it does not prove that the action taken was the optimum.

The essential task in all case study work is to analyse the situation presented in depth. A first reading is *not sufficient* to grasp the total dimensions of any case; very often the significance of the facts, data and information embedded in the case does not emerge until detailed qualitative and quantitative analysis is undertaken.

The significance of the extracted information can then be weighed, evaluated and decisions made as to the most appropriate course of action.

Good decisions do not just depend upon logic and facts, but also upon sound judgement and imagination. Decisions should be translated in terms of the underlying set or sets of problems to be developed into a positive plan of action.

This brief introduction to case studies indicates that this approach to education training and personal development has the following key benefits:

1. It uses real-life business situations to work on, but without the risks associated with the real world.
2. It applies a global view to a business setting – so often as a member of a team within an organization individual perspectives are narrowed owing to the limitations and responsibilities of the job and the time available.
3. It creates personal detachment from the problem setting so enabling a more objective understanding to be achieved.
4. Learning from complexity. Real-life business situations are rarely ordered; managers must

learn to cope and understand the complexity of problem areas. Using the case method helps to develop individual capacity to tackle complex business issues.

5. Using different roles in the context of the case study scenario develops wider perspectives. Evaluating the position from a number of different viewpoints assists the building of one vital managerial quality, sound judgement.

6. Applying 'in-depth analysis' provides a strong information base from which decisions can be taken. Opportunities are created for applying new techniques in a 'safe' situation before using these in the real world.

7. Identifying and prioritizing problems builds powers of evaluation required for rational decision making.

8. Making actionable decisions by applying logic, facts, judgement and imagination.

9. Designing strategic plans and the related controls stimulates creativity which encourages the individual to experiment and thereby to become conditioned to the dynamics of change.

10. Achieving group interaction to test out ideas and to learn from the experience of others helps the individual to develop interpersonal skills which are vital for success in marketing and business management.

Discrete skills can be learned by using case studies and these include basic analytical skills, skills of application, creativity, written and oral communication and, through awareness of one's self, social skills are developed.

A MODELS APPROACH TO CASE STUDY ANALYSIS

Many students experiencing a case study for the first time face a conceptual barrier.

1. What am I expected to do?
2. How do I make a start?
3. I have read the case study thoroughly but it appears too complex to tackle.

The most basic question to ask is 'What is wrong?' Then, 'What can I do to put it right?' Then, 'Do my suggestions overcome the difficulties I have identified in the case?' Figure 16.1 explains in diagrammatic terms.

The dimensions of analysing difficulties in organizations have to be considered in relation to the complexities involved. It is useful and, indeed, essential to attempt to discover and define the boundaries to the difficulties facing the organization to view the company in the case study as an 'analysis and decision system' (Fig. 16.2).

Two environments need to be examined:

– The internal organizational environment.
– The external organizational environment.

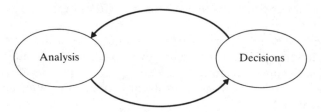

Figure 16.1   A simple model of approach to case analysis

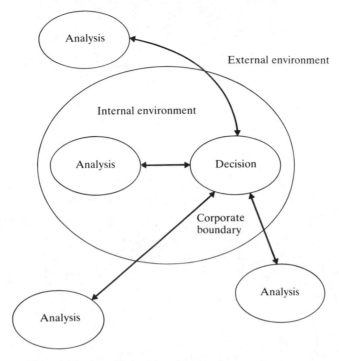

Figure 16.2   A sophisticated model of approach to case analysis

Analysis must be conducted both within the defined boundaries of the organization and beyond, in the external corporate environment.

Analysis conducted both internally and externally will then lead to decision proposals which relate to the internal organizational environment in the context of the wider external company environment.

Therefore, the analysis process must span and bridge the defined boundary to enable the company to be viewed as an 'open system' which interacts with its environment, both taking from and adding to the dynamic status of the 'world' beyond the immediate boundaries of the company.

To jump across the hurdle from analysis to decisions in the context of marketing case studies, a closer look is required at the essential components which comprise the analysis and decision system (see Fig. 16.3).

The components within this analysis and decision system are interrelated in many ways, the main relationships being demonstrated by arrows in Fig. 16.4. These relationships are the processes which cause the system to function. The relationship diagram in Fig. 16.4 demonstrates the dynamic qualities of the analysis and decision system, showing how the parts relate to the whole system.

To tackle marketing case studies, the relationships conveyed may be broken down into a set of systematic processes or procedures as shown in Fig. 16.5 to (a) prepare a case study, and (b) present the case for examination purposes.

The analysis and decision case study model can now be extended to a set of 20 stages for the preparation and presentation of complex marketing case studies. These stages are:

1. Familiarization.
2. The brief.

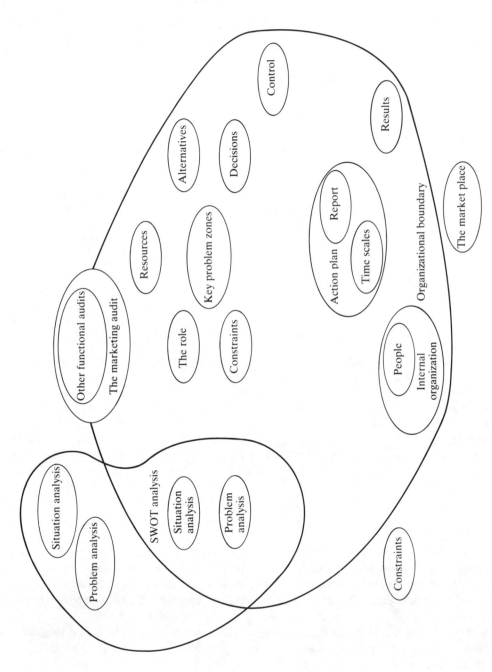

Figure 16.3   A marketing case study analysis and decision system

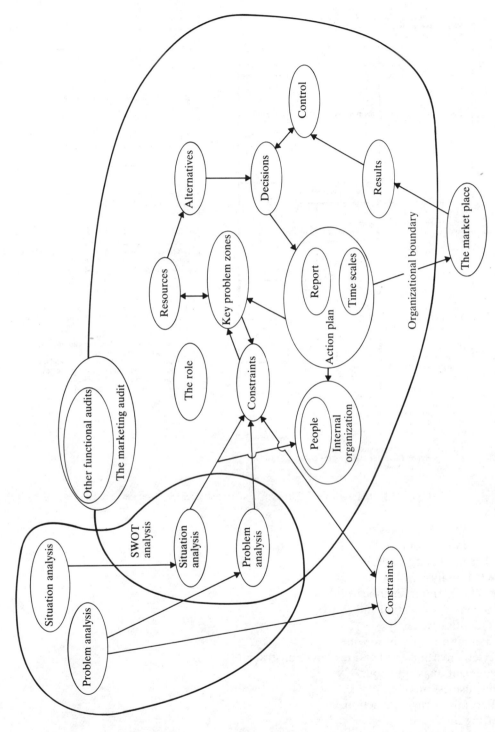

Figure 16.4   A marketing case study analysis and decision relationship diagram

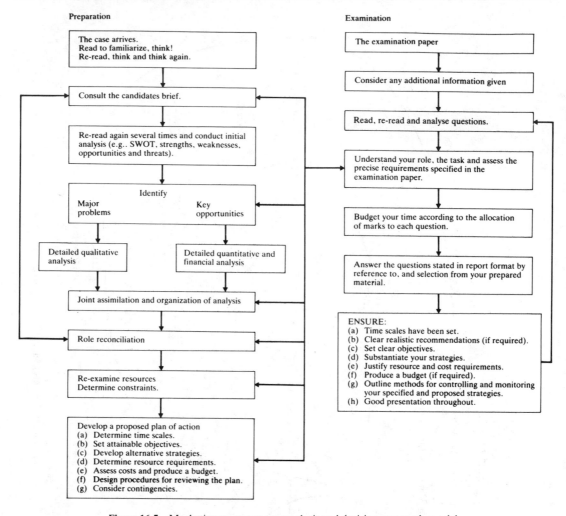

Figure 16.5   Marketing management: analysis and decision case study model

3. Initial situation analysis:
   – The information audit.
   – The marketing audit.
4. SWOT analysis.
5. Initial constraint identification.
6. Problem identification and analysis:
   – Quantitative analysis.
7. Redefinition of problem zones.
8. Review environmental and resource constraints.
9. Statement of assumptions.
10. The business mission.
11. Alternative courses of action.
12. Setting time scales.
13. Setting objectives.
14. Developing strategies.

15. Tactics.
16. Staffing and organizational responsibility.
17. Contingency planning.
18. Results.
19. Control.
20. Report presentation.

USING THE ANALYSIS AND DECISION MODEL

Stage 1   Familiarization

Read through the case study quickly several times to familiarize yourself with the case study scenario.

Read through again, this time more slowly to determine more about the organizational setting, the products/services, and people involved in the environmental context in which the case study scenario is set. Consider the facts presented and the information which can be gleaned from them. Consider how the information presented in the case can best be organized to help you refer back to it for more detailed analysis. At this stage do not discard any of the case material as being invalid.

This is not the time to identify problems or to suggest solutions.

If possible, it is time to leave the case for a few hours to help to digest the material to which you have been exposed for the first time.

Above all, remain global in the thoughts you may have marshalled.

At this initial stage avoid all temptation to tackle the detailed aspects with which you have been confronted.

Stage 2   The brief

In certain marketing case studies, as a potential candidate for assessment or examination, you will be given a brief which specifies the role you will be required to take with reference to the case study scenario. Consider your position carefully, in particular:

(a) Are you to be a member of the organization? If so:
    (i) In what capacity?
    (ii) Is this a staff or line capacity?
    (iii) What will be the boundaries of your responsibility?
(b) If you are an external consultant to the organization:
    (i) What is your position?
    (ii) What is your brief – actual or anticipated?
    (iii) Who will be affected by your actions, where, when and how, both within your own consulting organization and in the client company?

Now reconsider the case study material with which you are familiar, in the light of the position in which you are placed.

Stage 3   Initial situation analysis

The information audit It is time now to transfer your review of the case study into a more detailed description and clearer understanding of the situation and the role you have to perform with respect to the total scenario.

To develop your understanding it is necessary to interpret the case facts and data to build up an information bank to establish the actual information you have, assumptions about it and the additional information you may need in the real-life situation.

An assessment, therefore, must be made and the following questions should be posed.

– How reliable are the facts, figures and stated opinions?
– To what extent can the information presented be accepted as precise and valid?
– Are there gaps in the information presented?
– Are these gaps designed purposely by the case study writer for identification and explanation by students?
– Is the information presented likely to be subject to change either as a result of the dynamic conditions presented, or to be provided at the examination stage?
– Where are the weak links in the information?
– Are the sources of information given valid?

Students may find it helpful to structure the audit under a series of headings before asking these questions.

The structuring will depend upon the case being studied, although functional business areas, issues presented, processes in the organization, time dimensions, personal relationships, and financial and statistical issues are suggested for the beginner.

To complete the information audit, it must be remembered that case studies are rarely written to provide clear facts but to encourage the student to use deductive logic to infer or even speculate to stimulate ideas.

It is necessary, therefore, at the end of the audit to provide a set of assumptions from which to build.

The marketing audit Having determined the status of the information presented in the case study it now becomes necessary to conduct a marketing audit on the total case scenario in preparation for a SWOT analysis that will, in turn, lead to the design of a strategic marketing plan.

The marketing audit of the case study must build up an information base to check the validity and reliability of all facts and stated opinions which relate to marketing issues arising in the case study scenario.

A checklist of points needs to be examined. Although no checklist is completely comprehensive and hence foolproof in application, the following major headings distinguish the internal and external audit.

External company environmental factors

(a) Macro-economic environment:
     (i) Political/legal/fiscal.
     (ii) Economic.
     (iii) Social/cultural.
     (iv) Technical.
(b) The market environment:
     (i) Market profiles.
     (ii) Customer profiles.
     (iii) Product profiles.

   (iv) Pricing profiles.
   (v) Communication profile.
  (vi) Channel and physical distribution profile.
 (vii) Industry structural profile.
(viii) Competitor profiles and profitability.

It would be quite impossible to compile a complete list of factors under each heading. The student, to complete a 'profile' under each section, should answer the following: Who? What? Where? When? How? Why? and summarize the difficulties arising.

Internal company environmental factors The internal audit is a complete examination of the situation which currently exists. The internal marketing audit should examine every element which should be contained in an idealized marketing plan, together with the systems and procedures used to design, develop, implement, control, and review the plan (see Table 16.1).

    The marketing audit contributes to the student's SWOT analysis in the following way:

Table 16.1

	Current position		
Internal audit elements	Design systems	Implementation systems	Control systems
1. Corporate and market analysis			
2. Constraints			
3. Apparent and stated assumptions			
4. Key problems and potential problem resolution			
5. Resource evaluation			
6. Time dimensions for planning marketing			
7. Objective setting and achievement			
8. Strategic marketing planning			
9. Tactics employed			
10. Organization for marketing			
11. Forecasting			
12. Budgeting systems			
13. Sales analysis			
14. Sales achievement			
15. Market share(s)			
16. Profit performance			
17. Total marketing mix variables			
18. The marketing information system			

Internal audit →**Strengths and weaknesses**
External audit→**Opportunities and threats**

During the process of auditing the case study, where information presented conflicts, as often it does in the real world, candidates must apply common sense, make assessments and state their assumptions before proceeding.

Stage 4   SWOT analysis

The evaluation of the information and marketing audits can now be organized into a SWOT analysis.

Strengths and weaknesses→**Historic internal review to date**
Opportunities and threats→**External current review, forecast over a future time period**

The SWOT analysis provides the basis upon which later stages in the model depend. It should aim to condense the case information in an ordered form for easy subsequent reference.

By committing the SWOT to a written presentation a better understanding of the total case study emerges. In turn, this assists the student to focus on particular issues to help achieve clear problem definition.

The SWOT analysis should be conducted rigorously and is usually best achieved by syndicates working in groups, which often produce creative insights which can be developed to produce distinguished marketing planning proposals.

The content of the SWOT analysis should not appear just as a set of concise, static statements in the pro forma provided in Fig. 16.6, but be *used* to generate *thoughts* for clear problem definition. The real value of a SWOT analysis is to consider the implications that arise from it at corporate and marketing levels. A critical assessment can then be made of the main problem themes facing the company, priorities set for tackling them, and thereby the student can ensure that the key result areas of the business have been appraised.

Stage 5   Constraints

Constraints may impose problems upon an organization. They may also provide the limits within which problems can be both identified and researched.

The audits conducted, i.e., the case information audit, the corporate audit and marketing audit, and analysed in the SWOT analysis, will highlight the constraints, both internal and external, which provide limits to organizational performance.

Internal resource constraints and external market constraints provide a framework within which objectives can be set, maximized and achieved.

Stage 6   Problem zone identification and problem analysis

The next extension to the SWOT analysis is to interpret it in terms of key problem areas for attention.

The definition of, and distinction between, problem areas will depend upon the role the student adopts. With a specific role brief the boundaries of responsibility can be clearly drawn and provide the basis from which an actual perspective can be taken. Where the brief is vague then the case study student must take a variety of perspectives and hence will view the organization from different angles and hence identify a variety of problem areas.

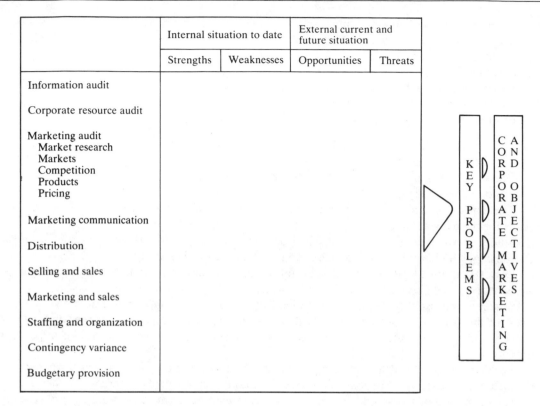

	Internal situation to date		External current and future situation	
	Strengths	Weaknesses	Opportunities	Threats
Information audit				
Corporate resource audit				

Marketing audit
  Market research
  Markets
  Competition
  Products
  Pricing				

Marketing communication				
Distribution				
Selling and sales				
Marketing and sales				
Staffing and organization				
Contingency variance				
Budgetary provision				

Figure 16.6 'SWOT'

The initial step must be individual or group brainstorming on problem areas so as not to discount anything at this initial stage.

The definition of problems is quite difficult because the nature of problems often means that they actually comprise sets of problems, which become problem zones and, in turn, there are often related difficulties which are hard to isolate for analysis and action. Complex sets of problems are known as messes. The task of the candidate, therefore, is to separate out those problem zones that are containable.

Handling problem zones is a matter of scale. Small-scale problems or difficulties:

(a) have an interdefinable boundary;
(b) involve a limited number of people;
(c) can be treated as a separate matter;
(d) have limited applications;
(e) are capable of being clearly prioritized;
(f) operate over a limited time scale;
(g) require information that is known;
(h) have a known problem;
(i) possess a known solution.

'Messy' problem zones are much larger and poorly defined:

(a) they have no readily defined boundary;
(b) they involve more people;

(c) they cannot be treated individually and disentangled from the context;
(d) they may have far-reaching implications;
(e) the time scale is uncertain;
(f) they are difficult to prioritize;
(g) information needed is not specified and difficult to specify;
(h) it is not sure what the problem really is;
(i) no immediate solution is known.

Within marketing case studies simple problems may be posed, but often the problem zone lies between the two extremes above.

One way in which problem zones can be detected is to distinguish between what commonly exists and the desired state for the future.

The tension which exists between the SW area and the OT area in SWOT analysis is a rich source for problem area detection.

Students often consider problems in isolation, where in effect there is usually a causal relationship, which can be quite complex and hence multicausal in origin.

Distinction must be drawn between symptoms and fundamental problems to ensure that the outcomes expected and planned for actually occur.

Students can usefully distinguish between existing problem zones and anticipated problem zones. In the latter area, using the SWOT analysis, this classification can be further divided into problem areas for opportunity exploitation and problem areas to avert the risk of impending threats.

Problem areas defined should be capable of action and hence they need to be prioritized with reference to the scale of the problem area specified and the time scale for overcoming them.

Hence the use of a time scale running from the immediate term to the long term over specified years and months is useful.

In many case studies problems may be difficult to define. The student should distinguish between the following problem zones:

– Actual explicit problem zones.
– Concealed problem zones.
– Potential problem zones.

The student should realize that in the first two zones some may be historic or recurrent problems.

The analysis of problem settings in case study scenarios must ultimately be assessed in terms of who and what is affected and to what extent the problem is zone controllable and by whom.

Problem zones can often be highlighted by the imposition of criteria for organizational assessment. It is against such standards that problems which previously had not been identified become revealed.

Detailed problem analysis – quantitative The identification of problem zones from the SWOT analysis may require, in certain case studies, the application of financial and statistical techniques to assist the depth of analysis required accurately to specify the level of problem(s) facing the company.

Within the space of this text we cannot provide a comprehensive résumé of such techniques.

However, one set of financial assessment techniques often of immediate use is financial ratio analysis.

Financial ratios The subject area of financial analysis is underpinned by ratio analysis. Financial ratios in use are numerous. The marketing student should not need to become a financial analyst to use them but rather be selective and know the implications of the main categories.

Ratios are not a standard formula for judging the performance of a business. Many ratios are in common use and express standard relationships but are only a guide since management cannot be reduced to a formula. What the standard relationships do convey is a logical and important operational sequence of related key control figures. The absolute figures by themselves are of limited value to management.

Ratios are not a substitute for judgement. Management is not provided with answers to its problems by ratios. Not only must judgement be used in the selection of key ratios to suit the business but also judgement in their evaluation. Ratios calculated on an industrial basis or for a group of companies operating in a similar type of business, where there is a common basis of calculation, also enable the student to compare company performance with industry performance.

Ratio analysis is a useful financial technique to assist management in the control of the business, providing its limitations are understood.

The marketing student in the analysis of case study profit and loss accounts and balance sheets should be aware of the importance of the following basic ratio types:

(a) *Liquidity ratios*

These are used to assess the company's ability to meet its current financial obligations.

   (i) *The current ratio*

      Formula: Current assets divided by current liabilities.

      Interpretation: The number of times current liabilities are covered by current assets. This is a fairly crude measure expressing the company's ability to meet current obligations with a margin of safety, which may arise from the varying quality of the current assets, particularly with reference to stocks and the status of debtors. A more critical measure of the company's solvency is the 'quick ratio', known also as the 'acid test'.

   (ii) *The acid test*

      Formula: Quick assets divided by current liabilities.

      Interpretation: The number of times current liabilities are covered by quick assets. Quick assets are cash and 'near cash' items, but *not* stock because it may not be quickly convertible to cash. Quick assets are often considered as current assets minus stocks. In most cases this is cash plus debtors, a critical measure which should be in 1:1.

(b) *Profitability ratios*

These are used to assess the company's profit performance with reference to the direct costs and indirect costs of the business and the associated control of both in relation to sales performance.

   (i) *Gross profit %*

      Formula: Gross profit divided by sales multiplied by 100.

      Interpretation: As a percentage of sales revenue gross profit is the margin created from absolute sales for the period minus the direct costs represented by the cost of sales.

   (ii) *Net profit %*

      Formula: Net profit before tax and depreciation divided by sales multiplied by 100.

      Interpretation: Net profit or loss is the result of charging the indirect costs as revenue expenses of the business against the gross profit margin. To present an ojective picture the net profit figure is taken before depreciation has been charged and corporation tax deducted.

(iii) *Return on total assets*

Formula: Net profit divided by total assets multiplied by 100.

Interpretation: The ratio measures the rate of profitability achieved on the total assets of the business. Much will depend upon the accuracy of the assets valuation in the company's balance sheet. There is frequent debate over which profit figure to use. The key is to be consistent throughout the analysis. Options include:

- the figure used in the net profit per cent ratio;
- net profit after tax.

In either case it is considered appropriate to add back the interest charged on long-term debt to demonstrate objectively the company's capacity to produce profits from total asset utilization.

(iv) *Return on capital employed*

Formula: Net profit before tax and long-term interest divided by total capital employed multiplied by 100.

Interpretation: This is considered to be the primary ratio from which family trees of ratios can be extended to form a pyramid. It expresses the efficiency of management and measures its performance to generate a *rate* of return on the total capital and reserves of the business.

(v) *Return on owner's equity*

Formula: Pre-tax profits divided by equity capital multiplied by 100.

Interpretation: This ratio measures the rate of return on the owner's investment in the business. As a percentage, absolute return can also be measured for every £100 invested.

(c) *Funds management*

These ratios are used to assess how efficiently the company uses the available working capital, particularly with reference to inventory holding, debt collection and payment.

(i) *Debtors collection period*

Formula: Debtors divided by sales multiplied by 365 days.

Interpretation: This ratio determines the time taken by the company to collect debts. It provides a clear indication of the efficiency of credit control.

(ii) *Average payment period*

Formula: Creditors divided by purchase multiplied by 365 days.

Interpretation: This ratio determines the average time taken for the company to pay its bills. The relationship between (c)(i) and (c)(ii) gives an indication of how the company manages cash flow.

(iii) *Stock turnover*

Formula: Sales divided by closing stock.

Interpretation: This ratio measures the rate at which stock moves through the business. A more critical measure can be made by taking the cost of sales figure. The ratio is expressed as the 'number of times' stock is turned. If this is then divided into 365 days one can assess the number of days' or months' stock which are tied up on the company shelves. Often less dynamic companies tie up a considerable amount of working capital through poor inventory control.

(d) *Ability to borrow*

These ratios demonstrate the position of the company in relation to the level of indebtedness and the management of the capital structures.

  (i) *Debt ratio*

     Formula: Current liabilities divided by total assets multiplied by 100.

     Interpretation: This ratio measures the percentage value of the current liabilities in relation to the total asset value of the business. This demonstrates the amount of current short-term indebtedness which is covered by the company's assets and hence the company's ability to pay off current liabilities from the sale of total assets.

  (ii) *Capital gearing ratio*

     Formula: Fixed interest capital divided by shareholders' funds multiplied by 100.

     Interpretation: This ratio reflects the percentage of fixed interest capital and business commitments in relation to the shareholders' funds. It shows the relative position of creditors to the business owner's stake in the company. The fixed interest capital figure is also called net debt and is calculated by adding long-term debt to debentures to overdraft and short-term loans less the cash the company has as a current asset.

Stage 7   Redefinition of problem zones

Owing to the length and associated complexity of some case studies it is necessary to conduct further financial and statistical analysis to gain a more complete understanding of the material presented.

The results of the quantitative analysis must now be set against the backcloth and market setting of the organization to provide a balanced view.

Hence it is the consideration of further quantitative and qualitative analysis that may force the student to redefine the problem zones before proceeding to the next stage of the model.

This provides a natural break, a time to sit back and reflect on the analysis progress to date before adopting a more focused view of the situation. Once the finishing process starts it is very difficult to revert to take a holistic view again. Therefore, allowing for the time constraints imposed, the longer one can take in problem analysis to provide a global situation summary, the better will be the design of the proposed action plan.

Therefore, it is at this stage, before confirming firmly the problem zones for attention, that the candidate should finally reconcile the role(s) in relation to the case study scenario.

Stage 8   Review environmental and resource constraints

Before proceeding to the action plan, students should check that the environmental and corporate resource constraints have been fully appraised and stated so that progress can be planned within these limitations.

In particular, modifications to the design and implementation of resource management can be considered, so that slack or wasted resources can be manipulated to maximize efficient resource utilization.

Stage 9   Statement of assumptions

Based upon the analysis conducted so far, students must state all assumptions before proceeding with the development of objectives and the strategic marketing plan.

Stage 10   The business mission

The corporate plan comprises a statement of the global business mission for the company. This direction is laid out as a set of corporate objectives, corporate strategies with the main tasks for the time period defined, plus corporate financial projections as a set of budgets.

The corporate plan should dictate the changes required for the period. These changes are operated by each strategic business unit in the organization.

The business mission must precede the setting of marketing objectives and the development of marketing strategy and therefore it provides the foundation for marketing planning.

Simple but demanding questions must be answered.

- 'What business is the company in now?'
- 'What business is the company *really* in?'
- 'How well is the company doing?'
- 'What assumptions can be made about the future?'
- 'Where should the company be, say, in five years' time and why?'
- 'What routes can be taken to get there?'
- 'What will be the market reaction?'
- 'What is the level of corporate risk?'
- 'Which direction should the company actually take?'
- 'What resources does the company have and what will it need?'
- 'How can it be ensured that the company will arrive at the intended destination?'
- 'What action needs to be taken to achieve the business mission and what will be the total cost?'

The answers to these questions should be summarized on a corporate statement which specifies the future business mission for the organization.

Stage 11   Alternative course of action

Students are now required to take a substantial conceptual leap from problem definition to suggesting alternative solutions.

Creativity is the key! Enjoy the process of generating ideas, have fun, be experimental. So far the process has been quite rigid, yet turgid courses of action are not really required and rarely do these provide the best solutions for strategic planning.

In some cases, alternatives may be explicit in the case study, the student is required to set up criteria by which to weigh the alternatives. Often, though, alternative courses of action are required to embrace, contain and resolve the key problems prescribed.

Students in these case situations must have an overall appreciation of the global alternatives which are feasible and provide a basis upon which to assess these alternatives to make a firm judgement.

Good solutions are often as good as the ability to define and separate problems for attention.

Problem zones may be too wide to handle in one attempt and hence students must aim to tailor the chosen course of action to lower level problems.

In all case study work there is no *one* solution, but rather defensible and justifiable courses of action which jointly attempt to resolve the difficulties which the organization faces. Owing to the 'soft' nature of many problem settings, solutions may be partial at one end of the continuum and one may resolve a whole set of problems at the other. Rarely will independent courses of action achieve an all-embracing solution to the complexities of a defined problem zone. Rather, it is a set of related and hence integrated combined solutions which serve to make real progress towards overcoming or containing organizational problems.

Courses of action will normally achieve systemic effects both within the organization and beyond into the environment of the marketplace, and hence alternatives must be assessed objectively to ensure optimization within the previously defined constraints.

Basic cost benefit analysis of the proposed alterations is suggested. Students should consider the negative outcomes of their proposals as well as the positive effects.

Above all, the selected course of action must be feasible and achievable within the defined limitations of the company scenario posed.

Stage 12   Setting time scales

Problem analysis and the selected course or courses of action must be set in the context of time. Realistic time scales must be set for the development of a strategic plan.

Plans are usually devised on a rolling planning basis and hence a one-year plan can be so rolled over, for example, a three- to five-year period with reviews scheduled at regular intervals.

Students should develop the time horizon for action both within a 12-month period and beyond. Even within the one-year plan these are events which require immediate action, say, within three months. These also should be clearly distinguished.

The complexity of a problem zone may require, for example, a series of sequential actions over a specified time scale ranging from three months to three years – in which case, students should demonstrate clearly the use of appropriate action phased clearly over the specified time period.

Stage 13   Setting objectives

Having chosen and justified the best course of action to resolve the problems presented, this decision must now be implemented in the form of a formally presented plan.

Many marketing case study students do not know the questions with which they may be faced in an examination and hence the most appropriate form of preparation is to prepare a comprehensive marketing plan from which sections can be selected on the day of the examination.

Objectives provide the basis for the plan and should be specified at corporate and marketing levels and then at marketing scale plan levels so that strategies are designed to relate to the specified objectives at the various levels of the plan.

Marketing objectives should be specified for the prescribed time periods in both quantitative and qualitative terms and be capable of action, measurement and achievement within the selected periods. They should be both consistent and attainable.

It is vital that objectives are specified clearly so that it can be communicated precisely what it is that you wish to do.

The SWOT analysis provides the stimulus from which objectives should be set. Objectives should be designed to overcome the key problems and problem zones which were determined from the SWOT analysis.

A useful technique is to develop an objective tree which starts at global higher level objectives and obtains a clearer focus for action at the lower marketing scale plan levels, i.e., a hierarchy of objectives. This hierarchy should specify *what* is to be *achieved* at each level.

The setting of marketing objectives should aim to achieve balance within the marketing mix and allow for a degree of flexibility.

Marketing objectives should embrace the company philosophy and encourage the development of revised policy.

Essentially the following areas cannot be ignored in the design of marketing objectives:

- Market position.
- Change.
- Output.
- Resource utilization.
- Staff performance and attitude.
- Social responsibility.
- Profitability.
- Cost control.

Stage 14   Developing strategies

Marketing objectives specify *what* is to be achieved. Marketing strategies should outline *how* the objectives are to be achieved.

Marketing strategies are determined from objectives, not the other way round – but the student must ensure that the proposed strategy is not over-embracing and does not go beyond the requirements of the specified objective. This is a common fault in student presentations, which in many cases extends to a total reorganization of the company both internally and with reference to its position in the marketplace – albeit to achieve a very modest objective.

Strategy is the route to the achievement of objectives over specified time intervals for which the objectives have been set.

Balance is a keynote to check the interval consistency of the plan to ensure that the marketing elements for which strategy is designed are integrated and not competitive. When presented, the designed marketing strategy should demonstrate where the emphasis has been placed to achieve marketing objectives and the wider business mission.

As a mechanism for marshalling the impact of the developed strategies, financial resource deployment must be specified clearly in the form of a total marketing budget illustrating capital sources, revenues and expenditure.

The strategic marketing plan should demonstrate the utilization of existing resources and those additional resources to be procured to implement the designed strategy.

Stage 15   Tactics

The detailed implementation of the strategic plan is conveyed as an action plan which specifies the actual individual activities to be undertaken with due dates for their achievement.

Stage 16   Staffing and organizational responsibility

People have problems, not organizations, and people design, implement, administer and review plans to overcome problems. Students preparing case studies often demonstrate a total detachment from the human activity system of the organization.

Human resource management is a key factor in the management of the marketing function. Therefore, attention to this critical area is essential in preparing marketing management case studies.

Case material will have varying levels of information about key personnel involved, but where it is provided students must analyse the staff profile, consider the existing position and detect where areas for change are required.

Change may not simply mean hiring and firing – even if this is within the remit given in the student brief – but also staff development, training, instruction and progression within the organizational structure.

In particular the deployment of staff to take responsibility for the implementation of the marketing plan is an essential part of case study preparation.

Staffing should be viewed in a global context to include the appointment and appraisal of external agencies and consultants.

Stage 17   Contingency planning

Strategic planning in the relatively safe internal corporate case environment is one thing. Implementing the plan to achieve the designed strategy is quite another!

The purpose of contingency planning is to enable and even force management to think ahead to answer the question, 'What if our expectations are not realized in the real world?'

Contingency thinking is designed to create answers to the 'What if?' questions so that management will have the answers ready ahead of time if the designed strategy goes wrong. In case study preparation the vital section on contingencies forces the student to think about a wider range of situations that might occur than when strategies were first designed to meet corporate and marketing objectives.

The student should consider how flexible the designed plan is should conditions change. Answers to the following questions are needed:

– 'What is the capability of the organization to adapt to changed conditions?'
– 'How quickly can the organization respond and with what internal and external effects?'
– 'In what way must the organization respond to avert a crisis or the partial achievement of objectives?'
– 'What options are open to the company in the light of anticipated change? How should these options be evaluated and what action should be taken?'

At an earlier stage in this case study analysis and decision model the student had to generate and decide between alternative courses of action. Reference back may provide a source for idea generation when designing the contingency plan.

Stage 18   Results

The case study student is often required to produce a strategic and tactical plan in a vacuum where the input is simply the case study material and the output is a well-presented strategic marketing plan. It is assumed that the results of the plan are the achievement of the specified plan objectives. If the objectives have been carefully and clearly communicated in a hierarchy and allocated to responsibility centres for action, monitoring, evaluation and adjustment, the task is usually deemed complete. It is often overlooked to answer the following questions:

– 'When implemented what will be the tangible results of taking the proposed action?'
– 'Can these results be quantified?'

Therefore, the projected outcomes should be considered not only in terms of qualitative contribution but in financial terms with reference to anticipated profit and profit contribution.

Stage 19   Control

The management process has been described as planning, organizing, directing, controlling, communicating, coordinating and evaluating organizations and individuals to achieve effective decisions.

The control function needs careful attention in the preparation of a marketing plan.

The control function should monitor feedback and assess performance so that appropriate adjustments can be made to achieve the desired goals and objectives of the organization.

A system of controls should be specified in both qualitative and quantitative terms in accordance with the time dimensions of the designed plan.

By designing a control system to review regularly actual performance against forecasted performance, management should be in a position of *knowing* what may go wrong.

The control system, efficiently administered, should avoid surprise, avert crisis and prevent the plan getting out of control.

To measure progress towards the achievement of goals and objectives responsibility centres should be designated. No student must consider these without reference to the culture of the organization and the ability to adopt controls.

Despite the stage of organizational development or size of the organization, all managers should be in a position to highlight impending problems that require immediate attention. This ability produces time in which to diagnose and analyse problem areas, then to design a strategy to resolve the difficulty. Levels of control to be designated should link with the management structure and organizational levels of the company.

To design a control system for the marketing plan every element in the plan should have a set of specified controls tailored to fit the plan and the organization. Students must be aware that there is not one ubiquitous control model that can be applied to all plans.

The control system should enable situational analysis, problem diagnosis, the setting of priorities for feedback, and specify the form and frequency of controls.

The main aim is for the designed marketing plan to succeed. The control system assists the progression towards success.

In the real world plans fail frequently owing to a number of often interrelated factors. Typical factors are shown in Fig. 16.7 and should be provided for by the structure in the design of the marketing plan control system.

To assist the control of the marketing plan the company must have a marketing information system. The complexity of the system will vary considerably depending upon the size of company and style of company management.

The system is a structured, interacting complex of staff, machines and procedures which should be designed to generate an orderly flow of pertinent information. Information is needed from the external and internal organizational environment to be used as a basis for decision making in specified areas of responsibility.

Therefore, the information system lies between the environment and the marketing executive user.

The student must consider what the marketing planning system needs, in what form and what is economically feasible within the financial resource constraints of the organization.

Budgetary control The most vital ingredient in business is planning for profit. Without profit rarely can business survive and grow. An essential activity is profit planning and control and budgeting is probably the widest ranging control technique used because it percolates the entire organization.

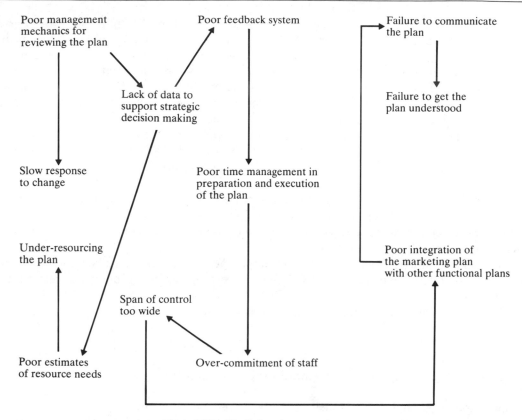

Figure 16.7 Marketing plan control system

Budgetary control in the context of the marketing plan is generally designed and adopted to coincide with the financial year of the company.

Correctly applied the process of budgetary control makes a penetrating, critical and almost uncompromising evaluation of the performance of the marketing plan.

Students must recognize that budgeting and the associated information system provide a major contribution to achieving the objectives of the marketing plan.

The system must be inspired at senior management level and used to set operational standards with accountability for performance. The budgetary control system must be set up to allow for measurement against planned and forecasted performance.

When compiling case study marketing plans, students must realize that budgeting involves more than just forecasting. It provides a framework for evaluating performance.

In the context of case study examinations students are often required only to list the appropriation of a total budget under appropriate cost/profit centres. This is usually the final stage of an exhausting examination. Students must realize that this is only the beginning and that the budget headings with forecasted income and expenditure have real organizational implications.

Stage 20   Case study report presentation

Written reports must be planned to achieve maximum impact on the reader.

The planning stage starts with the purpose of the report, to whom it is to be presented, what is to be included and how it is to be presented.

The purpose of a written case study report for students of marketing may be for course assessment or formal examinations. The function is to inform the reader of the facts, to explain the proposed course of action and to convince the reader that the recommendations and plans proposed are justifiable and hope that a favourable reading/assessment is awarded.

A report must be written with a clear understanding of who the reader is and what he knows of the situation, so that communication can take place at the reader's knowledge level. For examination case reports, assume the reader, your examiner, has a low knowledge level. Do not overestimate the reader's ability. You must be able to *demonstrate* your knowledge and understanding of the situation. The reader's attitude under conditions of assessment should be objective, but in the real world the writer must be aware of prevailing attitudes so as not to offend the reader.

In both the real world and for course assessment the writer must have vision about what the reader wants to receive in terms of content, style and presentation.

Remember reports are not extended essays but concise statements which set out your thoughts and proposals simply and clearly.

All recommendations should be justified to support your proposed plan of action, but do not bore the reader with in-depth analysis – this is in your working papers for subsequent reference if required.

It is important that the report is so structured that:

(a) the report is read;
(b) it is understood;
(c) it follows a logical sequence leading the reader along a particular path.

Planning the structure of your report before writing is absolutely essential.

For examination candidates, questions posed under examination conditions should be broken down into their component parts and a structure designed to ensure all component parts have been handled. This structure then forms the headings for your report. Remember to commit to paper the most important points first, just in case your time budget has been exceeded for that particular section of the examination paper. Ensure that conclusions and recommendations are labelled clearly to receive maximum attention by the reader.

The conventions for structuring a report vary considerably. One format used personally is as follows:

(a) *Title page*: containing the report title, to whom it is addressed, the date, author's name and company and the list to whom the report is to be distributed.
(b) *Summary*: a résumé of the terms of reference of the report with a short statement containing key functions, conclusions and recommendations. (This may provide also for a 'short report' for senior executives not wishing to indulge in the complete work.)
(c) *Detailed contents list*: showing clearly the structure of the report with a numbering system which is used throughout the report. Major headings and sub-headings should be shown and indexed by page number for easy reference.
(d) *The main report*: this section contains the detailed facts and plans to support the summary given in (b) above. The main report should substantiate the recommendations made to the company in the summary section.
(e) *Appendices*: this section should comprise three sub-sections:
  (i) Supporting data to back up the main body of the report but which is too detailed for inclusion in the main section and would otherwise disrupt the flow of the report.

(ii) Sources of reference, itemizing the bibliography and external sources consulted in the preparation of the report.

(iii) Glossary of terms, to assist readers not totally conversant with the more technical aspects of the report.

For examination candidates this structure may only be appropriate where one global question has been asked. Where questions are issue specific then the report must be tailored to the actual examination questions asked. This can be seen clearly in the worked examples included later in this textbook.

One alternative structure that may be applied by examination candidates is as follows:

(a) *The problem statement*: this is an interpretation of the specific examination questions stated in terms of a problem for solution.

(b) *The implications of the problem*: this section contains a concise résumé of the causes and effects of the problem.

(c) *Alternative courses of action*: A succinct statement of the options which could be taken to solve the problem area.

(d) *Conclusions and recommendations*: stating the selected course of action, justifying it and explaining in detail the recommended course of action to be taken.

Presentation is crucial for a report to be well received. Each page must appear interesting to appeal to the reader's eye.

The use of white space, headings, indentations and report numbering systems should be applied to create maximum impact.

Remember the reader's attention span may be quite short so sections and paragraphs should reflect this. In short, write simply, write briefly, write positively and avoid cluttering the main text with elaborate diagrams, charts and tables.

Finally, to complete what has been a comprehensive overview of case study analyses and how they should be approached, an appendix is provided giving some useful concepts and definitions. It is unlikely that you will ever need all of these definitions in the context of marketing case studies, but the list is as comprehensive as possible in terms of modern business policy cases analysis. The next chapter concentrates upon marketing case study analyses.

APPENDIX TO CHAPTER SIXTEEN: Some Useful Concepts and Definitions

(*Reproduced from material kindly supplied by E. C. Lea and B. Kenny, Huddersfield Polytechnic.*)

Accounts payable   Amounts owed by the firm to its creditors (US).

Accounts receivable   Amounts owing to the firm by its debtors (US).

Accumulation depreciation   The cumulative amount of depreciation written off a fixed asset.

Acid test   see Quick ratio

Amortization   The writing off, over a period, of an asset or a liability.

Asset   Any property, tangible or intangible, which can be expressed in monetary terms and which brings benefit to the firm, e.g., plant and equipment, stocks, goodwill.

Asset turnover   Ratio of sales to net tangible assets.

Authorized share capital   The maximum share capital which a company can issue at any given time. The amount, which can be altered by the shareholders in general meeting, is stated in the memorandum of association and must be disclosed in the balance sheet. Also called nominal share capital or registered share capital.

Average collection period   The frequency with which a company collects its debts:

$$\frac{\text{debtors} \times 365}{\text{credit sales}} \text{ days}$$

Bonus shares   Shares issued to existing shareholders without further payment on their part. Also referred to as a scrip issue or a capitalization issue.

Book value   The monetary amount of an asset as stated in the balance sheet. Usually represents acquisition cost less accumulated depreciation.

Business planning   Involves the process of establishing objectives and the development and implementation of strategy, extending down to the development of sales forecasts, establishment of budgets, anticipation of needs for capital and facilities and equipment.

'*Cash cows*'   Low growth products that usually generate more cash than is required to maintain market share. Generally regarded as the foundation of the firm.

Convertible loan stock   Loan stock which may be converted at the option of the holder at a future date or dates into ordinary shares at given price ratios.

Cost of capital   The cost to a company's ordinary shareholders of issuing shares or debentures, of retaining profits, or of other sources of funds.

Creditors   Amounts owing by a company resulting from, say, the purchase of materials.

Cumulative preference shares   Preference shares entitled to be paid the arrears of their dividend before any dividend is paid on the ordinary shares. Any arrears must be disclosed as a note to the balance sheet.

Current assets   Those assets which are either already cash or can reasonably be expected to become cash within one year from the date of the balance sheet, e.g., debtors, stock-in-trade. If the directors believe that any of the current assets will not realize their balance sheet values in the ordinary course of business this fact must be disclosed.

Current liabilities   Liabilities which are expected to have been paid within one year from the date of the balance sheet, e.g., trade creditors, proposed final dividend, current taxation.

Current ratio   Ratio of current assets to current liabilities. A measure of liquidity.

Debentures   Loans, usually but not necessarily secured on the assets of the company. Usually redeemable but may be irredeemable.

Debtors   Amount owing to the company, e.g., from the sale of goods. Usually shown in balance sheets net of provision for debts unlikely to be recovered.

Deferred taxation   Tax which is due beyond one year from the date of the balance sheet.

Depreciation   Expense recording the using up of fixed assets through operations. Usually measured by allocating the historical cost less disposable value of the asset on a straight-line or reducing-balance basis.

Discounted cash flow   The present value of future cash receipts and payment, i.e., their value after taking into account the delay in receiving or paying them.

Diversification   A strategy by which the firm's growth objectives are achieved by adding products or services to the existing lines. Concentric diversification takes place when the products added are similar to existing types, from a production, marketing channels, customers or technology point of view. Conglomerate diversification is growth into areas unrelated to the company's present product/market scope (often associated with acquisitions).

Divestment   Refers to retrenchment strategy. The selling off or liquidation of a division or unit of an organization.

Dividend   That part of the profits of a company which is distributed to the shareholders. May be interim (paid during the financial year) or final (recommended by the directors for approval by the shareholders at the annual general meeting). Both must be disclosed gross of tax in the profit and loss account. The proposed final dividend is shown gross in the balance sheet as a current liability.

Dividend cover   The ratio between earnings per share and the ordinary dividend per share.

Dividend yield   The relationship between the ordinary dividend and the market price per ordinary share.

'Dodos'   Term for describing low share–negative growth products. Used in context of product life cycle/product portfolio analysis.

'Dogs'   Products which are at a cost disadvantage and have few opportunities for growth at a reasonable cost. Generally low market share products needing cash to survive and, consequently, not profitable.

Earnings per share   Net profit after tax attributable to the ordinary shareholders divided by the number of ordinary shares.

Earnings yield   The relationship between the earnings per ordinary share and the market price per ordinary share. The reciprocal of the price–earnings ratio multiplied by 100.

Environment   Generally refers to *external* forces affecting the organization. These may be classified under legal, social, political, economic, technological and market forces.

Equity share capital   Defined by the Companies Act as any issued share capital which has unlimited rights to participate in either the distribution of dividends or capital. Often more narrowly defined to mean ordinary shares only.

Experience curve A postulate that suggests that as the firm grows in size and experience it is able to reduce costs and improve productivity, for a given activity.

Financial ratios Relationships among items in financial statements.

Fixed assets Assets held for use in the business rather than for re-sale.

Fixed overheads Those overheads whose amount remains constant over the usual range of activity.

Gearing The relationship between the funds provided to a company by its ordinary shareholders and the long-term sources of funds carrying a fixed interest charge or dividend.

Goodwill The difference between the 'value' of a company as a whole and the sum of the values of the tangible assets and liabilities taken separately. Usually recorded only when the company is being evaluated for, say, potential purchase.

Historical cost The usual basis of valuation in published financial statements. Favoured because it is more objective and more easily verifiable by an auditor. Its use is contentious, especially in times of inflation.

Holding company A company which controls another company, called its subsidiary. Balance sheet of holding company must show separately amounts owing to and owed by subsidiaries.

Intangible assets Assets such as goodwill, patents and trade marks.

Integration Growth strategy characterized by the extension of the firm's business definition, i.e., vertical (forward and backward) integration. In this case the firm may integrate forwards to assure control of distribution, or backwards to safeguard supplies of raw materials.

Issued expenses Expenses of making an issue of shares or debentures.

Issued share capital The amount of the authorized share capital which has been issued; the remainder is the unissued share capital. The amount of the issued capital must be disclosed in the published balance sheet. Not necessarily equal to called-up or paid-up share capital.

Issue price The price at which a share is issued. Since the issue may be at a premium or a discount, the issue price is not necessarily equal to the par value.

Liabilities Amounts owing by a company, which must be disclosed in the published balance sheet. For example:

- aggregate amount of bank loans and overdrafts;
- aggregate amount of other loans;
- amounts owing to subsidiary companies;
- recommended dividend;
- redeemed debentures;
- debtors.

Liquid assets see Quick assets.

Loan capital Funds acquired by non-short-term borrowing from sources other than the shareholders of the company.

Long-term debt Long-term sources of funds other than equity (share capital and reserves).

MBO (*m*anagement *b*y *o*bjectives)   A technique which establishes a formal approach requiring top, middle and lower management to operate by a system of objectives.

Market price   The price at which a company's securities can be bought or sold on a stock exchange. Not necessarily equal to the par value or the issue price.

Minority interest   That part of a subsidiary company's shareholders' funds that is not held by the holding company. Usually shown as a separate item on the net worth and liabilities side of a consolidated balance sheet.

MIS (*m*anagement *i*nformation *s*ystem)   A formal system of gathering intelligence – information to be used by the strategist. For example, economic data, market reports, technological development, etc., plus data on internal operations.

Net current assets   Another name for working capital.

Net profit ratio   Ratio of net profit to sales.

Net tangible assets   Assets except for intangible assets (goodwill, patents and trade marks), less liabilities.

Net working capital   Another name for working capital.

Net worth   Assets less liabilities. The proprietorship section of a balance sheet, usually referred to in the case of a company as shareholders' funds or share capital and reserves.

Nominal share capital   see Authorized share capital.

Non-voting shares   Shares with no voting rights. Non-voting ordinary shares are usually cheaper to buy than those carrying votes.

Objectives   Desired targets or results which at the basic level may be expressed in financial, product/mission or social–psychological terms; at the fulfilling level, objectives may be defined in more directed fashion such as relationships with customers or continuous improvement of resources.

Ordinary shares   Shares entitled to share in the profits after payment of debenture interest and preference dividends. Often referred to as the equity capital.

Paid-up share capital   The amount of the called-up share capital which has been paid up by the shareholders.

Par value   The face or nominal value of a share or debenture. Not necessarily equal to the issue price or the current market price. Dividend and interest percentages refer to the par value, yields to the current market price.

PIMS ('*p*rofit *i*mpact of *m*arket *s*trategies')   UK study relating to profitability analysis (see Schoeffler, Buzzell and Heany 'Impact of Strategic Planning on Profit Performance', *Harvard Business Review*, **52**, March–April 1974, pp. 137–45).

Policies   Broad guidelines to pursuing objectives, and designed to clarify or sharpen up those objectives.

Preference shares   Shares which usually are entitled to a fixed rate of dividend before a dividend is paid on the ordinary shares and to priority of repayment if the company is wound up. Participating preference shares are also entitled to a further dividend if profits are available. If a preference dividend is not paid the arrears must be disclosed as a footnote to the balance sheet. Arrears can only arise if the shares are cumulative as distinct from non-cumulative.

Price–earnings ratio The multiple of the last reported earnings that the market is willing to pay for a company's ordinary shares. The reciprocal of the earnings yield multiplied by 100.

Product portfolio (*analysis*) Relates to specific marketing strategies to achieve a balanced mix of products that will produce the maximum long-run effects from scarce cash and management resources.

'*Question marks*' Sometimes known as 'problem children'. High growth/low market share products. Cash generation is low and cash needs high.

Quick assets Current assets less stock-in-trade.

Quick ratio The relationship between quick assets and current liabilities. Also known as liquid ratio, or the acid test. A measure of liquidity.

Quoted investments Investments for which there is a quotation or permission to deal on a recognized stock exchange or on any reputable stock exchange outside Great Britain. Must be shown separately in the balance sheet.

Reserves Reserves arise either from the retention of profits or from specific capital transactions such as the issue of shares at a premium or the revaluation of assets. Must not include provisions – unless the directors consider they are excessive – or the taxation equalization account. Not a charge against profits; not necessarily represented by cash on the other side of the balance sheet. Movements in reserves during the financial year must be disclosed.

Reserve fund A reserve which is represented by specially earmarked cash or investments on the other side of the balance sheet.

Retained profits Profits not distributed to shareholders but reinvested in the company. Their cost is less than a new issue of shares, because of the issue costs of the latter.

Return on investments Ratio of profit (usually before interest and tax) to net tangible assets. A measure of profitability.

Revaluation The writing-up of an asset to its current market value.

Revenue reserves Reserves regarded by the directors as being normally available for dividend.

Rights issue An issue of shares in which the existing shareholders have a right to subscribe for the new shares at a stated price. The right can be sold if the shareholder does not wish to subscribe.

Share capital Unless limited by guarantee, a company registered under the Companies Act must have a share capital divided into a fixed amount. The ownership of a share gives the shareholder a proportionate ownership of the company. The share capital is stated in the balance sheet at its par (nominal) value.

Shareholder Member of a company whose part ownership of (share in) the company is evidenced by a share certificate.

Shareholders' funds The proprietorship section of a company balance sheet. Includes the share capital and the reserves (sometimes called net worth).

Share premium Results from issuing shares at a price higher than their par value. Must be disclosed in the balance sheet as a reserve. Cannot be used to pay dividends but can be used to make an issue of bonus shares.

'Stars'   Products that are market leaders and also growing at a fast rate. They represent the best opportunity for growth and investment.

Stock-in-trade   Consists for a manufacturing company of raw materials, work-in-progress and finished goods. Usually valued at the lower of cost or market value.

Stock turnover   Ratio of sales (sometimes, cost of sales) to stock-in-trade.

SBU (strategic business unit)   An operating division of a firm which serves a distinct product–market segment or well-defined set of customers. Generally it has the authority to make its own strategic decisions as long as they meet corporate objectives.

Strategy   As a concept, refers to the total system incorporating the firm's objectives, policies and the planning required to achieve objectives. In the managerial sense, strategy relates to the continuous process of effectively relating the organization's objectives and resources to opportunities in the environment.

Synergy   Exists when the strengths of two companies or units, when put together, more than off-set their joint weaknesses.

(a) Many products resulting in higher utilization of facilities, personnel and overheads (operating synergy).
(b) Many products using same plant and equipment (investment synergy).
(c) Management experience in one industry helping to solve problems in another industry (management synergy).

Synergy can thus be gained through application of production, marketing or financial expertise.

Time interest earned   The number of times that a company's interest is covered or earned by its profit before interest and tax.

Turnover   Sales. The profit and loss account must disclose the amount and basis of turnover for the financial year. The directors' report must disclose group turnover and profit (or loss) before tax divided among classes of business that differ substantially.

Unquoted investments   Investments for which there is not a quotation or permission to deal on a recognized stock exchange or on any reputable stock exchange outside Great Britain. If they consist of equity of other companies directors must either give an estimate of their value or information about income received, profits, etc.

Unsecured loan   Money borrowed by a company without the giving of security.

'War horses'   Term used to describe high-share/negative growth products. Used in context of product life cycle/product portfolio analysis.

Working capital   Current assets less current liabilities.

Work-in-progress   Partly completed manufactured goods.

Yield   The rate of return relating cash invested to cash received (or expected to be received).

SEVENTEEN

MARKETING CASE STUDY EXAMINATIONS

A marketing case study examination requires candidates to apply themselves in a managerial capacity to a simulated practical marketing situation.

The examination is often 'open book', meaning that candidates may bring into the examination hall material which they have prepared in advance of the examination. This approach enables the candidates to produce a more comprehensive answer within the examination period, provided that time is not lost in the sifting and searching of the prepared material. An efficient filing system is crucial to achieve effective management of examination time.

The candidate must be completely familiar with every aspect of the case to be able to approach the examination with confidence. Effective preparation for this examination depends upon effective training. Candidates must build up stamina for their final performance and hence practice up to and including a 'mock examination' is most advisable.

BEFORE THE EXAMINATION

While mini case scenarios may be presented at the examination, major case studies arrive in a time period before the examination. The candidate must plan, organize, coordinate, direct, control and evaluate the preparation of the case study in the context of the role specified in the candidate's brief.

The candidate must consider the following simple questions in depth:

1. What are the major problems and key opportunities?
2. Then, in order to resolve and exploit them:
   (a) What has to be done, to whom and by whom for what reason?
   (b) How should this be done?
   (c) When should this action take place and over what period?
   (d) Can these actions be justified?
   (e) How much will it cost the organization?
   (f) Can the expenditure be justified and are funds/resources available?
   (g) How can a check be made on what is to be achieved?
   (h) What should be done if circumstances change?

The candidate must reconcile the specified role(s) and understand fully the boundaries of power, influence, authority and responsibility. It is strongly recommended that the case study preparation includes the duties and responsibilities of key managerial positions within a variety of marketing and sales organizations and that a distinction be drawn between the position of executive directors, non-executive directors and external consultants. Candidates must realize that preparation involves preparing *themselves* as well as preparing the analysis and decision making for a major marketing case study. Candidates may benefit from role-playing exercises to assist the learning process of identifying with roles – this process is central to answering questions in the case study examination.

Consult the case study instructions to determine and understand instructions on information sourcing.

Much has to be achieved in a short time so do not waste a moment by researching beyond the boundaries of the case material unless there is stipulation. Case studies are designed to be self-contained exercises. Searching for additional material will undoubtedly lead to confusion and frustration. Credit will not be given for external information introduced into your examination answers unless this is part of the candidate's brief.

On a practical note, make sure you have a 'good night's sleep' the night before the exam. Burning the midnight oil until the dawn chorus breaks will drain both your physical and mental energy.

Set out for the exam with a full kit of well-documented notes, pens, pencils, ruler, calculator, etc. – candidates still rush out on the day of the examination and arrive late having forgotten their kit.

AT THE EXAMINATION HALL

Arrive in time, avoid having a *heavy* meal, bring a watch and try to have a calm, cool, clear and collected mind. Sitting examinations can be a traumatic experience for many, but do not forget the examiners are human, on your side and trying to pass you.

Arrange your prepared material and kit so that it can be easily accessed. Remember, the more that you bring into the examination hall, the more time that may be lost sifting through it.

THE EXAMINATION PAPER

Credit can only be given for what is written in the examination answer book, not for that which has been previously prepared. Read the rubric and make sure you understand and follow the instructions it contains. Determine how many questions are required to be answered and judge the amount of time to be given to each based upon the allocation of marks. The effective management of time within the three-hour time scale is critical to a candidate's performance.

Read all the questions and make sure that you understand precisely what is required. Carefully consider any additional information given.

ANSWERING THE QUESTIONS

1. *Your role*: the role specified in the candidate's brief may be expanded and thereby clarified on the examination paper, which means that candidates may need to restructure their thinking to respond to the situation stated and to answer fully the questions posed.
2. *Layout, style and presentation*: management report format is recommended. Essay style is inappropriate and too inefficient to convey fully the level and complexity of answer required within the three-hour period. Candidates should conceive headings and adopt a numbering system in a fashion similar to that used in the specimen answers in this textbook. A good

examination paper will use the facing page of the examination book to outline the contents of the report showing appropriate sections as dictated by the examination questions.

Presentation is the keynote in most reports. Candidates should create 'white space' to present their reports legibly and in a way which attracts the examiner's eye.

3. *Questions*: questions do not have a standardized format. They may vary in number but usually will be action oriented and inevitably require strategic marketing plans.

Make certain that you answer the *question stated* and not that which *you would have liked* to answer.

4. *Answers to questions*: there is no 'right' answer to case study questions. In the case of marketing analysis and decision cases, the examination paper should present clear, well-substantiated decisions. In open book examinations, the time for analysis has been provided with the issue of the case well before the examination. This analysis should enable the candidate to be completely familiar with the on-going situation. From this position appropriate action can be recommended in the examination room. Do not re-state the situation or give a lengthy, detailed analysis – the examiners are fully aware and attuned to the case situation! In a real-life marketing situation, problems have to be solved and opportunities seized by taking action, not by dwelling on a situation, doing nothing and losing out. Such is the emphasis required in the examination room!

Answers are to be succinct, to the point and with clearly outlined proposed courses of action; avoid a muddled list of alternatives.

Candidates are advised to follow the procedure outlined in the case study model illustrated in this textbook and observe the necessity for reiteration as indicated by the loops.

Pre-prepared answers rarely succeed to fit the requirements of open book examination questions. A lack of imagination by the majority of candidates is a major weakness. Creativity is highly rewarded. It is the candidate's individual ideas that the examiner is looking for, not a batch of identical scripts carefully dictated or rehearsed before the day!

CANDIDATES WHO FAIL – 'THE MAGNIFICENT SEVEN'

The waffler

The candidate who produces a large volume of written material which normally starts 'Before answering the questions I will review the company situation ...' Some 14 or 20 pages later, having strayed up many a blind alley, the candidate starts question 1 only to leave a hurried note 'Sorry, ran out of time'.

The backroom boy

All analysis and no action. Granted, there is a need for this type of person in certain avenues of marketing but the examination requires a strategic plan of action. Examination day is 'D DAY' – a day for decisions.

The waster

Produces little of anything remotely relevant to the subject being examined.

The non-conformist

Likes to sit for an examination paper that has not been set, has blatant disregard for the actual questions and produces a marathon marketing plan, probably directly copied from his pre-prepared material.

The syndicate member

Regurgitates answers that have been produced on a group basis without integrating the answers to the precise questions set, so relates poorly with what is required.

The dreamer

Fails to understand the role, and usually reorganizes the entire company, including firing key executives outside his orbit. The dreamer plans beyond the wildest hopes of the company.

The marginal failure

Tried hard but not hard enough to satisfy the examiners. May succeed next time.

EIGHTEEN

CASE STUDY WITH SPECIMEN ANSWER
Fisher plc (Handtools marketing)

Fisher, based in Swansea, Wales, is a public limited company (plc). The 'Fisher Works' in Swansea opened at the turn of the century to provide tools for Welsh industries.

The Welsh steel industry provided many of the raw materials needed in the manufacturing process and despite the recession in the steel industry, both nationwide and in the Western world, demand for Fisher products today remains active.

Fisher plc (hereafter referred to as Fisher), currently has an estimated 15 per cent share by value of the UK non-power hand tool market. Significant export trade has developed over the past 15 years to secure brand recognition in different countries. Certain Fisher products also are manufactured under licence in Germany and France and sold throughout Europe. Similar trade has developed in eastern coast states of the US. Direct exports from the UK to worldwide customers outstrip domestic sales within the UK.

The UK market for Fisher hand tools can be classified as:

(a) domestic purchasers;
(b) professional users (i.e., tradesmen);
(c) industrial buyers.

Recent research among distribution channels has revealed that approximately 40 per cent by value fall into section (a) with section (c) taking 20 per cent.

The Fisher brand has penetrated each of these market segments with considerable success to achieve its overall market position.

A variety of trading agreements on price and volume are used to secure a stable position within the distribution channels. The wholesale trade accounts for 47 per cent of UK turnover; retail trade some 35 per cent; 12 per cent to mail order houses with the residual sales to direct accounts.

These various channels reach a variety of end users. The company, to quote their marketing manager, have yet to achieve a *complete* picture of 'which type of purchaser and/or end user buys which type of tool from which source of supply – internal estimates rarely agree'.

Market segmentation by end user provides a variety of profiles – ranging from the owner of a screwdriver to the owner and frequent user of a complete range of tools. The end user can be classified on a continuum ranging from the 'non-user' through to the semi-skilled do-it-yourself enthusiast' to the 'skilled non-professional' and on to 'the tradesman'.

Among the market classified as 'domestic home purchasers' ((a) above), 50 per cent are considered 'skilled' users, 40 per cent 'non-skilled' users and the rest 'very occasional users'. The term 'skilled' can be variously defined, but refers to the frequency of use rather than the real ability of the end user.

Market development has been achieved through the trade user to the domestic user over time. This accounts for a wide discrepancy of market shares achieved by type of tool within the defined domestic, professional and industrial markets. To complicate the total market profile further, different types of tools are supplied to each market sector, although many of the tools in the Fisher range are purchased in each sector.

Despite market research findings which have revealed variations in brand quality perception, among end users, of the different types of tools, the Fisher brand is among the leaders in terms of brand recall and brand image when the market is considered as a whole. Furthermore, for specific tools, the Fisher brand has a consistently higher image rating than other market suppliers.

Overall the company considers itself, and is considered by the markets it serves, to have a good image. Favourable attitudes have been revealed by wholesale and retail distributors as well as tool users. The major attributes cited in recent in-depth research with distributors included 'Products in the range are distinctive', 'Good reliable tools', 'Good range of tools', 'Good variety in different sizes of tools', 'Effective support and good display materials', 'The terms of trade are fair – although we never keep pace with demand on certain items'.

Periodic market research is a feature in which the company takes pride. A recent survey covering the total market for Fisher tools completed in March 1984 revealed the following key findings:

- The major factors influencing all forms of household do-it-yourself (DIY) activity were:
  (a) number of years married
  (b) age and income of the end user
  (c) age and type of house
  (d) period of time in residence.
- Readership was confined to the popular national daily press, and most read DIY magazines.
- All types of consumers recalled a variety of brand names.
- There was an insignificant difference in the 'DIY habit' among the male 25–55 aged B, C1, C2, and D socio-economic groups.
- Domestic purchasers appear more brand loyal than their trade counterparts who tend to purchase a wide variety of brands and furthermore are more fully aware of suitable substitutes.
- A significant number of domestic purchasers will not accept a substitute for certain Fisher tools.
- Manufacturers' delivery from leading market suppliers appeared to be a general problem associated with this market.
- The need for DIY tools to be sold by specialist retailers is reducing substantially.
- Traditional tool retailers adhere to the manufacturers' recommended prices.
- All retailers offer a cash discount to trades persons.
- Growth in tool discounting for domestic purchasers is developing at retail 'discount outlets'.
- Many cheap, foreign tools are available on the market.
- A significant number of purchases of low priced tools are for replacement purposes.
- Quality perception is *the* prime brand purchase motivator among all types of buyers.
- Quality and durability are the key factors considered by the trade users.
- All groups considered the 'effect of advertising as minimal' in influencing the purchase decision.

Within Fisher plc, strategic marketing decisions have depended upon the internal management information system – a fully computerized system totally integrated throughout production, sales and distribution operations.

The board takes pride in the system, which is considered by key users at middle management and executive levels to provide regular up-to-date information at the required level to assist decision making.

The recently conducted market research now forms part of the marketing information system.

Detailed analysis has revealed the need to review and adjust the marketing plan in the following areas:

1. Pricing.
2. Distribution, stock control and ordering procedures.
3. New product development.
4. Marketing communication.

Initial internal discussions have taken place; the preliminary debates have considered:

- The market control which can be secured through a differential pricing policy throughout the various distribution channels and between channel members.
- A revision of minimum order levels to increase order size and thereby reduce the frequency of deliveries.
- More effective product screening and wider use of test marketing prior to the national launch of new products.
- The choice between a generic campaign to promote the Fisher brand across all market segments and product-oriented advertising.
- More effective control of current international business operations and the alternatives for the future.

Each area is considered to be a priority for future marketing operations.

Fisher's London-based advertising agency, Bowland Furness and Lonsdale (BFL), strongly favours a campaign to build the Fisher brand *per se*. Bill Bowland, the Account Director, has a clear vision for the next 12-month period. At a recent internal agency meeting Bill proclaimed:

> We've got to get right through to the end-user – this means promoting Fisher with a big push. The Fisher brand has a good image, we have to build this further to enhance credibility and awareness among non-users to create more sales and yet retain the brand-loyal customers.
>
> The Fisher account is a key plc account, we cannot risk their dissatisfaction – my hunch is that they may ask other agencies to pitch for this campaign if we cannot convince them that the brand image is more important than the product.

Lisa Furness, BFL creative head, claimed:

> The Fisher brand represents a set of consumer-type products, their hand tools are not in any way industrial, therefore, we are selling to people with competing demands for their cash. We must persuade them that Fisher is best. Above all the dimensions of the Fisher brand must represent not only quality, durability and good value for money, but also the 'human' dimensions.

Within the London advertising agency circuit Lisa's work was often considered distinctive and above all memorable. BFL accounts were mainly consumer; awards for creativity and poster design are among the accolades achieved. The current range of key accounts covers men's cosmetics, two government accounts, a confectionery manufacturer, a brand of toothpaste, hi-fi equipment, carpets and home computers.

Lisa continued:

> Fisher have a complex understanding, or misunderstanding, of their market. I believe that market segmentation has a place in their marketing strategy, but the bottom line is that tools are tools and people buy brands. The concentration for the campaign must be on media advertising, the integration required is around the Fisher brand so we should capitalize on this – use just one theme throughout the campaign and create maximum impact. We need a concept now to embody the Fisher brand, the copylines will follow. I will arrange for a brainstorming session – above all we must be bold, distinctive and simple. We must ensure that Fisher favours Furness – well, BFL – hey?

Within the Fisher marketing department at the quarterly review, sales were down on forecast and some concern was raised about current advertising effectiveness.

Ken Slater, as Marketing Manager, had recently quarrelled with Lisa Furness over some non-business matters and this may have coloured his comments to the marketing team:

> I wonder if BFL really understand our market, we have been with them for three years now and we have only just remained on target. I think that the sales force need more help to promote our range of products. We must put the product first and our trade relationship cannot be overlooked. Less advertising, more sales promotion and beef up the Public Relations activities may be the formula for the future. We must be ever mindful of the contribution of market research – we have defined clearly our market segments – each requires special and separate marketing communications activity.

Ken Slater, as a member of the Institute of Marketing had attended an open day event at Moor Hall in April and met a number of advertising personnel. Two individuals left favourable impressions, Lynne Barker and Colin Webb from the Barker Webb agency based in central London. Lynne and Colin had left a large international agency some 18 months previously to form a new outfit with three other young advertising staff from other London-based agencies. With luck, good judgement and the dedication to hard work, the new agency was billing £3.5 million. Good contacts throughout the advertising industry enabled Barker Webb (BW) to offer a full range of services from creative design, market research, sales promotion, display materials, exhibition work, direct mailing apart from the regular business of campaign planning and execution.

Ken Slater, without reference to BFL, had briefed BW. The accounts held by BW covered a broad spectrum of products and services, although its collective experience was much wider. Naturally BW was keen to pitch for the new account. Prior to setting up BW, Colin Webb, in his previous employment, was Account Director for one of Fisher's main competitors.

APPENDICES TO CHAPTER 18

18.1 Company Organization Chart and Personnel Profiles

18.2 The UK Market for Hand Tools – by Louse Dupont

18.3 Memorandum – Profit and Sales Performance

18.4 Sales Analysis – Year Ending 1 April 1984

18.5 Selected Abstracts from Market Research Report, April 1984

18.6 Memorandum – BFL Advertising Agency

18.7 Memorandum – New Product Development

18.8 Memorandum – Profitability

18.9 Memorandum – Profit to Sales Position

APPENDIX 18.1   Company Organization Chart

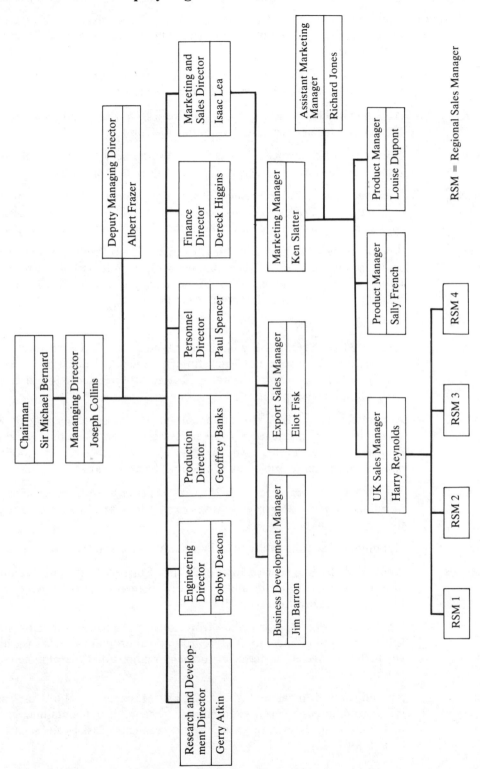

Figure A18.1   Company organization chart

RSM = Regional Sales Manager

Notes to Fisher plc organization chart

Sir Michael Bernard	Appointed 1978, Chairman of three other large manufacturing companies. Serves on a number of government committees. Former Member of Parliament. Aged 70.
Joseph Collins	Appointed 1979, a former Finance Director for 10 years. Aged 58, plans to retire at 60 to home in Spain. No other business interests.
Albert Frazer	Appointed 1982 by merchant bankers for a four-year period. Chartered accountant, former business consultant. Aged 46.
Gerry Atkin	Appointed 1968, former Research and Development Manager. Aged 45, joined company as a school leaver. All family links with Wales.
Bobby Deacon	Appointed 1980 on the retirement of former Engineering Director. American national. Process engineer by training. Previously Engineering Manager of Kansas Extruder Corporation. Wife born in Wales. Aged 43.
Geoffrey Banks	Appointed 1967. Retired July 1984. Former Group Product Manager of six years' experience. Five years' sales experience in household furnishing industry. Business graduate from Manchester Business School. Diploma holder from Institute of Marketing. Aged 38.
Richard Jones	See candidates' brief.
Sally French	Appointed 1982, from Fisher salesforce. Aged 26, single. Currently studying part-time for Institute of Marketing Diploma, ambitious to achieve a marketing management position by 30. Recently rejected a job offer by BFL. Handles new products.
Louise Dupont	Appointed 1983. MBA from Manchester Business School. Aged 24, single. Previous experience in market research. French national. Higher education in UK. Father owns an established French tools and tooling equipment company employing 120 people, based in Paris.
Harry Reynolds	Appointed 1965. Aged 55, with 25 years' experience with Fisher in sales positions, controls 16 representatives across four sales regions through four regional sales managers.
Paul Spencer	Appointed 1981 from Welsh Steel Works. Aged 37, single.
Dereck Higgins	Appointed 1979, to replace Joseph Collins. Former Chief Cost Accountant now Finance Director and Company Secretary. Works closely with the Managing Director. Aged 41.
Isaac Lea	Appointed 1979 by Joseph Collins from a major competitor with a brief to achieve marketing integration at board and subordinate levels. Task has yet to be completely achieved – further organizational development is planned. Aged 45.
Jim Barron	Appointed 1965, previous Fisher UK Sales Manager. Aged 61, responsible for international business development. Key role in maintaining links with European and American licensing agreements. Tasks quite separate from Eliot Fisk.

Eliot Fisk   Appointed 1980 from Kansas Extruder Corporation. Aged 39. Role con-
                            fined to direct export sales from the UK to worldwide customers. May
                            absorb Jim Barron's job in three years' time as Export Director.

Ken Slater   Appointed 1980 from fast moving consumer food products manufacturer.

APPENDIX 18.2   Report on The UK Market for Hand Tools

To: Ken Slater – Marketing Manager
From: Louise Dupont
Date: 18 July 1983

1. Secondary data

The market for hand tools is poorly documented. The problem, typical of most published statistics, is that figures never conform and estimates vary considerably. Therefore, the figures in this
report are to be considered as a guide only because they are very approximate indications. One
major reason for this statement is the complex distribution system and the various sources of
supply to the end purchaser/user.

2. Market trends

Overall there is a marked decline in the market for traditional hand tools. In volume terms this
has amounted to some 35 per cent over the past three years – as a conservative estimate.
     Approximately 75 per cent of the UK market is supplied by imported products, which norm-
ally are much cheaper at retail selling prices than the British manufactured product.

3. Industry sales (in £ million)

	1978	1979	1980	1981	1982
UK manufacturers' sales at ex-factory prices	132	135	112	104	95^E
Exports	82	81	87	89	n/a
UK manufacturers' sales to home market	49	54	25	22	n/a
Imports	63	82	82	83	n/a
Total UK sales	112	136	107	105	n/a

E – Estimate
Source: Government Statistics.

Market sizes of selected hand tools – 1981	Sales at manufacturer's ex-factory prices
Spanners,* socket sets* and wrenches*	35
Saws and blades	11
Pliers,* pincers* and rippers*	10
Measuring and marking tools	10
Screwdrivers	9
Files and rasps	6
Hammers	4
Wood chisels	2
Planes	2
Carpenters bits and braces	1
Other hand tools	15

Source: Government Statistics.
*Products not produced by Fisher.

4. Market behaviour

There is a distinct tendency towards the purchase of cheaper tools. The DIY sector appears, during times of recession and high unemployment, to be more price sensitive and less quality conscious. The concern appears to be for 'everyday tools' and not 'lifetime tools'. It is estimated that the DIY sector accounts for 35 per cent of the market by value at manufacturer's ex-factory prices (i.e., manufacturer's selling prices).

5. Changing pattern of distribution

Large supermarkets, superstores and DIY discount retailers are increasing in importance.

Specialist tool shops are a very important sector of the retail trade, where the consumer can obtain advice, but they are losing sales to the DIY supermarkets. Manufacturers who had ventured into the retail trade through vertical integration are now reversing this trend.

Builders merchants, a traditional channel, retain their position, although the majority of sales are made to professional users.

The decline in the volume trade to the UK market has led to considerable de-stocking at the retail end, and although this process has now ceased to a great extent, considerable selling effort is required to bring sales back to former levels. Most manufacturers are working as a result, at far below production capacity. Increased import penetration means that UK manufacturers must fight harder for domestic market sales.

6. Marketing implications

The implications for Fisher are wide reaching, a revised marketing plan must be drawn up to select the best strategy for the next three-year period in the hope that the market will be restored to former levels of buoyancy.

Over recent years there has been a marked tendency towards power tools to replace hand tools – further research should be conducted in this area.

APPENDIX 18.3   Memorandum – Profit and Sales Performance

To: Ken Slater   Date: 1 May 1984.
From: Isaac Lea

I have just received preliminary year end figures from Dereck Higgins. Our performance for the past four years has not improved in real terms.

The increase in total sales value is between 3 and 4 per cent per year and our ratio of profit before taxation to sales hovers at approximately 2 per cent. It has been made quite clear to me that, for a company of our size and reputation, this is just not good enough – we would be better employed on the money market than in the sale of hand tools. Our shareholders are becoming restless after the recent years of apparent stagnation. We must give active consideration to a revised marketing strategy for the forthcoming year.

Our increased dependence upon overseas trade may necessitate the appointment of an international advertising agency to supplement, or replace, BFL. I would suggest an annual advertising budget of £250 000 to cover home and export markets.

I would welcome your urgent attention to this matter.

APPENDIX 18.4   Sales Analysis – Year Ending 1 April 1984

Home and export sales – year ending 1 April

	1975 H (%)	1975 E (%)	1980 H (%)	1980 E (%)	1981 H (%)	1981 E (%)	1982 H (%)	1982 E (%)	1983 H (%)	1983 E (%)	1984 H (%)	1984 E (%)
Breakdown by Product Group												
Saws	81	19	55	45	50	50	48	52	45	55	45	55
Measuring tapes	90	10	83	17	82	18	80	20	76	24	75	25
Screwdrivers	78	22	70	30	62	38	61	37	60	40	57	43
Files and rasps	40	60	40	60	41	59	37	63	35	65	30	70
Hammers	41	59	43	57	39	61	34	66	32	68	31	69
Wood chisels	36	64	31	69	30	70	27	73	27	73	22	78
Planes	45	55	39	61	37	63	35	65	31	69	30	70
Carpenters bits	45	55	38	62	36	64	34	66	31	69	26	74
Vices	40	60	41	59	40	60	36	64	32	68	33	67
Hand drills	45	55	37	63	35	65	34	66	32	68	30	70
TOTAL FISHER PRODUCTS	74	26	53	47	49	51	44	56	40	60	38	62

H = Home
E = Export

Overseas markets for Fisher hand tools* – year ended 1 April

	1975	1980	1982	1984
Western Europe	2	5	8	10
Eastern Europe	2	4	5	7
Asia	3	4	5	7
Middle East	14	15	16	18
Africa	3	12	14	15
South America	2	2	3	1
USA		5	5	4
TOTAL % SALES	26	47	56	62

*All export sales are through Fisher appointed agents in the respective markets.

Direct home sales analysis – year ending 1 April

	1975 (%)	1980 (%)	1981 (%)	1982 (%)	1983 (%)	1984 (%)
Wholesale	42	23	21	19	17	16
Retail	20	18	17	15	14	13
Mail Order	6	6	5	5	4	4
Institutional/industrial	6	6	6	5	5	5
TOTAL % OF FISHER SALES REVENUE	74	53	49	44	40	38

Retail sales by type of outlet

	1975 (%)	1980 (%)	1981 (%)	1982 (%)	1983 (%)	1984 (%)
Builders merchants	1	1	1	1	1	1
Discount stores	1	1	1	2	3	3
Supermarkets	2	2	2	2	2	1
Department/chain store	2	2	2	2	1	1
Specialist tool shop	4	4	4	3	2	2
Ironmonger/hardware store	6	4	3	2	2	2
DIY shops	4	4	4	3	3	3
TOTAL SALES %	20	18	17	15	14	13

APPENDIX 18.5   Selected Abstracts from Market Research Report, April 1984

Hand tool market – competitor profile*

Conducted by Jackson Market Research
Project Leader: Richard Jones
Date of Report: April 1984
Research Commissioned: November 1983

1. Sample composition:
   Tradesmen   200
   Domestic users   500
   Institutional/
   industrial buyers   15
   Mail order   10
   Wholesalers   10
   Retailers   50

2. Sampling frames:
   Selected without regional bias to provide national representation.

3. Sampling methods and data collection method:

   Tradesmen: quota sampling – quota controls age and type of trade/profession. Personal interviews, on and off the job.
   Domestic users: random sampling – street interviews. Post-survey stratification into levels of skill by usage rate.
   Mail order companies: 100 per cent of all registered. Telephone interviews – for initial screening followed by personal interviews at company premises.
   *Institutional*industrial buyers*: a 25 per cent sample of Fisher key accounts. Personal interviews.
   Wholesalers and retailers: a 10 per cent sample of Fisher accounts stratified by size of account to provide a representative sample nationally. Personal interviews.

Structured interviews were used throughout the survey using recorded questionnaires.

*Abstract from full report

Competitor analysis – year ending April 1984

Company code	UK (%)	Export (%)	UK hand tool Market share (%)	Import (%)	UK manufacturer	Hand tool product range code	UK media advertising expenditure (£000)	Size of sales force	Year of market entry
A	65	35	3	nil	✓	Sp, Pl, F, H, C, Wr.	10	5	1937
B	42	58	8	10	✓	Sa, H, Wo, Me, C, V, Spi, O.	80	10	1951
C	90	10	2	nil	✓	Sa, Me.	5	4	1939
D	45	55	4	nil	✓	Me, H, W, C.	—	6	1928
E	20	80	4	5	✓	Wo, V, C, F, Wr, Sc, Pla.	10	5	1946
F	38	62	15	35	✓	Sa, Me, Sc, F, H, Wo, Pla, C, O.	120	16	1919
G	100	—	20	100	no	Sp, Sa, Pl, Me, Spi, F, H, Wo, Pl, O, Sp.	100	12	1968
H	100	—	15	100	no	Sp, Pl, F, H, Wo, O.	120	8	1975
I	100	—	29	100	no	Sp, Sa, Pl, V, Me, Spi, F, H, Wo, Pl, O.	250	n/a	1965 onwards

NB   Assume UK hand tool market = £100 million at manufacturer's selling prices.

Company code F = Fisher plc

Other codes   I = Other importers

            = Independent organizations

Product range codes

Sp	Spanners	Wo	Wood chisels
Wr	Wrenches	Me	Measuring tools
Pl	Pliers, pincers, rippers	Spi	Spirit levels
F	Files and rasps	V	Vices
H	Hammers	Sc	Screwdrivers
C	Carpenters' bits and braces	Pla	Planes
Sa	Saws and blades	O	Others

Competitor rating by tradesmen – Rating scale −5 to +5

	A	B	C	D	E	F	G	H	I
				Company codes					
Value for money	+3	+2	+3	+2	+2	+3	+1	+2	+2
Durability	+4	+2	+5	+2	+5	+3	−2	−1	−2
Appearance	+3	+2	+4	+2	−1	+3	+1	+1	−1
Design	+3	+2	+4	+2	+1	+3	−1	−1	−1
Reliability	+4	+3	+5	+3	+5	+3	−3	−2	−2
Range of products	+3	+3	−4	+2	+2	+4	+4	+4	+5
Advertising	−4	−2	−4	−4	−4	+1	+3	+3	+2
Quality	+4	+3	+5	+3	+4	+3	−1	−1	−1
Guarantees	+3	+1	+4	+2	+3	+3	−1	−1	−1
Packaging	−2	+1	+1	+1	+1	+2	+2	+2	+1
Availability	+1	+4	+1	+4	+3	+4	+3	+3	+5

Competitor rating by institutional/industrial buyers – Rating scale −5 to +5

	A	B	C	D	E	F	G	H	I
				Company codes					
Value for money	+4	+2	+2	+2	+2	+4	−1	−1	−1
Durability	+5	+2	+5	+3	+5	+3	−3	−2	−3
Appearance	+3	+3	+3	+1	−1	+4	−1	−1	−1
Design	+3	+3	+4	+2	+1	+3	+1	+1	+1
Reliability	+5	+3	+4	+4	+5	+3	−2	−2	−2
Range of products	+3	+4	−4	+2	+2	+4	+3	+2	+4
Advertising	−4	+1	−3	−4	−4	+2	+2	+2	+1
Quality	+5	+3	+5	+4	+4	+3	−1	−1	−1
Guarantees	+4	+3	+3	+2	+2	+3	−1	−1	−1
Packaging	−1	+3	+1	−1	−1	+4	+2	+2	+1
Availability	+2	+1	−1	+3	+3	+4	+4	+3	+5

Competitor rating by domestic purchasers – Rating scale −5 to +5

	A*	B	C*	D	E†	F	G	H	I
				Company codes					
Value for money	+3	+3	+1	+2	+1	+4	+4	+3	+3
Durability	+4	+4	+5	+2	+5	+3	+3	+3	+2
Appearance	+2	+3	+2	+2	−1	+4	+2	+3	+1
Design	+2	+3	+4	+2	−1	+3	+2	+3	+2
Reliability	+4	+4	+5	+2	+5	+4	+3	+3	+2
Range of products	+1	+2	−4	+3	+1	+4	+4	+3	+5
Advertising	−5	+1	−5	−5	−5	+2	+2	+3	+1
Quality	+4	+3	+5	+3	+3	+3	+2	+3	+2
Guarantees	+3	+2	+4	+3	+2	+3	+1	+1	−2
Packaging	−2	+1	+1	+1	+1	+4	+1	+2	−1
Availability	−4	+4	−3	+4	−2	+4	+4	+3	+5

*Small sample response (less than 15%).
†Limited brand recognition (35% response).

Competitor rating by wholesale, retail and mail-order channels* – Rating scale −5 to +5

	A†	B	C‡	D	E§	F	G	H	I
					Company codes				
Value for money	+2	+3	+2	+2	−1	+3	+3	+3	+2
Reliability	+4	+3	+5	+4	+5	+3	−2	+1	+1
Design	+2	+3	+4	+3	−1	+4	+1	+1	+1
Range	+2	+3	−5	+2	+2	+4	+4	+3	+5
Advertising	−5	+2	−5	−5	−4	+2	+2	+2	+1
Guarantees	+2	+2	+2	+2	+3	+3	−2	+1	+1
After sales service	+2	+2	+1	+2	+3	+3	−2	+1	+2
Customer satisfaction	+4	+3	+5	+3	+2	+3	−1	+1	+1
Trade discount	−1	+1	−2	−3	−3	+1	+4	+4	+5
Delivery service	−1	+1	−3	−1	+1	−1	+3	+4	+5
Packaging	−2	+2	+1	+1	−2	+3	+2	+2	+2
Profit potential	−1	+1	−1	−1	+1	+2	+5	+5	+5

*Results of surveys were very close, hence the mean scores have been applied in this table.
†Small sample response.
‡Restricted distribution.
§Not mail order.

APPENDIX 18.6   Memorandum – BFL Advertising Agency

To: Ken Slater
From: Richard Jones
Date: 10 May 1984

I realise that I am a very new member of the marketing team, but feel that I have a small contribution to make on the above subject, I hope, therefore, that you will treat this memo in the spirit in which it is written. I am not trying to 'teach my grandmother to suck eggs'.

Naturally you are concerned with BFL's performance and an immediate reaction may be to request another agency to provide a presentation – I would suggest two other agencies. This would keep BFL 'on its toes'. The agency I worked for, Bard, Klein and Mason, would be worth considering, there may have been changes since I left but the man to contact is Colin Webb, my former boss. I can also recommend one of my former market research clients, an advertising agency based here in Swansea, Fortnam and Golde.

Before any decision is taken it is fair to consider what BFL has achieved; I have a checklist for agency evaluation which you may find helpful.

Should you wish to proceed with other agencies we should offer BFL the chance to retain the account and notify the company of our intentions. We must not overlook BFL's 10 years' experience as an agency and the billing size of £27 million.

APPENDIX 18.7   Memorandum – New Product Development

To: Richard Jones
From: Ken Slater
Date: 15 May 1984

I have been aware for some time of the need to diversify beyond hand tools and yet remain within the DIY market.

An opportunity has arisen for Fisher to act as distributors for a Swedish company manufacturing paint applicators. The product range comprises paint brushes, paint rollers and a more recent innovation, paint pads. The latter I have no interest in whatsoever.

How do you suggest we proceed?

This is your first assignment with the company, please advise me of your progress, I would hope to receive your report by the middle of June.

On the subject of your memo of 10 May, I thank you for your comments and would ask you to supply the checklist you mentioned with your report.

APPENDIX 18.8   Memorandum – Profitability

To: Dereck Higgins
From: Ken Slater
Date: 16 May 1984

I refer to our conversation of some two weeks ago concerning our profit to sales position.

I have now had time to reflect upon the situation; appropriate attention is being given to the matter but this is under Mr Lea's direct authority. However, at present our information system does not carry financial trend information over the past five years; would you, therefore, provide an outline analysis of the cost impact areas which have a direct influence upon our net profit before tax position? Kindly send a copy also to Mr Lea for information.

My new assistant manager is keen to develop his interest in the financial control area. I am encouraging this and have asked him to talk with you directly.

I understand that Mr Lea approves fully of staff development initiatives.

APPENDIX 18.9   Memorandum – Profit to Sales Position

To: Ken Slater
              c.c. Isaac Lea
From: Dereck Higgins
Date: 17 May 1984

I understand that during Isaac Lea's vacation to the Middle East you have to deal with the running of the department.

The issue of profitability is a number one priority at board level.

I have appended a brief outline of cost trends which contribute to profitability. In marketing you really influence all these areas – including the reduction in numbers of the workforce through poor sales performance.

However, you may feel that additional ratio analysis and financial analysis would be helpful, kindly telephone my secretary to arrange a meeting and bring along your new assistant.

Analysis of Fisher plc profit to sales – year ending 1 April

		1980		1981		1982		1983		1984	
		M	F	M	F	M	F	M	F	M	F
Pre-tax profits											
Sales	%	4.5	2.2	4.5	2.1	4.0	2.2	3.5	2.1	3.5	1.9
Production cost											
Cost of output	%	82.1	76.0	81.5	73.3	80.1	72.1	78.3	72.5	78.0	72.5
Distribution cost											
Cost of output	%	6.1	9.6	6.3	12.3	6.8	12.9	7.3	12.9	7.5	13.0
Selling cost											
Cost of output	%	2.0	4.5	2.5	5.9	3.0	6.3	3.3	6.1	3.5	6.3
Administration cost											
Cost of output	%	9.8	7.7	9.7	8.5	10.1	8.7	11.1	8.5	11.0	8.2

M = Median of UK manufacturers A, B, C, D, E.
F = Fisher performance.

QUESTIONS

As Richard Jones you are forming a close working relationship with Ken Slater.

Your first report is now due for presentation and should comprise the following sections:

Section 1 Justified recommendations for proceeding with diversification into paint applicators together with a comprehensive specification of the information required at this early stage of new product development.

(20 marks)

Section 2 A checklist for advertising agency evaluation and your judgement of how best to evaluate the alternatives now open to the Fisher advertising account.

(20 marks)

Section 3 What you expect from BW at their forthcoming presentation.

(20 marks)

Section 4 An assessment of the current market position of Fisher plc both at home and overseas, with justified options for development to 1986.

(40 marks)

GENERAL APPROACH

The candidate must have adopted the role of Richard Jones, the newly appointed Assistant Marketing Manager.

The examination required the candidate to produce a report for Ken Slater, the Marketing Manager. It was expected that all candidates used management report format.

It was expected that all sections of the report would be answered.

The importance of questions has been shown and candidates should have observed the differential allocation of marks.

It is expected that time should be allocated to match this distribution of examination marks.

A good tip is to allow $1\frac{1}{2}$ minutes per mark, i.e., a 20-mark question should be given 30 minutes' writing time. This tactic should leave time for answer planning and reading through the final script before the end of the examination.

THE APPROACH TO EACH SECTION

Section 1 – Diversification

(20 marks)

Practical insights were required. No student was expected to make a 'go decision' on the basis of the case information. It was too early to make firm recommendations in this direction without a feasibility study. Half of the marks were allocated to the first part of the question; the second part was straightforward and required a simple listing of the required information before further interest was to be taken by the company.

Students should have adopted the role of Richard Jones with his background experience in market research and acted accordingly.

Section 2 – Advertising agency evaluation

(20 marks)

The first part of the question was to be fully anticipated by the student – 40 per cent of the mark allocation was given for the advertising agency checklist.

Part two required a method for evaluation of the advertising agency options:

- the international advertising agency; or
- the local agency in Swansea, Wales; or
- the existing account holders, BFL; or
- the new agency, BW.

Section 3 – Forthcoming BW presentation

(20 marks)

Each analysis and decision case study attempts to explore the varied dimensions of marketing. This case has featured advertising agency dynamics.

At a superficial level the candidate was required merely to state what would be expected at an advertising agency presentation.

To pass and attain higher grades, a consideration of the size of the budget and the importance of the marketing factors was expected. In the context of the case, the issue of segmentation, market position, distribution penetration and the export markets could not be overlooked. The debate between brand and product advertising could have been explored.

Section 4 – Future developments

(40 marks)

This question was deliberately open-ended, giving both the strong and weak candidate the opportunity to develop a theme within the context of the question.

The case study was broad based, stimulated interest in several directions, with sufficient material to fire the diligent student to prepare thoroughly in advance of the examination. The candidate was expected, therefore, to answer the following *implicit* questions:

1. Where is Fisher now, both at home and overseas?
2. What are the problems associated with the current state?
3. How can we best proceed to exploit these markets for the future?

ANSWER

REPORT

To: Ken Slater, Marketing Manager.
From: Richard Jones, Assistant Marketing Manager.
Subject: First report on diversification, advertising agencies, Fisher's current position and short-term development.
Date: 18 June 1984.

Introduction

I have been with the company for just a short while and have, therefore, much to learn about the organization, the market and the internal and external corporate environment. This report is a first attempt. I would welcome the opportunity to discuss the content, format and appropriateness of the document so that it may be amended before circulation and subsequent filing.

Section 1 – Diversification into paint applicators

Fisher plc is a multi-product company facing changing demand patterns for tools the company manufactures. Diversification is just one route to retain profitability. However, I feel that the company's product strategy should be subjected to a thorough scrutiny. A complete product audit would enable the marketing department to match the current provision with market demand. Perhaps it is time to 'put our house in order' before considering yet new ventures.

At this stage I would recommend most strongly that we *do not* proceed with an adoption decision until a feasibility study is conducted, completed and given full management consideration. There is simply not enough information currently available upon which to make a sound decision.

Before undertaking a feasibility study, initial corporate considerations must be given. These may save considerable management time on what may turn out to be a fruitless and costly exercise.

A few simple, yet penetrating, questions must be asked:

– Where is Fisher plc now?
– Where do the company and the shareholders want it to be, say, within five years?
– How do we get there?
– How does diversification into paint applicators contribute – if at all?
– What will be the effect on the Fisher brand name if the new product range does not receive trade, professional and/or consumer acceptance?
– Can the company afford failure?
– What is the real opportunity cost, i.e., the cost of other development options that are foregone should the company adopt the Swedish company's proposals?

– The proposed diversification is within the DIY market, but is this really the business the company is in? Painting and decorating is beyond the current sphere of company knowledge and outside the current technology orbit, which is based upon steel (not wood and bristles).

At this early stage I would advise a cautious approach. I would advise, assuming the above questions have been answered to management's satisfaction, that the following information is obtained.

Market information
– What is the size of the UK market, by volume and value?
– What are the secular, cyclical and seasonal trends?
– What is the rate, if any, of the real growth in the market?
– Who are the competitors?
– How well established are they?
– How are market shares distributed?
– What changes have taken place in market shares over the last five years?
– How brand loyal is the market at trade, professional and consumer levels?
– What are the main purchase motivations and how have these changed in recent years?
– Can market gaps be identified?
– What will be the real cost of market entry and what are the potential financial gains and over what period of time?
– When could Fisher expect to achieve break-even?

Product information
– How does the Swedish product compare on:
  product specification;
  appearance;
  actual quality;
  perceived quality;
  performance;
  raw material costs and hence price to the trade and final markets;
  supply and maintenance of supply;
  image (and brand image)?

Price information
– What are the unit costs?
– How price competitive will the product be on the UK market assuming import and transportation on-costs?
– What are the trends in Swedish raw material costs?
– How price sensitive is the market at trade, professional and consumer levels?
– What return does the company require from this investment and how does this affect price–volume relationships over specified periods of time?

Product information
– What is the level and form of support that we can expect from the Swedish company – can it be used to sell the product in?
– What is the cost of selling in and subsequently selling the product out in the final end-user markets?

– Does the Swedish brand have a marketable USP or will Fisher have to inject artificial product plus points?
– What is the likely response from competition?
– Will Fisher achieve trade acceptance and under which brand – Fisher or the Swedish brand?
– Can Fisher trade on existing brand image at all? As overseas distributor for a Swedish manufacturer it is unlikely unless the Swedish company adopts the Fisher brand name.
– How can we promote/merchandise the product effectively at the point of sale?

Distribution information
– Can existing channels be used – and to what extent?
– Will new channels be required?
– What is the real cost of distribution – what percentage can be absorbed within existing capacity?
– How will the introduction of the product affect trade relationships?
– Can we give the trade sufficient margin to fend off competition?

Sales information
– Can the product simply be added to the existing product portfolio?
– What is the level of additional selling effort required and the coincident need for training?
– What level of priority should be given to selling paint applicators – for how long and what will the effect be on other products?

The above sections are not exhaustive but are intended, within the time available, to raise a number of key questions, which must be answered before we can proceed further.

Communication with the Swedish company is advised as a 'holding operation' while we consider our options in this direction further.

Section 2 – Advertising agency evaluation

The checklist for advertising agency evaluation previously discussed is as follows. Some of the points may require clarification or de-jargonizing. May I suggest this can be achieved at our review meeting.

Checklist From personal experience, after visiting and meeting the agencies and discussing their services and client profile, short-listing agencies involves full consideration of the following points:

1. Creativity.
2. Experience.
3. Absence of internal conflict.
4. Reputation.
5. The size in terms of employees and billings.
6. International structures.
7. Management style and ability.

However, the appointment decision has hinged on the following criteria:

1. The understanding and interpretation of client marketing problems.
2. Creativity.
3. Management experience and style.

4. The real ability of the agency.
5. Compatibility between agent and client teams.
6. The presentation and agency track record.
7. The size of the agency.

In evaluating the existing agency and in making an assessment of the alternatives available the following points should be considered in detail.

1. Agency management structure.
2. Internal procedures.
3. Basis of remuneration.
4. Internal method of costing, plussing-up and charging: allocation of overheads.
5. Legal and financial status: major shareholders; issued capital; turnover.
6. Clients – names, industry groups, billings, number of years with named contacts for references.
7. Experience in relevant industries and markets.
8. Quality of advertisements in relation to brief of:
   (a) copywriting;
   (b) creativity;
   (c) visuals;
   (d) campaign continuity;
   (e) measurement of results.
9. Campaign assessment in relation to:
   (a) campaign plan;
   (b) copy platform;
   (c) visual mix;
   (d) visual continuity;
   (e) measurement of results.
10. Media services and expertise in:
    (a) press;
    (b) TV;
    (c) direct mail;
    (d) merchandising;
    (e) packaging;
    (f) point of sale;
    (g) sales literature;
    (h) technical publications;
    (i) exhibitions;
    (j) photography;
    (k) press relations;
    (l) public relations.
11. Research:
    (a) advertising;
    (b) media;
    (c) campaign;
    (d) market;
    (e) product.
12. Overseas connections.
13. Provincial branches.

14. Personal compatibility with and professional capability of:
    (a) Account Executive.
    (b) Account Director.
    (c) Creative Head.
    (d) Media Manager.
    (e) Research and/or Marketing Head.
    (f) Managing Director.

Evaluation of alternatives   The options open to Fisher at this time are:

1. The international advertising agency.
2. The local agency in Swansea, Wales.
3. The existing account holders, BFL.
4. The new agency, BW.

The choice may be subjective but the extent of subjectivity should be minimized. One method is to take the checklists above and to appraise each alternative on a rating scale from 1 to 5 as shown below.

Agency options

Checklist criteria	International agency	Local agency	BFL	BW
A	5	4	2	1
B	3	3	3	3
C	4	2	1	1
D	1	2	3	5
'N'				
Totals	xxx	xxx	xxx	xxx

At this level the analysis is too simplistic. Differential weights should be applied to each criterion so that a priority rating is determined. The total scores can then be assessed to rank the agencies accordingly. This is merely a simple technique to help the selection process but does not replace management judgement.

In my position as Assistant Marketing Manager with limited knowledge of some options and more knowledge of others, I feel my assessment would be biased. Had I considered myself to be in a more objective position I would have completed the task outlined above. Perhaps we could complete the matrix together and as a result of joint discussion complete the exercise. Having completed such in the past I found from personal experience the act and discipline of using the checklist in this way was more useful as a framework for evaluation than the actual achievement of a mathematical solution. In the same way the rigour and thought that are required in any planning process are often more beneficial than the published and agreed document. In short, the *process* of evaluation is often *the* most important factor.

Section 3 – The BW presentation

Advertising agency presentations vary considerably. This can be attributed to differences between agencies and how hungry they may be for the account. Differences as applied to the aforementioned criteria are diverse and hence the style, quality, time, *rapport* and content of the presentation will vary. Equally, what I expect from an agency presentation and the interpretation I will give to the presentation will be different yet again from other members of the client team. Once again we enter the realms, to an extent, of subjectivity.

My evaluation must depend, therefore, on what *we* actually expect of the agency – until we have agreed our terms of reference then we can only assess the presentation on the interpretation of the brief the agency has received from us. Since I have not been closely involved at the process level it is difficult for me to comment on the expected content of the presentation. Having stated the above caveats, I would in this situation expect to consider the agency on the criteria previously specified. However, there are some central points which BW should not overlook.

Apart from the creativity, a full consideration of the size of the Fisher budget must be given. I would be particularly keen to consider how the budget has been appropriated between media and non-media activity. The scheduling of advertising activity in relation to market demand is vital, as is the placement of advertising in relation to market weights. I would expect some consideration of the likely response in relation to the projected levels of exposure. The importance of market factors must be set in perspective – the agency must not consider the exercise in isolation from the market but rather as a means of bridging a communications gap.

Answers to the issue concerning product/brand advertising must be resolved.

The fundamental issues of segmentation, distribution penetration and export markets must be given full treatment against a prescribed market position for Fisher.

The above points must be considered by BW – how they are handled will depend upon the style of presentation – but answers must be forthcoming. If not, the agency should be probed to test its level of understanding of our brief.

On a more formal note I would expect a clear statement of:

– our marketing objectives;
– BW marketing communication, advertising, sales promotion and public relations objectives;
– BW creative strategy and media strategy to achieve the objectives;
– a research programme to pre-test and post-test the campaign;
– budget appropriation and designation of responsibility.

Much will hang upon the effectiveness of the presentation. The level of detail is a matter of judgement and how BW has judged the requirements and level of understanding of the client team.

Above all, a good level of agency confidence and commitment is vital. Agencies must convey that they know their business and what they believe is best for us. In so doing they should be able to impart a willingness for effective agency/client communication. Rapport, therefore, is a keynote and this is often difficult to achieve at the initial presentation stage.

Section 4 – Current market position

The market position of Fisher plc must be set in the context of prevailing market factors. The following factors are considered relevant.

1. Despite a multi-million pound market, maturity has been reached and there is little doubt that market decline has started. Within this overall position there is little evidence of growth sectors within the mass market.
2. Important consumer trends are in evidence. There is an apparent preference and hence significant trend towards power tools.

   A weakening in brand preference at trade level exists although the DIY sector is very brand conscious despite increasing consumer patronage of low price functional hand tools.

3. At industry level there is apparent over-capacity, which will further threaten the domestic market even in the short term.
4. A very significant percentage of industry production is exported, although companies cannot compete effectively with foreign imports. It appears that export markets remain an attractive target for further development and hence will offer survival opportunities for UK hand tool manufacturers – especially with the weakening position of sterling.
5. Owing to stagnant home sales, the effect of import penetration, declining markets and excess capacity, price flexibility is very limited in this very competitive domestic market.
6. There has been, and will continue to be, a shift in channels of distribution. Direct sales to retailers have increased at the expense of the wholesale trade.
7. As yet there appears to be only moderate promotional support to create a pull effect on the channel.
8. *Fisher's domestic market position – strengths*. The company is:
   (a) the largest in total sales value of all UK manufacturers;
   (b) the largest exporter of all UK manufacturers;
   (c) the largest in terms of domestic sales of all UK manufacturers.

   Despite the industry position outlined above and with the very real threat from imported products, Fisher has a confirmed market position which has not, as yet, been seriously affected. The company enjoys a dominant market position with a formal marketing organization to support and defend and furthermore protect this position.

   Fisher enjoys good trade/distributor relationships with good brand images at industrial, trade and consumer levels. The Fisher brand and associated quality image are maintained across a well-established product range.
9. *Fisher's overseas market position – strengths*. In addition to the extended Fisher organization structure overseas there is good potential to increase sales further in existing countries and to penetrate others – albeit from a position of strength and experience.
10. *Fisher's domestic market position – weaknesses*.
    (a) Despite Fisher's market stature profitability is very low.
    (b) In comparison with the industry, Fisher has high selling and distribution costs.
    (c) The opportunity to diversify into power tools to consolidate the domestic market position has been lost.
    (d) Capacity is under-utilized.
    (e) Service levels may be too high as reflected in high distribution costs.
    (f) The company is in a poor position to undertake cost effective innovation – and yet it cannot face further decline in pre-tax profits.
    (g) Selling costs far exceed industry average and these have considerable impact on the profit to sales position.
11. *Fisher's overseas market position – weaknesses*.
    (a) From our knowledge the exclusive use of agents until now implies little initiative has been taken for the further development of export international organization structures. With the dependence of the company on exports, planning is needed now in this direction.
    (b) Comment number 1 is, however, undermined by the widespread export activity – showing little real evidence of concentration.
12. *Fisher plc – short-term plan to 1986*. It is vital to realize that while much exists for attention, priorities must be given to defined problems and plans developed for those areas that are agreed priorities. Further discussion is needed to secure agreement and commitment to the key result areas for the immediate and short term.

I consider the following to be short-term priorities:

(a) *Market research*

    (i) As an independent exercise, the power tool market should be explored to confirm or otherwise market gaps that may exist for Fisher to exploit – provided that this does not contravene company policy.

    (ii) A feasibility study for paint applicators should be given full consideration, subject to board approval.

    (iii) A segmented end-user purchase profile is required to assist in the future development of sales and promotional strategy. Fisher knows who the buyers are but has insufficient knowledge of their purchase habits and restrictions. Adjustments to distribution/strategy should follow, especially with the degree of change occurring in the retail distribution of hand tools.

        Market and sales forecasts should be produced to assist with the interpretation of the internal company research proposed below.

(b) *Internal company research*

    (i) To assist in the management of future company profitability and hence to cultivate better relationships with Fisher plc shareholders, an independent study should be conducted as an immediate priority.

    (ii) Profit contribution analysis by product group, product item and by market segment should be undertaken to determine the high cost impact areas and those which make a contribution to corporate profitability.

    (iii) Accurate costing information is required together with accurate sales data.

    (iv) A combined effort between the marketing and finance sections is needed to ensure that organizational commitment is given to the task and that it is conducted thoroughly and professionally.

    (v) The implications of the findings should have a direct impact on marketing and sales planning.

    (vi) It is anticipated that product policy may be reviewed, pricing policy may be adjusted and new sales strategies implemented to ensure that every possible avenue is explored to maintain *and* improve pre-tax profitability.

    (vii) The findings of the study will assist in the revised targeting of overseas markets to help achieve further geographic expansion.

    (viii) It is anticipated that these developments will be fully documented in the company's export market development plan.

(c) *Staffing*

The findings of the research may have staffing implications. Notwithstanding this, manpower development and linked succession planning is required as a result of the positions of Geoffrey Banks, Jim Barron, Harry Reynolds and the ambitious product managers, Sally French and Louise Dupont.

    (i) The company must be aware of the staffing situation and not wait until a crisis occurs. The research programme will act as a stimulus to consider staff before new strategic plans are drawn up and agreed.

    (ii) Until the above work is undertaken it is inappropriate to outline specific development plans.

    (iii) The findings of the research will strongly influence the future direction of the company, which, of necessity, must change course.

    (iv) The probable areas for change are shown in the table.

Potential development areas to 1986

	Home market rating	Overseas market rating	Immediate action	Short-term action
Corporate research	5	5	✓	
Corporate objectives	2	2		✓
Marketing objectives	3	3		✓
Marketing research	3	2	✓	
Product development plans	2	2		✓
Pricing planning	5	5	✓	✓
Distribution planning	3	3		✓
Advertising and promotion plans	4	4	✓	✓
Sales plans	5	3	✓	✓
Staffing plans	2	3		✓
Controls on the marketing plan	4	4		✓
Budgeting	2	2		✓

Rating scale 1 to 5, where 1 indicates low adjustment levels and 5 indicates high adjustment levels.

13. *Review*

I look forward to discussing this report with you in the near future.

Signed: Richard Jones.

NINETEEN

CASE STUDY WITH SPECIMEN ANSWER

A. & C. Watson Ltd (Industrial Marketing)

A. & C. Watson Ltd, was founded at Coventry in 1954 by two brothers, Alan, an industrial chemist, and Christopher, a mechanical engineer. The brothers were inspired by their father who held a family tradition in managing Watson Steel Works Ltd. The 'works' has changed operations during its 100-year history from a sheet metal works to a firm specializing in the precision engineering of machine tools which today is managed by Michael Watson, the third and eldest son.

The 'Watson Brothers', as they were known locally, used customized business as their path to growth and business development, and operated successfully by making metal washers and shims* for special applications – albeit largely as a result of trade 'passed on by father'.

Today A. & C. Watson (UK) Ltd (ACW), one of some thirty gasket manufacturers in the UK, is a successful international company owned by an international conglomerate, the Neal Sanders Corporation, whose worldwide consolidated turnover far exceeds £200 million (see Appendix 19.1)

The 1960s saw a major development to the ACW product range; further differentiation of the basic washer and shim types led to considerable product depth by type, size and specification. Fibre washers were introduced made from both asbestos and simple plastic polymers.

Gaskets were developed for a wide range of end-use industries using various materials ranging from mild steel to special metal hardenings, laminated brass and metal–asbestos combinations.

In addition to the development of woven asbestos for insulation end use and special gasketing for 'ring joints', came the development of the Helitex gasket, which was a completely new concept in industrial sealing (see Appendix 19.2)

This new type of gasket is based upon a series of spirally wound concentric interfacings which combine stainless steel with an asbestos packing. The new gasket withstands much higher stress tolerances and extreme variations in temperature. It also produces a watertight seal and is highly resistant to vibration, corrosion and fire. The uses in the industrial and engineering sectors have consequently appeared almost limitless and are still developing on a worldwide scale.

The late 1960s saw further product development and the first stage of international business development. Export trade to the United States had been growing steadily and to exploit further the market a new company A. C. Watson (US) had been set up in 1969 to handle east coast busi-

---

* Thin metal packings used to make mechanical parts fit.

ness. Some seven years later a sister organization was formed in Chicago to supply west coast industry. Both factories have ensured a firm foothold in the US and Canadian markets and recently have acquired a majority shareholding in the Evans Corporation which manufactures automobile gaskets.

During 1973 and 1975 two sales subsidiaries were set up by A. C. Watson (US) in Nigeria and Singapore respectively, to supply Africa and the Far East. Currently no plans exist to commence manufacture in these countries but they will continue to be 'far off field storage depots'.

The latest factory, which operates as an independent manufactuing subsidiary of ACW (UK), was opened in June 1976 in Holland to exploit opportunities within the Dutch petrochemical refining industries. Over a further three-year period ACW (UK) appointed sales agents in Sweden, Venezuela and Mexico.

Coincident with this international expansion, a new depot was built in 1977 at Aberdeen to serve the North Sea oil industry.

Diversification into a range of industrial sealants and pneumatic sealing equipment has been achieved and a new sealants salesforce was appointed in 1978 to supplement the existing UK and European sales teams.

Just nine months have passed since the establishment of a special trouble-shooting team which offers technical specialism. Apart from routine maintenance of industrial installations, they have the range of equipment and products to handle most customer requirements in the petrochemical refining industries. This team of seven, highly trained, engineers has been named 'Force 10'.

Expansion has been at the cost of heavy research and development, re-equipping the manufacturing plant and ensuring the highest standards of precision for Helitex with the installation of micro-computer technology for application to micro-engineering and other production operations. The research and development team, which enjoys the opportunity for speculative research, has a reputation for innovative product designs, many of which are far ahead of the rest of the industry. Extensive tests of existing products, undertaken in the laboratory testing station, are supplemented by yet further research which is in response to technical and scientific leads. Currently, plastics and new polymer compounds are being tested for stress, tolerance, vibration, etc., in the hope that new product ideas will emerge.

Production, although operating at 70 per cent capacity, has not been without setbacks. All production machinery is imported from the US and delays in delivery times have been a constant source of frustration. The environmentalist lobby on the use of asbestos, and subsequent legislation, has caused an accelerated programme of research and development to produce substitute materials. A close watch is now kept on the market environment to keep the factory alerted to any future threats.

The company enjoys good working relationships at all levels and one worker representative from the trade union attends the monthly board meetings.

ACW enjoys a very low staff turnover, and despite the recent redundancy of 35 production operatives and early retirement agreed with 15 others at junior administrative levels, employees have remained loyal to the company.

The culture of the ACW organization is one of a high regard for the management hierarchy. The small board of five directors have a separate suite of offices, a separate dining room and kitchen on the first floor and car parking designated by name plates. A high sense of achievement and self-sufficiency is part of the charisma created by the Watson brothers.

Middle management, defined by those with the title 'manager', have a separate dining room adjoining the works canteen. ACW managers share an open-plan office on the ground floor of the main two-storey office building.

Corporate planning is a matter of basic group policy, with the emphasis to set objectives which match company resources to production requirements.

While lunchtime discussions are dominated invariably by internal influences and priorities, formal board meetings occur monthly with quarterly presentations made to the Neal Sanders board. Budgetary control, sales target achievement and technical considerations receive particular attention while a positive zest for new innovation permeates every meeting.

Christopher Watson firmly believes that it is the responsibility of his Sales and Marketing Director, Stephen Sutcliffe, merely to sell what ACW produces, an opinion which is also voiced by Mark Sutton, his Research and Development Manager.

A memo sent to Sutcliffe on his appointment gives a clear indication of the MD's convictions (see Appendix 19.3).

Following Stephen Sutcliffe's appointment, the seals salesforce was reorganized into three regions to increase the accountability of individual representatives.

A new 'Midlands' region (Area B) was designated under Bob Pearce, a former ACW representative of some 10 years' standing. Further appointments to the salesforce were made in 1978 when two engineering graduates were taken on to replace David Clarke and Andrew Smith who had been promoted from the seals force to regional sales management of the newly created sealants salesforce (see Appendix 19.4).

In all, eight new representatives were appointed and placed on an intensive six-month training programme organized by external sales training consultants.

These eight representatives still remain at ACW and two have recently obtained the IM Diploma by part-time evening study.

Sutcliffe has, on several occasions, consulted the mature salesmen about further training but the force resents the 'need for re-schooling'. They consider that technical representatives or sales engineers as they are known do not require high pressure selling techniques in this industry, and that success to date proves this.

All salesmen are paid on a 'salary only' basis, with a Christmas bonus usually amounting to a further month's money paid at the discretion of Stephen Sutcliffe. This discretionary bonus is on the basis of Sutcliffe's assessment of an individual's performance throughout the year. It is a system which Sutcliffe believes in and one which he considers works best after his 30 years' experience as a technical representative. However, his sales managers do not share the same view. Frank White firmly believes in the need for a commission system, but does not wish to press too hard for this, having been with the company for only two years, and having taken over the job previously handled by Sutcliffe himself!

Advice from Terry Porter has been heeded. 'Frank, don't rock the boat if you want to get on, I say the same to my regional managers and they appear content, Neal Johnson and Max Bennett have been with me for 12 years now and the company looks after them well. Bob Pearce, who has an ambitious wife, is my only potential mutineer.'

André Pascalle, the international member of the sales management team, is a major asset to ACW. Of French and Austrian parents he speaks French, German, English and Spanish fluently and has local working knowledge of the countries and operational areas of his sales agents, where he spends some 40 per cent of his time. He works closely with Stanley Reed on international contracts, and has four representatives in Germany who return to the UK after a six-week journey cycle. His sphere of influence throughout the company is considerable and he spends more time with the Watson brothers than with his immediate boss. He was offered the board appointment of Marketing and Sales Director before Sutcliffe but had turned it down on the basis that it would constrain his movements and stunt his job satisfaction.

Monitoring the movements of the salesforce is achieved by a mandatory 'Friday phone-in'.

The German reps are expected to call in each Friday between 10.00 a.m. and 12 noon to the Coventry office. In the event of André Pascalle's absence, they report direct to Stephen Sutcliffe.

The UK sales representatives telepone their regional managers, who, in turn, report in to Terry Porter and Frank White. Sutcliffe expects a report phoned to him at home by 10.30 each Saturday morning.

A monthly UK sales meeting is held at Head Office and this is supplemented by an annual weekend sales conference held in a London hotel each June after the publication of the annual accounts.

Internal sales office administration and ordering are handled by the Customer Service Department where complaints and after-sales service enquiries are dealt with swiftly and efficiently. Alan Humphreys, a former sales manager, has spent his entire working life with the company and after an unfortunate road accident decided to stay with paperwork and an office job, rather than be out on the road. As Customer Service Manager, he is a highly valued member of the management team.

The dispatch and onward distribution of products takes place from the main warehouse at Coventry but the recent downturn in business during the recession in European trade has, despite computerized stock control, produced unusually high stock levels.

ACW has a conscious policy of maintaining high customer service levels and prides itself on providing good delivery times irrespective of cost. Production is often disrupted by urgent orders for Helitex specials and this is a frequent source of conflict between Len Roberts and Alan Humphreys.

ACW vehicles and sales fleet are maintained to the highest standards and renewed regardless of mileage every two years.

All export orders are air freighted using the services of a local freight forwarding agency to handle the documentation requirements.

One distinguishing feature at the works is a helicopter pad, itself an attraction and source of newsworthy items. It was built in 1976 to handle the booming business with the oil exploration and refining industries in the North Sea, where a broken pipeline seal or flange can cause a considerable loss in production and delivery times must be kept to a minimum.

In accordance with the board policy 'marketing' activities are kept low key. No funds are consciously appropriated for media advertising although trade press coverage is enjoyed from the regular editorial coverage of new applications of Helitex. The majority of the small promotions budget is allocated to sales aids, samples, sales kits and technical data sheets. Being conscious of the firm's corporate image, Christopher Watson commissioned a new 12-page, four-colour brochure and found this to be well received by both actual and potential customers who were largely unaware of the total range of products manufactured by ACW. The success of this brochure has led to further work on the development of a new company logo, new house colours and new letter headings for stationery, etc., to make sure that a new dynamic image is effectively communicated on all company instruments.

Stephen Sutcliffe has read this new move as either a 'change of heart' or as a direct remit from the Neal Sanders Corporation, and to make sure he is fully aware of market reactions to ACW and the range of products, has commissioned a small market research survey – of which some desk research is detailed (see Appendix 19.5).

A lecturer at a local college, a personal friend, has also produced a short statement on the public relations image presented by ACW and its salesforce (see Appendix 19.6).

Meanwhile, John Mills's team has also been working on a detailed analysis of sales activities and market trends (see Appendix 19.7).

To complete the 'audit' detailed discussions have been held on pricing policy, pricing strategy and tactics – all previously the realm of Mark Taylor.

Sutcliffe believes that it is now time to take stock of his operations, and make significant changes to meet the challenge of the next five years so that he may be able to hand over the reins of a successful and well-managed operation upon his retirement. He is now giving careful consideration to the final accounts and profit contribution trends (see Appendix 19.8).

APPENDICES TO CHAPTER 19

19.1   The Neal Sanders Corporation

19.2   Typical Washers, Shims and Helitex Gaskets

19.3   Memorandum – Appointment of Stephen Sutcliffe

19.4(a) Production and Distribution Organization Structure
19.4(b) Sales and Marketing Organization Structure
19.4(c) Sales Areas

19.5(a) UK Market Trends by Value
19.5(b) Initial Appraisal of Market – 1979

19.6   Memorandum – Public Relations Perspective

19.7   Sales Analysis – Years Ending April 1976–82

19.8(a) Profit Contribution by Product Group – Years Ending April 1976–82
19.8(b) Profit and Loss Accounts – Years Ending April 1976–82

19.9   Summary Balance Sheets – Years Ending April 1976–82

APPENDIX 19.1   The Neal Sanders Corporation

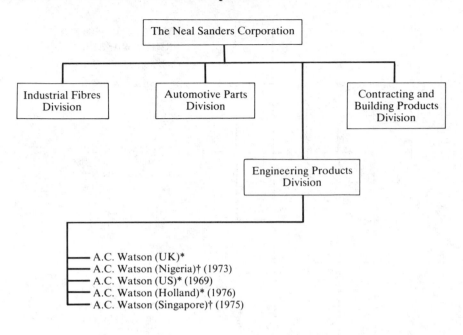

* Manufacturing companies
† Sales subsidiaries

Figure A19.1   The Neal Sanders Corporation

APPENDIX 19.2 Typical Washers, Shims and Helitex Gaskets

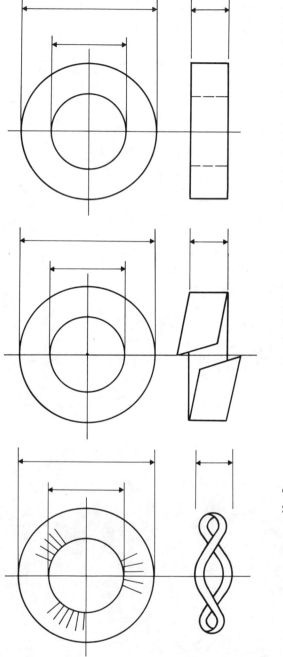

(ALL sizes in millimetres)

BRIGHT WASHERS

Cadmium plated or hardened brass:

Size range

D1	D2	T
1 to 40	2 to 77	0.2 to 6.6

BLACK WASHERS
Cold rolled steel strip-
option zinc plated.

Size range

D1	D2	T
5.5 to 75	9.2 to 120	1 to 11

SPRING WASHERS
Carbon steel hardened, tempered
phosphated oil or lanolin
coated.

Size range

D1	D2	T
3.1 to 50	5.5 to 66.5	1 to 8

CRINKLE WASHERS

Size range

D1	D2	T
1.7 to 21.2	3.5 to 34.7	0.2 to 2.6

(*continued*)

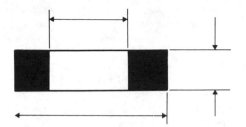

SHIMS

Laminum shim stock, also half
hardened brass aluminium and
stainless steel.

D	D1	T
10 to 150	15 to 190	0.15 to 3.20

OTHER TYPES PRODUCED

Tablock washers, tapered washers
with or without shaft keyways.

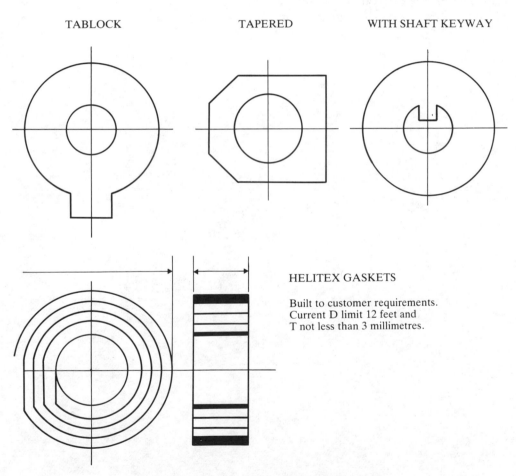

TABLOCK   TAPERED   WITH SHAFT KEYWAY

HELITEX GASKETS

Built to customer requirements.
Current D limit 12 feet and
T not less than 3 millimetres.

Figure A19.2   Typical washers, shims and helitex gaskets

APPENDIX 19.3   Memorandum – Appointment of Stephen Sutcliffe

To: Stephen Sutcliffe   Date: 18.9.75
From: C. Watson, Managing Director
Subject: Appointment

Welcome to the board, and to the new job of Marketing and Sales Director. It is a grand title and 'marketing' is included to be fashionable with the international scene. Frankly you are my *Sales* Director, I hope you will never forget it!

You have a Marketing Services Manager and a small team – do not let them interfere too much, their job is to generate more sales volume by discovering new potential for our products.

My view is that marketing is a luxury, it costs money and you can't measure the results of the achievement – all far too woolly – given a free hand I would rather have another four reps on the road. Sales are all that matter – they get the orders – or at least it's your job to make sure they do – our success to date has proven that good sales service is all that is required to run a business effectively and I don't want to be found wrong. I'm fully aware of the problems ahead, but our research and development team are second to none.

Good luck, it is good to have a man of mature years on the board.

APPENDIX 19.4(a)   Production and Distribution Organization Structure

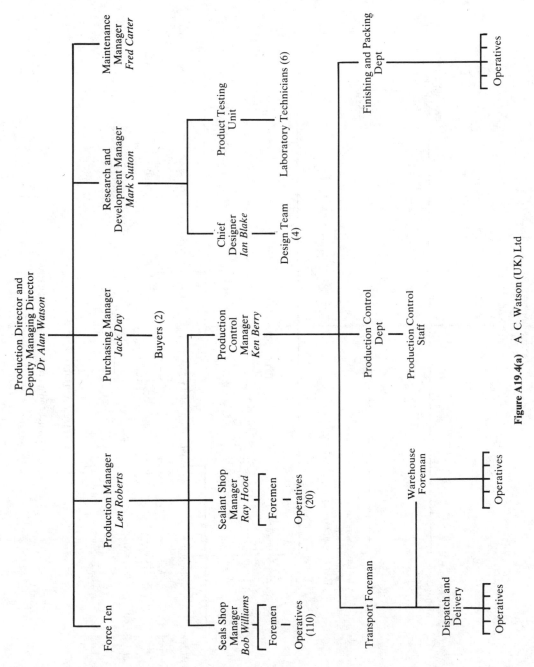

Figure A19.4(a) A. C. Watson (UK) Ltd

Production and distribution organization structure

APPENDIX 19.4(b)   Sales and Marketing Organization Structure

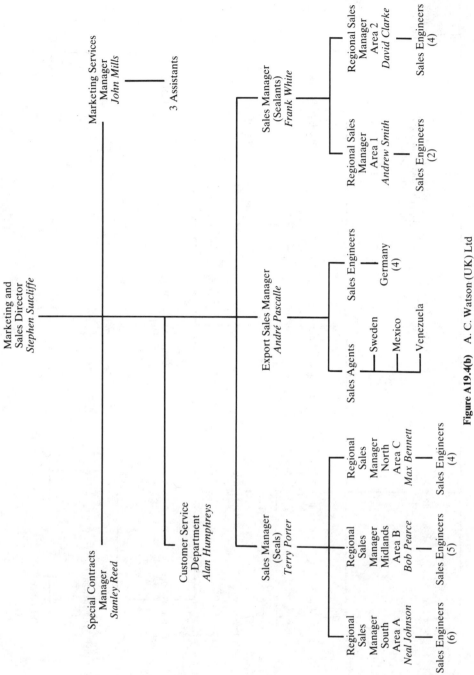

Figure A19.4(b)   A. C. Watson (UK) Ltd

Sales and marketing organization structure

APPENDIX 19.4(c) Sales Areas

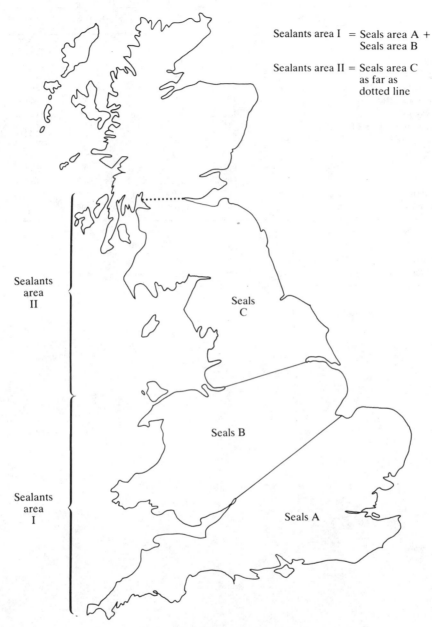

Sealants area I = Seals area A +
Seals area B

Sealants area II = Seals area C
as far as
dotted line

Sealants
area
II

Sealants
area
I

Seals
C

Seals B

Seals A

Figure A19.4(c) Sales areas

APPENDIX 19.5(a)   UK Market Trends by Value (Index 1976 = 100)

	1977	1978	1979	1980	1981	1982*
SEALS						
Washers, shims and metal packings	114	114	132	139	143	145
Helitex-type gaskets	129	142	180	201	211	223
Other gaskets for mechanical engineering end use	131	141	174	193	209	237
Fibre washers and jointings	125	146	150	129	141	172
Automotive gaskets	136	147	167	174	179	189
Laminated brass sheeting and foils	112	132	146	169	185	208
SEALANTS						
Mastics	112	123	156	167	189	203
Ring joint sealants	108	117	131	142	153	167
Compound sealant	118	132	147	167	197	213
Waterproof sealant	107	110	133	143	155	160
INDUSTRY						
Natural gas	124	167	208	239	272	301
Natural gas liquids	130	145	179	250	600	700
Crude oil production	150	352	444	903	1396	1514

*Estimate

Source: ACW Marketing Services Department.

APPENDIX 19.5(b) Initial Appraisal of Market – 1979

Major market segments	Major product groups						
	Washers	Other gaskets	Helitex gaskets	Compound sealants	Ring joint sealants	Fibre washers	Mastics
Oil refineries and petrochemical refining	✓	✓	✓				
Original equipment manufacturing (pumps, compressors and valves)			✓		✓	✓	
Building contractors		✓					✓
Heat exchange and exhaust manufacturing				✓			
The gas industry	✓			✓		✓	
The electrical industry	✓						
Oil exploration companies	✓	✓	✓				
The automotive industry (prime movers)	✓	✓	✓				
Engineering contractors			✓				
Specialist end use				✓	✓	✓	✓
Our competitors							

APPENDIX 19.6   Memorandum – Public Relations Perspective

Dear Stephen,

My observations are as follows:

1. On first arriving the company's name was only visible from one direction when approaching the ACW complex.
2. The reception area and visitors' waiting room do not convey a welcoming atmosphere despite a most efficient receptionist whose telephone manner was commendable.
3. The office staff speak well of the company, are happy in their work and operate with an air of efficiency and all appear most courteous to visitors.
4. The company has a positive sense of identity, but it is poorly conveyed. The company headed notepaper is old, inappropriate to an international image and does not represent the best possible impression.
5. Little use is made of the Neal Sanders centralized publicity facility in London.
6. The salesforce are motivated by goodwill and a positive sense of corporate identity but receive insufficient information and direction from Head Office. Particular weaknesses appeared to be no guidance for cold calling, no sales targets for product groups, an absence of profit contribution knowledge and infrequent individual assessments by their regional managers.

Yours truly,

Peter

APPENDIX 19.7   Sales Analysis – Years Ending 1976–82

Total ACW Sales by Product Group – years ending April 1976–82 (£000s)

Product Group	1976	1977	1978	1979	1980	1981	1982
SEALS							
Washers and shims/ metal packings	572	652	647	866	936	1017	850
Helitex	920	1276	1430	1882	2018	2310	2544
Other gaskets	370	415	497	642	678	688	791
Fibre washers	74	131	230	96	55	72	152
Automotive gaskets	303	474	535	651	704	624	560
Insulation materials	149	193	219	255	94	84	89
Laminated brass sheeting	99	131	153	170	209	123	103
SEALANTS							
Mastics	–	–	–	60	152	332	606
Ring joint sealants	–	–	87	167	180	198	190
Compound sealants	–	–	28	105	195	314	507
Waterproof sealants	–	–	–	11	53	93	132
Total UK sales	2487	3272	3826	4905	5274	5855	6524
Total exports	925	1241	1601	2416	3164	3759	4349
Total sales	3412	4513	5427	7321	8438	9614	10 873

Export Sales by Product Group – years ending April 1978–82 (percentages)

Exports to	1978				1979				1980				1981				1982			
	A	B	C	D	A	B	C	D	A	B	C	D	A	B	C	D	A	B	C	D
Germany	1.3	7.5	5.6	–	0.9	8.1	4.9	–	0.9	9.2	4.9	–	0.7	9.3	4.5	–	0.5	9.6	3.6	0.3
Sweden	–	1.9	0.8	–	–	2.3	1.3	–	–	3.7	1.5	–	0.3	4.6	2.1	–	0.4	4.8	2.2	0.2
Mexico	–	–	–	–	–	0.3	–	–	0.2	0.6	–	–	0.2	0.9	–	–	0.3	1.7	–	–
Venezuela	–	3.2	5.1	–	–	5.4	6.2	–	0.6	7.3	5.6	–	0.7	9.6	5.0	0.4	0.9	9.9	4.9	0.3
Others*	0.7	2.7	0.7	–	0.4	2.6	0.6	–	0.2	2.4	0.4	–	–	0.8	–	–	–	0.4	–	–
Total export % of ACW sales revenue	29.5%				33.0%				37.5%				39.1%				40%			
Representing (£000's)	£1601				£2416				£3164				£3759				£4349			

*Others to: Iran, Libya, United States of America, Nigeria, Singapore.

A Washers and shims.
B Helitex.
C Other gaskets for mechanical engineering end use.
D Fibre washers.

UK Salesforce Analysis for year ended April 1982

	Call rate		New prospects			
Salesforce	No. per week $\overline{X}$	Coefficient of variation† (%)	Each journey cycle	Number converted this year	Journey cycle (days)	Value of orders achieved (£)*
SEALS						
Area A						
B. Anstey	12	16.7	4	6	20	331 197
A. Majors	10	30.0	5	2	20	380 667
C. Whiffin	14	7.1	3	4	20	403 991
D. Allen	9	22.2	2	1	20	350 123
S. Lawrence	8	12.5	1	2	20	420 871
M. Aldred	13	23.1	3	3	20	397 151
Area B						
E. Lees	15	13.3	7	10	25	156 600
P. Fisher	19	15.8	9	6	25	171 417
C. Smith	20	15.0	6	2	25	233 921
S. Hudson	17	17.6	4	5	25	133 089
W. Tyler	13	15.4	3	3	25	87 089
Area C						
H. Brown	9	22.2	3	2	20	589 416
D. Young	11	18.2	3	2	20	617 032
N. Watson	8	12.5	2	3	20	505 473
K. Fletcher	7	28.6	1	0	20	310 079
SEALANTS						
Area 1						
J. Hood	23	21.7	14	11	30	212 327
K. Neal	25	20.0	16	13	30	246 921
A. Summers	19	10.5	12	9	30	202 427
J. Mason	21	14.3	9	6	30	186 325
Area 2						
T. Old	17	17.6	12	5	30	265 200
L. Raven	15	20.0	10	7	30	321 793

*A percentage of orders are placed and the sales accredited to the appropriate territory

† Coefficient of variation $= \dfrac{\text{Standard Deviation}}{\text{Mean } \overline{X}} \times 100$

NB   André Pascalle could not offer comparative data.

UK Sales Revenue Analysis by Region – years ending April 1977–82 (percentages)

	1977	1978	Seals 1979	1980	1981	1982		1978	1979	Sealants 1980	1981	1982
Area A	n/a	40	37	37	35	35	Area 1	2	4	7	10	13
Area B	n/a	23	24	20	18	12						
Area C	n/a	34	32	32	31	31	Area 2	1	3	4	6	9
TOTALS	100	97	93	89	84	78	TOTALS	3	7	11	16	22

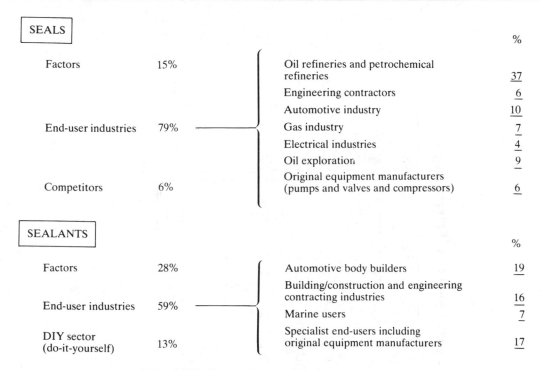

SEALS			%
Factors	15%	Oil refineries and petrochemical refineries	37
		Engineering contractors	6
		Automotive industry	10
End-user industries	79%	Gas industry	7
		Electrical industries	4
		Oil exploration	9
Competitors	6%	Original equipment manufacturers (pumps and valves and compressors)	6

SEALANTS			%
Factors	28%	Automotive body builders	19
End-user industries	59%	Building/construction and engineering contracting industries	16
		Marine users	7
DIY sector (do-it-yourself)	13%	Specialist end-users including original equipment manufacturers	17

Figure A19.7   Home sales breakdown by customer groups

APPENDIX 19.8(a)   Profit Contribution by Product Group – Years Ending April 1976–82 (percentages)

Product group	1976		1977		1978		1979		1980		1981		1982	
	H	E	H	E	H	E	H	E	H	E	H	E	H	E
SEALS														
Washers and shims	16.3	0.8	15.1	1.1	12.2	1.1	12.1	0.7	11.8	1.2	11.1	1.2	10.7	1.3
Helitex	41.1	5.3	37.1	9.4	39.2	10.6	38.0	12.9	37.6	13.0	37.9	17.1	37.8	19.4
Other gaskets	14.1	5.1	12.1	4.9	11.8	4.6	11.1	5.1	10.3	7.1	9.9	7.6	8.4	7.4
Fibre washers	0.3	—	0.6	—	1.1	—	0.2	—	0.1	—	0.2	—	0.7	0.2
Automotive gaskets	12.2	—	14.2	—	13.7	—	12.3	—	11.7	—	8.4	—	6.4	—
Insulation materials	3.2	—	3.7	—	3.7	—	3.9	—	1.8	—	1.0	—	0.7	—
Laminated brass sheeting	1.6	—	1.8	—	1.9	—	1.9	—	2.1	—	1.3	—	0.9	—
	88.8	11.2	84.6	15.4	83.5	16.3	79.5	18.7	75.4	21.3	69.8	25.9	65.6	28.3
SEALANTS														
Mastics	—	—	—	—	—	—	0.2	—	1.2	—	1.9	—	3.3	—
Ring joint sealants	—	—	—	—	0.2	—	1.0	—	0.9	—	0.9	—	0.8	—
Compound sealants	—	—	—	—	*	—	0.6	—	1.0	—	1.1	—	1.5	—
Waterproof sealants	—	—	—	—	—	—	*	—	0.2	—	0.4	—	0.5	—
	—	—	—	—	0.2	—	1.8	—	3.3	—	4.3	—	6.1	—

H – Home trade.
E – Export trade.
*Insignificant amount.

APPENDIX 19.8(b)   Profit and Loss Accounts

A. & C. Watson (UK) Ltd* Profit and Loss Accounts – Years Ending April 1976–82 (£000s)

	1976	1977	1978	1979	1980	1981	1982
Sales*	3412	4513	5427	7321	8438	9614	10873
Cost of sales	2146	2880	3526	4705	5218	6042	6904
Gross profit	1266	1633	1901	2616	3220	3572	3969
Expenses	921	1173	1315	1767	2309	2870	3230
Profit before tax	345	460	586	849	911	702	739
Tax	170	225	291	420	460	360	381
Net profit	175	235	295	429	451	342	358

*Note final accounts for ACW (UK) only, (ACW sales revenue worldwide currently exceeds £25 million).

APPENDIX 19.9   Summary Balance Sheets

A. & C. Watson (UK) Ltd Summary Balance Sheets – Years Ending April 1976–82

	1976	1977	1978	1979	1980	1981	1982
Fixed assets:							
Freehold land and buildings (at cost)	110	250	311	427	530	530	530
Plant, equipment and vehicles (depreciated)	220	320	460	710	779	800	840
Total fixed assets	330	570	771	1137	1309	1330	1370
Current assets:							
Stock and WIP	259	315	472	553	687	842	1064
Debtors	287	395	511	732	914	960	1087
Bank	72	89	121	185	472	585	635
Total current assets	618	799	1104	1470	2073	2387	2786
Current liabilities:							
Creditors	300	441	597	783	912	1025	1120
Dividends	10	11	12	20	20	35	27
Taxation	170	225	291	420	460	360	381
Total current liabilities	480	677	900	1223	1392	1420	1528
Current assets *less* Current liabilities	138	122	204	247	681	967	1258
Total net assets	468	692	975	1384	1990	2297	2628
Financed by:							
Share capital	175	175	175	175	350	350	350
General reserve – retained profit	293	517	800	1209	1640	1947	2278
	468	692	975	1384	1990	2297	2628

QUESTIONS

Stephen Sutcliffe retired on 1 May 1982 and has emigrated to live with his son and daughter-in-law in Australia.

As Duncan Morris you have been appointed at the request of the Neal Sanders Corporation to replace Stephen Sutcliffe.

Previously you were a divisional marketing manager at the Evans Corporation where your track record was regarded highly: much had been achieved during your five years with the company. Now you have returned home to Coventry where you were employed in sales and sales management positions in the automotive industries.

You have been given a clear brief to review the sales and marketing operations at A. & C. Watson Ltd, where there is now a desire at board level for the company to become more marketing oriented!

You are required to prepare a report for Christopher Watson, your Managing Director, for subsequent discussion at a special meeting of the Neal Sanders board which you will be required to attend.

Your report should comprise the following sections:

Section 1   Home and export sales and profit forecasts by product group for the next three years, i.e. until April 1985.

(25 marks)

Section 2   A strategy for the achievement of these forecasts to include the following:
(a) Internal reorganization of the sales and marketing functions.
(b) Management and control of field sales operations.
(c) Your marketing mix plans.

(60 marks)

Section 3   An outline budget itemizing expenditure levels for the achievement of Sections 1 and 2 over the specified period.

(15 marks)

REQUIRED APPROACH TO EACH QUESTION

Section 1 – Home and export sales and profit forecasts by product group for the next three years

The *total* question must be answered, *and* in sufficient depth because this section 'provides the foundation' for the rest of the paper.

Candidates should have prepared, well in advance, much of the requirement for this question.

Section 2 – Strategy to achieve Section 1

(a) *Internal reorganization*: the candidate is given an open brief. The important ingredient is *rationale* – change alone will not gain full credit without the *justification* for it. This section can easily take much more examination time than you intend! Remember that a well-balanced answer to all three parts of Section 2 is required to achieve a reasonable proportion of the allocated marks.

(b) *Management and control of field sales operations*: the distinction required here was between *internal* operations and *field* operations.

Again, with a wealth of data the danger is to overshoot the time allocation for the section. Therefore, a focus is required on key issues rather than a full dissertation on sales management and the control of field force operations.

(c) *Marketing mix plans*: the essense is on the *mix* and not to produce a full marketing plan, which alone would absorb the total three examination hours.

Again a focus on key points is essential. The marketing mix plan *must* be designed to achieve the sales and profit forecasts outlined in Section 1.

Section 3 Budgets

There are various ways to tackle this section but I suggest a reference back to Section 1 is necessary and the additional expenditures incurred should be itemized.

ANSWERS

Section 1 – Sales and profit forecasts – UK and exports to 1985

Total sales Total sales for ACW are expected to increase at between 10 and 12 per cent per annum taking the revenues to approximately £15.5 million by the year ending April 1985. The total forecast is based upon a straight line extrapolation of historic data and applying the forecast factors stated above.

Product group sales The method of forecasting *total* sales is considered legitimate in the light of known data on ACW overall performance.

This overall position is, however, not achieved by proportionate increases within each product group. Each group has different rates of increase and decline in accordance with the changes in market demand, the respective product life cycles and future marketing/sales policy.

Export sales Growth in total export performance is expected to continue and is forecasted to achieve a 45 per cent status on total ACW sales revenue, by year ending April 1985. This projected trend should achieve total export sales of approximately £7 million during this time period.

Sales forecasts These forecasts have been produced in the same format as the core data provided in Appendix 19.7 of the ACW case study (see also tables on page 380).

Profit forecasts The decline in the profit to sales position must be arrested. A 10 per cent profit to sales ratio should be achieved by the year ending April 1985 which will yield a projected net profit before taxation of £1.5 million.

The profit contribution projections have been extended in the format provided in Appendix 19.8 of the case.

In percentage terms a growth in contribution is expected from exports in accordance with the increase in sales revenue.

On the home market, sealants are expected also to increase profit contribution.

Jointly, the increase in contribution in these two areas will reduce the dependence on profits from home market seals sales, i.e., in *percentage* terms. Volume profits in *value* terms will naturally increase in accordance with profit projections. A percentage decline does not represent a decline in financial terms.

Profit contribution and profit forecasts are shown in the tables on page 381. Profit to sales ratios have been modified from the case data to account for the economics/diseconomics of scale and the associated 'on-costs' adjustments of each.

Total ACW sales forecast by product group – years ending April 1983–85 (£000s)

Product group	1983	1984	1985
SEALS			
Washers and shims/ metal packings	800	725	650
Helitex	2652	3400	3900
Other gaskets	850	1000	750
Fibre washers	180	200	200
Automotive gaskets	500	400	300
Insulation materials	50	25	–
Laminated brass	70	50	–
SEALANTS			
Mastics	995	1200	1550
Ring joint sealants	190	190	190
Compound sealants	600	700	800
Waterproof sealants	150	160	185
Total UK sales	7227	8050	8525
Total exports	5023	5950	6975
Total sales	12 250	14 000	15 500

Export sales forecast by product group – years ending April 1983–85 (percentages)

	1983				1984				1985			
Exports to	A	B	C	D	A	B	C	D	A	B	C	D
Germany	0.4	9.9	3.0	0.3	0.3	10.2	3.0	0.2	0.3	10.5	2.5	0.2
Sweden	0.5	5.4	2.5	0.2	0.6	5.9	2.7	0.2	0.6	6.5	3.0	0.1
Mexico	0.5	2.1	–	–	0.6	2.7	–	–	0.6	4.0	0.3	–
Venezuela	1.0	10.6	4.1	0.3	1.1	11.0	3.5	0.3	1.2	11.8	3.0	0.2
Others*	–	0.2	–	–	–	0.2	–	–	–	0.2	–	–
Total export % of ACW sales revenue	41%				42.5%				45%			
Representing (£000's)	£5023				£5950				£6975			

A Washers and shims.
B Helitex.
C Other gaskets for mechanical engineering end use.
D Fibre washers.
*Others to: Iran, Libya, United States of America, Nigeria, Singapore.

Profit contribution by product group – year ending April 1983–85 (percentages)

Product group	1983		1984		1985	
	H	E	H	E	H	E
SEALS						
Washers and shims	10.0	1.2	9.5	1.0	9.0	0.8
Helitex	37.5	21.6	37.5	24.8	37.5	28.2
Other gaskets	7.4	7.0	6.0	6.5	4.5	6.0
Fibre washers	1.0	0.2	1.0	0.2	1.0	0.2
Automotive gaskets	5.0	–	4.0	–	3.0	–
Insulation materials	0.3	–	–	–	–	–
Laminated brass sheeting	0.8	–	0.5	–	–	–
	62.0	30.0	58.5	32.5	55.0	35.0
SEALANTS						
Mastics	5.0	–	5.7	–	6.5	–
Ring joint sealants	0.8	–	0.8	–	0.8	–
Compound sealants	1.7	–	1.9	–	2.0	–
Waterproof sealants	0.5	–	0.6	–	0.7	–
	8.0	–	9.0	–	10.0	–
Profit forecasts*	£857 000		£1 190 000		£1 500 000	

*Before tax.
H – Home trade.
E – Export trade.

Profit forecasts by product group – year ending April 1983–85 (£000s)

	1983		1984		1985	
	H	E	H	E	H	E
SEALS	531	257	696	387	825	525
SEALANTS	69	–	107	–	150	–
TOTAL	857		1190		1500	

H – Home trade.
E – Export trade.

Section 2(a) – Internal re-organization of sales and marketing

The need The ACW sales and marketing organization has developed over time with the expansion of the company. The task that has now to be achieved is to attain the sales and profit targets outlined in Section 1 over the specified three-year period. As Duncan Morris, the newly appointed Sales and Marketing Director, my first duty is to the ACW organization, my peers and my subordinate staff.

Reorganization is disruptive and is conflict generating in its very nature. My objective will be to introduce change, effectively, with the minimum amount of upheaval and ensure that the change secures the full participation of all involved. This means that timing is vital, the 'new broom sweeps clean' syndrome may serve to alienate rather than to secure additional commitment.

To become known, accepted, involved and trusted is a first priority before the climate is right for further organizational development. Then it is a matter of personal judgement on when to initiate organizational change.

Before the plan is drawn up a series of formal meetings and more informal gatherings will be necessary to assess staff reaction and solicit views on a wide range of company-oriented issues.

Administration, sales records and the marketing information systems To achieve the forecasted growth, the internal organizational efficiency must be considered as a major priority – 'first put one's house in order!'

The need for two separate sets of sales territories, i.e., sealants and seals, appears largely historical. These should be rationalized into a new common format that is suitable and agreeable to all concerned, and also improves the internal efficiency of data search, administration and performance appraisal.

With the growth potential of sealants, these should be absorbed into the seals regions and be known geographically as Northern, Southern and Midland regions. The short-term effect would mean that Andrew Smith is Sealants Regional Sales Manager for the Midlands and Southern regions instead of Sealants Area I.

Sales management A distinction must be drawn between sales management, marketing management and the joint direction of both functions. As Duncan Morris my existing span of control is too wide, I do not need to be involved in 'day-to-day' operations, but more with the strategic and longer term plans for the future. Sufficient operational pressure will exist at board level; therefore, a new position of UK Sales Manager should be created and filled within the next nine-month period. This may present a promotion opportunity for one of the existing Sales Managers and create internal promotion opportunities for others – also stimulating additional motivation from within the sales organization.

The new sales structure would, therefore, be as follows:

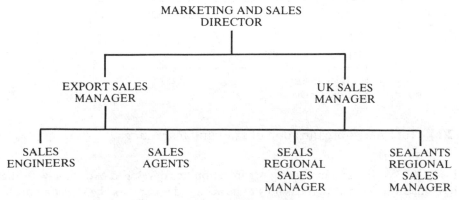

Figure A19.9   Sales management structure

The marketing function For the immediate term in my role of Marketing Director, I would plan and direct marketing operations. A careful assessment of the role, function and contribution of the marketing services *staff* function would be undertaken with a view to the assessment of the value of such a unit.

By the end of the three-year period, the marketing function should have *line* authority over sales at middle management level. The need for a Special Contracts Manager, a Customer Services Manager and a Marketing Services Manager reporting to me directly is questionable.

This could be overcome by introducing a Marketing Manager into the structure and leaving these as subordinate functions to the new Marketing Manager. The medium-term plan must wait until I can assess the abilities of existing Sales Managers and determine their strengths and weaknesses, likely response to retraining and reaction to another new executive. My objective is to ensure the ACW company becomes marketing oriented, but this cannot be at the expense of alienating the sales function.

Promotion and training *into* a marketing management position may be a more desirable alternative than bringing in yet more 'new blood'.

A career path for those IM Diploma holders within the sales staff could then be secured, and this may encourage others into training for these most worthy professional qualifications.

Marketing orientation As the director with profit responsibility, marketing planning is an essential process. A high priority must be placed on the integration of the marketing plan into the company's planning and budgetary control cycles. Liaison and agreement must be secured across the board, once top level commitment to marketing principles can be ensured then organizational development and restructuring can follow smoothly with the minimum of top level resistance.

Section 2(b) – Management and control of field sales operations

The following problems are apparent:

- Resistance to sales training among older reps.
- No commission system.
- Current method of payment not considered suitable.
- André Pascalle, the Export Sales Manager, appears 'a law unto himself'.
- Within the UK journey cycles are not standardized.
- Journey cycles are not coordinated between the UK and export sales teams.
- The 'phone-in feedback system' may have operational difficulties.
- UK and export reps meet only at the annual sales conference.
- An apparent lack of sales planning and control manifest by the variation of performance of reps and call rates, prospects, and order value between the two sales forces at national and regional level. To ensure that the company is 'geared up' to achieve the sales forecasted, the above problems must be considered as immediate, and, therefore, carry a high priority for action.

The following action is recommended for implementation with the next six-month period.

Training External sales training consultants should be appointed to design and implement a sales training programme based upon the training needs of the company and the individual needs of the representatives.

A simple sales training course is *not* envisaged but a consultative period, spent in the field, as a diagnostic exercise to determine accurately the specific needs and then design the most appropriate cost effective programme with periodic reviews.

Payment A new payment structure should be negotiated, with a commission element that:

(a) satisfies present complaints; and
(b) stimulates more sales.

Export sales Sales targets must be set for André Pascalle's team. While his 'power base' may be difficult to influence in the short term, he can still be made accountable for the achievement of targets. The operation must not only be tightened up but must also be communicated effectively to ensure that projected sales performance is attained. The German market must be considered as a first priority for increased accountability.

Journey cycles All UK and export journey cycles should be standardized and the most suitable period accepted. The four-week cycle, i.e., 20 working days, is recommended.

Phone-ins The operational difficulties must be investigated and remedied. If problems are insurmountable a new system should be implemented.

Sales conferences Two conferences should be held annually – one three-day *planned* event, one two-day with a social agenda for reps' wives.

'Special orders' Higher stock levels should be kept, if practicable, to avoid disruption to production and improve customer service.

Sales planning and control A *system* must be designed, implemented and maintained so that accountability starts with the representative and ends at my office as Sales and Marketing Director. The current system is weak at all levels throughout the organization.

Standards must be set and agreed in joint consultation with the regional sales managers. Once agreed, they will be responsible for the implementation of the sales control system.

A full investigation followed by a written report on regional performance followed by a set of reports on individual representatives will be necessary to evaluate current performance *before* imposing new standards.

Reasons for the differences between sales forces *and* reps within regions must be pursued.

Standards must be set for:

– Call rates.
– Variation in call rates per week.
– Number of new prospects each week.
– Targets set for new prospect conversion.
– Sales quotas set for each region.
– Sales targets set for each representative.

A new sales-maintaining feedback system must be designed and implemented to provide Head Office with regular current information on field activity and also to inform reps of their performance against standards and targets set.

Regular reviews, i.e., monthly, must be made with reps by regional sales managers (RSMs) and in turn between the RSMs and the sales managers.

The newly appointed UK Sales Manager will take overall responsibility for sales performance.

Section 2(c) – Marketing mix plans to year ending April 1985

Within the constraints of this paper these plans will be outline plans only and be designed to achieve the quantitative forecasts set in Section 1.

Corporate objectives

- Achieve continued development of ACW company operations both at home and overseas.
- Improve the rate of return on capital employed in the current climate of industrial recession.
- Re-establish ACW profitability through company-wide marketing orientation and action.

Marketing objectives Within the framework of ACW corporate policy and the agreed corporate plan:

- Achieve sales of £15.5 million and a net profit before tax of £1.5 million by year ending April 1985.
- Achieve export sales contribution of 45 per cent of total ACW sales revenue.
- Exploit profitable segments of the home and overseas markets.
- Rationalize the existing product range to eliminate cheap unprofitable products.
- Reorganize the sales and marketing functions.
- Maintain and expand the market dominance in the field of spirally wound gaskets (Helitex).
- Develop the market for sealants and further penetrate the mastics market.
- Provide a sound basis for marketing planning activities.

Market research To ensure that the company's marketing strategy is planned to achieve maximum profitability, in-house desk research should be conducted by the marketing services team. This research would comprise an in-depth pareto exercise to measure the profit contribution *vis-à-vis* sales volume by the end-use market and customer classification. This would determine with some accuracy the 'real' importance of the identified market segments and offer direction for future action.

The internal information system should be fully conversant with all sources of marketing information relating to the markets which the company services. A close watch must be maintained on uncontrollable variables and the future effects of further environmentalist lobbies.

Field research should be undertaken to determine the attitude towards ACW among customer groups and suppliers and test the reaction towards the new promotional material.

As Duncan Morris it is my impression that much has yet to be achieved in terms of corporate image.

For my benefit as the new Sales and Marketing Director I would require a full environmental review of the market to be conducted internally. This would include:

- Market(s) profiles.
- Customer/end-user profiles.
- Competitor profile.
- Product/service profile.
- Market segment analysis.
- Target market identification.

The product plan Upon joining the company, it was apparent to me that efficiency can be increased and profitability improved if we produce that for which there is a substantial market. Some products carried do not yield sufficient return and result in company working capital being tied up in 'dead stock'.

It is proposed that pending a more detailed analysis the following ranges are dropped:

- Laminated brass sheeting.
- Insulation materials.

Sealants Sealant sales should be restricted to the UK market to allow for a period of consolidation. The company cannot stretch the sales resource too wide, exploitation and further penetration potential exists on the home market.

The mastics market should be considered as a 'number one priority' for the sealants salesforce for the next three-year period.

Seals Helitex must remain the 'number one' product and be pushed hard to meet sales and profit targets both at home and overseas.

Sales of Helitex produce sales of 'other gaskets' and 'washers and shims' and the trade should not be overlooked.

Further product development in terms of specification, tolerances, etc., should be aimed for to attain further market development for this product. New market applications should be explained through product differentiation.

Products for export markets The major product groups should continue to be pushed, i.e., washers and shims, Helitex, other gaskets and fibre washers.

Helitex will remain the 'number one export' with further market penetration in all cited countries. Venezuela and Germany will remain the most important markets in sales volume terms. Mexico and Sweden are expected to achieve increased significance over the next three-year period.

It is not planned to extend 'width' of the export range at this stage but to search for development within the existing range, to improve 'depth' of products offered to actual and potential industrial buyers.

Increased production capacity utilization must be aimed for at this stage by increasing output from the existing production resource and thereby to increase company profitability.

Product development For the medium term the company must ensure that the sealants market is given substantial support to allow mastics to become the number two company product to reduce ACW dependence on Helitex for sales and profits.

The pricing plan It is apparent from the case that different pricing methods are being used for the different product ranges. This is shown by the variation in the profit contribution to sales situation. The figures below (all percentages) are for sales (S) and profit (P):

	1980		1982		1984*	
	S	P	S	P	S	P
Washers and shims	19.6	13.0	15.1	12.0	11.6	10.5
Helitex	61.5	50.6	65.4	57.2	72.2	62.3
Other gaskets	25.3	11.1	22.8	15.8	21.6	12.5
Automotive	13.3	11.7	8.6	6.4	5.0	4.0

* = Forecast

The position is clouded further by the different apparent pricing structure in export markets.

The projections for 1984 indicate the pricing strategies to be applied. 'Cost-plus' is not appropriate owing to the price sensitivity in certain competitive market sectors.

Sales of washers and shims are expected to assume less importance, but none the less a price increase will yield higher pro rata profit contribution.

The sales of Helitex dominate and the product USPs allow the company to change premium prices to maximize the profit margin from this product range. Price increases in the medium term for Helitex must be considered carefully; to achieve increased penetration in the 'multi-markets' prices will need to be softened accordingly, and hence the profit margin per unit reduced in real terms. Longer term pricing considerations must be given attention because ACW is heading into a situation where sales and profits are too heavily dependent upon the performance of Helitex.

It is assumed that the range of 'other gaskets' is various in nature, but also that a competitive market for these exists. It is also assumed that a significant percentage of other gasket sales is derived from Helitex sales, because the two key market segments of oil exploration and oil refining are serviced by Helitex and 'other gaskets'.

To retain market position, the margin on other gaskets will be reduced and by adopting this stance competition may be held at bay.

These markets represent 46 per cent of home end-user industry seals sales and should be handled with care. To substantiate further this recommendation there can be little brand loyalty for other gaskets, whereas Helitex, for the immediate term at least, remains unique.

Promotion

Above the line Above-the-line activity in the past has been limited to editorial coverage for Helitex. It is proposed to introduce advertising in the trade press to support the selling effort of the two field forces. In turn this will assist the re-motivation of the force brought about by re-training and the new payment structure.

Target audiences Advertising will be directed at the trade to 'push' additional products into the distribution pipeline.

The target audiences will, therefore, be factors, industrial specifiers and purchasing officers in end-user industries for both seals and sealants. This will take up 80 per cent of the press advertising budget.

The DIY sector should also be developed to create awareness and stimulate interest in ACW Sealants.

Budget A budget of £25 000 should be appropriated for 1983 and reviewed annually thereafter. This modest budget will not only be the first expenditure on advertising, but also overcome a threshold problem at board level of appropriating company funds to such a purpose.

All above-the-line activity will be restricted to press.

Impact To obtain additional mileage from editorial coverage, 'feature ads' should be used, and in addition advertising support to editorial offered to publications which are read by the identified target audiences.

The prime objective is to maximize exposure (OTS) among the target groups; therefore, matching readership profiles of the trade publications to the specified target audiences will be essential.

Below the line In accordance with the total review of sales planning, and the use of external sales training consultants, existing sales support materials must be appraised and modified/ supplemented where necessary. This includes sales aids, samples, sales kits and technical data sheets.

Keeping the ACW and Helitex names in the forefront of the market is vital.

In this market it is considered inappropriate to offer promotional gimmicks, but selective 'give aways' including pens, diaries, calendars and phone note pads are considered appropriate.

Budget It is considered that below-the-line activity is more important in this market and, furthermore, direct sales support is required now! A budget of £75 000 is proposed for below-the-line activity, which will total £100 000 with the proposed above-the-line activity.

Impact The combined effect of new sales incentives and sales planning plus a *planned* programme of advertising and sales promotion, will not only achieve an element of surprise in the market, but also stimulate sales because this is the first major promotional push in the company's stated history.

Feedback The effectiveness of advertising and sales promotion activities must be monitored closely to measure, as far as is possible, the effect in terms of changed attitudes and sales response. This will help me, as Duncan Morris, to press for an increased budget for the following and succeeding years.

Public relations A climate of uniformed opinion should be maintained between ACW and the identified publics.

Public relations activities should not be haphazard acts of public spiritedness which are aimed at securing maximum exposure through the exploitation of the press and other media, but planned events, integrated with the total ACW marketing communications activity.

Distribution It is assumed from Appendix 19.7 that the following main channels exist:

1.	ACW (UK)	——————	UK seals and sealant factors	—————— Indirect
2.	ACW (UK)	——————	UK seals and sealant end-user industries	—————— Direct
3.	ACW (UK)	——————	Export through sales agents	—————— Sweden Mexico Venezuela
4.	ACW (UK)	——————	Export through sales engineering	—————— Germany

To achieve the forecasted sales revenues in home and export markets, the volumes of products flowing down these channels will all increase.

With the increase in projected export business, and taking into account company UK sales projections and the trend analysis by *value* in Appendix 19.5, priorities between and within these channels will change.

The maintenance of trade channel alliances is vital to ensure that the company retains a balanced perspective with reference to these channels.

This may require a shift in selling emphasis to ensure equitable work loads and returns to gain maximum advantage from the existing channels.

The German market, in particular, must be reviewed to consider the cost/benefit of the attention currently given to this single market.

The development of German sales agents as used in Sweden, Mexico and Venezuela should be investigated.

A feasibility study should be conducted within the next 12 months to evaluate this alternative. Channel efficiency must be the prime consideration at all times.

Section 3 – Budgets

For Section 1 – Sales and profit forecasts for year ending April (£000s)

	1983	1984	1985
Total sales	12 250	14 000	15 500
Cost of sales	7 750	8 820	9 750
Gross profit	4 500	5 180	5 750
Profit before tax	857	1 190	1 500

For Section 2 – Sales and marketing expenditure levels during the period to April 1985

The following items are areas of *additional* expenditure, that would not otherwise have been incurred. These items have been absorbed within the cost of sales figures above.

	£
MARKET RESEARCH	
Desk and field research	7 000*
Feasibility study (distribution)	2 500*
SALES	
Sales training and consulting services	10 000*
Administration and MIS changes	8 000*
Sales planning system design and implementation	5 000
New UK Sales Manager (incl. on-costs and car)	20 000
Sales conference	5 500
MARKETING	
New Marketing Manager (incl. on-costs and car)	25 000
Marketing planning administration	5 500
Advertising	25 000
Sales promotion	75 000
Public relations	5 000
CONTINGENCY	16 500
	210 000

*A substantial proportion considered as non-recurring charges.
NB   Should the feasibility study result in a sales agency decision for Germany, savings may be made by the reduction/re-deployment of the representatives involved.

TWENTY

CASE STUDY WITH SPECIMEN ANSWER

A. & R. Baxter Ltd (Service Marketing)

Albert and Robin Baxter founded their private limited company in 1953 following the coronation of Queen Elizabeth II. They started in business by hiring caravans for touring holidays in England.

Ten years later caravans were available for short period hire for touring holidaymakers for destinations throughout the United Kingdom and Western Europe.

In addition, caravans on permanent sites at coastal resorts throughout the South of England could be hired.

Today, A. & R. Baxter Ltd designs and manufactures caravans of a variety of sizes and specifications which are sold direct or through concessionaires throughout the United Kingdom. The touring caravan hire business has been retained in addition to the hire of caravans on permanent holiday village sites and caravan parks throughout the EEC countries and Spain. The association in the leisure industry between caravanning and camping provides a common need for equipment and related supplies. This inspired the Baxter brothers to open specialist retail outlets to meet the demand from people who joined the growth in popularity for this form of holiday.

Currently, despite development problems, several retail outlets known as 'BAXTER'S' serve the counties of Yorkshire and Lancashire. Sensing a change in the market and with the coincident growth in the 'package holiday' business for overseas destinations – and the sun – the company took a bold step into the travel agency arena.

Currently six 'BAXTER'S Travel Shops', as they are known, have been opened. Plans have been agreed to extend this number to ten within the next two years.

The most recent outlet opened specializes in the 'flight only' business – a market segment which appears to be growing rapidly, particularly in London where immediate access to international airlines and the associated travel trade may be enjoyed.

Company interest in Spain has very recently stimulated yet further diversification to the Canary Islands, in particular the island of Tenerife. To exploit the very real growth in tourism to Tenerife, Baxter's have linked up with a property development company on the island to build a new holiday village complex of 500 units. A new Spanish company, Parque Montana s.a., has been formed as a joint venture with financial backing from a leading London based merchant bank in addition to funds from Spanish and Middle Eastern sources.

Planning permission has been granted, building works have commenced and initial sales have been taken on site.

The estimated completion date of the development now known as Parque Montana is December 1987.

Building works have been planned in three phases of 160 housing units with provision for shops, restaurants and community services in the remaining 20 units.

Phase I will be completed for occupancy by December 1985 with Phases II and III planned for the month of December in succeeding years.

The new development is just 2 kilometres from Playa de las Americas, the largest international tourist resort on the south side of the island and less than 10 kilometres from the beautiful resort and harbour of Los Cristianos, a major tourist attraction.

Phase I of Parque Montana is to be sold to private buyers, principally from the United Kingdom but also from France and West Germany.

The development and popularity of 'time sharing', the ownership of property within the Canary Islands and throughout the world, has led the board of Parque Montana s.a. to consider seriously the option of a time-sharing model for Phase II.

Baxter Ltd is now experiencing a significant transitionary period in the organization with growth, diversification and decline occurring simultaneously.

Concerned about the next five years, Albert and Robin, inspired by Sir Adrian Baxter, have instructed a team of management consultants to conduct a total review of business operations.

It is expected that the consultants will identify the key problem areas the company currently faces and could reasonably anticipate in the next five years, then produce corporate and marketing plans with the detailed financial implications of each.

APPENDICES TO CHAPTER 20

20.1   Company Organization Chart and Personnel Profiles
20.2   Baxter's Camping and Caravanning Retail Outlet Profile
20.3   Baxter's Camping and Caravanning Sales Revenues – Years Ending 31 March 1981–85
20.4   Baxter's Range of Caravans and Related Sales Revenues
20.5   Baxter's Travel Agencies – Profile and Turnover
20.6   Parque Montana s.a. Organization Chart and Associated Notes
20.7   Tenerife – a Profile
20.8   Introductory Letter to Clients
20.9   Typical Investment Appraisal on Purchase of a Parque Montana Property
20.10 Price Profile and Availability of Housing on Selected Developments at Playa de las Americas and Los Cristianos
20.11 Time-Sharing Models on Tenerife
20.12 Maps
20.13 Typical Apartments on Parque Montana
20.14 Baxter's UK Retail Sites

APPENDIX 20.1   Company Organization Chart and Personnel Profiles

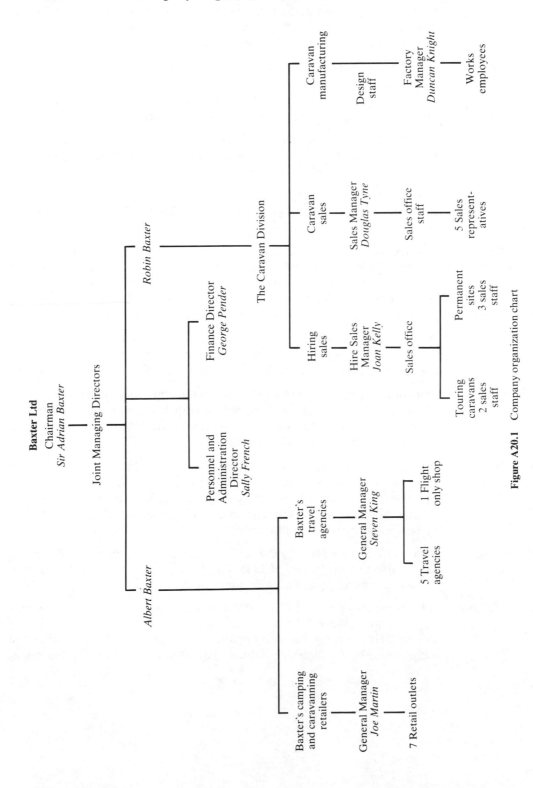

Figure A20.1   Company organization chart

Sir Adrian Baxter	Appointed 1953. Chairman of two other large companies associated with travel and related leisure industry. Senior committee member of the English Tourist Board Advisory Body. A respected figure in city finance circles. Fellow of the Institute of Marketing. Aged 76.
Albert Baxter	Aged 54. Elder of the two brothers. Former noted mountain climber, sportsman. Other financial interests in sports clothing and yachting accessories companies in each of which he holds a 20 per cent shareholding. Wife, Spanish, owns banana plantations in Canary Islands.
Robin Baxter	At 50, a dedicated workaholic. Single. Few interests outside the business. Enjoys visiting the European sites 'in season'. Has developed expertise in caravan design. No other business interests.
Sally French	Appointed June 1983 after three years as Assistant Personnel Officer in a confectionery factory. Distant relative of Sir Adrian. Her position and job specification are under review.
George Pender	Chartered accountant with developed expertise in the financial management of foreign investments. Appointed April 1983 on the basis of personal recommendation through Sir Adrian's 'friends in the City'. To date has set up profit centres within Baxter's and contributed significantly to company profitability. He is expected to take up an equity option in Baxter's this year.
Joe Martin	Appointed as an office junior 20 years ago. Seven years in current position. At 43 he holds the respect of the shop managers but would like to move to another area of the company to avoid 'becoming stale' in his current job.
Steven King	Appointed April 1984 from a national travel agent chain after seven years in the travel business. At 29 he is highly motivated, has won the confidence of Albert Baxter, has a Diploma of the Institute of Marketing and could be promoted further within the organization.
Joan Kelly	Married, three children under ten years of age. Started with the company five years ago as a Sales Assistant and since then has replaced all sales staff under her control to overcome the frustration and personality clashes she previously experienced. The young team are ladies under 25. She will be taking maternity leave in two months' time.
Douglas Tyne	With the company for 14 years as Sales Manager. At 62 he will be taking early retirement at the end of 1985. He owns a caravan site in the south of France, at which he plans to enjoy some more time.
Duncan Knight	A long-standing personal friend of Albert Baxter – both were active climbers together. At 56 Duncan is content to spend the rest of his working life with Baxter's. He has a good working relationship with the works employees and has a reputation for meeting production deadlines within specified budgets.

APPENDIX 20.2   Baxter's Camping and Caravanning Retail Outlet Profile

Outlet number	Town	Date opened	Current number of staff (incl. manager)		Manager	Manager's date of birth	Date of appointment as manager
			FT	PT			
1*	Sheffield	1.1.61	3	3	Don Adams	1.7.30	1.1.61
2*	Leeds	1.1.66	3	3	Don Adams	1.7.30	1.1.66
3*	Halifax	1.6.67	2	4	Fred Long	6.7.29	1.1.73
4	Manchester	1.3.68	4	3	Alan Bailey	16.5.22	1.3.68
5	Bolton	1.9.68	2	1	Alan Bailey	16.5.22	1.9.68
6	Stockport	1.6.73	2	1	Keith Longton	18.8.41	14.3.81
7	Wigan	1.1.77	2	2	John Galpin	23.11.43	17.5.80
8	Manchester	1.1.79	–	–	Alan Bailey	16.5.22	1.1.79
9	Huddersfield	1.2.80	–	–	Tom Daley	19.5.29	1.2.80

FT = full-time; PT = part-time.
*Freehold sites owned by Baxter Ltd.

APPENDIX 20.3   Baxter's Camping and Caravanning Sales Revenues – Years Ending 31 March 1981–85 (£000s)

Outlet number	Town	1981	1982	1983	1984	1985
1	Sheffield	190	200	253	278	290
2	Leeds	178	194	236	250	275
3	Halifax	83	89	93	96	100
4	Manchester	213	243	225	196	185
5	Bolton	67	73	81	83	87
6	Stockport	81	88	76	58	30
7	Wigan	57	65	73	77	81
8	Manchester	43	51	31	–	–
9	Huddersfield	37	26	–	–	–

NB   Outlet 9 closed end February 1982.
Outlet 8 closed December 1983.
Outlet 6 closing July 1985.
Gross margin on sales averages 35 per cent.

APPENDIX 20.4   Baxter's Range of Caravans and Related Sales Revenues

Baxter range of caravans

Model†	Design year	Price (inc. VAT)*	Berths	Width (ft-in)	Total height (ft-in)	Body length (ft-in)	Shipping length (ft-in)
		£					
Robin	1981	2689	2	5–05	6–06	9–10	13–00
Swift	1983	4247	4	7–03	8–00	14–05	18–06
Kite	1984	6372	3–4	7–02	8–02	17–07	20–10
Buzzard	1980	4920	6	7–01	8–03	18–03	22–05
Hawk	1982	6357	4	7–01	8–01	17–05	20–09
Eagle	1983	7125	5	7–03	8–03	19–01	23–05

*Value added tax at 15 per cent. Price increases net of
VAT: 1980   1981   1982   1983   1984   1985
     +9%   Nil   +10%   +6%   Nil   +5%
†The Kestrel is to be launched in June 1985.

Baxter range of caravans – standard fittings

Model	Toilet compartment	Shower	Provisions for mains electricity supply	Oven	Water heater	Space heater	Refrigerator	Double glazing
Robin	Y	N	N	N	N	N	N	N
Swift	Y	N	N	N	N	Y	Y	Y
Kite	Y	Y	Y	Y	Y	Y	Y	Y
Buzzard	Y	N	N	N	N	N	Y	Y
Hawk	Y	Y	Y	Y	Y	Y	Y	Y
Eagle	Y	Y	Y	Y	Y	Y	Y	Y

Y = Yes; N = No.

Baxter range of caravans – unit sales

Model	1981	1982	1983	1984	1985*
Robin	77	179	243	312	400
Swift	–	–	103	196	250
Kite	–	–	–	127	225
Buzzard	174	260	270	250	185
Hawk	–	65	190	103	75
Eagle	–	–	60	90	125

*Estimate
NB An add and drop policy is applied, with an average model life
of four years. Sales in 1981, including former models, amounted to
£1.5 million.

Baxter's Caravan Division
Sales Revenue from Hiring on Permanent Sites within EC and Spain† (£000s)

	1981	1982	1983	1984	1985*
Belgium	–	–	8	17	27
Denmark	–	–	–	–	–
France	104	110	121	152	178
Greece	–	–	–	–	15
West Germany	–	–	4	8	11
Irish Republic	–	–	6	8	8
Italy	–	5	10	15	19
Luxembourg	–	–	–	–	–
The Netherlands	–	–	–	–	–
United Kingdom	110	114	126	140	150
	(125)	(215)	(163)	(83)	(30)
Spain	–	15	40	40	60

*Estimate.
†The entry of Spain into the European Community (EC) is expected in 1986.

APPENDIX 20.5   Baxter's Travel Agencies – Profile and Turnover

Baxter's travel agencies – outlet profile

Outlet number	Town	Date opened	FT	PT*	Manager	Manager's date of birth	Date of joining as a Baxter's employee
1‡	Sheffield	1. 3.79	4	2	David Rosen	3. 8.55	15. 6.83
2	Leeds	1. 4.81	3	2	Julie Birch	4.11.60	1. 3.82
3‡	Huddersfield	1. 4.82	4	3	Andrea Lamb	16. 5.63	1. 3.82
4‡	Manchester	1. 2.83	6	–	John Wood	11.12.56	3. 5.83
5	Doncaster	1. 1.84	3	–	Kate Minster	17. 1.62	1. 2.84
6†	Manchester	1.11.84	2	1	Mary James	15. 7.50	5. 6.82

Current number of staff

FT = full-time; PT = part-time..
*Saturdays only part time
†Flight-only sales.
‡Freehold sites owned by Baxter Ltd.
NB Baxter's is a member of the Association of British Travel Agents (ABTA).

Baxter's travel agencies – sales revenues for years ending 31 March 1981–85. Sales in holiday/flight booking value (£000s)

Outlet number	Town	1981	1982	1983	1984	1985^E
1	Sheffield	0.505	0.655	0.790	0.950	1.150
2	Leeds	0.360	0.785	1.125	1.750	2.250
3	Huddersfield	–	0.336	0.671	1.230	1.950
4	Manchester	–	–	1.125	2.150	3.300
5	Doncaster	–	–	–	0.565	0.780
6†	Manchester	–	–	–	0.020	0.185

NB Baxter gross income from commission on bookings averages 10 per cent; net profit approximately $2\frac{1}{2}$ per cent on bookings.
†Flight-only sales.
E Estimate.

APPENDIX 20.6   Parque Montana s.a. Organization Chart and Notes

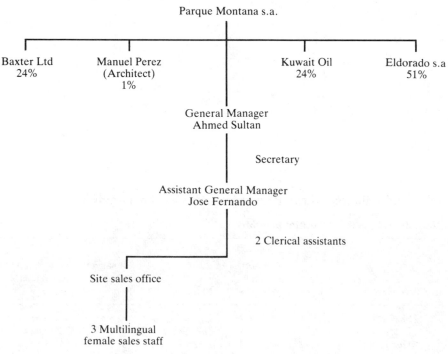

Figure A20.6   Parque Montana s.a. organization chart

Notes to Parque Montana s.a.

The company was formed in 1983, with the shareholdings designated in the organization chart. Ahmed Sultan was jointly appointed as General Manager by the board of directors, which comprised the Managing Directors or their nominees from each organization. Albert Baxter has taken responsibility for the venture for Baxter Ltd.

General Manager   Ahmed Sultan, known to all as 'Andy', is single, 39 years of age, studied building and construction engineering in England, and had five years' experience in construction management in Kuwait, his birth place, although until his current appointment he was General Manager of the Sultan family export trading business based in Madrid, and hence is a fluent Spanish speaker.

His responsibilities to Parque Montana s.a. are diverse, but cover the total management of the Parque Montana site. He controls the building contractors and hence the building works, is responsible for the maintenance of building schedules and for the quality of the finished units to the customer.

While the initial selling process is conducted by the site sales office, he personally handles all details relating to the financial and legal elements of each transaction. He is thus well known by the banks and government administration departments in Playa de las Americas and in the island's capital, Santa Cruz.

Assistant General
Manager   At 27, Jose Fernando is young, inexperienced and just three months in the position. His appointment has been made to enable him to learn the job and take more responsibility as Phase II of the building operations commences. He is the son of the Managing Director of Eldorado s.a. and is fluent only in Spanish.

Site Sales Office   The office is housed in one of the units and hence represents a 'show house' for prospective purchasers to view.

A small-scale model of the total development is available to view to enable interested parties to consider their purchase in the context of the completed development – albeit in three years' time.

Deposits are taken of £500, or 100 000 pesetas, to secure the site. Units sold are marked on the model to enable the buyer to consider availability.

Sales are either made direct with customers or through estate agents. The sales staff, aged 22–24, comprise two Spanish, born in Madrid, and Elizabeth Baxter, Albert Baxter's daughter, bilingual in English and Spanish.

The three staff are paid a salary, given free accommodation and enjoy a commission on confirmed sales.

Office hours are 10.00 a.m.–1.00 p.m./4.00 p.m.–7.00 p.m.

APPENDIX 20.7   TENERIFE – A PROFILE

Everything in this island contributes to the appeal to its visitors. The sun, combined with a climate in which extremes are unknown, and the island's natural beauty complement the up-to-date facilities for tourists. The island's greatest appeal is the people who inhabit it in their overwhelming friendliness and hospitality.

The tremendous attraction of Tenerife forces its charm on all. This Atlantic island provides the fresh air and the balanced background of tranquillity that the holidaymaker needs to restore lost energy and to enjoy life to the full. Its beaches, coasts, mountains and woods are all subordinate to the all-embracing peace.

Tenerife has increased its tourist facilities in spectacular fashion. It has had the vision to add to its incomparable climate and splendid never-failing sunlight, hotels which enjoy considerable prestige, residential areas and magnificent holiday housing estates full of plants and flowers. It has been given an impulse to sports, especially water sports and to the organization of attractive excursions.

Mount Teide, majestic and imposing, is the dominant element around which nature takes the most varied forms. The north of the island is cool, shady, green and flower-filled. The south has the warm sun, a dry atmosphere and blue sky which make it a success all year round. Among a wide range of the island's charms are the tourist enclaves of Playa de las Americas and Los Cristianos.

The hotel industry in the island, including the state-run hotels, constitutes one of the most important pillars of the island's tourism. The chief hotels have first-class discothèques, flamenco dancing and sports facilities. Year round programmes are organized for the visitor to Tenerife – 'Touristic Folk Music Festivals' all over the island, and the colourful and amusing carnivals of Santa Cruz de Tenerife. Shopping is, of course, a great attraction in Tenerife. The bazaars offer the widest variety of excellent, modern and exotic goods at very moderate prices.

All tourist centres are surrounded by vegetation. The climate is always mild, with an average range of temperatures throughout the year between 23°C and 31°C – that of an eternal spring. In winter the snow-covered Teide overlooks the tourists who bathe in the warm waters. The shops, especially in Santa Cruz and in the south of Tenerife, are a temptation for tourists and those with a few hours to spend in a port from the transatlantic liners.

The water of these seas has an average temperature oscillating between 22°C in summer and 19°C in winter.

Tenerife is a natural magnet for tourists all over the world during all four seasons of the year. Wild nature and a cosmopolitan atmosphere live side by side on this island, blue over the sea and blue under the sea – a blue which envelops the pure air of the Atlantic.

Like a jewel set on the Atlantic Ocean, Tenerife is probably the most interesting of the Canarias. It is the largest island and has the best provision for tourists. It has the best and most modern airport of all the Canarias Islands. It has the best and most modern port of all the Canarias Islands and one of the most important of all Spain. The sight of Teide, the highest mountain of Spain, 3718 metres, is spectacular.

The island displays fantastic contrasts, landscapes of great diversity, from colourful valleys to woods of giant trees, from little hamlets to volcanic sceneries of almost frightful shapes and colours.

Very few places around the world can offer you all year long and so close to each other so many sports, fishing and surfing. Since there is a legal limit to the building density, there will never be the disturbing massification of concrete jungles common to other tourist traps.

APPENDIX 20.8 INTRODUCTORY LETTER TO CLIENTS

Parque Montana s.a.

Dear Client,

Tenerife is a place where you can live happily, dream-like and untroubled, especially when you are living in a beautiful place like Parque Montana. Lush green areas, bars and restaurants – every detail has been cared for. First quality construction, designed and conceived and of careful planning, keeps the community costs at a very low price.

Services on Parque Montana are intended to meet any requirements you may think of – 24-hour security guards, reception, supplies and furniture in stock. If you wish we will take care of the legal and financial details as well. For instance, since south Tenerife is often booked out during the whole year, you could obtain an excellent rent by letting your property through our management service and we will guarantee you nine months' rent over the year.

Maintenance costs are thus kept at a minimum level. Parque Montana's technical staff always manage the disposition of the sites in a way to guarantee maximum possible sunlight. Of course, you too can become one of the happy people living on the Parque Montana site. You might not be a millionaire, but you do not need to be one! Remember, you are buying at Spanish prices and you benefit from a very special way of payment which is:

- You pay a holding deposit of £500 or 100 000 pesetas.
- You pay 25 per cent of the amount when the contract is signed.
- The second 25 per cent is payable when the walls and the roof have been built.
- The third 25 per cent is payable when the interior of the house is finished, i.e., the floor, the windows and the bathroom.
- The fourth and final payment is paid when we give you the key to your property and we go to the offices of the notary to sign the *escritura* (deeds).

If our developments should be of interest to you or your friends and you require further information, please do not hesitate to contact us again. We will be only too pleased to help.

APPENDIX 20.9   Investment Appraisal

Investment appraisal of individual purchase of Parque Montana studio. Cash forecast 1985–90

Year		Cash outflow (£)	Cash inflow (from renting) (£)
1985(including legal costs)		20 000	2 000
1986		500	3 500
1987	Flights/	500	4 500
1988	maintenance and	750	4 500
1989	associated 'on-costs'	750	4 500
1990		1 000	5 000
		23 500	24 000

Capital growth at 15 per cent per annum

Year	Purchase price (£)	+15% (£)	Projected value (£)
1985	18 000	2700	20 700
1986	20 700	3105	23 805
1987	23 805	3570	27 375
1988	27 375	4106	31 481
1989	31 481	4722	36 203
1990	36 203	5430	41 633

Return on investment to 1990

$$\frac{\text{Total realizable revenue}}{\text{Original investment}} = \frac{42\,133}{18\,000} = 234\% \text{ or } 39\% \text{ per annum}$$

APPENDIX 20.10   Price Profile and Housing Availability at Selected Developments

Freehold prices of property – fully furnished* at selected current developments

	Studio apartment (£)	1 Bedroom apartment (£)	2 Bedroom apartment (£)
PLAYA DE LAS AMERICAS			
Parque Montana			
Phase I	18 000	27 500	35 000
Parque Marina			
Phase II	14 600	19 500	27 250
Oasis			
Phase I	16 750	25 500	n/a
Parque Las Vegas			
Phase II	17 500	24 500	33 500
Club Botanico	n/a	29 500	39 250
LOS CRISTIANOS AREA			
Park Horizon		23 100 to	
Phase II	16 600	28 600	38 500
Playa Shoto	15 600 to	22 500 to	29 500 to
Phase I	17 500	27 000	32 500
Torres del Teide			
Phase III	21 500	29 000	n/a

*Assuming £1 sterling = 200 pesetas.
NB Living area in square metres varies between developments. Internal specifications vary in quality and style.

Parque Montana – apartment breakdown

	Studio apartments	1 Bedroom apartments	2 Bedroom apartments
Phase I	60	70	30
Sold	20	10	Nil
Phase II	40	80	40
Phase III	30	90	40

Selected developments – apartment profile

	1 Studio apartments	2 1 Bedroom apartments	3 2 Bedroom apartments	Total
Parque Montana	60	70	30	160
D/A 6.10.84	(20)	(10)		
Parque Marina	150	100	35	285
D/A 1.5.84	(110)	(75)	(5)	
Oasis	100	75	–	175
D/A 1.3.85	(60)	(35)		
Parque Las Vegas	50	100	150	300
D/A 1.6.84	(40)	(30)	(40)	
Club Botanico	–	15	45	60
D/A 1.4.84		(12)	(10)	
Park Horizon	25	200	75	300
D/A 1.7.84	(25)	(100)	(20)	
Playa Shoto	400	200	50	650
D/A 1.11.84	(100)	(40)	(5)	
Torres del Teide	75	25	–	100
D/A 1.1.85	(15)	(5)		

1 Sleep 2 persons.
2 Sleep 4 persons.
3 Sleep 6 persons.
NB Figures in brackets refer to confirmed sales at time of going to print.
D/A = Date announced.
Estimated building time on average 12–15 months from D/A.

APPENDIX 20.11   TIME-SHARING MODELS ON TENERIFE

There are many different ways in which time sharing can operate to provide co-ownership of property. Parque Montana may need to develop a separate model to achieve corporate and client objectives. Two typical models in operation are described below.

Los Cristianos model

There are now apartments available for co-ownership on a three-monthly basis in the development which is the most sensible and convenient way to acquire a holiday home of your own in the sun.

For a once-only payment of around £9000 you can own three months of an apartment for-ever! You may choose to use your three months as a holiday home for the family and friends *or* letting your apartment will give you a return of around £120 per week on your investment.

Your new apartment will be fully furnished and equipped. Immediately before your arrival an efficient management service will have checked that everything is in its right place in perfect condition.

The development is ideally situated with breathtaking views of Los Cristianos harbour and the surrounding hillside. Another unique feature is the heated swimming pool with the same magnificent view of the harbour as from your balcony.

The fishing village of Los Cristianos offers an excellent choice of restaurants, plenty of bars and fashionable shops (a new shopping complex is to be completed by the end of 1985). There is a sandy beach for bathing and plenty of water sports – water-skiing, wind-surfing and skin-diving. You can fish off the harbour wall or spend a pleasant day at sea on one of the many pleasure boats available.

For golf enthusiasts a 27 hole course will be completed by the end of 1985, the first on the south of the island only ten minutes' drive from Los Cristianos.

Close by a new clinic has recently opened with all modern facilities.

Since the construction of the new airport on the south of the island new properties have soared in price. At present one bedroom apartments with a sea view are selling at between £30 000 and £40 000.

With co-ownership you avoid all the headaches. For a modest annual management fee you have no need to worry about maintenance, water, electricity, sewerage, furnishing replacement, repairs, etc.

You will be one of four owners holding clear and free title (*escritura*) to the property.

With sun all the year round where the average daily temperature rarely drops below 21°C (70°F) and rainfall is minimal you could not ask for more!

Playa de las Americas model

In the time-share scheme you purchase your holiday apartment for as many weeks in the year as you wish. You own it for that period forever. Best of all, for a one-off payment you will experience years of holiday enjoyment – freezing future holiday costs at today's prices.

The complex offers a total of 412 units comprising one bedroom, two bedroom or studio apartments in an exclusive club environment with bars, cafés, restaurants and sports facilities that will match five star standards through the world.

An annual management fee of between £35 and £50 per week owned, at current prices, will organize almost every aspect concerning the apartment owned. The fee covers: cleaning; decorating; servicing; replacement of breakages; electricity; insurance; renewal of furnishings; security; provision of total complex facilities; reinvestment in site facilities; guaranteed limit to no more than 6 per cent increase per annum in management fees for the next six years; staffing the complex.

With a time-share apartment you can:

1. Use it for holidays.
2. Loan it out.
3. Let it for the period you own.
4. Watch it grow in terms of capital appreciation – currently at 30 per cent per annum.
5. Will it to beneficiaries.
6. Sell it at any time.
7. Exchange it for other places for the specified time owned (subject to availability) throughout the world, for a nominal administration cost.
8. Enjoy a holiday for life for just the cost of a flight – plus your spending money of course.

Typical costs for one week prime time at Christmas*

	Prime site ocean front views (£)	Secondary site swimming pool and coastal views (£)	Tertiary site mountain view (£)
Studio apartment with balcony	3500	2500	2250
1 Bedroom apartment with balcony	4500	3000	2750
2 Bedroom apartment with balcony	5500	3500	3250

*Costs vary according to international peak holiday times.

APPENDIX 20.12   MAPS

TENERIFE AND THE CANARY ISLANDS

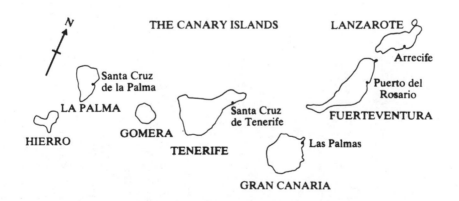

Figure A20.12   Maps of Tenerife and the Canary Islands

APPENDIX 20.13   TYPICAL APARTMENTS ON PARQUE MONTANA

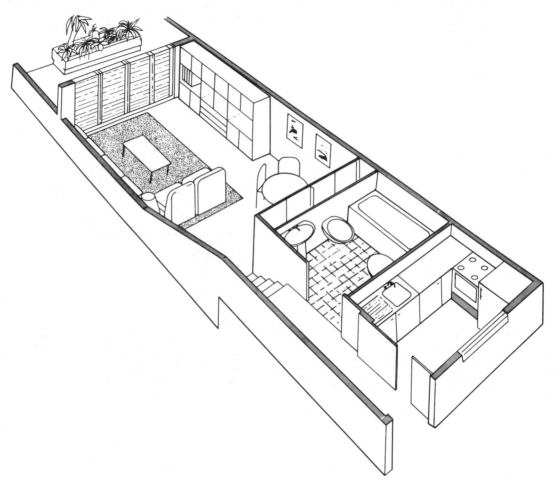

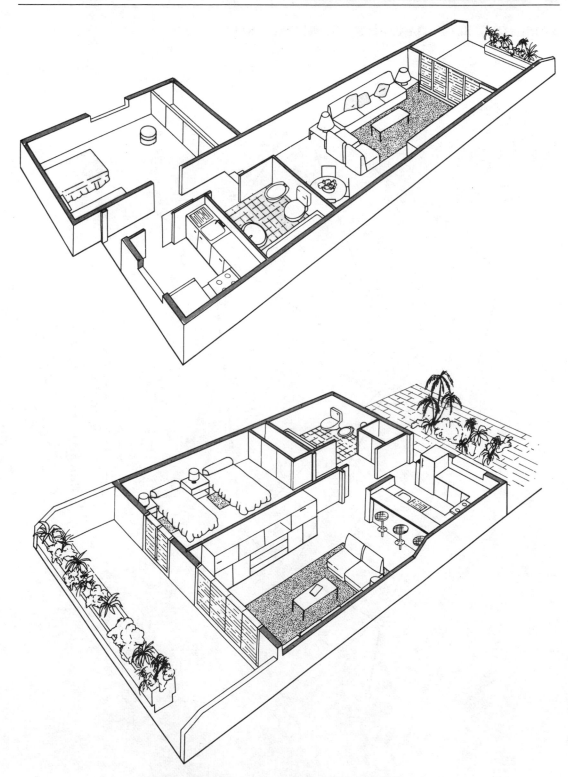

Figure A20.13 Typical apartments on Parque Montana

APPENDIX 20.14 BAXTER'S UK RETAIL SITES

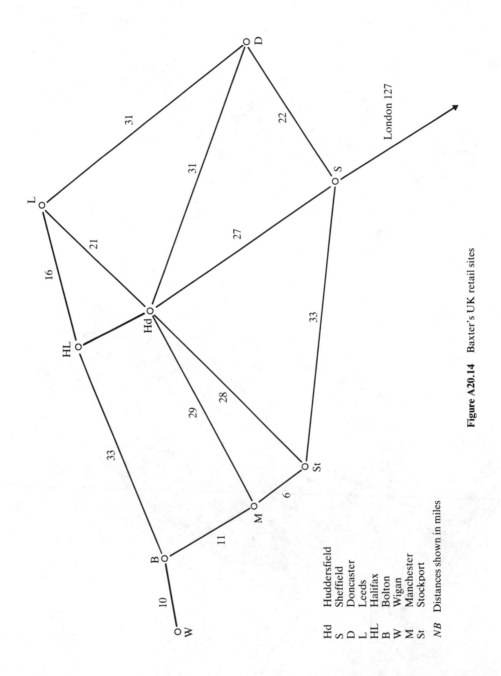

Hd	Huddersfield
S	Sheffield
D	Doncaster
L	Leeds
HL	Halifax
B	Bolton
W	Wigan
M	Manchester
St	Stockport
NB	Distances shown in miles

Figure A20.14 Baxter's UK retail sites

QUESTIONS

As Roger Mead, your first task is to organize your team to complete a fact finding mission derived from your client's brief.

You have learned since your appointment and original briefing of the following changes:

1. A policy decision has been taken to discontinue the hire of touring caravans. Existing used caravan stock is to be moved to permanent sites in France and Belgium or sold.
2. The new Baxter Kestrel is an 18-ft four-berth luxury caravan to be sold at £6750 including VAT, which is to replace the Baxter Hawk which will be withdrawn in December 1985.
3. Don Adams has been taken seriously ill and is not expected to rejoin the company.
4. The decision on time-sharing Phase II at Parque Montana has been confirmed by the board of the Spanish company.

YOU ARE REQUIRED TO REPORT ON THE FOLLOWING

Section 1 The implications, in brief, of the new information at your disposal for A. & R. Baxter Ltd business opportunities.

(20 marks)

Section 2 Detail the additional information requirements you would require Brenda Gardner and Nigel Harding to obtain to assist in the achievement of the consultancy assignment.

(20 marks)

Section 3 The methods you would employ to market the time sharing of Parque Montana Phase II and the financial potential to be realized.

(40 marks)

Section 4 Make justified recommendations on the future siting and official opening of three additional travel shops and one flight-only retail outlet over the next two years.

(20 marks)

GENERAL APPROACH

1. Allocation of time to questions
   Too many candidates ignored the differential allocation of marks between questions. Question 3 was the major question on the paper, carrying 40 marks, and hence time should have been apportioned accordingly. The approximate allocation of time to each question should have been:

Question	1	2	3	4
Minutes	35	35	70	35
Marks	20	20	40	20

   leaving five minutes to check the paper.

   By the time candidates have reached this stage in the progression towards achieving the IM Diploma, a good number of examinations must have been attempted and passed, and yet this simple tactical expedient of budgeting time has yet to be learned.
2. Answering questions
   It appears that candidates under the pressures imposed by the examination and the environment of tension in the examination hall fail to take several deep breaths to relax sufficiently to

actually read the examination questions. It is evident that little more than a superficial scanning takes place because many students are not answering the actual questions which have been asked. Candidates must read each question carefully and slowly several times in order to identify:

(a) the objectives of each question; and
(b) how to prepare an answer covering all the dimensions of the question and thereby achieve the question objectives.

It is recommended strongly that key words are underlined so that candidates do not lose sight of the content and direction they are required to follow. For example, the words printed in italics below should be underlined:

Section 1: 'The *implications*, in brief, of the new information at your disposal for A. & R. Baxter Ltd *business opportunities*.'

A simple question: in short, 'How does this new information affect the business?' Far too many students did not consider the *implications*. Few seemed to be able to respond to new information, synthesize this and consider the potential impact on A. & R. Baxter Ltd.

Section 3: 'The *methods* you would employ to *market* the *time sharing* of Parque Montana Phase II and the *financial potential* to be realized.'

Students appeared to have difficulty in interpreting and answering this question and yet in brief the question asked is 'What marketing methods would you use and what financial return could be expected?'
    The word 'market' was variously defined in the context of the question, and students were not penalized for the approach taken. However, on completing the Institute of Marketing Diploma and gaining a cherished professional qualification, a potential employer may legitimately ask 'How would you suggest we market X?' A professional answer would be expected!
    Too many candidates ignored the second part of the question, or tried to bypass it.
    Questions should be attempted across the total dimensions in which they are set; candidates choosing to avoid a statement of the financial potential limited their chances of passing the question.

Section 4: 'Make *justified recommendations* on the future *siting* and *official opening* of three additional travel shops and one flight-only retail outlet over the next two years.'

In answering Section 4 *recommendations* alone were not sufficient without *justification* for them. Hence the question asked for *justified recommendations*.
    Too few justified; most merely proposed.
    Again the 'blind spot' in the questions was 'official opening'. Most candidates proposed new sites but then overlooked the official opening of them.
    Questions are not designed to trick candidates but are conceived to test understanding and to provide an opportunity for students to demonstrate that understanding.
    Until students devote more time to reading questions carefully, areas of each question will, therefore, be missed and hence failure grades will continue to be awarded by examiners.

APPROACH TO EACH SECTION

Section 1

(20 marks)

Four pieces of additional information were provided: equal allocation of marks was given to the response to each. Clearly there is not a stock model answer. Examiners were testing students' grasp of the case study through the response received to the new information. Implications and, hence, marketing insights were required.

Subsection 1 'I am pleased that touring caravans have been discontinued, this is what we would have recommended' is *not* enough. Candidates should have considered the resource implications: on staff, management time, financial position, and the opportunities this now presents A. & R. Baxter for the future.

Subsection 2 'It is good that they have introduced a new caravan. Sales should increase in the future.' Again such shallow comments gain little credit. What are the product policy implications here? How do these affect product planning for the future? What are the sales implications and how is product positioning perceived and projected? Will old stock be discontinued? Why has the Hawk sales performance not been upheld? Are they not repeating the same mistake? These are typical issues which could have been aired.

Subsection 3 'This is such a shame. He was a much valued senior manager in the company. Arrangements must be made for a retirement gift, although if he recovers we could have him back one day a week.' Such comments have not really grasped the impact of this new information.

Don Adams is a key manager with considerable responsibility and success to date. The immediate problem is succession management. Who is to replace him? When? How? And what short-term effect will this have on staff morale, retail sales and company profit? How can this situation be resolved with the minimum amount of risk to the organization? Again a series of questions can be asked and the implications considered by potential suggestions in each area.

The emphasis must be on the future. Candidates should not dwell on past events and yet some suggested marketing audits should be conducted!

Subsection 4 This piece of information on time sharing was an ideal lead into Section 3 and yet many students failed to make the connection. Whereas Section 3 asked for marketing methods and financial implications, the wider implications of the decision should have been considered at this point. Again resource implications are a major issue to be explored and, similarly, these new dimensions of further development for A. & R. Baxter in the Canary Islands could have been considered.

Section 2

(20 marks)

Apart from the necessary marketing information and information requirements which were specific to the areas of the company, many candidates overlooked their role, and hence missed two vital areas of information search.

As Roger Mead, a senior consultant and partner of Mead & Franklin Associates, you lead a team of consultants; Brenda Gardner, a chartered accountant and chartered company secretary, and Nigel Harding, qualified in law and marketing. Naturally you should know the respective strengths of your team. It was, therefore, expected that both legal and financial information should have been specified as part of the additional information requirements you felt necessary for the achievement of the consultancy assignment.

Section 3

(40 marks)

This was the major question on the case study. Therefore, sufficient depth in answers was expected. Candidates who failed to budget their time according to the marks allocated rarely succeeded in producing sufficient depth to secure a pass grade. Candidates should have specified clear objectives, in particular quantitative objectives relating to units to be sold over prescribed time scales. A clear understanding of market segmentation was required to distinguish between direct outright sales and sales of time shares. The target audiences by profile and nationality must be given consideration so that marketing communications activities can be tailored to the needs of the identified target groups.

Some candidates concentrated on a promotional plan to market time-sharing Phase II of Parque Montana. However, a wider view was also considered legitimate since other marketing mix elements cannot be ignored.

The pricing dimension in relation to existing or proposed time-share models was an important element to be considered. This, in turn, relates to the promotional plan.

Candidates did recognize the international dimension of the promotion and the need for media/non-media and sales activity not only on the island of Tenerife and the other Canary Islands, but also in the major population areas of holidaymakers' countries of origin, particularly Europe and, in particular, France, Germany and the UK. Few considered the budgeting implications of this!

The second part of the question required a statement of the financial return over a specified time scale based upon the time-sharing model proposed. Naturally the financial projections will differ depending upon the time slots sold, but this is where students were weak.

In the live situation this is probably the most important factor – what return will A. & R. Baxter yield from time-sharing Parque Montana Phase II and how can this be achieved – through which time-share models and at what marketing costs to the company?

Section 4

(20 marks)

Comments in the earlier section identified the particular weakness of candidates. Currently the organization is quite parochial, located in Lancashire and Yorkshire, albeit large UK counties covering a wide geographic area. The question of debate must be: 'Should A. & R. Baxter extend within the geographic boundaries of the current organization – even using existing sites – or should a bold move be made to the South of England with the higher population and potentially higher levels of disposable income?'

Siting near airports was suggested by a large number of students, but without any real concern for the resource implications, and rarely were such recommendations fully justified by those candidates. Hence often these appeared as unsubstantiated proposals.

Few candidates took advantage of the time scale for development. The significance of the difference between travel shops selling package holidays and flight-only shops selling airline tickets was rarely appreciated, and even if it can be argued that such operations could be combined, this point was overlooked.

The largest area of weakness, however, was the lack of concern for the official opening of these outlets. Few took the opportunity for exploiting local markets – using local press plus the use of PR to obtain maximum exposure for such a newsworthy event. In practice, the PR planning and execution has really paid dividends to the company, not only in official openings but with a substantial planned programme of PR activities.

ANSWER

A. & R. Baxter Ltd
Report

From: Roger Mead, Senior Consultant.
            Mead & Franklin Associates.
Subject: A. & R. Baxter Ltd.
Date: June 1985.

Section 1 – Implications for A. & R. Baxter Ltd business operations of new information

Touring caravans The decision to discontinue the hire of touring caravans will have the following implications for the company:

- In recent years this sector of the business has yielded little real return on company investment. Therefore, the resources consequently freed up can be re-deployed to the key result areas of the business.
- Joan Kelly as Hire Sales Manager will have one section of her job responsibility reduced. Two sales staff are now freed up to work within the Caravan Division or within the wider Baxter organization where staff shortages prevail.
- An opportunity now exists for organizational development within the Sales Departments of the Caravan Division, especially as Joan Kelly is to take maternity leave in two months. Robin Baxter should make plans for organizational change now before the impetus of the decision on discontinuing touring caravans is lost. In turn, his top management time can be re-apportioned to the profit earning areas of the Caravan Division.
- With a reduction in touring caravan hire from £215 000 to £30 000 (estimate), currently this section of the business must be making a negative profit contribution. The decision to discontinue will stop this drain.
- The sale of used caravan stock may help to redress the position on profit contribution in this financial year, but the caravan stock moved to France and Belgium may continue to produce sales revenue for the company for some years hence.

Product development As consultants recently commissioned by the company we have had no opportunity to become involved in the product development programme for Baxter Caravans. As a result of the information received the following observations have been made:

- The company's product planning for the caravan range appears to be to use an 'add and drop' policy over a relatively short product life. We would wish to investigate further the rationale for this, in particular to discuss the reasons for the tail off in sales by model type.

- Without further knowledge of the design and features of the Baxter Kestrel, we cannot comment in detail. However, it would appear that the Kestrel is a 'relaunch' of the Hawk; there is little to discriminate between the two models. We are concerned about the sales implications of our observations.
- Without further research into the industry product provision for caravans by type, design, manufacture and price we cannot proceed. However, Baxter's must consider the product positioning as perceived by owners and potential buyers in relation to how they project the Baxter range of caravans. In particular, how will this new model be received in the context of:
  (a) Baxter's existing range; and
  (b) current models produced by competitors?
- What is the company planning for the launch of the new model? To gain maximum sales for the Kestrel and to sustain sales of the Baxter caravan range a marketing and sales plan is required. We have no evidence of this!
- The sales of the Baxter Hawk have not been upheld; the company has decided to withdraw the model. However, during the interim period when both the Baxter Kestrel and the Baxter Hawk are on sale it may be considered appropriate to discount the Hawk to clear stocks to enable the new Baxter Kestrel to compete more openly in the market.

Don Adams's illness With nearly 25 years' service with the company Don Adams is a key manager, with considerable responsibility and success to date. His management of the Leeds and Sheffield outlets contributes over 50 per cent of the sales revenue derived from the retail sales of caravanning and camping equipment. In absolute terms, he is responsible for sales in excess of £0.5 million. This problem is serious. The company must take action to ensure that sales loss is minimized.

The implications therefore are:

- Succession management. Recruitment advertising must be placed to replace him, even allowing for some internal movement of retail management from smaller outlets.
- It is a shock to the company to lose a key manager of only 50 years of age, but also it should be a warning that management succession must be planned for.
- In the immediate term, a key manager from the company must be temporarily appointed to retain control and maintain staff morale.
- Joe Martin has a long history with the company and is well respected. He seems to be an obvious choice to step into the breach as General Manager until he can find a replacement. This restricts his capacity for overall control of the seven outlets in the interim period.

Time-sharing Parque Montana Phase II The involvement of A. & R. Baxter in the Canary Islands presents a stimulating opportunity for diversification, despite the limited power position the company holds as a minority shareholder. The decision by the board of Parque Montana s.a. to time-share Phase II has the following implications:

- Time-sharing apartments on Tenerife are 'in vogue'. Parque Montana s.a. are therefore providing what customers need – they are meeting an identified demand and hence this is a start towards marketing orientation which otherwise appears absent from the organization.
- Time sharing produces more 'owners' which encourages yet more business to the island of Tenerife, which in turn boosts tourist traffic to the island, which in turn builds a tourist market of a profile suitable for further exploitation.

- Time sharing is the way to hold down prices of future holidays, i.e., at today's prices. The market for outright ownership appears to be softening and price will become a more sensitive issue. This boosts demand for time sharing – which must stimulate the demand for yet more building. In turn, Baxter Ltd must benefit, having a foothold both in the market for outright purchase and now time-sharing apartments.
- The market segments for:
  (a) outright ownership; and
  (b) time sharing
  are distinct and discrete. Parque Montana can now effectively compete in both markets at a time when the level of building development suggests that 'boom conditions' prevail on the island of Tenerife.
- Baxter must now consider the staffing implications of this move – who is to represent the company's interests on the island at this time of rapid organizational development?

Section 2 – Information requirements

Apart from the information we have to hand we consider the following information would assist us in the achievement of our consultancy assignment. Detailed market and company profiles must be drawn up. In addition to marketing information the professional expertise of Brenda Gardner and Nigel Harding should be used in the legal and accounting areas.

Company information

- Stress placed on the organization as a result of organizational problems and, in particular, resulting from the involvement with Parque Montana s.a.
- Intentions for change to the organizational structure and/or personnel within the structure.
- Staff development plans, if any.
- Contingency plans for the appointment of a new chairman should the need arise.
- Intentions of Albert Baxter and his Spanish wife with reference to future involvement in the Canary Islands.
- The review criteria for the position of Sally French in the company.
- The size of the equity option to be taken up by George Pender and the associated shift in the balance of power.
- The personal development plans for Stephen King.
- Plans for the replacement of Douglas Tyne and how these will impinge on the members previously identified for the restructuring of the Caravan Division.
- Succession management plans for the camping and caravanning retail outlets. Alan Bailey is due for retirement in two years and now manages three key outlets. With Don Adams's illness there is now an opportunity for a major re-think for the management in this area.
- What is the anticipated impact of Spanish entry into the EEC on the total Baxter organization?
- The travel agency management is young and very new to the company. What factors commit this management to the company? What are their motivations? Are these managers fulfilled and what is the level of staff turnover?

Financial information

- Profit contributions by main areas of business activity.
- Profit contributions within each main area of business activity.
- The real cost and the trends therein of maintaining caravans on permanent sites in the UK and Europe.

- Growth in sales revenue against growth in net profitability in each area of business activity.
- How can the gross commission on holiday/flight bookings be improved beyond 10 per cent? Would membership of other trade associations, e.g., IATA and ATOL, improve not only the image of the Baxter travel outlets but also the profit contribution?

Legal information

- What is the liability to Baxter's travel customers in the event of tour operator or system failure? How is Baxter insured against this?
- What is the company's legal liability concerning ownership and fulfilment in Parque Montana s.a.?
- What is the financial risk, the legal risk, against the return on the opportunities currently being exploited?
- How will Baxter's opportunity for increased control improve after Spanish membership of the EEC?
- What is the potential threat to the company of any sudden change in the Spanish legal system relating to the building works on the Spanish owned island of Tenerife?
- What is the history and stability of the directors of Parque Montana s.a.? In the event of collapse what is the limit to Baxter's liability?

Marketing information

Products

- The rationale for the company's product strategy on caravan manufacture.
- Industry trends in the purchase of camping and caravanning equipment.
- Industry trends in the form of holidays taken by caravanning and camping.
- Competitor market shares by volume and value for caravan sales.
- Industry trends on the success or failure of travel agencies and the growth in market preference for Tenerife.
- The strength of local competition among travel agents in the town in which Baxter's operates and proposes to operate.
- Growth in the flight-only business in London.
- Detailed competitor profile with projections for apartment building in the southern part of Tenerife.
- Future problems on building regulations following Spanish entry into the EEC in 1986.
- The life cycle for time sharing as a concept and as a viable operation internationally.
- The strength at consumer level of branding with particular reference to caravans.
- Product positioning for the Baxter's caravan range.
- The reason for projected sales decline in the caravan model Buzzard. Is this product policy or the effect of the product life cycle?
- What is the most effective time-sharing model currently being sold in Tenerife and what factors can be attributed to its success?

Pricing

- How price sensitive is the market for Tenerife property? If the Spanish peseta moved against sterling what would be the impact on apartment sales in the short term?
- To what extent is price a key motivating factor for Tenerife property sales and how is the issue of price presented to the consumer by Parque Montana s.a. and its competitors?

Promotion

- The specific target markets for private buyers and for time-share owners.
- The specific target markets for caravan sales.
- The level of advertising expenditure and the projected advertising appropriations in the future.
- The media used and the effectiveness of these media.
- The use of art studios and/or associated agencies.

Sales/distribution

- Breakdown of direct sales versus sales through concessionaires for Baxter caravans.
- The geographic profile of caravan sales by region.
- Profile of the caravan salesforce and detailed performance of each representative.
- Lease renewal dates on Baxter's retail outlets.
- The sales revenue from the hire of caravans on permanent sites appears to be ahead of inflation. How does this compare with industry trends and with Baxter's projected revenues in this area for the next three to five years?
- How can Baxter's influence the marketing and sales strategy for apartments and time sharing of Parque Montana properties?

Section 3 – The marketing of time sharing for Parque Montana Phase II over two years

Introduction

The growth in property development around the southern island resorts of Playa de las Americas and Los Cristianos has been almost exponential. Parque Montana s.a. must ensure that sales momentum is achieved both to spur on and finance further building development. The marketing methods to be employed will, therefore, cover the major elements of the marketing mix with an emphasis placed upon the design and implementation of effective marketing communications. To date, direct outright sales targets have been under-achieved owing to the level of competition and the coincident threat of over-supply. Time sharing is a new venture for Parque Montana s.a. on Phase II. Therefore, again, to compete effectively the promotion must be right first time. At the same time outright sales effort must be maintained and increased to ensure that Phase I is fully sold before Phase II development gains too much momentum and the company becomes overstretched financially.

Marketing objectives

- To design and implement an effective plan to introduce to the market time-sharing for Parque Montana Phase II properties.
- To achieve sales of:
    - 40 studio apartments
    - 80 one-bedroom apartments
    - 40 two-bedroom apartments
within a two-year estimated building development period (allowing for time scales slipping on development).
- To maintain a high profile image in all marketing activities.
- To achieve profit contribution levels specified by the board of Parque Montana s.a. and its financiers.

Marketing research

Field research among holidaymakers in the form of 500 street interviews should be conducted to discover:

- What is understood by time sharing.
- The prevailing attitudes towards the concept as understood.
- The percentage interested sufficiently to find out more and to visit a time-share complex.
- Knowledge of other companies currently promoting time sharing in the key resorts of Playa de las Americas and Los Cristianos.
- A profile of potential purchasers and their purchase motivations.

This market information will assist in the production of promotional material and help in the development of personal sales technique.

Time scale: 6 weeks.

Target start date: mid-July 1985.

Time sharing Parque Montana Phase II The time sharing of Parque Montana properties must appeal to the target groups specified, be more flexible than current competitors' offerings and be attractive on price and benefits. The benefits of time sharing *per se* are universal (cf. case study on page 403). Therefore, the Parque Montana (PM) package must be distinctive. The key result areas must be on the 'PM product offering' and the pricing strategy (see later section).

From our understanding, a time share is literally sharing of time with others for the benefit of holiday-making in a specified apartment or complex for a fixed time interval, normally for a specified time in the year (e.g., the first two weeks of July). While this 'time slot' is 'owned' for life and can be exchanged internationally, the owner may wish to return to Tenerife but not at the same time as purchased. *Therefore, an exchange opportunity within PM Phase II* within, say, three-month time bands exists. Time-share owners could thus present an attractive selling point. These time bands could be colour coded:

WHITE TIME – January, February, March;
YELLOW TIME – April, May, June;
RED TIME – July, August, September; and
GREEN TIME – October, November, December.

Different pricing levels should apply to each colour time zone to coincide with the peaks and troughs of the volume of holiday trade to Tenerife, which, although it is a twelve-month holiday resort, has obvious peaks at UK school holiday times (Christmas, Easter, summer and even half-terms).

The basic time-share unit should be one week, allowing potential buyers to purchase in multiples of one week. It is anticipated that most will buy two weeks as this corresponds to the traditional holiday period of most holidaymakers.

PM operations will manage the time-sharing complex where the services provided will be typical of those specified in the Playa de las Americas model (cf. case study on page 404).

Part of Parque Montana *Phase I* should be converted into fully furnished time-share apartments to be used as show apartments to allow potential buyers to visit the complex to view typical units in which they may invest.

Pricing Following research on price as a purchase motivator or inhibitor and being led by typical costs for prime time at Christmas, it is proposed that the following matrix be considered as a basis for further discussion. The matrix is based upon a penetration pricing principle with differential prices to be charged for different time zones to reflect demand.

Suggested costs (net of service charges for one week (£ sterling)

	White	Yellow	Red	Green
		Time zone		
Studio	2500	2000	3000	2500
1 Bedroom apartment	3500	3000	4000	3500
2 Bedroom apartment	4500	4000	5500	5000

NB It is recognized that within these time zones seasonal peaks occur, e.g., Christmas and New Year. These weeks can be surcharged at +30 per cent.

Discount scheme It is proposed that, as an incentive to purchase and to assist in the direct selling activities, a discount scheme operates as follows:

Provided the interested parties sign up on their first visit to the complex, 15 per cent reduction be offered, plus 10 per cent on three weeks or more purchased. This reduction is seen to be considerable and will induce buyers to place a deposit. All funds are to be remitted within 28 days of signing the contract.

Promotion

Objectives

1. To build credibility for the Parque Montana time-sharing organization.
2. To create awareness of PM time-sharing apartments and to encourage holidaymakers to visit the PM complex.
3. To ensure that 100 people visit the PM time-sharing show apartments each day.

Target groups

1. Holidaymakers in Playa de las Americas and close resorts who are:

   (a) UK, German or French nationals;
   (b) married couples;
   (c) singles;
   (d) families;
   (e) ABC socio-economic groups;
   (f) aged 30 plus.

Media selection and justification To reach the target audience above-the-line activity will be very limited. It is recommended that local newspapers written *not* in Spanish but in English, French or German, plus monthly magazines directed at holidaymakers, should be used. Limited use could be made of poster sites assuming availability exists.

Sales promotion The majority of communications activity will be below the line supported by personal selling.

The sales promotion task is to entice 100 people each day away from their immediate relaxation to take time to visit the PM time-share complex. Furthermore, the resistance level must be overcome because holidaymakers may fear a 'rip off' or may have visited other time-share complexes.

Incentives are required which will encourage people out of the holiday inertia.

It is suggested that the following incentives be offered.

In the street Invitation cards handed out highlighting:

1. 2000 pesetas to visit the site, paid after completing the tour plus free taxi to and from the PM time-share complex.
2. 1000 pesetas bonus to visit in off-peak hours – between 9.00 and 10.30 a.m.
3. Free drinks on arrival during the tour.
4. The chance to enter a competition
   (a) to win one week free, and
   (b) to draw a prize from a raffle based upon the number of the invitation card.

At the complex A 15 per cent discount on the purchase price of a time share on the PM complex offered at the end of the tour with a sales representative. Full-colour brochures are to be given to all visitors on leaving.

Sales

Sales targets

No. of property units		Total no. of weeks to be time shared	No. of customers required at two-week purchase level	No. of customers at 75% occupancy
Studios	40	2080	1040	780
1 Bedroom	80	4160	2080	1560
2 Bedroom	40	2080	1040	780
		8320	4160	3120

Over a two-year period *at least* 3120 customers are required to purchase assuming a minimum two-week time share and 75 per cent take-up overall. Therefore, to allow for flexibility and contingencies, 3500 buyers should be targeted over a two-year period. This averages, let us assume, 30 per week. Over six days we require a minimum of five buyers per day. Assuming a 10 per cent conversion rate, at least 50 enquiries must be received each day. This means at least 50 persons must be enticed to visit the PM time-share complex and this momentum must be maintained over two years. Allowing for the tail off in demand over the two-year period, at least 100 potential buyers are required to visit each day.

Sales strategy Two key points exist for selling:

1. In the street.
2. At the time-share complex.

In the street Short-term 'personality girls' should be appointed to approach people from the target group, explain briefly about the PM time-share complex and invite them to visit the site. Invitation cards should be handed out which can be used for redemption of moneys and gifts previously specified.

To maintain the interest of the 'personality girls' a flat rate of 2000 pesetas per day should be paid *plus* 1000 pesetas for each person or couple visiting the complex. This can easily be determined by coding the invitation cards so that the correct girl receives the incentive. In addition, if a deposit is taken for the sale of a time share a further 2000 pesetas will be paid.

For the girls who work hard, earnings are potentially high. The financial incentive is strong to encourage maximum effort in approaching holidaymakers in the street, to achieve the daily target of 100 visitors. Assuming 10 per cent conversion, 1000 contacts must be made each day. Twenty girls should be recruited with a target of 50 contacts each per day. To avoid drop-off in motivation a shift system should operate, e.g., mornings or afternoons or three-day blocks. This means that a pool of at least 40 girls should be obtained. One source is young holidaymakers/students assuming there are no restrictions for casual labour on the island. In addition, local labour with English-speaking ability should be employed.

At the complex Trained commission-only sales representatives should be appointed and, subject to a trial six-week period, be offered a one-year contract renewable for a further 12 months. A one-month notice period would be required by either party.

On arrival at the complex each visitor would be joined by a representative who, over a 45-minute tour, would extol the virtues of time sharing, provide a guided tour of the complex and apartments and, finally, present a sales pitch plus offering the first-visit discount package to close the sale.

Sales representatives will receive 0.5 per cent commission on each sale when funds are remitted in full by the buyer.

Section 4 – Recommendations for new outlets

Résumé of current position The development of Baxter's travel agencies has been a good example of consistent growth which, over the past five years, has produced and maintained six retail outlets with just one shop specializing in flight-only sales.

A. & R. Baxter Ltd, throughout the history of the organization, has been northern based, and hence it has been natural for this development to be located in towns that are both familiar and logistically convenient for exploiting the geographic markets of Yorkshire and Lancashire. It can be argued, therefore, that the outlook of the company with reference to the UK market could be considered at least regional if not parochial. The future siting of the new outlets must consider, therefore, the culture of the organization.

Options Three distinct alternatives exist:

1. To site the new outlets within the existing geographical network.
2. To relocate to the South, in particular the London region, to take advantage of the larger although more competitive market.
3. To site the outlets at major international airports.

Option 3 is considered impractical, costly in administrative terms and would remove much of the real business from its marketplace, the high street, or main trading area in towns and cities. Moreover, the city of Manchester has two outlets with easy access to Manchester International Airport.

Option 2 is undesirable for the following reasons:

- Fixed costs of setting up business in the South are much higher, particularly rent and rates.
- Staff costs will be higher; the best staff go to the highest paying employer.
- The return in percentage terms from sales is the same throughout the country. Therefore, more

volume business would need to be achieved to produce the same profit contribution as northern outlets.
- The marketplace is fiercely competitive.
- The travel trade depends on good contacts and quick reaction to enquiries and bookings. Baxter's have this in the North and would have to invest two to three years to achieve the same impact in the South.
- A split operation would be wasteful in resource terms and communication/control would become increasingly difficult.

Selection   Therefore, at least in the short term, it is recommended that option 1 is adopted, justified on the practical weaknesses of options 2 and 3. Furthermore, the time scale to achieve the opening of these new outlets is just two years! In the context of the Baxter organization, the most expedient method for expansion must be adopted to achieve short-term objectives.

A phased operation for development is envisaged approximately at the intervals shown in the table.

Action plan

Outlet	Timing	Location	Justification
1	Within 6 months	Stockport	The outlet is closing in July. Assuming that the lease is current or renewable, a shop conversion and new staff could be achieved in the immediate term. The difficult period following the opening could be further supervised by staff at Manchester, just six miles away. In real terms a low risk option.
2	Within 16 months	Halifax	Logistically it is well placed for access to Huddersfield and Leeds, yet is an independent town of stature. The existing site, which has performed moderately for some years, should be reviewed as to the actual contribution made to company profitability. If this is positive a second site should be acquired.
3	Within 24 months	Huddersfield	Within this two-year period the success of the Manchester flight-only shop will have been confirmed as a concept. This will strengthen the conviction to open a second flight-only shop. Huddersfield, with one travel shop, is a large town which may accept the concept and we trust will have enough volume business to sustain the introduction of another travel outlet. Huddersfield is at the hub of the existing network with relatively easy access to Northern airports.

The above plan of action is just a series of structured suggestions at this stage. We would wish to conduct a full feasibility study to confirm or modify or review before the scheme was proposed for adoption.

Three sites only   Furthermore, within the time scale proposed we feel that the company would be ambitious within the staff resources available to achieve the successful opening of *three* additional outlets. It is felt that to open *four* within two years, i.e., one every six months, is *far too* ambitious. New business links in Tenerife may, within the immediate term, present opportunities for further expansion for the A. & R. Baxter travel business and these must, if presented, be evaluated carefully against the backcloth of the total Baxter organization. Moreover, the organization must have sufficient flexibility to exploit new directions. Therefore, based upon our current knowledge, it is our firm conviction that three new outlets in two years should be the upper limit.

The official opening(s) With an organizational history in the travel trade for the last five years, with A. & R. Baxter a well-known company and with six outlets open to date, the consecutive opening of more shops is newsworthy and of particular local interest. There is here a core of planned programme of public relations activities linked to a launch advertising strategy.

The proposed plan is as follows:

Advertising objectives
1. To create a rapid, high level of awareness that Baxter's is to open a new travel shop in town.
2. To encourage people to go to the new shop to collect brochures and see the staff.
3. To convert awareness into flight and holiday bookings.

Public relations objectives
1. To announce that Baxter's is expanding its chain of travel shops to take professional care of the town's holiday and flight needs.
2. To create a climate of informed opinion among the town's people of what Baxter travel shops do to convey a sense of trust between the travel shops, their staff and the general public.
3. To convey a corporate image for the shops that results in key opinion leaders projecting a favourable attitude towards the organization.

Advertising strategy It is vital to secure advertising coverage, before, during and after the event of the official opening.

Media selection and justification
1. *Local press*: This will penetrate the target audience of the local members of the general public. Two full-page ads should be placed weekly on Friday two weeks before the opening to act as a 'teaser' (Baxter's is coming to town!) followed by supportive half-page ads following the official opening. Free sheets can be used in the same way. Essentially local press and free sheets have potentially a high readership in relation to circulation and hence have a low cost per thousand and a coincident high OTS.
2. *Local radio*: a short campaign covering five days before the opening should be used to support the press advertising and PR activities.

Public relations strategy Good press relations are important not only to gain coverage of the 'official opening' but also to broadcast newsworthy times about the Baxter organization on an on-going basis. A press kit should be produced with a news release and associated photographs but, in addition, editorial coverage of the opening should be aimed for. A full-page advertising feature could be booked to entice editorial coverage.

To ensure press coverage is achieved, local dignitaries should be invited to the 'official opening', with one local person of public note to 'cut the ribbon' and to unveil a small commemorative plaque.

While this plan is quite 'low key' it is tailored to meet the needs of the Baxter travel organization and its development. A similar 'model' could be applied as each new unit is opened in different towns.

INDEX